THE DICTION OF POETRY

FROM SPENSER TO BRIDGES

THE DICTION

OF POETRY

FROM SPENSER

TO BRIDGES

BY BERNARD GROOM

Professor of English, McMaster University

UNIVERSITY OF TORONTO PRESS

In association with McMaster University

To my sister Ida Sutherland Groom

PREFACE

THIS WORK is the result of an almost lifelong study of the diction of English poetry. It is the fulfilment of several preliminary articles which I have published on the subject, most notably two contributions to *Essays and Studies by Members of the English Association* (volumes XV and XXIV) and two *Tracts* in the series published by The Society for Pure English (Nos. XLIX and LIII).

The book is primarily an essay in literary criticism. The chapters are in part studies on the choice and use of words by certain English poets, but an attempt is also made to relate the diction of each poet to the quality of his work. The standpoint of the book is mainly historical, for it accepts a long-established tradition of English poetry without any attempt at radical revaluation. No such attempt appeared necessary: the poets dealt with have shown, and still show, a power of survival which has so far defied the onslaughts of time and change: their works, and therefore their language too, are matters of enduring interest.

It would be an endless task to acknowledge all the debts which I owe to the writers, past and present, who have thrown light on this vast and many-sided subject. Much of the best criticism is embedded in articles on individual authors; and it is impossible to record the source of every illuminating remark which has brought into prominence some special word or phrase. Such authors as Logan Pearsall Smith, J. W. Mackail, and Ernest de Selincourt scattered their verbal criticism broadcast, and I can only acknowledge my debt in the most general terms. Many living writers, such as Professor Geoffrey Tillotson and Miss Ethel Seaton, have laid me under the same kind of obligation. Where, however, I have been indebted to books and articles dealing with entire aspects of the subject I have made the acknowledgment which is due.

It is a great pleasure to record my obligation to the Humanities Research Council of Canada for a grant most generously made to assist the publication of this work, and to McMaster University which, as sponsor, made a similar grant. I also thank my colleagues, Professors G. C. Haddow and R. M. Wiles, for valuable suggestions and encouragement.

Several of my former students, Miss Marguerite Anne Manson (now Mrs. T. Olson), Mr. John Bell, Miss Joan MacDonald, and Miss Jocelyn Ann Cayley gave much help in the typing of my manuscript and in other ways, and I gratefully associate their names with the work. Finally, my thanks are due for the valued co-operation of the University of Toronto Press, and in particular to its Associate Editor, Miss Francess G. Halpenny, who gave me the benefit of her experience and skill.

B. G.

McMaster University
Hamilton, Ontario
June 1955

ACKNOWLEDGMENTS

Acknowledgment is due for leave kindly given by the owners of copyright works, as follows: to the Clarendon Press, Oxford, to reproduce my Tract (no. LIII) in the Society for Pure English Series, and to quote some passages from Edward Thompson's *Robert Bridges* and G. S. Gordon's *Shakespearian Comedy and Other Studies*; to Messrs. Macmillan and Co. Ltd. (London) to quote a passage from Alfred Noyes's *William Morris*; to the Cambridge University Press to reprint three excerpts from Caroline Spurgeon's *Shakespeare's Imagery*; and to Messrs. Henry Holt and Company, Inc., to reprint some passages from Mark Van Doren's *John Dryden*, copyright, 1920, by Harcourt, Brace and Howe, Inc., copyright, 1946, by Mark Van Doren.

CONTENTS

THE DICTION OF POETRY

FROM SPENSER TO BRIDGES

THIS WORK deals mainly with the diction of poetry, not with "poetic diction." It is concerned with the outstanding poets of some three centuries whose practice shows them to recognize an "essential difference between the language of prose and metrical composition."[1] The diction of poetry, then, consists of all the words and phrases in true and creative poetic writing which are in any way distinguished by their form or function from those in ordinary use. It includes synonyms which heighten or embellish style; also felicitous phrases which, even if often repeated in later use, still confer honour on their true inventors; and finally, certain imaginative and expressive words which exist only in the world of poetry.

The term "poetic diction" (in quotation marks) is used where I have meant to imply a charge of convention or of mechanical repetition. In this I am following the example of Wordsworth in his Preface to *Lyrical Ballads*, where "what is usually called POETIC DICTION" is subjected to searching adverse criticism. For example, the phrase "amorous descant"—almost a cliché in the middle of the eighteenth century—is "poetic diction" in the sonnet by Gray which Wordsworth analyses in his Preface, but it belongs to the diction of poetry in Milton's beautiful description of the nightingale (*Paradise Lost*, IV.603), where it originated. The expression, though often abused, remains intact in its earliest setting.

The borrowing of a word or phrase from one poet by another does not, of course, at once transform it into "poetic diction." Such borrowing is often an act of brilliant poetic invention. On the other hand, a poetic word or phrase must, if carelessly repeated, fade and finally die. A reader of poetry, sensitive to language and to style in general, may train himself to distinguish with some confidence between the living and the lifeless use of such expressions; but those experienced in such delicate work will not flatter themselves that their judgment is infallible.

No poet can compare with Spenser in the strength of his continuous influence, direct and indirect, on the diction of English poetry. He was

[1] Wordsworth's Preface to *Lyrical Ballads* (dated 1800, but published Jan., 1801; G. M. Harper, *Life*, I. 416). Wordsworth, of course, takes the opposite view.

the earliest master of the school to which Milton, Gray, Keats, Tennyson, Bridges, and a host of other poets, belong. To say that all the major poets of England for three centuries after 1600 were Spenserians would be untrue in one sense and an exaggeration in another. Yet his example remained operative beyond that of any other poet in the language. The word "Spenserian" may, of course, imply various degrees of discipleship. Few poets reproduced the minuter details of his diction so closely as Thomson or Shenstone did in certain of their poems. The widespread vogue of the Spenserian stanza in the eighteenth and nineteenth centuries is more significant. Yet even this is far from indicating the full extent of his example and influence.

The word "Spenserian" as used by later poets has a wider connotation than might appear at first sight: it cannot be briefly defined, and its full sense demands a somewhat elaborate description. Spenser stood for the fullest liberty of word-usage and word-formation conferred by the use of metre and the nature of poetry. Spenser's diction is of a kind which suits a smooth and even versification, and though not remarkable for energy, it contains resources which may be developed into energy by more vigorous minds. It is diction drawn from various sources, and has itself many "colours." It gives ready admission to polysyllabic words and compound epithets, and is a widely representative literary dialect, susceptible of adaptation. It especially lends itself to use in intricately rhymed stanzas, but may also be fitted to blank verse and certain forms of the heroic couplet. For dramatic writing it is eminently unsuitable. From the nature of its inventor it has always been associated with the romantic epic or episode, and it has something also of a pastoral flavour. It is an excellent vehicle for description and for some kinds of narrative. The weaker features of the original Spenserian style are archaism and redundancy; these have generally been avoided or reduced by the greater writers in the Spenserian tradition. Poets of very different character may be Spenserian by fundamental affinity. Both Milton and Dryden, for instance, were declared Spenserians, though their relation to their original is expressed in widely divergent ways.

The history of Spenser's continuous influence on the diction of poetry begins with *The Faerie Queene* rather than with *The Shepheardes Calender*. No doubt the earlier poem is of great significance to the philologist in its use of archaic and dialectal words. But it was *The Faerie Queene* mainly, if not exclusively, that was in the mind of Milton, Dryden, Gray, and the rest, when they mentioned the name of Spenser. Moreover, it was not until he came to write *The Faerie Queene* that Spenser's style attained its full maturity. In his earlier work, the poet is experimenting in various styles. Even within the compass of *The Shepheardes Calender* there is variety: the style of the July eclogue, for instance, is more rustic than that of some others. In *Mother Hubberds Tale*, the diction is near to that of ordinary usage, and the poet disclaims the need for any lofty terms:

> No Muses aide me needs heretoo to call;
> Base is the style, and matter meane withall.[2]

To discuss the varieties of style in Spenser's minor poems would, in our present study, be no more than an interesting preliminary, for *The Faerie Queene*, which gives him his position in the history of poetic style, contains all the types of diction which he ever used. Touches of dialect even, the marks of his bucolic style, are not wanting: the poem is, in fact, representative of his entire treasury of words and phrases. We may therefore concentrate our attention on his greatest work, with no more than occasional glances at *The Shepheardes Calender* and the other poems.[3]

I

In his formation of a poetic style, Spenser was a daring innovator. There was no adequate model for the varied effects which he wished to produce in *The Shepheardes Calender* and *The Faerie Queene*: he therefore framed a style of his own from diverse sources, not excluding the work of his immediate predecessors. His earlier poem was accompanied by notes which explained, and sometimes sought to justify, the more unusual words; but the style of *The Faerie Queene* was allowed to make its way in the world alone. Spenser adopted a defensive attitude. He had no wish to impose words on the language, but merely claimed a freedom necessary to his special purposes. His problem was not peculiar to himself: it arose from the general condition of the art of poetry at the time. Since the death of Wyatt there had been great progress in versification, and in the last quarter of the century the writing of smooth regular iambic lines required no unusual skill. The question troubling ardent minds like Marlowe and Spenser was how to raise insipid correctness to the level of true poetry. It was a difficulty widely felt; and word-hunting, as we know from many allusions in the drama

[2]Quotations follow the Oxford *Spenser*.

[3]For aspects of the subject not discussed here, the reader is referred to W. Renwick's "The Critical Origins of Spenser's Diction" and "Mulcaster and Du Bellay" (*Modern Language Review*, XVII, 1922); to B. R. McElderry's "Archaism and Innovation in Spenser's Diction" (*Publications of the Modern Language Association of America*, XLVII, 1932); and to C. L. Wrenn's "On Rereading Spenser's *Shepheardes Calender*" (*Essays and Studies by Members of the English Association*, XXIX, 1943).

of the time, became a common pastime. Spenser's poetry was written in the full tide of this new fashion: it belongs to the buoyant age of expansion. Well before the death of Shakespeare the tide was turning, and though new words were still freely coined, their quality was more critically scanned. But by 1599, the year of Spenser's death, the reaction had barely begun.

A complete examination of Spenser's diction would lead us into byways far from the general course of English poetry. Many of his formations and borrowings are no more than oddities and curios. In its entirety Spenser's diction could never have served as a model. Apart from his archaism, his practice is startlingly inconsistent. His skill in versification and his mastery of the vocabulary are admirable: but he is an unequal and—by later standards—a somewhat unscrupulous artist. Fortunately the exuberance and licence of his style were saved from unduly influencing his followers, by the strong reaction in taste to which I have alluded. The post-Elizabethans admired precision, neatness, and economy. The best qualities in Spenser's diction survived this and many other changes of fashion, and every subsequent generation of poets found fresh suggestions in it. For Spenser's diction is, like his poetry, of rich variety. His style is of many moods: sometimes high, sometimes homely; sometimes compact, sometimes redundant. His diction is equally varied: and his characteristic words, even when taken from their context and examined as mere lists, often reveal themselves as good, bad, or indifferent. In retrospect, Spenser appears as the main founder of our poetic diction,[4] but we must not be dazzled by the glamour which later poetry has cast over many of his phrases. He was a craftsman as well as a poet, and much of his conscious effort was directed to the task of choosing *appropriate* terms—rustic words for his eclogues, stately words for his similes, fitly varied words for his rhymes. When all is said, he had much of the "prodigality" which Gray admired in Shakespeare and Milton.

II

Readers of *The Faerie Queene* will always be impressed by Spenser's mastery of versification and the apparent ease with which he overcomes the difficulties of his rhyme-scheme. But his technique is attained at a certain cost, and without the help of numerous licences the lines would not flow with their familiar smoothness. Some of Spenser's liberties came to be regarded as the general prerogative of verse-writers, and

---

[4]The phrase, not in quotation marks, is used here and elsewhere in this study without the implications noted on p. 3.

therefore attract little attention in the modern reader. Others, however, were too obviously makeshift devices to pass into correct use. But on a broad view, Spenser is clearly revealed as one of the main founders of the principles of English versification. Before considering his *poetic* diction, therefore, we must examine the main features of his *verse* diction.

If Spenser sometimes abuses the freedom traditionally allowed to poets, the fault must be partly laid upon the spirit of his age. The right of reason and analogy to regulate the English language was as yet hardly acknowledged, and no authoritative English grammar was in existence. The verses of "the new poet," however, were so flowing, so musical that much of his technique obtained a lasting prestige. His use of affixes to supply a needed syllable was a common Elizabethan licence, and a certain number of words thus formed were retained. He is much more moderate in his use of "aphesis," and hence a higher proportion of his aphetic words long remained in verse.[5] It is in the arbitrary alteration of vowels to obtain needed rhymes that his freedom seems most audacious, but perhaps the practice is too rare to constitute a real feature of his style. Such a licence deserves mention only because it is possible.

Redundancy is a true feature of Spenser's style. Just as he will not only use but will even repeat phrases like "equall peares" and "readie prest," so he is constantly adding affixes to eke out the syllables required by the metre. The archaic y- is mainly a device of this kind; it is added indiscriminately to the past tense or participle of any verb when the metre so requires. Though the practice is employed by other Elizabethans, such as Sylvester and Arthur Hall, it is pre-eminently a Spenserian feature.[6] Later, it is a mark of avowed imitation of Spenser's style, and otherwise was not generally adopted. But in his lavish use of prefixes and suffixes to form new words or modify the meaning Spenser is following the general practice of his time: in Elizabethan poetry the free handling of affixes gives the impression of a growing and expanding language. No author indulges in this form of word-making more than Spenser, and though it is not always possible to determine whether he was the first user of a particular word, the number of his genuine creations was certainly very considerable. Of prefixes his favourites are: *a-, dis-, en-*; of suffixes, *-full, -less, -ment, -y*. Spenser was anticipated in this method of enriching the vocabulary, notably by Golding, translator of Ovid's *Metamorphoses*; and among his contemporaries, Peele and Marlowe are conspicuous for the same practice.

Whether Spenser's formations are in any sense new words, expressing

[5]E.g., 'mongst, 'scape, 'stonisht.
[6]See *O.E.D.* y-(4).

a shade of meaning not to be conveyed otherwise, or whether they are mere metrical makeshifts, it is not always easy to determine. The *Oxford Dictionary*, after discussing the varied origins of the prefix *a-*, states that it was "looked upon as vaguely intensive, rhetorical, euphonic, or even archaic, and wholly otiose. With this vague feeling *a-* was often prefixed by Spenser and other artificial archaists of the 16th century to words both of Old English and Romance origin, where it . . . can only be explained as due to vague form-association." The quality of these new words varies considerably. In the following passage (*F.Q.*, IV.iii.50):

> Where when she saw that cruell war so ended,
> And deadly foes so faithfully affrended,

the reader will probably consider that "affrended," though only a nonce-word, is permissible and not unpleasing in a fluid language like Elizabethan English. Another of Spenser's creations, *attune*, became a special favourite of poets. It is found in Book II of *The Faerie Queene*[7] (a part of the poem specifically alluded to by Milton) and was then used in *Paradise Lost*,[8] and afterwards by Pope, Thomson, Shenstone, Wordsworth, Coleridge, and others. But many formations with *a-* are of a less fortunate kind, and were never repeated, or repeated only once or twice by imitators of Spenser's style. Examples are *accourage, accourt, addeeme, aggrate, awarm*. They are among the poet's failures, and contribute to the "obsolete" effect which has limited the appeal of his work.

A similar difference of quality marks the members of the other groups. The formations with *dis-* are less numerous, and some of the most effective examples are in the work of other poets. Among the *Oxford Dictionary*'s "first instances" are Spenser's *disattyre, disloign, dispaint* ("to paint diversely"), *disprofesse*. But the most notable of these words is *dispread*, which apparently first appeared in the description of the coach of Lucifera in the pageant of the Vices (I.iv.17):

> Drawne of faire Pecocks, that excell in pride,
> And full of *Argus* eyes their tailes dispredden wide.

Used by Spenser in more than one graphic description, it could not escape the notice of poets, and accordingly we find it repeated by Fairfax, Sandys, Daniel, Thomson, and various others. Probably the most frequent of all prefixes was *en-* which, apart from its other uses, was, according to the *Oxford Dictionary*, at times "merely intensive" or "in poetry often merely to give an additional syllable." In a line like the

---

[7] II.xii.76; also in I.xii.7.
[8] IV.265 (the sense is slightly changed).

following (*F.Q.*, I.ix.48), which immediately follows the eloquent persuasions of Despair,

> The knight was much enmoued with his speach,

the prefix is perhaps intensive, though many times it is certainly no more than metrical. None the less, in employing such words, Spenser was not only following a well-established practice of the time,[9] he was helping to create a long-continued poetic tradition. At least one of his words, *empurple*, first recorded in Book III of *The Faerie Queene* (vii.17), was repeated in descriptive passages by Drummond of Hawthornden, Milton, Coleridge, and Mrs. Browning. To Gray the use of such words appeared to be a main feature of Spenser's style. Writing to his friend West in 1740 he remarks: "Now I talk of verses, Mr. Walpole and I have frequently wondered you should never mention a certain imitation of Spenser, published last year by a namesake of yours [Gilbert West], with which we are all enraptured and enmarvailed."[10] Though Spenser overtaxed the prefix, it has long been accepted in versification, both in forming new verbs like *enisle*, and as a euphonic adornment or at least a convenient extra syllable, in words like *engarlanded*.

In the large group of adjectives ending in *-ful(l)* one is aware again of a difference of quality. Some have perhaps never been repeated, and others have either been adopted by later writers, or have at least helped to create a tradition in which similar words have been formed by analogy. Thus there are the bad examples like *duefull*,[11] which the *Oxford Dictionary* brands as "an anomalous Spenserian formation," also the good ones like *wailful*[12] (used by other Elizabethans besides Spenser) which was found to have an expressive value by later poets in the Spenserian tradition such as Shenstone, Keats ("in a wailful choir the small gnats mourn"), and Bridges. Intermediate between the two classes are sundry formations which are rather Elizabethan than poetic, such as *discordfull, deuicefull, intreatfull*, and others.

It has long been recognized that epithets with certain affixes, especially *en-, -ful(l)*, and *-y* are marks of Spenser's style, though his originality in coining such words has sometimes been exaggerated. Mr. H. C. Hart, for instance, quotes a list of epithets in *-y* from Spenser's poems which includes: *hoary, frothy, dewy, foamy, rosy, finny, fleecy, plumy, snowy, pearly, fenny, balmy, ashy*, adding the comment, "many of them

---

[9]Dr. George Gordon thinks it was Skelton who first enlarged the range of the prefix. *Shakespearian Comedy and Other Studies* (Oxford, 1944), p. 148.

[10]*Works*, ed. W. Mason, 2 vols. (London, 1807), I, 256–7.

[11]*F.Q.*, IV.xi.44; VII.vi.35 (*dewfull*); and elsewhere.

[12]*S.C.*, Feb. 82.

are his own undoubted introductions."[13] A number, however, are not, and the only one in the list just given of which earlier examples are not quoted in the *O.E.D.* is *finny*.[14] None the less it is possible that the currency of such words in verse was largely due to the popularity of Spenser's poetry. Like other poets of the time, Spenser not infrequently adds the suffix -*y* to words which are already adjectives, as in *calmy, paly, moisty*. Such forms are often indistinguishable from mere "metrical alternatives." Shakespeare uses *paly* and *vasty*; but this type of epithet tends to drop out of later seventeenth-century verse. The disappearance is probably due to a stricter sense of grammar, as the regular use of -*y* remained popular far into the eighteenth century.

A few remarks must be added on Spenser's licences in varying the forms of words to suit rhyme and metre. A certain licence in varying the forms of proper names was one of Spenser's inheritances from Chaucer, but he surely used the privilege to excess. Other poets might have changed the name "Una" to "Un" and "Archimago" to "Archimag," but in Spenser such variations are unusually numerous and startling. For example, the mother of Belphoebe is called *Chrysogonee* in one stanza and *Chrysogone* in the next (*F.Q.*, III.vi.4, 5). In the story of King Lear, the name *Cordeill* changes with the same rapidity to *Cordelia* (II.x.28, 29). In the same spirit, Spenser, taking the fullest advantage of the ambiguous usage of the time, creates alternatives on occasion, when they did not already exist. Thus in his verse *moue* alternates, legitimately, with *mieue; wrist* with *wrest*. So, too, *daint*, a favourite in Spenser, for "dainty" is found elsewhere. On the other hand, *loring* for "lore" (V.vii.42) and *cherry* for "cherish" (VI.x.22) seem to have originated in *The Faerie Queene; aband* (II.x.65) is described by the *Oxford Dictionary* as "an artificial contraction of *abandon* used by Spenser and other of the Elizabethan affecters of archaism"; *graile* (I.vii.6) "perhaps a contraction for *gravel*," after its first appearance in *The Faerie Queene* was repeated by Henry More and by Browning in *Sordello* and is probably unknown outside poetry.

These specimens give a representative picture both of the fluidity of Elizabethan English and of Spenser's individual freedoms. Something of his commanding influence on poetic style is also indicated by the instances in which his example was followed. Still, the whole matter is one of philological interest rather than critical significance, and we may now turn to aspects of his style which are of more general importance.

[13]See the Arden edition of Shakespeare's *1 Henry VI* (1909). The *O.E.D.* was not completed until 1928.

[14]Spenser, however, perhaps originated the figurative sense of "snowy." "Snowy lockes" (*F.Q.*, I.x.48) is the first example quoted by the *O.E.D.*

III

Spenser's style declares him clearly to be a poet of the Renaissance. He did not, of course, introduce into English verse the practice of classical allusion—that existed already and was one of the "rhetorical" features of Chaucer's style—but he noticeably confirmed and extended it. Many of his allusions are part of the ordinary routine of contemporary verse: "Golden Phoebus," "wrathful Boreas," "silver Cynthia," "swelling Neptune"—no special invention is needed to form such phrases as these, in which the familiar name is coupled with some obvious epithet. At times, however, his descriptive phrases recall the words of Latin verse more distinctly. He was apparently the first of our poets to use the word *liquid*, after "liquidus" in Latin poetry, in the sense of "bright, transparent (like pure water)"[15] as in the description of a bird that cleaves "the liquid firmament" (*F.Q.*, III.iv.49).[16] He also introduced the word *daedal* (*F.Q.*, III.Prol.ii.), both in the sense of "cunning to invent" and as "a vague poetic use after Lucretius: natura daedala rerum."[17] But much of the classicism of *The Faerie Queene* is of the popular type that lingered on from the Middle Ages, and the spirit of the poem allowed it to appear by the side of the exacter type which arose from scholarship.

There are, in fact, many levels in Spenser's style. The popular proverb is there, also the stately reminiscence from Homer or the Roman poets. Classical names, as used in his verse, seldom contain such wealth of music or mythical suggestion as they have in *Paradise Lost*, yet his periphrases often give a clear anticipation of that poem. "That strong Tirynthian swaine" (*F.Q.*, VI.xii.35), "that great Oetean knight" (V.viii.2), "that sage Pylian syre" (II.ix.48), have very nearly the authentic stamp of Milton's manner. The range of such expressions is wide and is not confined to classical references: Samson, for instance, is "that mighty Jewish swaine" (V.viii.2), and Tasso "that famous Tuscan penne" (IV.iii.45). Sometimes, as in Shakespeare, periphrasis indicates a mood of tenderness, as in the lines (V.ix.50) in which Mercilla's "princely breast" is touched "with piteous ruth" for Duessa, so that she lets fall

Few perling drops from her faire lampes of light,

but more especially it is associated with similes, which in *The Faerie Queene* are often momentary elevations above the routine style of the poem. In the lines on Iris (V.iii.25):

[15]Quoted from *O.E.D.*
[16]Cf. "the liquid air" (Dryden), "the liquid noon" (Gray), etc.
[17]*O.E.D.* Cf. "daedal landscapes" (Warton), "the daedal earth" (Wordsworth).

> As when the daughter of *Thaumantes* faire,
> Hath in a watry cloud displayed wide
> Her goodly bow, which paints the liquid ayre;
> That all men wonder at her colours pride,

and throughout *The Faerie Queene* the periphrasis within the simile often marks the "exornation" (to use a term from the Rhetoric of the time) in a long stretch of narrative or allegory.

In *The Faerie Queene*, as in all long poems of any merit, there are moments when the style attains a colour or warmth above its usual tenor. The action takes a turn at which the emotion deepens, or some imaginary object is visualized with unusual vividness. At these rare moments the compound epithet often fulfils the function of adding force to emotion or stimulating the fancy to a wider survey. Spenser stands near the beginning of the large development of this poetic device,[18] and he was surpassed by many of his successors in the power and beauty of their formations. None the less, his compound epithets, both in number and in quality, form a notable element in his poetic style. A few of them, like *rosy-fingered* (morning) (I.ii.7) are echoes from classical poets, but many are original and felicitous formations of his own, and his example did much to establish the use of the compound epithet in English poetry at this time since it helped to give Nature-verse a much-desired resemblance to that of Greek and Roman poetry. Among his descriptive epithets one notices: *shaggy-bearded* (goats), *firie-mouthed* (steeds), *froth-fomy* (steed), *fire-spitting* (forge), *sea-shouldring* (whales)—formations which in their number and variety contribute towards making *The Faerie Queene* a main link between the classics of the Ancient World and three centuries of English verse. A peculiarly English quality of Spenser's epithets is their use for expressing an intimate or deep emotion. A constant feature for generations to come in imaginative writing was the creation and use of epithets in which the first element is the word "heart." Some examples of such epithets may be found in Sidney, but the man who firmly planted them in the soil of English verse was undoubtedly Spenser with his *"hart murdring loue"* (II.v.16), *"hart-thrilling* throbs" (III.ii.5), *"hart-percing* dart" (III. xi.30), *"hartfretting* payne" (IV.v.45), *"hart-murdring* paine" (V.v.30), and many more. It would be impossible to give any idea of the extent to which Spenser's example has been followed: one can only quote a few representative instances, such as Shakespeare's *"heart-easing* words," Drayton's *"heart-moving* music," Milton's *"heart-easing* mirth," Francis

---

[18]Such epithets occur in Chaucer, e.g., *laurer-crowned* (*Troilus*, v. 159), *tendre-hearted* (*ibid.*, v.118), but they are not common.

Quarles's "*heart-corroding* fangs Of griping care," Thomson's "*heart-expanding* view," Cowper's "*heart-chilling* fears," and—in the rhetorical prose of De Quincey—"*heart-shattering* music."

Spenser's formation of compound epithets does not correspond in all respects to later practice, and some types occur in *The Faerie Queene* which afterwards became rare, at least until the late nineteenth century. For instance, *vine-prop* (elm) is of an unusual pattern, seldom found outside the unconventional styles such as that of G. M. Hopkins. The epithets *bare-head* and *light-foot*, both in Spenser, belong to a type which has long gone out of use. The latter word, described by the *Oxford Dictionary* as "poetic" and "very common in the Sixteenth Century," is particularly common in *The Faerie Queene*, which is perhaps the reason why it has survived in verse almost to the present day, being used by Tennyson, Swinburne, and Housman.

IV

One of the most prolific sources of poetic words is the process known to philologists as "differentiation." During periods when the usage of a language is still unfixed, two forms of the same word may easily exist side by side, and in course of time, when the vocabulary comes to be sifted by critics and grammarians, one of the words in such a pair will drop out of use unless it has a new function assigned to it. A familiar illustration of this process is the emergence of a new word *humane*, which originally was only an alternative spelling of "human." Another form of differentiation takes place when an old or obsolescent word is retained in the vocabulary of poetry, while its rival and synonym remains in ordinary use. Indeed, this second kind of differentiation, which extends to many words retained in verse for their associations, covers a considerable part of the poetic vocabulary. It is natural that in the work of Spenser who did so much to build up and perpetuate the diction of English poetry, we should find the process of "poetic differentiation" abundantly illustrated.

On the surface, Spenser's principal means of forming a differentiated diction for poetry appears to be his use of archaism. One cannot help wondering how far he weighed the consequences of this practice to his future reputation. In any case, the risk he took was abundantly justified, for even at this day the style of his poem, though archaic, is not obsolete, since many of his archaisms have received new life in the work of his imitators. There are, of course, varying degrees of fidelity among the Spenserians to the details of their master's style. Certain of his characteristic words and types of words are seldom found outside such poems as *The Schoolmistress* and *The Castle of Indolence*—words like *dreeriment, covetise, riotise, drowsyhed, lustyhed, livelyhed*. These are "Spenserian" rather than "poetic" words.[19] But many of his archaisms, like *eld, shend, certes, nathless, beldame, eftsoons, uprist, ywis*, have a wider currency, and without being precisely "poetic" are not definitely "Spenserian." They will be found, not only in the work of the professed imitators, but here and there as elements in the individual style of Milton, Coleridge, Keats, and others.

Spenser's archaism is conspicuous enough, but its imaginative and emotional character is the main source of its interest to the critic. Yet it must be remembered that the apparent poetic quality of certain phrases is due to the general character of the poem rather than to the deliberate verbal skill of the poet. To the modern reader many expressions in *The Faerie Queene* seem to belong wholly to the realm of romance. This impression, however, is partly the result of time and association. There are expressions in the poem which originally had a more practical and matter-of-fact quality than they appear to possess today. A favourite word of both Chaucer and Spenser, "emprize," illustrates the point. Up to the end of the sixteenth century an "emprize" was much the same as an "enterprise." The former word is now obsolete except in imaginative writing, and we can see from Spenser's poetry how it obtained this romantic colouring. When words are beginning to grow unfamiliar, and are known to a reader only from a few contexts, they naturally take on the associations of such contexts. The chivalrous spirit of *The Faerie Queene* was powerful enough to give various words an association with chivalry. Thus "emprize" was obviously ear-marked for the poetry of the future when it occurred in such lines as the following (IV.x.4), in which Scudamour describes his quest of the "shield of Love" and the "fair Amoret":

> I boldly thought (so young mens thoughts are bold)
> That this same braue emprize for me did rest,
> And that both shield and she whom I behold,
> Might be my lucky lot. . . .

To readers of the eighteenth and nineteenth centuries Scudamour's quest would indeed seem an "emprize" rather than an "enterprise"—a chivalrous adventure, not a mere speculation. Here it is time that allows a new sense, almost a new word, to be created by association.

But the romantic touch was sometimes added by Spenser himself, for to him the language of Chaucer and Gower was much the same as

---

[19]Many such words occur in Chaucer, e.g. *coveityse* (*Romaunt of the Rose*, 1. 4129, Skeat's edition); *drerihed* (*ibid.*, 1. 4728); *falshede* (*ibid.*, 1. 4141), etc. But their survival in Shenstone and Thomson is of course due to Spenser.

his own language became to readers two centuries later. Thus *chevi-saunce* which was originally a commercial term, sometimes even having the meaning of "gain in a bad sense," was used by Spenser for a "chivalrous enterprise or achievement," as in the words (III.xi.24):

> for shamefull thing
> It were t'abandon noble cheuisaunce,
> For shew of perill, without venturing.

So too there are various vaguely attractive words in his poetry of which the precise meaning will perhaps never be discovered. Thus his *Astrophel* (l. 186) is described by the *Oxford Dictionary* as the "name of a plant mentioned by Spenser, which has not been identified," and *bell-amour* (*Amoretti*, lxiv) as "applied to some unidentified flower." A word he uses for "sword," *brondiron* (*F.Q.*, IV.iv.32), repeated by Quarles, is wrongly supposed to have the sense of "brand."

Poetry has a natural tendency to keep certain alternative forms of words, when such exist, on a kind of "reserved list," for use in a possible emergency. The difference of a single syllable or letter may easily make or mar the euphony of a line. Thus *margent* and *marge* have both been retained in verse as alternative forms of "margin." In Spenser such "poetic" words are numerous, but as often as not their stylistic value is rather potential than actual: the refinements of style remained to be cultivated in a later and less creative age. Thus in Spenser's lines (*F.Q.*, V.x.3):

> From th'vtmost brinke of the *Armericke* shore,
> Vnto the margent of the *Molucas*,

the form "margin" might be substituted without injury to the sound. But in Gray's line:

> Disporting on thy margent green,[20]

a similar change would be disastrous. Many so-called "poetic" words, such as *steed, damozel, gride, sheen* (adjective), *puissant, verdant, guerdon*, have in Spenser's work little of the distinctive quality which they were to receive in later times: the delicate verbal precision of a Tennyson or a Rossetti was impossible in the sixteenth century. Yet the presence of such words in *The Faerie Queene* is significant: it is significant for criticism, not merely for lexicography. Even if Spenser did not consciously use the form *damozel* "to express a more stately notion than is conveyed by *damsel*"; if he did not feel the "echoic expressiveness" of *gride* "suggested by words like *grate, strident*, etc." (*O.E.D.*), he at least gave such words an association with the world of imagination. Many of them are used again and again in *The Faerie Queene*, and a

[20]*On a Distant Prospect of Eton College.*

perceptive reader would inevitably, and perhaps unconsciously, associate them with romance and poetry.

The influence of Spenser on his disciples has been of a gentle and
unobtrusive nature. Less impressive than Milton, he is a more helpful
teacher, encouraging his pupils in their self-development, rather than
imposing the pattern of his own mind on theirs. Compared with many
of his mediaeval predecessors Spenser has an individual style, but compared with Milton, he is impersonal. His readers must often have felt
that they were reading the old authentic language of English poetry
rather than a special form of it shaped for the ends of a single writer.
They would not have been mistaken. His principal debt is, of course,
to Chaucer. Within the first hundred lines of *The Faerie Queene* he is
proclaiming his discipleship in his list of trees: "the sayling Pine," "the
builder Oake" (I.i.8).[21] Elsewhere (IV.ii.32) he repeats the first line of
The Knight's Tale,[22] and in another place, the three well-known lines in
The Franklin's Tale which declare that Love takes wing at the coming
of "maistery" "and soon away is gone."[23] There are "poetic" words
which pass from Chaucer to Spenser through almost the whole course
of English poetry, such as *reign* (as in "Pluto's grisly reign")—a word
repeated by Milton, Dryden, Gray, Shelley, and many others. Lydgate
is also the source of certain "poetic" words in Spenser. There is too the
possibility that Spenser knew something of the alliterative rhyming verse
which is used so beautifully in *The Pearl*. In such lines as

> So faire and fresh, as freshest flowre in May,

and

> The blazing brightnesse of her beauties beame,

there seems to be something older and finer than the Elizabethan trick
of "hunting the letter." It would be the merest speculation to suggest,
on these grounds, that Spenser had read *The Pearl*, a poem which in
some ways anticipates his own style; but I am glad that for reasons of
his own Professor C. L. Wrenn comes to a similar conclusion: "Spenser," he writes, "may have known something of the work of the Gawain-
poet."[24]

The conservatism and the variety of Spenser's diction, its "archaism
and innovation" are equally remarkable. Like the language of the 1611
Version of the Bible it preserves the past and anticipates the future.

---

[21]Cf. *The Parlement of Foules*, ll. 176, 179. Spenser transfers "sayling" from
the fir to the pine.
[22]"Olde" is changed to "antique."
[23]They reappear slightly changed in *F.Q.*, III.i.25.
[24]"On Rereading Spenser's Shepheardes Calender."

Its influence, like that of the Bible, operated in many different ways: the borrowers took according to their various needs, not after much the same fashion, like the imitators of Milton. To trace the influence of Spenser on the succeeding course of English poetry will be one of the main tasks of the following chapters, but a few points, by way of anticipation, may be fitly mentioned here. Shakespeare, as one might suppose, is most Spenserian in *A Midsummer Night's Dream*, and in one or two other plays of his early period. Pastoral poetry owes its diction to Spenser more than to any other English writer, and among the phrases which he may have originated are: *oaten pipe*, (*S.C.*, Jan. 72) *shepherd swain*, and *fleecy flock* (*F.Q.*, III.vi.15). The debt of Milton to Spenser is well known: he is indeed the greatest of the Spenserians, and his modifications of his master's style will be mentioned in a later chapter. Passing reference may here be made to Latinizing,[25] which in Spenser is only an occasional feature of style compared with its frequency in Milton; also to rare or striking phrases such as "buxom air"[26] or "scum the dross"[27] which are common to the two poets. In Spenser too are clear beginnings of what came to be called the "poetic diction" of the eighteenth century: "the *watry* Gods" (*F.Q.*, IV.xi.10), "the *nation* of . . . birds" (II.xii.36), "his *finny* droue" (III.viii.29). The story continues with the next century. A phrase from *Colin Clouts Come Home Againe* (l. 245):

> *Triton* blowing loud his wreathed horne

is obviously the original of Wordsworth's line:

> Or hear old Triton blow his wreathed horn.[28]

To this handful of examples may be added a few of a different kind—instances of unconscious testimony to the vogue of *The Faerie Queene*. Well known as the fact is, we may recall that two words, *blatant* and *braggadocio*,[29] are formations of Spenser's which have become part of the common vocabulary. The phrase "bower of bliss" which occurs in Book II of *The Faerie Queene* has been repeated, sometimes no doubt with conscious reference to Spenser, as in Cowper's poem *Hope* (l. 164); but it is strange to find it surviving—presumably without recognition of its source—among the rustic folk of Hardy's *Jude the*

---

[25]Examples of Spenser's "literal" Latinizing in the manner so familiar in Milton are: "rusticke *horror*" (*F.Q.*, I.vi.11); "*redounding* teares" (I.iii.8); "heauy *ruine*" (downfall) (II.vii.28).

[26]*F.Q.*, I.xi.37; *Paradise Lost*, II.842.

[27]*F.Q.* ("scumd the drosse"), II.36; *P.L.* ("scum'd the bullion dross"), I.704.

[28]"Wreathed horn" is also in John Fletcher's *The Faithful Shepherdess* (III.i).

[29]In Spenser "Bragadocchio."

Obscure, where it is bestowed as a nickname upon a somewhat unsavoury character. We shall notice other "poetic" expressions whose history illustrates the well-known "downward tendency of language."

Our line of approach has necessarily brought one aspect of Spenser's diction into prominence: its power of suggesting and stimulating the expression of later poets. Spenser stands for certain qualities and practices in the style of poetry, and it is possible, with due caution, to call these "Spenserian" without necessarily implying that they originated in his work. That he was the originator of many "poetic" words and phrases, subsequently used, has already been shown, but it should be remembered that he was often the channel through which certain expressions passed, rather than their fountain-head. His claim to the title of "the poet's poet" is clearer than his claim to be called the founder of our poetic diction. Indeed, as we have seen, Chaucer himself has a place in that tradition: so too, among the poets of the sixteenth century, has Sackville. But what is important is the continuous admiration which Spenser inspired among our poets from Milton onwards. His style was a fruitful source of suggestion to other poets at a time when Chaucer, to be read at all, had to be modernized, and when the "Induction" to the *Mirror for Magistrates* was scarcely known. Readers of Mr. B. R. McElderry's admirable article "Archaism and Innovation in Spenser's Diction" are warned against regarding Spenser as the creator, in the strict historical sense, of "modern poetic diction."

He made substantial additions to the literary language. . . . But language, even in its most changeable periods, is extremely conservative. No one person can "create" a poetic diction. The most he can do is to embellish incidentally a relatively standard idiom. The main poetic effect is latent in that standard idiom, and it is the poet's business to bring it out. This is what Spenser did. . . .

As for there being no such thing as a more narrowly conventional poetic diction before Spenser, a casual reading of Tottel's *Miscellany* will correct that impression. Or a reading of *O.E.D.*'s sixteenth-century quotations for such words as *adieu, adown, agone, babe, bedecked, bedight, clad, corse, locks, pine* (vb.), *ruth, sere, slay, sprite,* and *surge* will make clear that these words had an acknowledged poetic connotation not much different from what they have for us. These words are all used by Spenser, and they show that he was not of the opinion that a conventionally poetic word is necessarily undesirable. Spenser wished a richer, not an impossibly new or old diction.

Spenser is indeed the poet's poet, but he does much more than furnish hints on which others have improved. In many passages of *The Faerie Queene,* to say nothing of the best among the shorter poems, there is no room for improvement. Even in the pure technique of verse-writing he is often equal to poets with a far longer succession of models to guide them. For instance, in manipulating proper names for their sound and suggestion Spenser is—apart from Milton—the equal of any poet that can be named. Let the reader examine Spenser's four stanzas on the fifty Nereids (*F.Q.*, IV.xi.48–51) and the parallel passage in Bridges's *Eros and Psyche* ("March," 27, 28), and then ask what the earlier poet has to fear from comparison with his accomplished successor. To recall the many passages in *The Faerie Queene* in which Spenser's highest verbal skill is applied to great imaginative or ethical effects would here be impossible. It is enough to remember the great canto on the Cave of Mammon, the Masque of Cupid, the episode of Pastorella, the Masque of the Seasons and Months, and the concluding stanzas of "Mutability." It is a nice question, and one which need not be settled here, whether Spenser, as the creator of a poetic style, is more remarkable for the faultless quality of such passages as these or for the larger legacy of his diffused descriptions and narratives, pregnant with suggestion to succeeding poets.

THE EARLY SPENSERIANS

The Fletchers

The early Spenserians adopted the diction of *The Faerie Queene* largely because their poetic aims had a certain resemblance to those of the master. In Fairfax's translation of the *Gerusalemme Liberata*,[30] for instance, Spenser's language is used to render into English another epic of chivalry. Though not in the first rank of English translations, it is an accomplished work and was a favourite with Charles I. The brothers Giles and Phineas Fletcher borrowed a large portion of Spenser's spirit as well as his manner. Phineas is the closer follower of the two, in that his *Purple Island* is a poetic allegory: its subject being the human body, or "isle of Man," and its various enemies. Giles adopts perhaps as many Spenserian words as his brother. His sacred poem in four parts on the Life of Christ in Heaven and on Earth is the finer work of the two, and contains more original features.

In translating Tasso into English verse, Fairfax uses the *ottava rima* of his Italian original, but his diction—though somewhat less archaic and dialectal—may be described, with some latitude of sense, simply as Spenser's. He does not confine himself to Spenser's actual words, but introduces some new analogical forms of his own. He also varies spelling for purposes of rhyme with something of his master's freedom. To

[30]Published under the title of *Godfrey of Bulloigne* (1600).

illustrate the archaic colouring of Fairfax's style it is enough to quote such words as *gent, leasing, gan, eft, yclad, stowre, eath, emprise, semblant, ensample, mote, algates, ycleped, treen* (plural), which all occur within a few hundred lines.

The Purple Island (1633) of Phineas Fletcher[31] is written in a stanza based on that of Spenser. It consists of seven instead of nine lines—the fifth and seventh being omitted—and concludes with an Alexandrine. The shorter form lacks the structural unity of its original, for it falls into two distinct parts, the first consisting of a quatrain (*abab*), the second of three consecutive rhyming lines (*ccc*). The Spenserian words are not so frequent as in Fairfax, though it is impossible to forget *The Faerie Queene* for long. The poem is a blend of pastoral and allegory, and the stanzas in Spenser's praise (I.19,20,21) declare the school to which Fletcher belongs. The poet's training in the style of *The Faerie Queene* is shown by such phrases and words as *flaggy wing, merrie-make* (noun; Spenser, "merimake"), *dispreads, derring-deed* (cf. Spenser's "derring doe" and "derring doers"), *dreeriment, aggrate,* and *bounty head* (VI.26; Spenser, "bountihed").

The four parts of Giles Fletcher's poem (published 1610)—*Christs Victorie in Heaven, Christs Victorie on Earth, Christs Triumph over Death,* and *Christs Triumph after Death*—form a religious sequence of considerable beauty. Though the style presents some original features, the Spenserian colouring is always apparent. The stanza employed stands midway between that of *The Faerie Queene* and *The Purple Island,* being the Spenserian with the seventh line omitted. Fletcher's diction recalls other poets besides Spenser. In the frequency of the "verbs" transferred from other parts of speech, such as *sad, lanke, bowre, jolly, hermit,* it shows an interesting resemblance to the contemporary style of Shakespeare. In using the rare type of verb *elamp, elong* (to retard), *eblaze,* Fletcher seems to have followed his own counsel, and he is perhaps the one poet on record in whom this stylistic feature is to be found. But the Spenserian element is especially prominent. Like a true disciple of his master, he forms many derivatives with the prefix *en-,* such as *enwave, enslumber, englad, embeame.*[32] The Spenserian[33] words and forms borrowed directly reach a considerable number. Examples are: *belgards, empassion, aggrate, empurple, embay* (bathe, steep), *languishment, disentrayle, flit* (swift, nimble) *dispred.* However, the less precise evidence of "style" gives a stronger and a truer impression of Fletcher's Spenserianism. One or two phrases and passages are

[31] Giles and Phineas Fletcher, *Poetical Works,* ed. F. S. Boas (Cambridge, 1908).

[32] All are "first examples" in the *O.E.D.*

[33] "Spenserian" here means that the first quotations in *O.E.D.* are from Spenser.

incorporated in Fletcher's poem without change, the most noticeable being two lines from Spenser's stanzas on the Cave of Despair which reappear in the later poet's description of the Cave of "Desperation":

> Dark, dolefull, dreary, like a greedie grave,
> That still for carrion carkasses doth crave.[34]

These lines, identical with Spenser's except for slight differences in spelling, harmonize perfectly with their new content—a proof of the Spenserian quality of Fletcher's general style.

It is, however, right that we should recognize this poet's originality, for in many passages he passes far beyond the rank of a mere follower. The finest parts of his poem are those on the Temptation and the Passion. Two stanzas from the latter passage illustrate the work of the early Spenserian school at its best:

> It was but now their sounding clamours sung,
> Blessed is he, that comes from the most high,
> And all the mountaines with Hosanna rung,
> And nowe, away with him, away they crie,
> And nothing can be heard but crucifie:
>   It was but now, the Crowne it selfe they save,
>   And golden name of King unto him gave,
> And nowe, no King, but onely Caesar, they will have:
>
> It was but now they gathered blooming May,
> And of his armes disrob'd the branching tree,
> To strowe with boughs, and blossoms all thy way,
> And now, the branchlesse truncke a crosse for thee,
> And May, dismai'd, thy coronet must be:
>   It was but now they wear so kind, to throwe
>   Their owne best garments, whear thy feet should goe,
> And now, thy selfe they strip, and bleeding wounds they show.[35]

Sylvester

Joshua Sylvester (1563–1618) was the translator of Du Bartas and the author of several original poems. His place and importance in the history of the diction of English poetry will appear somewhat differently according to the relations in which his work is regarded. On a limited view of the subject, he might appear to be a figure of considerable magnitude. His translation of Du Bartas' *Semaines*[36] seems to have introduced into English usage a number of words and phrases which later formed the basis of the vocabulary employed by the "Creation-poets"

[34]*F.Q.*, I.ix.33; *Christs Victorie on Earth*, 23.
[35]*Christs Triumph over Death*, 32, 33.
[36]*Du Bartas his divine weekes and workes*, tr. 1591–1608.

of the eighteenth century, and their associates. But whether a direct connection between Sylvester and these poets can be established is a question which admits of much doubt. In his excellent book *The Language of Natural Description in Eighteenth-Century Poetry*,[37] Mr. John Arthos remarks (p. 79, note): "Though the diction of eighteenth-century English poetry owed immeasurably to Sylvester, many of the individual poets may have been quite ignorant of his work. They may have modeled themselves upon Lucretius and Virgil, and have been quite unaware that their English vocabulary came from Sylvester at second or third hand." The statement here made as to Virgil and Lucretius deserves the attention of all who are interested in the "poetic diction" of the eighteenth century, for the Latin character of that diction is more striking than has been commonly recognized. The argument of Mr. Arthos, if I may venture to paraphrase it, is as follows: Certain words and phrases, corresponding to philosophical notions of the universe and its Creator, passed from the Greek and Latin poets to Renaissance authors such as Du Bartas, and these, converted into English, entered our language by way of the translation of Sylvester. But it may well have happened that the later English poets whose diction in some respects resembles Sylvester's drew upon the same sources as Du Bartas himself, and need never have read the translation of his poem.

This argument is, I believe, substantially true. The main force which preserved in English poetry phrases like "feathered kind" (Dryden), "feather'd people" (Pope), "feathery people" (Thomson) for so long was the prestige of Latin poetry by which similar phrases, such as "genus alituum" (Lucretius) and "agminis aligeri" (Virgil), fixed themselves in the memory of generation after generation of schoolboys and students. No doubt, as Mr. Tillotson reminds us,[38] there were other causes: "The diction ... is not simply 'poetic' diction: it is also 'physico-theological' nomenclature." In any case, it is the power of thought and style that is important. Sylvester's diction is a phenomenon of language rather than of style. His own style is exuberant, unequal, heterogeneous—without the force or individuality to preserve his diction beyond the changes in literary fashion.

Sylvester, indeed, was the poet of a limited period only. Whatever his vogue may have been in the earlier part of the seventeenth century it rapidly declined after 1660. Dryden rejects him decisively. "I remember, when I was a boy," he writes, "I thought inimitable Spenser a

[37]University of Michigan Press, 1949.
[38]"Eighteenth-Century Poetic Diction" (*Essays and Studies by Members of the English Association*, XXV, 1939).

mean poet, in comparison of Sylvester's *Dubartas*"; and, after quoting a passage of four lines by which at one time he "was rapt into an ecstasy," continues "I am much deceived if this be not abominable fustian."[39] The significance of a poet's diction is obviously determined in part by his merit as a poet, and as Sylvester cannot be regarded as more than a minor writer, his diction cannot have a major importance. Two facts, however, make his case somewhat exceptional. He was the effective translator of the most important poem on the Creation to be written in the sixteenth century, and he was read by the youthful Milton at a highly susceptible age. These two considerations constitute his claim to a place in the present study, and an attempt will therefore be made to offer an estimate of the historical interest of his diction.

It has been asserted that Sylvester's work shows little of Spenser's influence: still, his style shows many of the same general features which were common to the age. It is true, however, that he is not one of Spenser's close disciples. His diction is somewhat flavoured with archaism, though he had none of Spenser's enthusiasm for Chaucer. Sylvester uses occasional archaisms like *treen* and *eyne*, and some participial forms like *yblent* and *ypend*: but these are not frequent enough to form a marked feature of his style. He is extremely fond of the termination *-full*, and in a short reading of his work one may gather a list such as *lampfull, presagefull, scopefull, shiftfull, stormfull, flamefull, strangefull*. His "verbs" often show the full measure of Elizabethan licence: e.g., *quintessence, retrograde, with-childe*, the last being something of a favourite. Such qualities of style show Sylvester simply as a poet of his age.

He is most interesting in his use of periphrasis, though here too he shows more of Elizabethan exuberance than of classical restraint or economy. The point may be illustrated in several ways. If, for example, we examine his method of forming periphrases for the word *fish*, we shall find it consists in applying a generic epithet like "scaly" in varied combinations: thus, we have "scaly *shoales*," "scaly *Nation*," "skalie [*sic*] *legions*," "scaly *folke*," "scaly *crew*."[40] But the neo-classical combinations show less variety, and tend to be limited to words corresponding to such Latin nouns as *genus, pecus, natio*, and *grex*. *Kind, race, tribe, nation*, and *people* are repeated frequently, as if a small but select "classical" vocabulary was an inexhaustible fund of elegance. There is another respect in which the periphrases of Sylvester differ widely from

[39]*Essays of John Dryden*, ed. W. P. Ker (Oxford, 1900), Dedication of *The Spanish Friar*.

[40]For first four phrases, see Arthos, *Language of Natural Description*, p. 369. "Scaly crew" is in *Du Bartas*, I.v.34.

those of his neo-classical successors. Sylvester's expressions are often those fanciful "conceits" which the later age condemned as "false wit." Thus, he calls snow "a heav'nly wool" (*Du Bartas*, I.ii.573); the sun a "radiant Coach-man" (I.iv.548), and (in an apostrophe) "pure goldy-locks" (I.iv.400). A crocodile is "Nile's poys'ny Pirate" (I.vi.284); lips are "two moving Leaves of Corall, soft and sweet" (I.vi.601). Not only are stars *studs*, but the fancy is elaborated into an astronomical conceit (I.iv.106–7):

> So those gilt studs in th'upper story driv'n,
> Are nothing but the thickest part of Heav'n.

Likewise the notion that snow is *wool*, is elaborated into the passage (*The Handy-Crafts*, 184–7) by which the youthful Dryden was "rapt into an ecstasy":

> But, when the Winter's keener breath began
> To crystallize the Baltike Ocean,
> To glaze the Lakes, and bridle-up the Flouds,
> And perriwig with wool the balde-pate Woods. . . .

That Milton had once read Sylvester and adopted some of his words and expressions has long been recognized. Perhaps the fact has been somewhat discounted in reaction against the attempt of the Rev. Charles Dunster (1750–1816) to prove that Milton's indebtedness amounts to plagiarism. Milton, says this writer, "has done little more than refined Sylvester's language, the translator of Du Bartas, with a few additions and variations, according to his usual custom. From this author Milton has borrowed many elegant phrases and single words, which were thought to be peculiar to him; such as *palpable darkness*, and a thou-sand others."[41] The case is, of course, greatly exaggerated; and though Milton certainly borrowed or "stole" some of Sylvester's words, Dunster overlooks the crucial fact that he was—in Swinburne's quoted phrase—a "celestial thief." Sylvester, nevertheless, appears to have had the same fascination for the youthful Milton as he had for the youthful Dryden. A number of his words and phrases lingered in Milton's memory, and were repeated in new contexts. *Palpable darkness*, however, is not one of these, since the phrase (traceable to the Vulgate: Exodus x.21) had appeared in English a century before Sylvester's time.[42] Still some sig-nificant parallels between the two poets are to be found. Thus, the *day-star* of *Lycidas* is an expression used by Sylvester.[43] The epithet for the

---

[41]Quoted by A. B. Grosart, editor of *The Complete Works of Joshua Sylvester* (1880).
[42]In *O.E.D.* (quotation "*c.* 1450").
[43]*Du Bartas*, II.ii *Babylon* 577 (*O.E.D.*).

Mincius, *smooth-sliding*, also in *Lycidas*, appears earlier in Sylvester's *Eden* (l. 117): "the chrystall of smooth-sliding floods." "The *Erythræan* main" in Milton's translation of Psalm 136 "don by the Author at fifteen yeers old" looks like a reminiscence of "th'Erithraean Deep" of Sylvester (*Du Bartas*, I.iii.77). A passage from Sylvester's *Eden* on a forest (ll. 518–19):

> Whose arched boughs, for Frize & Cornich bear
> Thick groves, to shield from future change of air

perhaps suggested the phrase "Cornice or Freeze" of *Paradise Lost* (I.716)—a conjecture one would hardly entertain if Milton had not almost certainly read Sylvester's *Eden*. One might be tempted to dwell on other "noticeable" words common to both poets, e.g. *rathe, swart, paranymph*, and phrases like "Amalthean Horn" (Sylvester), "Amalthea's horn" (Milton), but they are not rare enough to establish the certainty of Milton's indebtedness. When all is said, the influence of Sylvester on Milton (and therefore on English poetry) was one of temporary duration, and not of major importance. Much of the interest which might be found in Sylvester's diction is discounted by the general mediocrity of his poetic style.

THE DICTION of Shakespeare considered in its relation to English poetry in general presents an aspect much simpler than that which it shows when viewed as a part of its author's self-revelation in drama, narrative, or lyric, or which seen against the background of Elizabethan literature. A complete examination of Shakespeare's use of words from the critical point of view would embrace various questions of dramatic interpretation as well as many philological problems, and their purely poetic quality would be simply one aspect among several: his place in the succession of poets who have formed the traditional diction of poetry might easily be overlooked or crowded out altogether. It is, of course, impossible to draw an absolute distinction between Shakespeare the dramatist and Shakespeare the poet: in fact, his greatest scenes and plays are precisely those in which the two sides of his creative activity are most completely fused. The question is one of emphasis. For our present purpose, there is a special importance in the purely poetic or less dramatic parts of Shakespeare's work. These are closer to the general traditions of English verse. From these in particular Milton drew hints and suggestions for the diction of his early poems. For in the early plays Shakespeare does much to develop and enrich the capacities of the language for the description of Nature. There, his style is not over-charged with passion, not dazzling with excess of metaphor, not compressed to the verge of obscurity, but in passage after passage an exquisite model of poetic English. It is in *Romeo and Juliet*, in *A Midsummer Night's Dream*, and in *Richard II* that we find the loveliest descriptions of Nature as a source of refreshment and joy, whether in harmony with, or in contrast to, the passions of men.

But the descriptive passages of Shakespeare's later plays, especially those in the great tragedies, have immensely extended the expressive capacity of the English language. Such passages have already influenced the style of many poets and prose-writers in the past, and it is conceivable that they should exert a like power in the future. The poetry of *Hamlet, Othello,* and *Macbeth* is different in some vital respects from that of the earlier plays. In these tragedies, Shakespeare has solved the problem of charging the speeches of his characters with splendid and powerful poetry, without making us feel that the speakers themselves are necessarily poetic. No one is misled as to the true character of persons like Laertes, Gertrude, or Banquo because they utter certain lines and expressions of great beauty, and Iago is not to be deemed a poet at heart because, in a tense moment of the play, he speaks of poppy or mandragora, or "the drowsy syrops of the world." In these tragedies, poetry may be uttered by anyone. The men and women have a gift of creative expression in their choice and use of words no less than in the metrical rhythm of their speeches. Great poetry is here an integral part of the play. It keeps the imagination and emotions at the pitch of excitement required for the characterization and dramatic action to produce their full effect. Nor is this poetry of an esoteric nature or limited appeal. The language of Shakespeare, even if not critically appreciated, has a sure and general effect comparable to that of the Bible. Persons not conspicuously "poetic" in ordinary character are wrought upon by the heightening splendour of the words to an increased awareness of the action.

The diction of Shakespeare's later plays—say, from 1600 to 1611, the period of the great tragedies and the late romantic comedies—is marked by an intensification of passion and vitality as compared with the diction of the earlier work. Vitality, as we shall see, often expresses itself in terms of activity, agitation, *movement*. It is these elements of passion and movement that made Shakespeare's diction appeal to the Romantic poets, especially in their Nature-poetry, for they needed something different from the more stately and placid manner inherited through Milton from Spenser. The diction of Spenser is contemplative rather than impassioned, static rather than dynamic. It tends to dwell on the invariable aspects of things, and one of its chief effects is the finding of epithets for what seems immutable in a mutable world. Hence its conservatism, its love of tradition, its cult of the generic phrase. It is a diction fit to characterize the general virtues and vices of man, the forces of Nature, the species of animals, the seasons. It is a modification of language rather than a recreation of it. In all these aspects it appealed to Milton and the "Creation"-poets who followed him, whose aim was to represent Nature as the handiwork of a divine and unchangeable Being, perfect in Himself, and superior to the varying passions of men. One of its principal resources was the epithet, for as that could best convey the constant aspects of Nature, so it could best indicate the attributes of the Deity:

Immutable, Immortal, Infinite.

Spenser's diction, even as modified by Shakespeare from the first, was totally unsuitable for the effects to be produced in the tragedies. After the passing of Shakespeare's Spenserian period, there follows the comparatively unpoetic work of his best histories (*1* and *2 Henry IV, Henry V*). *Julius Caesar* shows promise of the new diction to come, but it is in *Hamlet* that it appears for the first time in full strength—the diction of intensified passion and movement.

The impression of movement produced on the imagination by Shakespeare's poetry is admirably described in Professor Caroline Spurgeon's book *Shakespeare's Imagery*:[1]

The more we study [the] main groups of images which constitute the greatest part of Shakespeare's imagery, the clearer it becomes that there is one quality or characteristic in them all which overpoweringly attracts him throughout, and that quality is *movement*: nature and natural objects in motion.

In other words, it is the life of things which appeals to him, stimulates and enchants him, rather than beauty of colour or form or even significance.

This fact of Shakespeare's love of movement is a good example of how a study of the subject-matter of his images may throw light on his poetic technique, for I believe it supplies a clue to one of the secrets of his magical style. Thus it leads us to note how constantly in description it is the aspect of movement or life he seizes upon and portrays; so that many of his most memorable and unapproachable lines are charged with this quality, often conveyed in a single word. How many epithets, for instance, have poets used for the moon—wan, silver, watery, inconstant, fruitful and so on—but has her particular quality of movement in relation to this planet, that of coming and going, ever been so magically caught as by Shakespeare in one word?

> And there is nothing left remarkable
> Beneath the *visiting* moon.[2]

Miss Spurgeon proceeds to give other instances of vivid effects produced by a single word, noting in particular "his favourite verb *peep*—a human action—to convey the quick darting movement of an object desiring to escape unseen:

> the borders maritime
> Lack blood to think on't, and flush youth revolt:
> No vessel can peep forth, but 'tis as soon
> Taken as seen."[3]

Miss Spurgeon develops this point at some length, but she draws no distinction between Shakespeare's earlier and later styles, though her

---

[1](Cambridge, 1935), pp. 50–1.

[2]*Antony and Cleopatra*, IV.xiii.67. Line-references in this chapter are from the one-volume Oxford *Shakespeare*.

[3]*Ibid.*, I.iv.51–4; Spurgeon, *Shakespeare's Imagery*, p. 53.

examples are in fact taken from the later plays, and by far the most striking ones are from *Macbeth* and *Antony and Cleopatra*. Now it was precisely in their passion for Nature and their sense of her life and movement that the great Romantic poets differed from their predecessors of the eighteenth century, to whom love of Nature was little more than an elegant taste. Miss Spurgeon hints at this relation when she remarks that "this excessive susceptibility to movement, this passionate absorption in the life of things, Shakespeare shares with two other great English poets," namely Wordsworth and Keats.[4] And in the Preface to her *Keats's Shakespeare*, she notes that the plays most marked by the younger poet were *The Tempest, A Midsummer Night's Dream, Measure for Measure*, and *Antony and Cleopatra*—one belonging to the Spenserian period of Shakespeare's diction, three to the later or "impassioned" period. We shall notice in the sequel that an admiration for Shakespeare's language in general was a mark of the taste of Romantic poets and critics as distinguished from the more limited admiration of his earlier style, of which we see proof in Milton and Milton's imitators in the eighteenth century.

In broad perspective, then, Shakespeare's diction has two main phases, which in the light of what has been said may be named the "Spenserian," and the "tragic," "impassioned," or simply "later." In both styles Shakespeare can write creatively, with a full exertion of his poetic power, but their prevalent quality differs in the manner already described. The Spenserian diction is perhaps more "beautiful," the "impassioned" diction more vital and powerful. The Spenserian type reaches its highest point of excellence either in *A Midsummer Night's Dream* or in *Romeo and Juliet*, but there are many Spenserian expressions in some of the earlier plays such as *1 Henry VI* and *The Two Gentlemen of Verona*: in general, however, this preliminary work is marked by a much greater indefiniteness of style than the masterpieces of the earlier period which followed it. Nor does the Spenserian type of diction ever entirely disappear. It survives in some of the less powerful passages of the great tragedies, and it reappears, in a modified but very beautiful form, in the late romantic comedies, especially *The Winter's Tale* and *The Tempest*. One mark of the Spenserian style is the high proportion of epithets, while the special mark of the "impassioned" style is the vital and often metaphorical verb. In both styles, Shake-

---

[4]*Shakespeare's Imagery*, p. 55. Miss Spurgeon draws attention to "a most delightful and suggestive article on 'Wordsworth's *Prelude*,' by Helen Darbishire [*Nineteenth Century*, May, 1926] in which Wordsworth's use of the word 'motion' is examined."

speare produces poetry which is often independent of, but not opposed to, the representation of action and character, though in the greater plays such poetry, by heightening effects of contrast, atmosphere, irony, and the like, contributes much to the sum-total of dramatic power.

But besides these two main aspects of Shakespeare's diction, there is a third, which though far less poetic in the good sense, and often not poetic at all, is important both from the critical and from the dramatic points of view. This is the diction which may be described as "conventional" or "traditional." Certain forms of it may be found in the less characteristic and inferior parts of Shakespeare's work: in *The Two Gentlemen of Verona*, for instance, even in the verse of *2 Henry IV*, there is much conventional diction of a somewhat colourless nature. Such writing is of no significance for our present purpose. But Shakespeare often employs a more vital form of conventional diction for interesting and even exciting dramatic effects. Diction of this kind had associations in the mind of his audience, and he knew how to use them. The finer points in a dialogue, even a turn in the action, may depend on the author's deft use of conventionally poetic idioms, phrases, or single words. Sometimes, too, this inferior poetry sets off by contrast the superior quality of the poet's original expressions. It is necessary to include this aspect of Shakespeare's diction in our present survey, and it will be the first of the three to claim our attention.

I

Of all Shakespeare's characters, the most dependent upon his creator's fund of "poetic diction" is Ancient Pistol. No doubt he has "a gift of comic magniloquence,"[5] but his ranting verse, judged on its own merits, is mostly worthless. His mind, such as it is, has been nourished on the bombastic and noisy diction of certain contemporary plays, and cut off from that soil would wither away, just as Osric is no longer himself when "all's golden words are spent." Though few characters in Shakespeare are so dependent upon a peculiar style of speech as these two, there are many moments in the dialogue and action of the plays which turn on the associations of words and phrases in the minds of the audience. One of the surest and richest sources of such effects was the familiarity of the Elizabethans with the supposed humours and language of lovers. Nearly half the plays contain passages in which the unreal and comic side of love is glanced at, and Shakespeare's favourite instrument for making his point was the known language of the love-sick man before he had felt the touch of real passion. Instances of this from

[5]W. R. Rutland, Preface to *2 Hen. IV* (Oxford, 1946).

Romeo and Juliet, As You Like It, and *Hamlet* will at once occur to the reader. But love, whether real or unreal, is not always in earnest: sometimes it is merely complimentary, and in such a mood its accepted diction might be no more than such hackneyed epithets as *red and white, golden, coral,* or *crystal.* Even for words like these Shakespeare often found the fit dramatic use, as for instance in *Twelfth Night* when the disguised Viola cannot answer with the sincere emotion expected by Olivia, and therefore takes refuge in a polite compliment, expressed in a conventional phrase:

> 'Tis beauty truly blent, whose red and white
> Nature's own sweet and cunning hand laid on.

The audience of the time, familiar with the phrase *red and white* in scores of love-sonnets and lyrics, would at once recognize Viola's "poetry" as a faded hothouse bloom rather than a fresh flower of the field. Still quite unmistakable today is the falsetto of Demetrius's exclamation in *A Midsummer Night's Dream* when he awakes with the action of the love-juice in his eyes:

> O Helen! goddess, nymph, perfect, divine!
> To what, my love, shall I compare thine eyne?
> Crystal is muddy,

and it is no wonder that Helen spurns all such titles as:

> goddess, nymph, divine and rare,
> Precious, celestial.

Phrases like "the roses in her cheeks," "her snow-white hand," "her coral lips," "the war of red and white" mostly occur in the love-scenes of make-believe or mistake in Shakespeare's early or romantic comedies, and they are on a par with the oxymoron which Romeo indulges in so freely while his thoughts are still on Rosaline. At first Shakespeare regarded such language with an indulgent smile: later he dismissed the trick of belying "with false compare" in the saturnine verses of his hundred-and-thirtieth sonnet.

That Shakespeare was fully aware that certain words and phrases, too trite for serious use, could be exploited dramatically is evident in scores of passages. As specimens of beginners' words in verse-writing, the quality of *golden* and *silver* is no doubt obvious enough. When in *Love's Labour's Lost* a fit of rhyming seizes the four lovers, the King of Navarre's sonnet (by no means a bad first attempt) is marked by the triteness of its phrasing: "the golden sun," "the silver moon," and so on. This is part of the comedy. But the same obvious epithets may be used with a very different effect. The King of Navarre is not quite sincere; but another insincerity, this time ghastly and terrible, is conveyed by the same words when Macbeth describes his murdered victim:

> His silver skin lac'd with his golden blood.

It has been said that, strictly speaking, no word is used twice in precisely the same sense. Shakespeare gives this truth a most vivid and startling demonstration.

Echoes from classical mythology are in general among the more lifeless parts of Shakespeare's diction. At all stages of his career he was content to use names like Phoebus, Cynthia, Neptune as the merest equivalents of "sun," "moon," "sea." Their presence in his writing is as it were a frank recognition that the use of verse itself is, after all, artificial. There is no sign that he had any profound sense of the poetry latent in classical names, and even when they appear as elements in phrases such as "dreadful Neptune," "Neptune's empire," "ebbing Neptune," "Neptune's yellow sands" the myth-making imagination, so strong in some poets, is barely perceptible. Shakespeare found mythological names more useful for a dramatic or technical than for a purely poetic purpose. Such expressions may serve well to "fence off" one type of diction from another, to indicate that a certain speech is in a different mood from the surrounding dialogue. Thus, in Act III of *Hamlet* when *The Murder of Gonzago* is performed, the conventional allusions of the opening lines,

> Full thirty times hath Phoebus' cart gone round
> Neptune's salt wash and Tellus' orbed ground,

at once distinguish the artificial play from the real one. A somewhat different effect is produced by similar means in *King Lear* when Kent, disguised as the King's messenger, has been abused by Cornwall for his "saucy roughness": he instantly goes to the opposite extreme of affected diction and sarcastic compliment:

> Sir, in good sooth, in sincere verity,
> Under the allowance of your grand aspect,
> Whose influence, like the wreath of radiant fire
> On flickering Phoebus' front. . . .

Such passages offer proof, if any were needed, that the classical commonplaces were at best tolerated by Shakespeare as harmless artifices which were hardly worth the trouble of avoiding and might serve the special needs of a moment.

There were, it is clear, many words and phrases which for an Elizabethan audience possessed associations which have since been forgotten.

It sometimes suited Shakespeare to play upon such associations as they then existed without creating the new associations which, when he chose, he could always command. The distinction is important: Shakespeare's diction is itself Elizabethan in one sense, but it is also "his own." The difference has always existed, and though it may be more accurately defined by the student of today it must have been perceptible to the intelligent reader or spectator of the time. Shakespeare could command various types of diction for dramatic purposes which, from a poetical standpoint, were not "his." The best illustration of this is to be found, I think, in the Player's Recitation in *Hamlet*. The style of this speech belongs to a dead tradition, and it is therefore impossible to recapture its true spirit. In consequence, some of our greatest critics have differed sharply as to its true quality. The view of Dryden is unfavourable in the extreme: "What a pudder is here kept in raising the expression of trifling thoughts!" Coleridge is equally emphatic on the other side: "This admirable substitution of the epic for the dramatic," he writes, "is well worthy of notice. The fancy, that a burlesque was intended, sinks below criticism: the lines, as epic narrative, are superb."[6] Coleridge at least makes the distinction between the usual style of Shakespeare and the style of the Recitation, but, though the piece can be effectively declaimed on the stage, his praise seems excessive. The most useful approach, however, is by way of analysis, and the following features of the diction are to be noticed: (1) the unusual quality, whether forcible or violent, of certain phrases—"o'ersizèd with coagulate gore," "head to foot Now is he total gules"—and the use of curious or rare words, e.g. *mobled, bisson*; (2) the *frequent* use of the sounded participial ending in -ed (*couchèd, damnèd, o'ersizèd, unnervèd, arousèd, o'erteemèd*); (3) the epic similes; (4) incomplete lines; (5) the rhetorical allusions to Fortune.[7] The general tone of the speech is barbaric, and its purpose seems to be to make violent appeal to the emotions of pity and fear. Something of the same manner is to be found in other speeches which aimed at rousing, without loss of time, feelings half savage, half heroic. A similar style and spirit are found in the Choruses of *Henry V*, and in the Prologue to *Troilus and Cressida* which, within the compass of its thirty-one lines, contains such unusual words as *orgulous, sperr up, fraughtage* as well as the rhetorical phrase

[6]Dryden: Preface to *Troilus and Cressida*, in *Essays of John Dryden*, ed. W. P. Ker (Oxford, 1900), I, 225. Coleridge: Notes on *Hamlet*, in his *Lectures on Shakspeare and Other Poets and Dramatists*.

[7]These points are repeated from the author's article: "The Varieties of Style in *Hamlet*" (*Essays and Studies by Members of the English Association*, XXIV, 1938).

crownets regal. The report of the bleeding Sergeant at the beginning of *Macbeth* has much the same style and the same purpose, and—apart from other resemblances—it contains two allusions to Fortune, one in the true rhetorical vein. In all these passages, style and diction are used by Shakespeare not in his own creative way—which is also the way of his drama and poetry—but in the blood-stirring fashion of a flourish of trumpets. There is no doubt a difference between the martial Choruses of *Henry V* and the ghastly report of the Sergeant, but broadly speaking they both belong to Shakespeare's "prologue style" as does also the Player's Recitation. The distinction between bombast and epic is here of small account: the hypnotic effect of abrupt rhythms, strong words, and rousing images is all that matters. As Dryden well says, "bombast is commonly the delight of that audience which loves Poetry, but understands it not."

The use of periphrasis by Shakespeare produces various effects. Sometimes it is pure mannerism or convention, sometimes it has a dramatic purpose, sometimes it is genuine, even splendid poetry. Conventional periphrasis is naturally more conspicuous in plays of inferior dramatic power: there, it is sometimes a stylistic habit based on associations which were perhaps common to the poet and his public. Certain notions appear to have been associated with feelings so strong that a periphrasis often seemed preferable to the direct name. Thus, the notion of royalty and its appurtenances was so august that the word "crown" was often too poor for the occasion, and a phrase had to be invented like "this golden rigol," "this inclusive verge of golden metal," "the circle of my glory," "the imperial metal circling now my head"; in *Macbeth*, which is a special tribute to the British throne, the crown is "this golden round," "the round and top of sovereignty." The notion of kingship lent a kind of vague aura to the word *royal*: it could even be applied redundantly to the word "king" itself ("so many royal kings," *A.&C.*, V.ii.321) and the *Oxford Dictionary* notes that "in a number of Shakespearian passages, the adjective [i.e. *royal*] has a purely contextual meaning, the precise force of which is not always clear." Again, the notion of tears gave rise to many fanciful phrases, the prevailing note of which is a kind of sentimental tenderness, not in the best taste. In *King John* they are "crystal beads," "heaven-moving pearls," "this honourable dew That silverly doth progress on thy cheeks," "wiry friends" that "glue themselves" to "a silver drop"; and there is a line in *The Two Gentlemen of Verona*, spoken by Proteus, which even suggests that the fancy is truer than the fact:

A sea of melting pearl, which some call tears.

How far such phrases have any dramatic value, as being expressive of character, may admit of dispute: often, no doubt, they are pure "poetic diction." Yet such is Shakespeare's power in his greatest moments that conventional or fantastic phrases are often subdued completely to the quality of the context. In Act IV of *King Lear* (Scene iii) the grief of Cordelia when she learns of her father's sufferings is described by a Gentleman in a lengthy passage full of far-fetched comparisons. So strong, however, is the emotion of the scene that it completely overcomes the artifice of the narrator's style, and even the exaggeration of

> There she shook
> The holy water from her heavenly eyes

suggests the exquisite beauty of Cordelia's character and the devotion she inspired in her friends. In the highest creative writing the ordinary associations of language may be completely obliterated.

The great forces of Nature, the sun, the moon, the stars, the sea, and the earth, are often described by synonym or periphrasis. The indirect phrasing of invocations is common enough to be regarded as a regular feature of style. Thus Silvia swears "by this pale queen of night"; Troilus "by the flame of yonder glorious heaven"; Bassanio "by those blessed candles of the night"; Aaron in *Titus Andronicus* "by the burning tapers of the sky"; and Viola rises to the occasion when she assures the Duke of her constant love, appealing in periphrasis to the constancy of the sun:

> And all those swearings will I overswear,
> And all those swearings keep as true in soul,
> As doth *that orbed continent the fire*
> *That severs day and night.*

But in countless passages, Shakespeare appears as the pure Nature-poet delighting in the evocative word or phrase for its own sake, or at least for its power of creating atmosphere. "The moist star Upon whose influence Neptune's empire stands" is a kind of suggestive scene-painting: "this terrestrial ball" is an anticipation of the eighteenth-century manner. In the single-word synonyms Shakespeare's diction is often most happily inspired: *zodiacs* for "years," *moons* for "months," and the like, and no one has shown a finer sense of the fit use of accepted equivalents, e.g., the various words for "sea": *surge, deep, main, flood.*

From a critical standpoint, the most interesting part of this study is to observe how the diction and the context interact upon each other. The effect already noticed of the periphrastic description of "tears" in *King Lear* is typical of Shakespeare's writing in the great tragedies. In *Mac-*

beth the emotional or imaginative value of phrases like "this filthy witness" for "blood," "the Lord's anointed temple" for the body of King Duncan, and "mine eternal jewel" for Macbeth's soul is even more evident: such expressions both give and receive poetic value. That the choice and use of such phrases truly belongs to Shakespeare's art both as poet and dramatist may be proved, if proof be needed, from the examination of a passage in *Julius Caesar*. Thus, if the periphrasis for "blood," *ruddy drops*, be viewed in isolation, there is no saying what its quality is, but in the dialogue between Brutus and Portia its power to convey passionate feeling appears unmistakably. In writing the dialogue in which the phrase occurs (*Julius Caesar*, II.i.233–303), Shakespeare follows the language of North's *Plutarch* pretty closely until Portia declares that she was married to Brutus not to be his "bedde fellowe and companion at bedde and borde onlie, like a harlot." In the original she pursues her speech, but in *Julius Caesar*, Brutus interrupts her at this point with a passionate assurance:

> You are my true and honourable wife,
> As dear to me as are the ruddy drops
> That visit my sad heart.

It is not surprising that Thomas Gray, one of the first critics to express general admiration for Shakespeare's language, should have seized on this impassioned phrase and inserted it into *The Bard*:

> Dear, as the ruddy drops that warm my heart.

Remembering Gray's fastidious taste we may estimate the significance of an "imitation" of this kind.

Antony and Cleopatra is perhaps the play of Shakespeare which depends most for its total effect on the magic of language, and a typical instance from it may be quoted of the poet's handling of "poetic diction." One underlying motive of the tragedy is well expressed in the sub-title of Dryden's imitation, "the world well lost." To Antony the glory of Rome is rivalled by the glory of Cleopatra, and at the height of his passion, the world hardly gets a good word from his lips:

> Kingdoms are clay; our dungy earth alike
> Feeds beast as man.

Such is Antony's style as long as Cleopatra is in the ascendant, and the undertones of imagery and diction keep this fact ever present in our minds. What the world prizes is not what the lovers prize, and there are moments when this opposition is vividly expressed in the choice of phrases. When Alexas arrives in Egypt bearing a gift to Cleopatra from

Antony he sees it with the eyes of the world and gives it the title consecrated by memories of the "gorgeous East": it is an *orient pearl*.[8] But
the next moment we hear the lover's own words: the breathless admiration of the messenger yields to the cool estimate of Antony: his gift was
nothing but the "treasure of an oyster." The point, small in itself, illustrates in epitome the half inspired, half infatuated vision of the lovers
who see or think they see that all things are on one level: Caesar and
the beggar (V.ii.8). The opposing view of the world is likewise expressed
in the undertones of the style, as for instance when one of Antony's
disappointed followers exclaims indignantly:

> We have kiss'd away
> Kingdoms and provinces;

indeed the marvellous diction of the entire play is largely a poetic elaboration of these two conceptions.

An examination of this one aspect of Shakespeare's diction brings us
face to face with the "myriad-mindedness" of the poet which makes
generalization so difficult. Two main points, however, are clear: one,
that Shakespeare—though not free from mannerisms of his own—had
generally a detached view of the existing associations of words and
could manipulate them for numerous kinds of dramatic effect; the other,
that he could handle words as if no associations existed and suffuse
them with new and vivid colours of his own. Beyond this, it is perhaps
possible to make one further distinction: namely, that when writing
comedy, especially the comedy of manners, and when engaged with the
development of a dramatic situation or action, he observes and manipu-
lates the existing associations of words; but in painting the passions, he
is as independent and original as the nature of language allows. In the
great speeches of *Hamlet, Othello, Lear,* and *Macbeth,* and wherever
he attains the same height in other plays, his diction is, in the fullest
sense of the word, creative.

II

Of Shakespeare's earliest plays, *Henry VI* and *The Two Gentlemen
of Verona* are those in which Spenserianism is most evident. H. C. Hart,
one of the Arden editors of Shakespeare, draws attention to some interesting touches of Spenser-like diction in *1 Henry VI. The Two Gentlemen of Verona* contains a number of passages of gentle undramatic
verse which sound much like lines from *The Faerie Queene* without the

---

[8]The phrase belonged to the romantic diction of western Europe: cf. "preciosas
perlas orientales" (*Don Quijote*, chap. xvi).

rhyme. Such is the effect produced by the simple thought, unemphatic epithets, and redundant syllables of such a piece as this (III.vii.25–32):

> The current that with gentle murmur glides,
> Thou know'st, being stopp'd, impatiently doth rage;
> But when his fair course is not hindered,
> He makes sweet music with th' enamelled stones,
> Giving a gentle kiss to every sedge
> He overtaketh in his pilgrimage;
> And so by many winding nooks he strays
> With willing sport, to the wild ocean.

A particular point of interest is that in this play (III.i.88) Shakespeare uses the epithet *sun-bright*[9] first recorded in *The Shepheardes Calender* and repeated in *The Faerie Queene.*

But in *Romeo and Juliet* we are on different ground, for there diction and imagery play a really principal part in the general effect. The imagery, Miss Spurgeon notes, is harmonized under the dominating image of *"light,* every form and manifestation of it."[10] The diction contributes to this effect, but it is also closely linked with the poetic description of Nature—Nature, in particular, as seen in "the revolving year" and in the enduring qualities of things. This is illustrated by some of the many phrases which begin with a compound epithet, such as *"well-apparel'd* April," "the *dew-dropping* south," "the *lazy-pacing* clouds," *"precious-juiced* flowers," "the *grey-ey'd* morn." Perhaps it is not too fanciful to see in these stable and Spenser-like epithets a hint of the law and order of Nature which are tragically contrasted with the fate of the "star-cross'd lovers." In this play too, as in *The Two Gentlemen,* there are many lines which need nothing but rhyme to be precisely in Spenser's manner:

> But all so soon as the all-cheering sun
> Should in the furthest east begin to draw
> The shady curtains from Aurora's bed. . . .

But at times the resemblance is even closer, for in the beautiful speech in which Juliet implores the night to hasten its coming, "fiery-footed steeds" is practically a reproduction of Spenser's "fyrie-footed team." Indeed, the whole speech occupies a capital position in the history of poetic style, for just as it links Spenser with Shakespeare, it links Shakespeare with Milton. Juliet's lines:

> Come, civil night,
> Thou sober-suited matron

[9]In Spenser and Shakespeare the epithet means "bright as the sun." An O.E. word *sunbeorht* exists in the sense "bright with sunshine" and in its modern form it is common, with this meaning, in later descriptive poetry.

[10]*Shakespeare's Imagery,* p. 310.

clearly suggested the epithet *civil-suited* in *Il Penseroso* applied to morning.

Without exaggerating the Spenserian qualities of *Romeo and Juliet* and *A Midsummer Night's Dream* we may notice that these two plays have other links with the diction of Milton. For instance, the lines from the former (II.ii.161–2):

> Else would I tear the cave where Echo lies,
> And make her airy tongue more hoarse than mine,

suggested the even finer lines in *Comus* in which the Lady remembers the fantasies of "airy tongues, that syllable men's names." Another evident link connecting the descriptive diction of the two poets is the "spangled starlight sheen" of *A Midsummer Night's Dream* (II.i.29) and "spangled sheen" of *Comus* (l. 1003).[11] And it was inevitable that the most beautiful of Shakespeare's Nature-plays should contribute from its diction to the Nature-poetry of the future. It was, one may conjecture, from the lines on Titania's bower, rather from any other Shakesperian passage, that the verb *canopy* came to be used in descriptions of overhanging foliage, and from the same source the "nodding violet" has been transplanted into many contexts in which, unhappily, its delicate life has not always thriven.

Richard II has less of the poetically conceived atmosphere which plays so large a part in *Romeo and Juliet* and the *Dream*, and its Spenserian quality lies chiefly in the rich addition of undramatic ornament to the diction of the dialogue. It abounds in Spenser-like phrases such as "time-bewasted night," "eagle-winged pride," "sky-aspiring thoughts," "rival-hating envy," "harsh-resounding trumpets"; *time-honoured* is a well-known epithet evidently coined in this play. One notices both in *Richard II* and in the *Dream* the metaphorical use of "lap" in Nature-description—twice in the former play, "the fresh green lap of fair King Richard's land" and "Violets . . . That strew the green lap of the new-come spring." These were phrases too beautiful to escape the notice of a selective poet like Milton who, in *Lycidas*, repeats the "fresh lap" of Shakespeare, expanding it into "Earth's freshest softest lap" in *Paradise Lost*.

The verbs also offer an interesting field of study in this group of plays: some of them belong to the diluted manner of the Spenserian stanza and of Shakespeare's earlier period rather than to the compressed and impassioned style of the tragedies. Shakespeare, like Spenser, is fond of using or creating verbs in which the prefix *en-* is used somewhat

---

[11]See also the excellent article by Ethel Seaton "Comus and Shakespeare" (*Essays and Studies by Members of the English Association*, XXXI, 1945).

vaguely or as a mere extra syllable as in *entwist, enring, endart*. It is curious, however, that verbs formed with this prefix appear most abundantly in the impassioned language of *Othello*. Examples are *"enshelter'd* and *embay'd"* (of the Turkish fleet), *"enchafed* flood," *"encave* yourself," *"enfetter'd* to her love," "traitors *ensteep'd*," "the grace of heaven . . . *enwheel* thee round." Such verbs seem to belong more properly to the romance of *The Merchant of Venice*, where Salarino dreams of some disaster at sea which might

> Enrobe the roaring waters with [his] silks.

Here the verb is as picturesque as an epithet, and it is in the use and formation of new epithets that Elizabethan English at the time of Spenser was most prolific.

The commonest method of forming epithets was to add a suffix— most often *-y, -less*, or *-ful*—to a noun (less regularly a verb or adjective). Adjectives in *-y* are very common in Shakespeare's earlier work: they are especially numerous in the *Dream* where, as George Gordon says,[12] they have "a special meaning and appropriateness." He quotes *rushy, unheedy, sphery, brisky, barky* and goes on to say that "in some twenty-eight lines between Oberon and Puck [III.ii.356–84] the further complement of *starry, testy, batty, wormy* are drops in that delicate rain of nicely calculated rusticity with which Shakespeare has sprinkled the language of this play. Four of the nine, *sphery, brisky, batty, barky*, he made for the purpose. There is a simplicity about this suffix which pleased the pastoral Spenser." Shakespeare continued to choose and invent adjectives of this form in his later plays, but they are more sparingly used and often of a more forcible nature. *Flinty*, first used by Shakespeare in *1 Henry VI*, remained a favourite metaphorical word right through his career, and one notices what emphasis he gives to it in the powerful writing of *Othello* where the phrase "my flinty and steel couch of war" is enforced in the next line by its contrast with "my thrice-driven bed of down." In the *"rooky* wood" of *Macbeth* he invented the epithet for a single use, and the word *corky* (*King Lear*) applied to the pithless arms of Gloucester caught his eye, along with the names of certain spirits, in Harsnet's *Declaration of egregious Popish Impostures*. Such forceful epithets, used with strict economy, are in strong contrast to the Spenserian group. Another set, *paly, vasty, steepy*—adjectives with a superfluous termination—seem more akin to rhetoric than poetry ("vasty deep," *1 Henry IV*; "vasty fields of France," *Henry V*). Among other epithets formed with suffixes we may notice *dateless* (first used in *Richard II*), a word with a good record in poetry

[12]*Shakespearian Comedy and Other Studies* (Oxford, 1944), p. 152.

and rhetoric, and *fitful*, which the Romantic writers adopted, with changed meaning, from the great line in *Macbeth*.

Spenserian diction and style reappear in Shakespeare's latest plays, but in a somewhat different form. The early Spenserianism is nearer to the original pattern. The style in its simple and pure form would be a little out of place in Shakespeare's tragic world. Hotspur in *Henry IV* finds Glendower too poetical, and Shakespeare himself knew that Glendower's style was dangerously undramatic as a model. But Glendower had been trained up in the English court and had framed "many an English ditty lovely well." His interpretation of Lady Mortimer's Welsh speech is perhaps the latest and certainly one of the purest specimens of Shakespeare's early Spenserian style:

> She bids you
> Upon the wanton rushes lay you down
> And rest your gentle head upon her lap,
> And she will sing the song that pleaseth you,
> And on your eyelids crown the god of sleep,
> Charming your blood with pleasing heaviness,
> Making such difference 'twixt wake and sleep
> As is the difference between day and night
> The hour before the heavenly-harness'd team
> Begins his golden progress in the east.

III

The transition to the tragic mood in Shakespeare's dramatic work is accompanied by a change in the character of his diction which is more easily felt than defined. This change in the character of his verbal style has, indeed, more than one aspect. Just as "tragedy" in Shakespeare signifies a closer and more passionate grasp of the realities of life, so the diction of the period, especially what is most original in it, is marked by a more emphatic and more continuous "energy." The change is not confined to the pure tragedies, but extends over the entire work of the tragic period. *Troilus and Cressida*, which is commonly attributed to the same year as *Hamlet*, has much of this new power, and *Measure for Measure*, which is of the period of *Othello*, shows the impassioned style at its height. In its essentials this new type of diction continues in the fullness of its mature power through all the later plays as far as *The Tempest*: *Henry VIII* has less of it than any other. "Maturity" is of course distinct from "variety." Shakespeare very early attained the art of varying his style both for dramatic and for poetic effects. Variety is delightfully used in *Love's Labour's Lost*, and with exquisite skill in *A Midsummer Night's Dream*; in *1 Henry IV* it is complex and masterly, but not until *Hamlet* is the entire range of variety within Shakespeare's power revealed, for there, for the first time, the impassioned note is heard in its full strength. From this time onwards maturity and variety generally go together, though *Coriolanus* has more of the first quality than the second, while in *The Winter's Tale* and *The Tempest* we hear the Spenserian note in addition, though with a difference.

If *Troilus and Cressida* belongs to the year 1602 and thus introduces the group of great tragedies beginning with *Hamlet*, the peculiarities of its diction have a special significance. For perhaps no play of Shakespeare, judged from style alone, gives a stronger impression of the poet's desire to break with his own past and to create a new method of expression, if necessary by violent means. One notes a kind of angry intellectual impatience in the style, as if a repressed side of the poet's nature were forcing itself to the surface. There is a profusion of new words, mostly of Latin origin, some peculiarly harsh in form. Many are previously unrecorded, and it is surely not fanciful to find the kind of impatience just mentioned in new formations such as *abruption, assubjugate, mappery, multipotent, oppugnancy, persistive, protractive*. Some are first recorded in previous plays of Shakespeare and are now repeated: *deracinate, expressure, impressure*; others, though not invented by Shakespeare, have the same character: *commixtion, maculation, vindicative*. No other play either before *Troilus and Cressida* or after shows so marked a departure from Shakespeare's usual methods of forming his diction.

But the genuine new method was to be less revolutionary and more creative. It lay in the development of old practices now fully exploited. The main element was the creation of new verbs, and as early as *Richard II* we may find Shakespeare using both the chief Elizabethan licences for verb-formation in such a passage as:

> Then am I king'd again; and by and by
> Think that I am unking'd[13] by Bolingbroke.

Grammatically this is the essence of the whole system: one new verb formed directly from a noun, and another by the addition of an affix. But the grammatical aspect is of course no more than the formal side of the process. A supply of new verbs greatly enriched the expressive power of Shakespeare's style: they added new vitality and movement, and they also increased the capacity for metaphor. Hitherto expressions like *unhappied* had been little more than a peculiarity of Elizabethan accidence: they were now to become, far more distinctly than before, a vital principle of poetic style.

[13]The verb *unking* is first recorded in *The Paradise of Dainty Devices*, 1576.

It is in *Hamlet* that the new method first appears in its full strength. The triumph of its style is proved not only by the wealth of its contribution to the general language in words and phrases but by its success in determining the pattern of the following plays. The vitality of the diction, which every reader feels, often consists in almost impalpable touches. But many of the bolder novelties take rank as new words and are listed as such in the *Oxford Dictionary*. Before giving examples of these I will briefly consider the fundamental features of the "new" diction in a broader light. As already mentioned, the change largely consists in a bolder use of the opportunity provided by Elizabethan grammar for the creation of metaphor. Writers on Shakespeare's English have often repeated Dr. Abbott's summary that in the language of the plays "you can *happy* your friend, *malice* or *foot* your enemy, or *fall* an axe on his neck." This is true, but from the critical point of view it is only half the truth. When Shakespeare writes in *The Merchant of Venice* (II.v.48)

Drones *hive* not with me

he is not only illustrating a grammatical freedom: he is creating a new verb because he wants it. The two actions are of course complementary and interdependent: even Shakespeare could not have won his freedom by a mere act of the will. But no other writer of the time can compare with him in the advantages he draws from the liberties allowed.[14] One has only to examine a single branch of this subject to obtain some notion of Shakespeare's achievement. Let us take, for instance, the names of parts of the body which are converted into new "verbs." The word *lip* becomes an equivalent for "kiss" (*Oth.*, IV.i.72; *A. & C.*, II.v.30); *fist* for "grasp or seize" (*Cor.*, IV.v.131); *knee* for "crawl" (*Cor.*, V.i.5); *tongue* for "denounce" (*M.M.*, IV.iv.28); *heel* for "dance" (*T. & C.*, IV.iv.86); *foot* for "kick" (*M.V.*, I.iii.119); *womb* for "enclose" (*W.T.*, IV.iii.503); *mouth* for "rant" (*Ham.*, V.i.306). Of these "verbs," *lip, fist, knee, heel*, and *foot* are listed as first used by Shakespeare in the senses mentioned, and it will be noted that every instance but two is taken from the later group of plays which begins with *Hamlet*. Other new "verbs" of a more general kind but similar in type to those quoted may be found in any of the later plays.

The diction in *Hamlet* is outstandingly vivid and creative, and it contains striking words of various kinds. Yet it is probably the unfamiliar

---

[14]The value of enriching vocabulary by this process is discussed by Ronsard in his *Art poétique*: "Sur les vocables receues en usage comme *pays, eau, feu*, tu feras *payser, euer, fouer* . . . et mille autres tels vocables." Quoted by W. Renwick, "The Critical Origins of Spenser's Diction" (*Modern Language Review*, XVII, 1922).

verbs which form the largest and most interesting group. A few of them such as *wan* (" all his visage wann'd") had already appeared in poetry, but a large number, perhaps the majority, are apparently used for the first time in *Hamlet*. Among them may be mentioned: *harrows* ("lacerate feelings"); *shark'd up*; *nighted* ("made black or dark as night"); *sicklied*; *inurn'd*; *down-gyved*; *sugar o'er*; *shuffle off*[15]; *candied* ("sugared," "honied"); *rivet* ("fix intently the eye or mind"); *apoplex'd*; *bedded* ("laid in a smooth lair"); *reword*; *film*; *unpeg*; *muddied*[16]; *uncharge* ("acquit of guilt"); *incorps'd*; *sanctuarize*; *be-netted*. This list leaves out the numerous new phrases such as "towering passion" and "cudgel one's brains," yet even so it gives an impressive picture of Shakespeare's creative diction in this play.[17] A comparable wealth of verb-creation will be found in the plays written just after *Hamlet*— *Measure for Measure, Othello, Lear,* and *Macbeth*—but the diction of *Antony and Cleopatra* perhaps surpasses that of *Hamlet* itself. The reader may judge of this from the following specimen-list of "new" verbs: *dumb'd* (I.v.50); "*barber'd* ten times o'er" (II.ii.232); *stale* (II.ii.243); "*beggar'd* all description" (II.ii.206); "the good Brutus *ghosted*," i.e. "haunted" (II.vi.13); "disguise hath . . . *antick'd* us all" (II.vii.132); "the n'er-yet beaten horse of Parthia We have *jaded* out o' the field" (III.i.33); "Cleopatra Hath *nodded* him to her" (III.vi.66); "Wouldst thou be *window'd* in great Rome?" (IV.xiv.72); "Octavia with her modest eyes . . . *Demuring* upon me" (IV.xv.29); "he *words* me" (V.ii.190); "some squeaking Cleopatra *boy* my greatness" (V.ii.219). It is tempting to pursue this study and note how this diction continues through *Coriolanus* down to *The Tempest*, but the point has already been illustrated as far as a few specimen quotations can do so: the true spirit of the diction is more impalpable than single words can show, and it is diffused over the entire play.

One common feature of Shakespeare's verbs is very characteristic of the diction of English poetry in general. The Elizabethan practice of the free use of particles such as *en-* and *-less* to form new derivatives has already been mentioned, but a special importance attaches to the creation of new verbs by means of the negative prefixes *un-* and *dis-*. It should be noticed that *un-* has two functions: to express pure negation, and to indicate the reversal of a process or action as in *undo*. The possession of this second means of verb-creation is of the greatest value in poetry, and there is hardly a limit to the number of new verbs which

[15]But also in *Twelfth Night*.
[16]The "verb" was used before in *All's Well*.
[17]Among the other "new" words in *Hamlet* are *credent, skyish, primy*.

might be formed in this way. Many volumes of poetry in the English language produced in the last hundred years and more have added one or two verbs of this kind to the common stock, though naturally most will never be used more than once. The value of this practice was realized by Shakespeare quite early. In *Richard II*, for instance, we find phrases like "*undeaf* his ear" (II.i.16), "*uncurse* their souls" (III.ii. 237). Words of the same grammatical type but of more memorable character appear frequently in the more energetic phases of Shakespeare's diction: examples are the well-known *unhand*[18] first used in *Hamlet*, and the vigorous *unsex*, created for Lady Macbeth. Other verbs, more or less memorable, of the same type are: *unbuild* (*Cor.*, III.i.97), *unclew* (*Timon*, I.i.169), *unclog* (*Cor.*, IV.ii.47), *unfix* (*2 Hen. IV*, IV.i.208), *unheart*,[19] *unmask*,[20] *unshout* (*Cor.*, V.iv.70). It is not unusual for negative words to appear in pairs, as in the following lines from *The Winter's Tale* (IV.iii.578–80), where both words are recorded for the first time:

A course more promising
Than a wild dedication of yourselves
To unpath'd waters, undream'd shores.

A miscellaneous list of various formations first found in Shakespeare[21] may be quoted: *unaching, unaneled, unattainted, unbacked, unbated, unbefitting, unbless, unbloodied, unbonneted, unbosom, unchary, uncropped, undinted, undistinguishable, undress, unearthly, uneducated, unfather'd, unfilial, unfirm, unfool, unfrequented, ungrown, unhelpful, unhidden,[22] unhooked, unhoused* (homeless), *unlicked, unlink, unqualitied, unshunnable.*

The prefix *dis-* is of Latin origin, unlike *un-* which is native, and in Shakespeare's time it had not long been freely applicable in new formations. It must have been especially popular about 1611, for in that year a re-issue of Florio's Italian-English dictionary appeared with many new additions of words in *dis-* coined to render Italian words beginning with the same prefix. Among the poets of the time it was perhaps Sylvester who was most prolific in verbs of this type, and some of his

---

[18]"Unhand it, sir!" said Mrs. Proudie. From what scrap of dramatic poetry she had extracted the word cannot be said; but it must have rested in her memory. *Barchester Towers*, chap. xi.

[19]Recorded 1593, also *Cor.*, V.i.49.

[20]Also in Sidney: used by Shakespeare in various senses.

[21]That is, of course, earliest citations in the *Oxford Dictionary*. But Shakespeare's practice of forming such words is so well established, that there is little reason to suspect the substantial accuracy of the list.

[22]*Unhid* is older.

creations, e.g. *disleaf,* have won a place in the vocabulary of description. Shakespeare's most memorable contribution to the general language is probably *dishearten,* which appears in a prose passage in *Henry V.* One can trace the process of creation in a passage like the following from *The Winter's Tale* (IV.iii.668–70), where the use of one word prompts the poet to coin another in the same pattern on the spur of the moment:

> Muffle your face;
> Dismantle you, and (as you can) disliken
> The truth of your own seeming.

Disbench (*Cor.,* II.ii.75), *disedge* (*Cymb.,* III.iv.96), *disorb* (*T. & C.,* II.ii.45), *discandy* (*A. & C.,* III.xi.165), *disquantity* (*Lear,* I.iv.272) are examples of Shakespeare's free and fearless handling of vocabulary in his later period. They belong to the language of passion rather than of description, but the picturesque quality of *dislimn* in Antony's reverie on the rapid changes of cloud-forms took the fancy of certain Romantic writers and we find it repeated more than once by De Quincey, as in "The nocturnal pageant has dislimned and vanished." It was too the Romantic and descriptive poets of the nineteenth century who most fully appreciated the picturesque value of new words beginning with *un-,* and among Shakespeare's principal followers in this type of diction are Shelley, Keats, and Arnold.

Shakespeare's diction may be richly enjoyed in *The Winter's Tale* and *The Tempest.* In these late plays, various types of expression previously mastered are brought to a focus. The language learned for the portrayal of passion is now applied to less distressful purposes, and at the same time, the finest art of the Spenserian period is revived for some of the poet's loveliest passages of Nature-description. In this ample variety of style room is found for mythological and pastoral diction, also for dramatic prose comparable to that of the great days of *Henry IV* and *Hamlet.* At moments one may forget the profound humanity of these plays and feel that Shakespeare is aiming at no more than pure expression for expression's sake. In *The Winter's Tale* the variety may be briefly indicated as follows: there are mythological touches, "Cytherea's breath," "Bright Phoebus in his strength"; pastoral phrases, "the queen of curds and cream"; poetic periphrasis, "Nine changes of *the watery star*"; new words by conversion of the parts of speech, "shook hands as over a *vast,*" "*horsing* foot on foot," "whilst you do *climate* here"; epithets in the Spenserian manner on the essential character of the thing described, "violets *dim,* but sweeter than the lids of Juno's eyes," "*pale* prime-roses, that die unmarried"—phrases accompanying the lovely description of daffodils; and in addition there is the finished comic prose of Autolycus, as well as a reminiscence of the "prologue style" in the speech of Time. In *The Tempest* there is a like variety. The style, as has been well said by Edward Thompson, shows "a swift and masterly carelessness of detail." Shakespeare is using with perfect ease the accumulated skill acquired in all his earlier work. One feature calls for special comment: the almost ultra-Spenserianism of the diction of the Masque. Nowhere else in Shakespeare is the style so entirely built up on epithets: *turfy* mountains, *spongy* April, *pole-clipt* vineyard, *short-grass'd* green, *windring* brooks, and the like—scarcely a significant noun in the first forty lines of the Masque but has its "rare," if not always felicitous epithet. The student of Shakespeare's diction must remember that the curious is not always the significant. What is most wonderful about him, as a stylist, is his power to produce such varying effects from the same means: for example, the verb *gild* may be brilliantly decorative (Sonnet xxxiii), grimly ironical (*Macbeth*, II.ii.57), satirical (*Hamlet*, III.iii.58), bitterly hostile (*Lear*, V.iii.85), or powerfully repulsive (*A. & C.*, I.iv.62). A study of Shakespeare's diction is not a study of his poetry, but only of the means which he used to produce incalculable effects.

THE SPENSERIAN TRADITION
AND ITS RIVALS UP TO 1660

BETWEEN 1579 and 1660 there is no poet whose style presents an interest comparable in its many-sidedness to Spenser's or Shakespeare's. These poets may almost be said to have invented a new language. Spenser's diction affected generation after generation of subsequent poets: Shakespeare carried expression to the highest point of energy of which language is capable, and his achievement remains one of the high-water marks in the poetry of the world. Although the period from Spenser to Dryden is crowded with interesting figures and contains many great ones, no new style so wide in its range or so lasting in its effects as that of *The Faerie Queene* appeared until the publication of *Paradise Lost* in 1667. Even Donne, one of the most powerful figures in our poetry, commands only a narrow range of expression in comparison with Spenser, Shakespeare, or Milton.

During this period, great changes took place in the English language and in the principles of taste which governed its use in literature. For some twenty years, the Elizabethan exuberance of diction flourished almost unrestrained. The general love of fluency and "copiousness," though an encouragement to eloquence, leads to tautology in good poets, and bombast in bad. About the turn of the century, a reaction begins to set in. First, it takes the form of a greater demand for economy and precision; poets cut out the inexpressive phrase and seek for the single significant word. This taste encouraged the use of far-fetched and curious expressions which still delight the reader by a flavour and piquancy not found elsewhere. A little later a new style begins to appear, designed to avoid the earlier fault of redundance as well as the new danger of obscurity and pedantry. Its aims are regularity, sobriety, and the avoidance of excess, and it issues finally in the style and diction of the orthodox couplet. In addition to these contrasts of period and aim, there were various conventions belonging to the different types of poetry which were at their height in the last years of Elizabeth. Of these conventions, the two most prevalent and definite are those of love-poetry and of the pastoral, which often merge and unite. To these must be added the technical convention of words or forms of words admitted to ease the difficulties of metre and rhyme. Every poet of the age shows some traces of these conventions in his work, and a brief consideration of them must precede the discussion of individual poets.

I

A certain part of poetic diction must always be determined by the forms of verse, and in Elizabethan times metre and rhyme were nearly always used in the various kinds of non-dramatic verse. In our examination of Spenser and Shakespeare, we have already noticed some of the means used to obtain smooth and easy versification. Spenser's archaisms, which sometimes supplied a needed syllable, could not be generally copied; but devices which Shakespeare used in his early work, and abandoned more and more as he developed an increasing pregnancy of style, were freely used by writers who were never destined to find their thoughts outrunning their words. Elizabethan taste preferred fluency to concentration, and knew nothing of that horror of the expletive word which has haunted English verse since Pope's *Essay on Criticism*. Even so good a poet as Sidney could use an expletive in three successive lines:

> For nothing from my wit or will *doth* flow,
> Since all my words thy beauty *doth* indite,
> And love *doth* hold my hand and makes me write.[1]

We have already noticed the superfluous prefix *en-* in some of Spenser's verbs and in the early work of Shakespeare. It is a fashion of the time: for instance, Daniel uses *enveil* and *encheer*. Other prefixes could be added at will, as in *bemoisten* (Lodge) and the very common *depaint*. Archaic words were sometimes used for the sake of an extra syllable, e.g. *withouten*, and the disyllabic forms *whereas, whenas*, and *withal* were also convenient. The superfluous syllable -*y* was added to a limited number of adjectives (as in *steepy, calmy, vasty*); but there seems to have been a feeling that this licence must be restricted, and some audacity was needed to write—as an anonymous poet did—"upon the *greeny* grass." If abbreviation was necessary, the device known as "aphesis"—clipping off the first syllable—could be widely applied. The most removable syllable was *a-* (*ar-, ap-*, etc.): we find, for instance, '*bate*, '*gainst*, '*pointed*, '*ray*, '*parel*, '*paritors* and many similar shortenings; but the loss of *be-* is also common as in '*cause*, '*gan*. The insertion of unnecessary words is the typical fault of Elizabethan verse. It was recognized as such, and the current term "bombast" was frequently

---

[1]*Oxford Book of Sixteenth Century Verse*, No. 105 (xv). Further citations of numbers in sections I–III of this chapter will refer to this collection or to the *Oxford Book of Seventeenth Century Verse*.

used in the mutual criticism of writers. But redundancy continued, aided by the popularity of the long iambic line of seven feet, which it is almost impossible to write without a kind of vapid fluency. Drayton, for instance (No. 316), wishing to say in this metre: "To beat back the winds and calm the showers" extends it into the mechanized sing-song of:

To beat the stormy winds aback and calm the raging showers,

but even in the slightly stricter Alexandrine, the same poet—an excellent writer in many ways—can be guilty of such inflation as:

To wipe away the drops and moisture from her hand.

A certain number of words, suitable for gilding description at small expense, stood ready for the pen of the Elizabethan versifier, and were not altogether disdained even by the best poets. Many of them do not disappear from verse for several generations, and are found as late as the time of Johnson. They are on much the same footing as the common mythological names which also survived many changes in taste, and were not wholly banished even by the efforts of Wordsworth. It is about the time of Sidney and Greene that *Phoebus, Titan, Flora, Cynthia, Boreas, Philomela,* and the rest are at the zenith of their popularity. The words for "poetic" description were mostly adjectives, which slipped easily into the place of significant words. There is no reason to treat them indulgently. They bring description down to a lower level than it reached in much good work of the fourteenth century, and would no doubt have been more severely handled had not "Elizabethan" so often meant "semi-sacred." The following is a stanza by Lodge which has found its way into the *Oxford Book of Sixteenth Century Verse* (No. 241):

O shady vales, O fair enriched meads,
    O sacred woods, sweet fields and rising mountains,
O painted flowers, green herbs where Flora treads,
    Refreshed by wanton winds and watery fountains.

"L'epithète rare, voilà la marque du poète" may be an over-refined dictum, but even the sober Beaumont of the seventeenth century demands "descriptions clear, yet rare." Could anything less rare in the range of poetic description be found than vales which are shady, mountains which rise, herbs which are green, and fountains which are watery? So much is evident to common sense; but anyone who has read the verse of the time knows that *painted* too is far from being a rare epithet, and that *wanton* is one of the most hackneyed words in the whole Elizabethan vocabulary: e.g. "*Wanton* music," "*wanton* brook" (Sidney); "*wanton* fish," "*wanton* sweets" (Lodge); "plenty's *wanton* store" (Daniel). Diction in the late sixteenth century was common property; this may not matter for verse which is sung, but it is fatal to description. Among other "poetic" words, one notices in particular *crystal*, an epithet for anything which shines, whether a "fountain" (Spenser) or "eyes" (Greene). *Sugared* had a short, but very active life, as in "*sugared* joy" (Oxford), "*sugared* thrall" (Greene), "*sugared* times" (Davies). *Sable* was an especial favourite with the Elizabethans: Daniel, for instance, writes of "*sable* hair," "*sable* clouds," and "*sable* Night." *Purling* is the usual epithet for a small river, as in Sidney's "*purling* stream" and Jonson's "*purling* brook." In description, *azure, orient,* and *balmy* were all common, but even more popular was the verb *enamel*, as in "rose-*enammelled* meads" (Brooke), "*enamelling* the banks" (Marlowe). This last word is an instance of the application of terms of art to description of Nature, a practice which was widely extended in the early years of the seventeenth century. Herrick, for instance, writes of "*spangling* dew" and of moonlight "*tinselling* the streams." Metaphors from ornament and dress are very frequent as in "*damask'd* meadows" (Herrick), "the *new-livery'd* year" (Wotton), "clouds in thousand *liveries* dight" (Milton), and the same feature appears in Drayton's pleasing simile in *The Muses Elizium* (6th Nimphall):

> Cleere had the day bin from the dawne,
> All chequerd was the skye,
> Thin clouds like scarfs of cobweb lawne
> Vayld heaven's most glorious eye.

The Elizabethans loved "golden words," and a few of their poets—in particular, Spenser, Marlowe, Shakespeare, and Drayton—wrote some brilliant pages of imaginative description. A little later, one sees the beginnings of a school of landscape poetry, but its full development had to await a more settled age. The Elizabethans were of too restless and animated a spirit; the Jacobeans and Carolines were too much absorbed in political and religious strife; not until the eighteenth century did civilization and security create the impulse to describe the real landscape, seen daily, in poetic words.

The Elizabethan love-song is really incomplete without its music, and to study it in the nakedness of print may seem unjust. But many of these songs have long survived in anthologies, though one often feels a want of character in the verbal style. A number of the lyrics are anonymous, or of disputed authorship, and seem to be almost a spontaneous growth of the age. In style and wording, something of the medieval tradition survives, but with a difference. The lady is protected, not by

Danger, Wicked Tongue, Shame, and the rest of the allegorical figures of the *Roman de la Rose*, but by her own Cruelty, Pride, and Disdain. "Fair is my Love, and cruel as she's fair," is the opening line of a sonnet by Daniel; "Lady Disdain" is Benedick's title for Beatrice at their first meeting in *Much Ado about Nothing*. The disdain of the lady is opposed by the desire of the lover, and desire sometimes rises into delight, sometimes declines into despair. Desire as the foe of Disdain (Oxford); Disdain as a deadly wound (Peele); Cupid, enemy to Disdain, parent of Desire (Greene); "Despair in me, Disdain in thee" (Constable)—such are the commonplaces of Elizabethan love-poetry, and the poet "A.W." (No. 141) marshals the four reigning emotions into a single line:

> Desire, despair, delight, disdain.

Cupid with his *darts* or *arrows* lurks in the background, and the colours which the lady's presence brings with it are added to the picture. They are two: *red* and *white*, with an occasional gleam of *yellow* or *amber*. "Thou art not fair, for all thy red and white," writes Campion. Lord Brooke's mistress is "Enamelled o'er with beauties white and red." Peele's is a "fair maiden, white and red." Lord Oxford sings of "This pleasant lily white, This taint of roseate red." The reader may be excused for recalling, in a new sense, the line of "A.W.": "Nothing else but red and white." Greene's description in *Tullie's Love* (No. 217) gives the ideal portrait in full:

> Sitting by the river side
> Lovely Phyllis was descried.
> Gold her hair, bright her eyne,
> Like to Phoebus in his shine.
> White her brow, her face was fair;
> Amber[2] breath perfumed the air;
> Rose and lily both did seek
> To shew their glories on her cheek.

It is a relief to turn from the direct to the dramatic use of the convention. There is a fine example in *England's Heroical Epistles* by Drayton. Dramatic truth and passion meet in the lines which the Earl of Surrey addresses to Geraldine (No. 325):

> When time shall turn those amber locks to gray,
> My verse again shall gild and make them gay . . .
> That sacred power that in my ink remains
> Shall put fresh blood into thy withered veins,
> And on thy red decayed, thy whiteness dead,
> Shall set a white more white, a red more red.

[2]The poets "vaguely confuse" the senses of *amber* (*O.E.D.*).

The Faerie Queene, as well as *The Shepheardes Calender*, is an important source of our pastoral diction. The phrase *oaten pipe*, of classical origin, occurs in Spenser's January Eclogue. *Swain* in its special sense of "shepherd" is found in *The Faerie Queene* (e.g., III.vi.15) and it is a conspicuous word in the later pastoralists, Greene, Breton, and Jonson, who often give it the additional meaning of "lover." *Silly*, in the sense of "innocent, harmless," occurs several times in *The Faerie Queene*, and reappears a little later as a more specific epithet for "sheep" and "shepherds."[3] The much-used pastoral phrase *curds and cream* is traceable to Spenser's November Eclogue ("curds and clouted Creame") and is found, with slight variations, in Breton, Drayton, and Jonson. It even reappears in *The Winter's Tale*, where Camillo calls Perdita "The queen of *curds and cream*" (IX.iii.161). Some pastoralists—for instance, Drayton—carry on the Spenserian tradition of antique or dialectal words, and Jonson does this in parts of *The Sad Shepherd*. Yet the Elizabethan pastoral is not hide-bound by convention. Breton, for instance, draws upon real life. In *Olden Love-Making* (No. 255), the lovers are not "Phillis and her swain," but in plain English "Susan and her sweeting"; and in his song of the forsaken mother (*A Sweet Lullaby*, No. 248) his language is as direct as Wordsworth's. There is a good deal of vitality in the Elizabethan pastoral, and it is sometimes a framework for real pictures of rural scenes and manners.

The Faithful Shepherdess of John Fletcher (printed by 1610) shows the vitality of the pastoral in the generation after Spenser, and its diction is a true part of the poetic beauty which, rather than dramatic effect, is its chief merit. Old and dialectal words are few, but the ordinary counters of pastoral diction are present in force, as well as some more inventive expressions which link the pastoral with the later poetry of Nature. The familiar expressions such as *swain, silly, jolly, enamelled, white* and/or *red* are all in evidence, and Fletcher makes special play with the word *wanton*, which he seems to associate with the freedom of pastoral life in contrast with the rites and rigours of the court: the passions are wanton (wanton heat, fancies, flame, etc.) and Nature is wanton (wanton spring, bed of leaves, etc.). But conventional phrases are no more than the groundwork of Fletcher's style, and the reader is more impressed by the decorative and picturesque expressions which are felicitous in themselves and prophetic of the future. *Golden-tressed*, for instance, is repeated by Milton (*Psalm 136*) and "straight-grown pine" is a perfect anticipation of Keats and Ruskin.

---

[3] Cf. "*silly* flocks" (Lodge), "*silly* swain" (Breton), "*silly* sheep" (Milton).

II

The future of the Spenserian tradition was much in doubt during the
first half of the seventeenth century. Ultimately, the example of Milton
was powerful enough to maintain a modified form of Spenserianism
throughout the eighteenth century, and the Romantic Revival renewed
its life, in fresh forms, for another hundred years. But between 1600
and 1660 the tradition had some vigorous rivals. Spenser's language is
not—to borrow the phrase of Gray (see below, p. 108)—"the language of the age"; its rhythms are not modelled closely on those of
real life; it is not marked by "strong lines." Certain poets desired a
masculine and rugged energy not found in Spenser; others wanted a
style based more closely on contemporary usage. Some critics suggest
that these reactions against Spenser may appear some day as nothing
but the assertion of a sound natural instinct against a false model. But
within the range of three centuries—from Spenser to Bridges—these
were minority movements, and whatever the future course of English
poetry, it will surely be long before they can be regarded in any other
light.

Satire was but a by-product of the Elizabethan genius, and it was
apt to be disfigured by mere rant and violence. But passing notice must
be given to the satirist John Marston, if for no other reason than that
his work shows the seamy side of Elizabethan diction. Improving on
the example of his masters Juvenal and Persius, he openly avows his
abusive intention (Book I, Satire II):

> Who can abstain? What modest brain can hold,
> But he must make his shamefac'd muse a scold?[4]

and he alludes to his superiority to restraint in phrases like "my respect-
less free-bred poesy." Contemptuous of "ill-pac'd far-fetch'd words"
designed "to get an undeserv'd repute Of deep deep learning" (Book
II, Satire VI), he draws a large proportion of his own words from popular speech, though without severing his connection with literary sources.
The modern reader may well be puzzled by such words as *slup, lusking*
(and *luskish*), *jobbernoules* which are sufficient in themselves to indicate
the distance between Marston's manner and that of classical English
satire, and when he assures us in a characteristic passage (No. 374):

> My spirit is not puffed up with fat fume
>   Of slimy ale, nor Bacchus' heating grape.
> My mind disdains the dungy muddy scum
>   Of abject thoughts, and envy's raging hate,

[4]Spelling modernized.

we feel how much Elizabethan diction needed to be refined by selection, when not kindled either by imagination or by the higher passions.

A similar effect of violence and strain is found in choicer spirits than Marston. We meet it in Chapman, who made repeated efforts to attain an epic diction, achieving a partial success in his translations of Homer. He sometimes reacted against the diffuseness of the earlier Elizabethan manner, producing in certain moods a stiff density of far-fetched words. Now and then his use of a single word recalls the pregnancy of Shakespeare's later manner, as in the lines from *The Shadow of Night* (No. 362):

> Since Night brings terror to our frailties still,
> And shameless Day doth *marble* us in ill.

The compressed character of his diction tending to violence appears in the experimental epic manner of his poem on Guiana. The effort to attain sublimity introduces a note of over-strain into the style. Guiana, we are told (No. 365), is a land

> whose rich feet are mines of gold,
> Whose forehead knocks against the roof of stars.

In the same style of over-emphasis, the nation is exhorted not to put forth its whole strength in one spasmodic effort:

> Then be not like a rough and violent wind,
> That in the morning rends the forests down,
> *Shoves* up the seas to heaven, makes earth to tremble,
> And tombs his wasteful bravery in the even.

The denunciation of self-seekers, with their "dunghill pride" and "poison'd souls, like spiders lurking In sluttish chinks" reminds one of Marston's abusive tongue, though Chapman has a higher motive; and the whole poem is summed up in the unmelodious but forceful couplet:

> Natures, that stick in golden-gravell'd springs,
> In muck-pits cannot 'scape their swallowings.

The style of the classical as distinguished from the romantic epic was unattainable by the Elizabethans. Chapman had the daring and aspiring spirit of his own age, but not the intellectual and moral self-discipline of the greatest of the Puritans. At their best, the Elizabethans could make the moment immortal, but they could not engrave enduring characters in granite. The spirit of the age was reflected in the condition of the language. Elizabethan English was inclusive—it was capable of a Gothic but not of a classical excellence. Sustained elevation was impossible at a time when the grading of words had scarcely begun. The study of the Bible, especially of the Version of 1611, was an important step towards the creation of an epic style, for vast numbers of words then became endowed with sacred associations. A growing sense of the gulf between the things of time and the things of eternity marked the outlook of the Puritans, and its effect was felt in the higher forms of literature. Shakespeare's power of holding the English language—virtually, the whole of it—in the hollow of his hand enabled him to become the master of poetic drama; Milton's power of judging between words and of excluding the unworthy, enabled him to attain the elevation of *Paradise Lost*.

III

The chief leader of simplicity in diction between 1590 and 1660 was Ben Jonson, though the best examples which his own work provided were on the small scale of his neatly written lyrics. But there was a somewhat earlier cult of simplicity, though it was not widely influential. It was less the result of a critical consciousness than of contact with the realities of life, and its chief exponents belonged to the practical world, being soldiers, priests, and men of affairs. On the edge of the group stands Sir Philip Sidney, who, had he been born later, might have become its leader, but he belonged to the generation of Lyly, and therefore found simplicity particularly difficult. Sidney wishes to be true to nature, to look in his heart and write; he wishes to be unaffected, and avoid repeating "poor Petrarch's long-deceased woes With new-born sighs," and in a few of his lyrics, such as "My true love hath my heart," he combines an effective simplicity with a grave charm which are rare in Elizabethan verse. In some of his lyrics, however, the sobriety of the diction only brings into relief the extravagance of the sentiment. But there were other Elizabethans who could write good sense in sober diction yet still be poets. The lines of Sir Edward Dyer, for instance, on a modest love ("The lowest trees have tops," etc., No. 119), though a little touched with Euphuism are of this order. So too is some of the work of Robert Southwell. No doubt Southwell's intention of making spiritual love his subject rather than "unworthy affections" confirmed his bent towards plainness of diction, and it is a pity that changes in taste have now made some of his work, sincere though it is, sound slightly trivial. The *Nosce Teipsum* (1599) of Sir John Davies, a poem explaining the riddle of man ("a proud and yet a wretched thing") by the doctrine of Immortality, has in its finer passages a fervid lucidity of thought which needs few ornaments of diction to sustain its poetic quality. In this respect it resembles the occasional verse of Sir Walter Ralegh which is often plain to the point of ruggedness: all is brought to the test of experience. There is probably more sincerity than usual in the customary compliment to Queen Elizabeth when expressed by Ralegh (No. 274):

> They that are rich in words must needs discover
> That they are poor in that which makes a lover.

Ralegh also uses verse for his darker moods, but his bitterness is not unbroken. The flood of denunciations in *The Lie* (No. 276) ends in a "brave" defiance: "No stab the soul can kill," and in a like spirit of idealism (*Affection and Desire*, No. 275) he condemns the amorous poets because they ignore the passion of the mind:

> As if wild beasts and men did seek
> To like, to love, to choose alike.

In the disjointed stanzas of *Cynthia, the Lady of the Sea* (not completed) one notices how naturally Ralegh's thoughts shape themselves into verse when he is wrestling with the hardest problems. The right diction for him, as for all the poets of this group, is "the real language of men."

The name of Samuel Daniel has long been associated with the notion of an unpoetic want of warmth and colour in diction. The epithet "well-languaged" applied to him by Browne was turned by Coleridge into a term of disparagement in his attack on Wordsworth's theory of poetic diction. Before this, Drayton had called him "too much historian in verse," and there is no doubt that his diction, fluent and refined as it is, has little to distinguish it outwardly from that of eloquent prose. But in certain characteristic poems this seems not to matter, for Daniel had the rare gift of a poetic ardour for abstract truths. The little poem called *Ulysses and the Siren*, a debate between the claims of Duty and Pleasure, is a model of phrasing. The best of his Epistles, such as those to the Countesses of Cumberland and Bedford, contain some of the finest passages of ethical poetry in the language, including the stanza so much admired by Wordsworth, which ends with the couplet (No. 300):

> And that unless above himself he can
> Erect himself, how poor a thing is man.

To accept such a line (No. 299) as

> Errors, demurs, essoins, and traverses

one must, it is true, enter into the rare mood of lofty fervour with which Daniel exhorts Sir Thomas Egerton to remove the abuses of the Law. The sympathetic reader may perhaps feel that certain effects were possible in the "inclusive" diction of the Elizabethans which would not be permissible in other ages. In any case he will respect the experiments of Daniel, the best critic of his time, and the author of the famous poetic prophecy of the future of the English language.

IV

Marlowe and Drayton are among the poets who used a modified Spenserian style for occasional descriptive effects. Although the Elizabethans did not cultivate the landscape poetry of which Milton was an early master, their notion of romantic narrative, in which action and sentiment are the chief elements, left room for scenic backgrounds on a small scale. Such descriptions are a feature of the romantic epics of Spenser, Ariosto, and Tasso. Spenser's descriptive manner is developed especially in his allegorical pageants and processions, and the continually appearing descriptions throughout *The Faerie Queene* were an inspiration to poets who had no use for his archaisms. One of his best pupils in his own century was Marlowe, whose *Hero and Leander* has passages of breathing human passion such as Spenser himself never equalled. Marlowe's admiration for Spenser had already been shown in *Tamburlaine* (Part II, IV.iv) where six lines from *The Faerie Queene* (I.vii.32) are embodied in the text with some verbal variations. There is not much Spenserianism in Marlowe's other plays, but in *Hero and Leander* (completed by Chapman) there is some brilliant imitation of Spenser's compound epithets. "Gote-footed Satyrs and up-starting Fawns" (II.200) is quite in the manner of *The Faerie Queene*; so are "steepe pine-bearing mountains," "blood-quaffing Mars," and "flint-brested Pallas" (I.116,145,311).[5] Marlowe has none of Spenser's prolixity, and his style, neither too dense nor too rare, has an almost classical rightness.

The work of Drayton calls for somewhat extended treatment, for it is closely linked with that of Keats, one of the great masters of descriptive diction. Drayton's *Endimion and Phoebe* (1595) is, by virtue of its style, a poem of unusual interest. There are hints that it was known to Milton,[6] but its connection with the early work of Keats appears again and again. *Endimion and Phoebe* made a vital contribution to the diction of the author of *Endymion*. There are lines which seem to bear the very stamp of Keats's earlier style, such as (91–2):

> And tasting once the nectar of his breath,
> Surfeit with sweet, and languish unto death,

or the description of moonlight (78) which

> Embalmed the banks with precious lunary,

or the line (51)

> Shadowed with roses and sweet eglantine.

[5]Quotations from *Works*, ed. Tucker Brooke (Oxford, 1910).
[6]Cf. "Of tufted Cedars and the branching Pine" (*Endimion and Phoebe*, 25) and "Cedar, and Pine, and Firr, and branching Palm" (*Paradise Lost*, IV.139).

Some of Keats's most characteristic descriptive words were suggested by Drayton: "the *patient* palm" of *Endimion and Phoebe* (33) recalls Keats's willow which "keeps A *patient* watch over the stream" (I.446–7); *covert* is an expressive word in both poets; and had Drayton not written (165–6),

> Upon each tree she carves Endimion's name
> In gordian knots,

Keats would not have described locks of hair as "*gordian'd* up and braided" (I.614). *Endimion and Phoebe* is an experiment, and Drayton did not himself mature the beauty latent in its style: that task was performed by the richer imagination of his successor.

But Drayton has other styles besides the picturesque, and in his later poetry he appears rather as a judicious artist in the choice of diction than an inventor of new effects. If one had to select from the later Elizabethans the author whose judgment was most surely rooted in the good work of the past and most marked in its anticipations of the future, Drayton might well be that man. In his poem *The Barons' Wars* (1603), enlarged from his earlier *Mortimeriados*, we find a representative picture of English verse in the Spenserian tradition after the Spenserian archaisms had been strained away, and at the same time a more flexible and more restrained use of those verse-devices which became standardized in the work of Dryden and other Restoration poets. The style of *The Barons' Wars* is, in fact, related by natural character to the style of social and political satire, for Drayton's muse in that poem is the muse of History not of Epic. The diction is near prose though in general not prosaic, being saved as much by its vigorous rhythms as by energy or finesse in word-selection.

Coming to details, we notice among the marks of verse-diction such features as the following: the quasi-Latin use of the participial epithet which was to become a recognizable feature in verse-diction in a phrase like Milton's "thoughts more elevate": Drayton himself has *elevate* (*B.W.*, I.33), also *repudiate* (I.30), *indubitate* (V.15), etc. The compound epithet based on "heart"—long recurrent both in verse and in rhetorical prose—is also found with moderate frequency: "*Heart-goring* wound" (I.20); "*heart-swoln* lords" (I.24); "*heartrending sight*" (II.67). Among epithets formed with affixes frequent in verse we find: *moisty* vapours (II.35), *grassful* ground (VI.34), *remissful* doom (I.11), and *plumy* crest (*Mortimer to Queen Isabel*). Some trace of standardization is beginning to appear in certain phrases of epithet with noun, such as "hollow" with "winds" and "pale-faced" with "night," as also in rhyme-words such as the archaic *trode* and *eyne*. But for any

one on the watch for the continuity of verse-traditions, the most striking "finds" in Drayton are certain expressions and uses which were to
become standardized in the "gradus" diction of the eighteenth century:
for example, the generalization of *gale* for any kind of wind, and of
war for "troops" (*B.W.*, IV.18), etc.:

> Ships of all burthens rigged and manned are,
> Fit for invasion, to transport a war;

also *watery plain* (IV.19) for "sea," and *scaly creatures* (III.48) for
"fish." And in Drayton too, who is so typical in his diction, one notices
that curious association of the word *ebon* with "night" (*Barons' Wars*,
IV.39):

> To write those plagues that then were coming on
> Doth ask a pen of ebon and the night—

a deeply embedded piece of tradition in English verse, found in Hey-
wood, Pomfret, Young, Cowper, Coleridge, and others.

v

The transition in the poetic style of the Elizabethans to that of the
Jacobeans and Carolines corresponds to a change in the national spirit
and temper. Religion is steadily becoming the dominant concern of the
nation. Religion might mean Royalism and the Church of England (or
the Church of Rome, for a minority), or it might mean Puritanism and
a godly reformation. Much of the poetry written between 1625 and
1642, as well as that which continued to be produced after the closing
of the theatres up to 1660, breathes the finer spirit of the age, and is,
in the wider sense of the word, "religious." A poet might worship God
as a Christian, or honour as a Cavalier, or intellectual and political
freedom as a Republican. It is a general spirit of self-dedication that is
felt so pervasively. But the new spirit is not present in the drama, which
was living on its impulse from the past. It is felt in the poetry of personal expression, especially in the lyrics of the Cavaliers and of the
religious poets. The Elizabethan style has changed. Some breadth of
outlook and some freedom of movement are lost, but there is a gain in
precision of style as there is in simplification of purpose.

These matters will be illustrated in the work of several of the poets
about to be considered, but some attention is first due to Ben Jonson
who, though neither a Cavalier nor a religious poet in the Caroline
sense, was the leader of the new lyric. Although Jonson was born in
1572 he is, for our present purpose, chiefly interesting as a post-Eliza-
bethan; for in his best and most finished work, that is to say, in his

lyrics and non-dramatic rhyming verse, he shows a quality in which most Elizabethans were deficient: he is selective. His diction shows a sense of the rank, station, and pedigree of words which, as already mentioned, was a prerequisite for the development of a classical epic style. In his dramas, Jonson never quite succeeds in forming a poetic style. The reason is plain: his realism was not in harmony with the true spirit of his time. The greatness of the Elizabethans lay in their power of transcending their ordinary selves, and Shakespeare's genius is a sublimation of this power. It is expressed in inspired improvisation. Jonson's declared aim was to write "language such as men do use"— in verse. His knowledge of the current vocabulary and idiom was immense, but his artistry is more evident in his lyrics and other short poems than in the vast exhibition of humours which fills his comedies. There were two Jonsons: the man of the exuberant comic spirit and the man of the precise and critical sense of language. The finest quality of Jonson's style is the unstudied neatness of phrasing in such well-known pieces as "Drink to me only with thine eyes," the *Hymn to Diana*, and the *Epitaph on Salathiel Pavy*. His favourite undertones of diction appeal to the reader's sensibility through his literary knowledge. He makes unobtrusive allusions to the Bible and the classics, as in the lines *To Heaven*:

> O, be thou witnesse, *that the reines dost know,*
> And hearts of all, if I be sad for show,

or *To Celia*:

> Sunnes, that set, may rise againe:
> But, if once wee lose this light,
> 'Tis, with us, *perpetuall night.*

The rightness of his diction can be best enjoyed in pieces like the evenly composed lines *To Penshurst* or the select language of *The Sad Shepherd* in which the representation of "humours" is effected by an agreeable use of dialect.

Herrick, in his *Hesperides* (1648), is a Horatian, like his poetic master, whom he celebrates in an ode. But "lexis" plays in his work a larger part than in Jonson's. His choice of words is often wantonly "curious," and his style has more than a trace of preciosity. Often, in his little lyrics, the high light is thrown on a single rare word, a spot of bright colour in a tiny picture: *liquefaction, dardanium, zonulet.*[7] The teeth of Julia are named in the last and culminating line of a poem, "those quarelets of pearl."[8] His cult of the curious in diction is stamped

---

[7]*Upon Julia's Clothes*; *To Julia*; *Upon Julia's Riband*.
[8]*The Rock of Rubies: and The Quarrie of Pearls*.

with the pedantry of the age when he addresses his conscience as his *protonotary* or calls the fancy-forming cells of the brain *fantastic pannicles*.[9] But he is often simply playful, as in his Latinisms: "*lautitious meat*," "this *fetuous* board."[10] Reminiscences of Horace are everywhere: "my retorted hairs," "untaught, to suffer poverty,"[11] and he is never better than when he reproduces the spirit of Horace in diction coloured but not disfigured by Latin memories.

Herrick delighted in prettiness of every kind, whether in children, or fairies, or clothes, and he finds the right word for the little things of country life, such as a *miching* mouse, the *chirring* grasshopper, *papery* butterflies, the *creeking* of a hen.[12] There is a light sprinkling of rustic words in his diction (especially in his fairy poems): *bruckel'd* children, *snugging* (nestling), *chit* (shoot).[13] Like his master Jonson, he is a collector rather than a maker of words, and in word-formation he does not venture much beyond hybrid compounds (in fashion at the time) like *intertalk, circumbind, circumwalk, circumflankt, circumspangle, circumcrost*.[14] In the description of Nature, he sometimes succumbs, like so many poets of the time, to the vogue of favourite words, and he will write of "some *crystal* of the spring" or "fields *enamelled* with flowers"[15]: indeed his poem *Farewell Frost, or Welcome Spring* is almost a *locus classicus* of conventional diction. Unlike the more contemplative Milton and Marvell, he does not much vary the vocabulary of description with inventions of his own.

George Herbert, though not among the "sons" of Ben Jonson, had their taste for a classical neatness and conciseness of style. His later life was one of service to God; and his poetry was a natural union between religion and art. He was interested in words and style: "I like our language as our men and coast," he tells us (*The Sonne*)—and it is true; for right idioms, words, and phrases his "liking" is evident. He had been public orator at Cambridge, and his family connections would have opened the way to a great career, had he chosen to pursue it. In *The Pearl* he says justly: "I know the wayes of learning . . . of honour . . . of pleasure." On becoming a parish priest, he reformed both his life and his literary style. The way of the world did not agree with the humility and plainness proper to his own primitive Christianity:

9*To His Conscience; Not Every Day Fit for Verse.*
10*The Invitation; The Temple.*
11*To Live Merrily, and to Trust Good Verses; A Country-Life.*
12*His Grange, or Private Wealth; Oberon's Feast; ibid.; His Grange.*
13*The Temple; Upon Roses; The Beggar to Mab.*
14*Mrs. Eliz. Wheeler; The Temple; His Sailing from Julia; To Sir J. Berkley; To Master John Crofts; To Silvia.*
15*To the Water-Nymphs; A Country-Life.*

> But when I view abroad both Regiments,
>   The worlds, and thine:
> Thine clad with simplenesse, and sad events;
>   The other fine,
>   Full of glorie and gay weeds,
>   Brave language, braver deeds,

—when he made the comparison (in *Frailtie*), he prepared the way for the controlled fervour and the precision of his unaspiring style. And with explicit reference to the diction which he will avoid, he asks, in *Jordan*:

> Is it not verse, except enchanted groves
> And sudden arbours shadow coarse-spunne lines?
> Must purling streams refresh a lover's loves?[16]

"Enchanted groves" and "purling streams" went the way of worldly ambitions, and Herbert became at the same time a true priest and a true poet. Traces of the conceit and of epigram linger in his verse, but his chief effects come from some simple phrase tellingly reserved, unerringly placed. Herbert's diction is not only plain: those who do not enter into the spirit of his poetry find it sometimes "quaint." He has the spirit of the primitive Italian painters who made homely things sacred, and sacred things homely. The aptness of his unceremonious words is often undeniable, as in the ending of *The Pulley*, when God appoints the lot of man:

> Let him be rich and wearie, that at least,
> If goodnesse leade him not, yet wearinesse
>   May tosse him to my breast,

or the line in *Antiphon* "The church with psalms must shout"; and it is a fastidious taste that is offended by the simplicity of lines like these (*Miserie*):

> O foolish man! where are thine eyes?
> How hast thou lost them in a crowd of cares?
>   Thou pull'st the rug, and wilt not rise,
> No, not to purchase *the whole pack of starres*:
>   There let them shine,
>   Thou must go sleep, or dine.

Herbert's use of everyday language in the style of true poetry was justly praised by Coleridge in his *Biographia Literaria*, and he quotes at length the beautiful poem *Love-unknown* to illustrate how such diction may be far removed from the prosaic.

[16]*Jordan* (1). H. J. C. Grierson calls the poem "a protest . . . against . . . the pastoral allegorical poetry of the Cambridge Spenserians" (*Metaphysical Lyrics and Poems*, p. 230). In another poem with the same title, *Jordan* (2), Herbert deplores his former habit of writing, when he "sought out quaint words, and trim invention."

VI

A detailed survey of seventeenth-century diction would include a consideration of Drummond of Hawthornden whose language shows lingering traces of the "aureate" fashion which marked the work of the last Scottish Chaucerians. A typical product of this school is Rolland's *Court of Venus* (*c*. 1560), which is characterized by some extreme examples of rhetorical Latinism, e.g. *suddant mort* (sudden death), *hylair vult* (joyous countenance). Drummond's use of words like *vive* and *decore* is perhaps a survival of this fashion. He had also a taste for highly ornamental words such as *diamantine* (introduced by Sylvester), *ensaffron* (his own invention), *enchristall'd*. He is, however, something of an anomaly in the present study, and his diction more properly belongs to the history of Scottish poetry.

Donne is also an anomaly. There can be no question about his greatness in both verse and prose, but his place in the tradition of English poetry is a different matter. The peculiar appeal which he makes to the present century should not disguise the fact that the general consensus of opinion for centuries was that his methods were opposed to the true genius of the language. On the historical aspects of Donne's diction two points are clear. One is the general truth of the statement made by Grierson and Smith that "Donne's avoidance of words felt at once to be 'poetic' is almost without parallel in English poets";[17] the other is the attraction which his "strong lines" and "masculine expression" exercise at certain times—though not always. By his special adherents in his own day he was recognized as an innovator: and Carew, in his *Elegie upon Donne*, praises him in terms which his modern admirers are glad to echo:

> The subtle cheat
> Of slie Exchanges, and the jugling feat
> Of two-edg'd words, or whatsoever wrong
> By ours was done the Greeke, or Latine tongue,
> Thou hast redeem'd, and open'd Us a Mine
> Of rich and pregnant phansie, drawne a line
> Of masculine expression,

and the panegyric culminates in the words:

> to the awe of thy imperious wit
> Our stubborne language bends.

The statement that Donne avoids words "felt at once to be 'poetic' " may be accepted as true in general, but a qualification is necessary. A

---

[17] *A Critical History of English Poetry* (London, 1944), p. 150.

close examination of his diction shows his position to be similar to that of Robert Browning: that is, he read widely in other men's poetry, reproducing various words and phrases—including "poetic" ones—but giving to what he borrowed the impress of his own character. Naturally the alchemy of his style is much more powerful in his mature work. In his *Epithalamion made at Lincolnes Inne* he is actually a Spenserian, and at moments no more than a nondescript Elizabethan, as in the featureless line:

> As gay as Flora, and as rich as Inde.

In the *Holy Sonnets*, which are written from the depths, traces of Spenserian diction are evident, but a new character is superimposed. For instance, the word-pattern of these lines in *The Faerie Queene* (II.v.16):

> Outrageous anger, and woe-working iarre,
> Direfull impatience, and hart murdring love

is reproduced by Donne in:

> Th'hydroptique drunkard and night-scouting thiefe,
> The itchy Lecher, and selfe tickling proud,

but the effect is more "masculine," at least, much rougher. Again, it was an occasional practice to borrow liturgical terms for use as high lights among ordinary words: Constable does so in a sonnet where he says that he may one day raise his style

> as others use,
> And turn *Eleison* to a higher strain.

This is effective, but it pales before the powerful line in the *Second Anniversarie*:

> As till Gods great *Venite* change the song.

The formal novelty of Donne's diction lies largely in its grammar; he uses words according to the logic of his meaning, not for metaphor, but for impassioned emphasis. His use of *self*, for instance, is characteristic in (*Twicknam Garden*):

> But O, *selfe* traytor, I do bring
> The spider love, which transubstantiates all,

and (*Holy Sonnets*, XVIII):

> Is she *selfe* truth and errs?

So is his use of *truth* in lines from *The Dreame* (*Songs and Sonnets*):

> Thou art so *truth*, that thoughts of thee suffice,
> To make dreames truths.

His aim is to give his words, whatever they may be, a preternatural force and intensity, an effect produced powerfully by the rhythms and repetitions in his *Hymn to God the Father*, and the greatest of the sonnets. Certain lines of this quality stand out unforgettably, as in *The Extasie*:

> And whil'st our soules negotiate there,
> Wee like sepulchrall statues lay;
> All day, the same our postures were,
> *And wee said nothing, all the day.*

Donne was less a lover of words than their imperious master and he left no impress on the language of poetry—at least for nearly three centuries—equal to the measure of his greatness.

VII

Of the four poets now to be considered, Vaughan, Crashaw, Quarles, and Marvell, the first three were products of the new poetic culture which was growing up as a rival to Spenserianism: men who were affected by both the discipline and the enthusiasm of religion, and who were finding in the new verse of the century, especially that of Herbert, a guide to original effects true to the spirit of the age and the genius of the language. They were neither Spenserians of the direct line, nor members of either of the new schools of Spenserianism which were to appear in the second half of the century. Vaughan and Marvell have a sure place in the English tradition, thanks in part to the quality of their feeling for Nature, and Crashaw's sensibility is of the same kind, though it is coloured by exotic religious emotions. Quarles belongs to a different rank, but he was the most popular poet of his time, and certain features of his diction have an historical interest.

Henry Vaughan had no marked habitual style, but his sensibility produced some fine and delicate effects of diction. His preface to *Silex Scintillans* (Part I, 1655) acknowledges his discipleship to "the blessed man, Mr. George Herbert, whose holy life and verse gained many pious converts, (of whom I am the least)." In style as in spirit, Vaughan belongs to Herbert's school and frequently echoes his master's phrasing. For instance, the rare compound *silk-twist* in *The Pearl* (Herbert) evidently suggested the *love-twist* of *Retirement* (Vaughan). The verb *interline*, used figuratively in Herbert's *Longing*, is again used figuratively in Vaughan's *White Sunday*. Both poets use the rare verb *snudge* (Herbert, *Giddinesse*; Vaughan, *Misery*). *Hope* (Herbert) concludes:

> With that I gave a vial full of tears:
> But he, a few *green ears* . . .

and the last line of *Love and Discipline* (Vaughan) ends with the same
two words: "And all the year have some *green ears*." There are many
parallels besides.[18] Another source of Vaughan's diction is the 1611
Version of the Bible which was now playing an increasing part in forming the literary style. Vaughan's memory was saturated with biblical
expressions, and they meet the eye everywhere in his religious poems:
"The cool o' th' day (*Son-Days*); "till the day Break, and the shadows
flee" (*Dressing*); or, from *Man*,

> The birds nor sow, nor reap, . . .
> The flow'rs without clothes live,
> Yet Solomon was never drest so fine.

It will be noticed from the quality of Vaughan's borrowings that he felt
the poetry of the biblical language.

Vaughan is less of an artist than Herbert, and is more unequal, but
in his best moments he soars higher. Herbert looks to Nature, like a
saint, for parables: Vaughan, a mystic, loses himself in contemplation—
as in the wonderful poem, *Night*. His best descriptions have a dawnlike
freshness in which familiar things are shown as if seen for the first
time, as in the lines from *The Rain-bow*:

> How bright wert thou, when Shem's admiring eye
> Thy burnisht, flaming arch did first descry!
> When *Terah, Nahor, Haran, Abram, Lot,*
> The youthful world's grey fathers in one knot,
> Did with intentive looks watch every hour
> For thy new light, and trembled at each shower!

No one can read these lines without remembering them, and Thomas
Campbell, who speaks slightingly of Vaughan, pays him an involuntary
tribute by repeating one phrase—somewhat robbed of its lustre—in his
own *To the Rainbow*:

> How came the world's grey fathers forth
> To watch thy sacred sign!

Scattered phrases in Vaughan's work like "the now *primros'd fields*"
(*Ascension-Day*) suggest that he might have excelled in description.
But he did not care enough for the variety of Nature; he preferred to
seek like qualities in different things. This desire appears in his diction,
which is apt to repeat itself. One wonders how often he uses the words
spice and *spicy*. Here are quotations enough to show that they are
favourites: "some *spicy* cloud," "*spicy* mornings," *spiciness* (of leaves),

[18]Many are pointed out in Mr. L. C. Martin's edition of Vaughan's *Works*.

"The Sun doth *spice* the day," "*spicy* mountains," "*spicy* whispers."[19] His language has traces of symbolism, as, for instance, in his use of the word *white* to suggest certain ideal qualities. Such expressions as "*white* days," "a *white*, celestial thought," "the true *white* Prince,"[20] are both common in Vaughan and characteristic of him.

There is one feature in the style of Francis Quarles, author of *Emblems*,[21] curious enough to deserve special mention. We have already noticed Herbert's practice of handling religious ideas with a familiarity born of simple and deep devotion. The language of Quarles at times goes further, and seems to court and defy ridicule.[22] This is the manner in which he describes in *Divine Fancies* (1632) "the infancy of our Saviour" in lines beginning "Hail blessed Virgin":

> O! what a ravishment 't had been to see
> Thy little Saviour *perking* on thy knee!
> To see him *nuzzle* in thy Virgin-Breast:
> His milk-white body all unclad, undrest! . . .
> And when his forward strength began to bloom,
> To see him *diddle* up and down the Room!

And there is a like eager familiarity in his lines *On Zacheus* from the same collection:

> Me thinks I see, with what a busie haste,
> Zacheus climb'd the Tree: But O, how fast
> How full of speed, canst thou imagine (when
> Our Saviour call'd) he *powder'd down* again!

Quarles like Vaughan is steeped in the Bible, and in his more earnest poems there is that touching use of simple language which was the birthright of his generation.

Richard Crashaw, bred as an Anglican, entered the Roman Catholic Church, and adapted his earlier style to the spirit of his adopted religion. His religious poems of the volume *Carmen Deo Nostro* (1652) illustrate the bolder features of his style more clearly than the better-known ones contained in *The Delights of the Muses* (1646). But Crashaw's diction is always warm and animated, and in *Musicks Duell* (freely translated from a Latin original) he shows himself master of a

---

19*Isaac's Marriage*; *The Relapse*; *Unprofitableness*; *Christ's Nativity*; *Fair and Young Light*; *To the River Isca*.
20*The Search*; *The Retreat*; *The King Disguis'd*.
21Douglas Bush states that "*Emblems* (1635) was the most popular book of verse of the seventeenth century." *English Literature in the Early Seventeenth Century, 1600–1660* (Oxford, 1945).
22Grierson and Smith remark that "The public sneered at a homeliness that often sank into bathos." *A Critical History of English Poetry*, p. 152.

rich poetic vocabulary. The synonyms he uses to express the smoothness of the nightingale's song illustrate his resources in language: "a cleare *unwrinkled* song," "the plyant series of her *slippery* song," "her *lubricke* throat," "*liquid* melodie." Crashaw's nature was clearly not at home in the austerity of the Anglican ritual; he craved for fervent emotion, richer colour. The imagery and diction of his poems in the 1652 volume remind one vividly of the florid art fostered by the counter-Reformation—its languishing postures and theatrical raptures. Crashaw rises at times to a burning eloquence, which is, however, often marked by extravagance, as in the lines *Upon the Body of our Blessed Lord, Naked and Bloody*:

> Thee with Thy self they have too richly clad;
> Opening the purple wardrobe in Thy side.

He delights in a soft and sensuous imagery which is often handled with much poetic skill, as, for example, in the *Hymn of the Nativity*:

> We saw Thee in Thy balmy Nest,
> Young Dawn of our Eternall Day,

and

> I saw the obsequious Seraphins
> Their *rosy fleece* of fire bestow.

This last epithet is a favourite: it occurs in "*rosy* princesse," and in "my *rosy* love"[23]: "*milky* soul"[24] is similar. But there is a virile vein in Crashaw, expressing itself in many turns of phrase and reminding one of the healthier side of his opulent imagination.

The work of Andrew Marvell (1621–1678) makes a special appeal to those who admire "curiosa felicitas" in poetic style. But he did not always keep to the same manner, and in his later poems there is much of the new style associated with Waller. Politics was one of his chief interests, and his *Horatian Ode upon Cromwell's Return from Ireland* is a brilliant adaptation of Horace's manner in Book III of the Odes to the career of the Lord Protector. The rare polysyllables of the Roman poet as in "aut Lacedaemonium Tarentum" are paralleled by Marvell in passages like

> And to all states not free
> Shall clymacterick be,

and

> But thou, the war's and fortune's Son
> March indefatigably on.

[23] *On the Glorious Assumption of Our Blessed Lady; A Hymn to the Name and Honour of the Admirable Saint Teresa.*
[24] *Hymn to Saint Teresa.*

A few years later, Marvell was already an adherent of the new manner. A couplet like the following from his poem on Cromwell's death:

> As long as rivers to the seas shall runne,
> As long as Cynthia shall relieve the sunne

shows the new cult of rapid smoothness in rhythm linked with polite, unemphatic diction. It is much the same in his *Last Instructions to a Painter*, where the Dutch Admiral Ruyter is described as sailing among the British rivers to survey the "bashful Nymphs" of their "crystal Streams."

He is at his best in the earlier work, written to please himself before politics engrossed him. To praise the lucent phrasing of such poems as *The Garden* would be superfluous. It is enough to notice how, at his touch, familiar words become select and rare (*The Bermudas*):

> He hangs in shades the Orange bright
> Like golden Lamps in a green Night.

But in his metaphysical love-poems the effective word is often "curious" in itself, as in the stanza (*The Definition of Love*) where he deplores the separation of himself and his mistress at opposite poles—

> Unless the giddy Heaven fall,
>   And Earth some new Convulsion tear;
> And, us to join, the World should all
>   Be cramp'd into a *Planisphere*.

No metaphysical poetry is more delightful than Marvell's: its union of the sensuous with the witty gives it a unique piquancy.

VIII

So far our survey of the seventeenth century has shown us a landscape of graceful but irregular beauty, in which Nature has preserved a certain harmony, but has created one feature after another according to her own will. But looking in another direction, we shall see the first outline of that formal garden which was continued after the Restoration and completed in the early years of the eighteenth century. The movement towards a limited uniformity of metre and diction was due to very complex causes, social as well as literary. The first of the "reformers" has traditionally been regarded as Sir John Denham, author of *Cooper's Hill* (1643). But there are earlier and perhaps more significant signs of the movement in various verse criticisms of the period, high among which stands a passage "concerning the true forms of English Poetry" in Sir John Beaumont's *Bosworth-Field* (1629). A certain amount of

what Beaumont says is commonplace, but some of his statements have
more point. He recommends in particular:

> Pure phrase, fit Epithets, a sober care
> Of Metaphors, descriptions cleare, yet rare . . .
> A language not affecting ancient times,
> Nor Latin shreds, by which the Pedant climes.

Beaumont mentions no names, but his plea for "a sober care of metaphors" is an oblique reflection on the Elizabethans, and had his principle
been observed, much of Shakespeare's poetry could not have been written. Similarly, the condemnation of obsolete language rules out one part
of the method of Spenser. By implication, the view of the two chief
Elizabethan poets as men of irregular genius, the heretics of poetry, has
already come into being. Stray hints of this view are common: but
Beaumont's couplets not only name the "disease," they also, by their
form, point to the cure. Other poets of the age, e.g. Carew and Cart-
wright, used couplets for verse criticism, whether in panegyric or elegy,
but do not, like Beaumont, anticipate the regular metre and cautious
diction of the later style.

Signs of the growth of that "poetic diction" so familiar in eighteenth-
century verse are also evident in the early seventeenth century, and are
not confined to the "Creation-poetry" of Du Bartas. Campion, for instance, writes of the "scaly nation," Drummond of Hawthornden of
"the scalie flocks," Carew of "the scalie herd," Fanshaw of "Nature's
feathered quire." "Flowery meads" is used by George Sandys and again
by Edmund Waller, who by the middle of the Civil War was writing in
that style of polite insipidity for which there was soon to be a demand.
As early as 1645 Waller's couplets were flowing with their famous
"smoothness" (*The story of Phoebus and Daphne applyed, &c*):

> Thirsis a youth of the inspired train,
> Fair Sacharissa lov'd, but lov'd in vain;
> Like Phoebus sung, the no less amorous boy;
> Like Daphne, she as lovely and as coy;
> With numbers, he the flying Nymph pursues,
> With numbers, such as Phoebus' selfe might use;
> Such is the chase, when love and fancy leads
> O'er craggy mountains, and through flowry meads,
> Invok'd to testifie the lovers care,
> Or forme some image of his cruell Faire.

"Nymph," "numbers," "flowery meads," and "cruel fair" are all recognizable as marks of the diction cultivated by amorous and pastoral poets
in Restoration and Augustan verse. At their first appearance Waller's

lines must have worn an air of smart novelty. Ten years later he has carried his reform of poetic style a stage further. Thus in the following lines from his *Panegyrick to my Lord Protector*:

> To dig for Wealth we weary not our Limbs,
> Gold, though the heavy'st Metall, hither swims;
> Ours is the Harvest where the *Indians* mowe,
> We plough the Deep, and reap what others Sowe,

the "sober care of metaphors" enjoined by Beaumont is faithfully observed. To Shakespeare, "plough" was a generic verb which could be applied to any movement analogous to the action of a ploughshare: sailors could plough the deep with a keel, a woman's face might be ploughed by her rival's finger-nails (*A. & C.*, IV.x.51–2). To Waller "plough the deep," though familiar, is evidently a harsh phrase, and he therefore eases it by the witty addition "and reap what others sowe." Metaphor for him is a kind of "ruggedness" which needs smoothing. It was in the spirit of Waller's easy transition, ploughing to reaping, that Johnson saw fit to amend the sudden leap in Shakespeare's lines:

> My way of life
> Is fallen into the sere, the yellow leaf

into the easy step of

> My May of life
> Is fallen into the sere, the yellow leaf.

Abraham Cowley, like Waller, is interesting for his negations. His style did nothing to secure his position among great poets. Johnson states that "his diction in his own time was censured as negligent." Unlike the group of religious poets, Cowley did not cultivate his talent in seclusion. He became a man of the world, who made love and learning the two great occasions of his poetry. But he had neither a lover's passion, nor an imaginative delight in the classical mythology which he knew so well. To these subjects he brings the temperament of the scholar and of the scientist. In his volume *The Mistress* (1647) his attitude towards the time-honoured themes of love-poetry is purely analytical. He notes, for instance, in his poem *The Spring*, that although Nature ought to be weeping in sympathy for the absence of his mistress, she is in fact as gay as ever. In his lines *On the Death of Mr. Crashaw* he praises that "hard and rarest union" of "poet and saint" which he cannot attain himself, and speaks his mind on the two chief poetic superstitions of the day: the worship of Jupiter, and the worship of woman:

> Nor have we yet quite purg'd the *Christian Land*;
> Still *Idols* here, like *Calves* at *Bethel* stand.
> And though *Pans Death* long since all *Oracles* breaks,
> Yet still in rhyme the *Fiend Apollo* speaks:
> Nay with the worst of Heathen dotage We
> (Vain men!) the *Monster Woman Deifie*. . . .
> What different faults corrupt our *Muses* thus?
> *Wanton* as *Girles*, as old *Wives, Fabulous*!

Cowley advocated the foundation of the new Royal Society which recommended such language as the plainest man could understand. His work as a poet was somewhat analogous. His mind was stored with learning and teeming with wit, but the words in which his thoughts are conveyed have a transparent simplicity. When he writes familiarly, whether in prose or in verse, his ease is delightful, and special praise is due to his sprightly Anacreontics. His "epic and pindaric art" was intended to excite and surprise, but as Pope remarked, it is "the language of his heart" that lasts. In the elegy *On the Death of Mr. William Harvey*, affection moulds his language into beautiful cadences; but the want of warmth in his love-poems and of colour in his imaginative ones has been fatal to much of his work. His diction was not naturally poetic, and he did not study the means to make it so. Johnson mentions and illustrates two of its prevalent features, the excessive use of *do* and *did* and of heroic lines wholly composed of monosyllables. Cowley's verse, like Butler's in a different way, acted as a dissolvent. The task of re-fashioning the style of poetry on positive lines was left to the assertive genius of Dryden.

MILTON

THE STYLE of Milton is not only a matter of great moment in literature, it is a fact of the first importance in the history of English culture. Compared with the achievement of the Elizabethans, his work is like that of the Emperor Augustus following the Roman Republic: it preserved and made available for an age of culture what was best in a freer and more experimental world. This, however, is most true if one thinks of Milton simply as the author of *Paradise Lost*. To the eighteenth century with its deep veneration for epic poetry, the view was natural; and it needed a certain independence to assert that he wrote not one masterpiece, but several. The mistake has not wholly disappeared. It lies at the root of the belief, now fortunately weakening, that Milton is a petrifying influence in English poetry. Yet his style, the expression of a proud and dominating mind, is never static, even in *Paradise Lost* itself. Milton was constantly adapting his metre and diction to new occasions. *Comus* differs in style from *Il Penseroso*, Book I of *Paradise Lost* differs from Book IV, and Book IV again from Book XII. *Paradise Regained* has a style of its own, and *Samson Agonistes* resumes the continuous tale of experiment and discovery.

Milton's aspiring and independent spirit is impressed in every part of his work. Coleridge's saying that John Milton is in every line he wrote is indeed true: he was one of the strongest individualists in religion and culture. He was not bound to live by pleasing a popular taste. Poetry for him is a sacred office, and the Muse he invokes is the Holy Spirit. Further, he was familiar with the whole body of European culture, and was qualified by both genius and learning to attempt the immense task of a universal poem. Yet again, he follows immediately one of the greatest ages of our own poetry of which he is a student and lover. He salutes Spenser, Shakespeare, and Jonson by name: he has also read and remembered the works of others—Fletcher, Drayton, Sylvester. But he was not merely learned in books. He was sensitive in the highest degree to physical and natural beauty, and his poetry is as great when he draws direct from observation and experience as when he writes from imagination and memory. No man was ever better equipped by education to do great things in literature; no man was ever more bent upon serving his Maker to the utmost of his endowments.

The crucial event in Milton's literary life was the choice, after long deliberation, of the story of Man's Creation and Fall as the object of his most elaborate effort. The loss of Paradise was the theme which offered his powers amplest scope. After a long enforced confinement to little pieces, he was in the mood to undertake a vast canvas. For years he had been accumulating the stores of knowledge needed in a work of immense scale. He was also the possessor of a style capable of great width and grandeur. The author of *Il Penseroso* and *Comus*, of *Lycidas* and the *Epitaphium Damonis* had tried his powers of description and knew that they were equal to a much vaster task. *Paradise Lost*, once finished, created the impulse to write more concentrated work, the result of which was *Paradise Regained* and *Samson Agonistes*.

In a criticism of Milton's language, the significant clue to follow is the development of his descriptive style. It is the perfection of Heaven, the vastness of space, and the loveliness of Eden that call forth and strain to the utmost the resources of his vocabulary. In the later books of *Paradise Lost* and in *Paradise Regained* he develops a quieter and more inward style, and his language is simpler. The last phase of his art is as great as any: but a study of diction is necessarily concerned more with the elaborate than the plain, and for that reason it is the style of *Paradise Lost*, especially in the descriptive parts, not of *Samson Agonistes*, that demands the closest attention.

I

Milton was an apt pupil, and he had the self-confidence which can borrow without feeling the loss of freedom. Other poets of the time imitated their predecessors: the Fletchers followed in the steps of Spenser, Vaughan modelled himself on Herbert. But in wide and fruitful reading of the best Elizabethan poetry, Milton had no superior. The signs of these studies are most evident in the poems which he wrote before 1645.[1] In *Paradise Lost,* there are traces here and there of Spenserian diction, but they are commoner in the looser and more relaxed verse written at Cambridge and Horton. Archaisms such as *ychain'd* (*Nativity Ode*), *ycleap'd* (*L'Allegro*), and *whileare* (*Upon the Circumcision*) are marks of his earlier style; and the epithet *feast-full* (Sonnet IX) points backward to Spenser rather than forward to the epics. There is also in his earlier poems a fair sprinkling of the "conventional" diction already described, e.g. "*enameld* Arras of the Rainbow" (*Nativity Ode*), "*enameld green*" (*Arcades*), "*Crystall* Fountains" (*Psalm 114*). Some of his happiest touches are traceable to

[1]Quotations are from *The Poetical Works of John Milton*, ed. Beeching (Oxford, 1919).

memories of other poets, re-minted for his own use. It was noticed by Swinburne that the phrase in *Lycidas* "the opening eye-lids of the morn" occurs in a beautiful passage by Middleton,[2] and there are many parallels with other Elizabethans. Drayton, for instance, whose descriptions have already been noticed, writes of "a *chequer'd* sky," of "*tufted* cedars" and the "fairest *livery*" worn by heaven: Milton writes of "the *chequer'd* shade," "*tufted* trees," and of "clouds in thousand *liveries* dight" (*L'Allegro*). Drayton's epithet *large-limb'd* is in Milton's translation of Psalm 136,[3] and Drayton's *smooth-sliding*[4] is in *Lycidas*. Milton's oft-repeated epithet for the primrose, "rathe" (*Lycidas*), also occurs (as an adverb) in Drayton, but there is a closer parallel in a line by E(dmund) B(elton) in *England's Helicon* (1600):

> And made the rathe and timely primrose grow.

The *Orchestra* of Sir John Davies has several resemblances in style and diction to Milton's work: Davies writes of "the axletree of heaven," Milton of the sun's "burning Axletree" (*Nativity Ode*); the rare word *cynosure* is in *Orchestra* and also in both *Comus* and *L'Allegro*; "number numberless" is in *Orchestra*, "numbers numberless" in *Paradise Regained* (III.310). The "printless feet" of *Comus* was evidently suggested by "printless foot" in *The Tempest* (V.i.34), the earliest known use of the epithet.

This list does not indicate the extent of Milton's borrowings, nor does it necessarily point in every case to his actual sources. It merely gives some idea of his debt to the Elizabethans, and some hint of his skill as a selective reader.

Besides these particular words and phrases, Milton also adopted certain general features of the current style. Some conceits disfigure a few of his early poems and make havoc of the unfinished *Passion*. His choice of words in description was especially affected by the prevalent habit of clothing nature in human attire. Apart from the metaphor of *livery* already quoted, one notices that the Morn is *civil-suited* and *Cherchef't* in a cloud; that the woodbine is *well attir'd* and flowers wear a *gay wardrop*, or *sad embroidery*; also that in *Comus*, a cloud has a *silver lining*. But such language is a comparatively late growth in Milton's style. He began composing while he was still a boy, and the earliest strata of his style are to be found in his paraphrases of Psalms, which give a remarkable foretaste of his mature work. The outstanding features of these compositions are the compound epithets and the allusive

[2]Swinburne, *The Age of Shakespeare*, chapter on Thomas Middleton.
[3]*Golden-tressed*, common to Drayton and Milton's *Psalm 136*, has already been mentioned; see p. 53.
[4]Also in Sylvester's *Du Bartas*.

periphrases. From what source Milton derived his practice of forming epithets as in "*froth-becurled* head" (of the sea, *Psalm 114*) or "*thunder-clasping* hand" (*Psalm 136*) cannot certainly be told: perhaps from Spenser, more likely from Greek or from Latin poetry. No doubt a taste for such words was formed by his discovery of them in various quarters, in Homer, in Spenser, and in the favourite Ovid. In any case, the practice was adopted by the author "at fifteen yeers old," and it remained a constant feature of his earlier style, and an intermittent one later. He used these words freely in his own Latin verse, e.g. "*racemiferis* vitibus" (*Elegia tertia*), "*salutiferum* gramen" (*Elegia quinta*), as well as in his English poems of earlier date. In *Paradise Lost* and the later poems they are less frequent, but they abound in the descriptive parts of his earlier work, especially in *Comus*, to the style of which they add much beauty. A few examples may be recalled: "*gray-hooded* Eev'n," "*flowry-kirtl'd* Naiades," "*silver-shafted* Queen," Sabrina's "*amber-dropping* hair" and "*coral-pav'n* bed," Thetis' "*tinsel-slipper'd* feet," "*rushy-fringed* bank." One example, "*earth-shaking*[5] Neptune," is a direct translation from Greek. The other feature in the paraphrased Psalms must have been due to a natural taste for majestic words. The allusive phrase, as we have seen, was employed by Spenser, but it was not from Spenser that Milton learned to expand "When the Children of Israel" into the sonorous line (*Psalm 114*):

> When the blest seed of *Terah's* faithfull Son. . . .

The earlier poetry of Milton is sometimes imaginative, sometimes descriptive, and different diction is needed for the different effects. The distinction is not absolute, but on the whole *Comus* and *Lycidas*— *Lycidas* more so than *Comus*—are imaginative poems: the scenes they describe are idealized or ideal. *L'Allegro* and *Il Penseroso*, though not confined to the literalness of precise local accuracy, are based on the English scenery which Milton saw daily at Horton, and are in large part a distillation of the sights and sounds in the rural life of southern England. The treatment and language reflect this distinction between the two pairs of poems.

Comus is in part a garland of the choicest flowers of late Elizabethan diction; but it also gives glimpses of imaginative vision in pure Miltonic phrase. Sometimes there is a passage in the mysterious or romantic vein (ll. 205–9):

[5]This epithet has now been traced back to Chapman, as have also *all-conquering*, *blue-haired*, and *never-ending*, which are first attributed to Milton by the *O.E.D.* See G. G. Loane's article, "Chapman's Compounds in the *N.E.D.*," reviewed in *The Year's Work in English Studies*, 1941.

> A thousand fantasies
> Begin to throng into my memory
> Of calling shapes, and beckning shadows dire,
> And airy tongues, that syllable mens names
> On Sands, and Shoars, and desert Wildernesses;

sometimes there are lines in that style of melodious vagueness for which Milton found the most proper use in his epic poems (ll. 311–14):

> I know each lane, and every alley green
> Dingle, or bushy dell of this wilde Wood,
> And every bosky bourn from side to side
> My daily walks and ancient neighbourhood.

Both passages are at the opposite pole from realistic distinctness, and there is the same effect in those phrases of blended English and Latin which are used later so vigorously in the descriptions of Eden. To write of "the nodding horror" of a wood (*Com.*, l. 38) does not give a clear picture, but it does stimulate the reader, familiar only with the English scene, to imagine in terms of general landscape; and the same result is produced in a line like:

> By grots, and caverns shag'd with horrid shades,

(l. 429) where the word "shades" performs the function of the Virgilian "umbræ." A small point in the diction of *Comus* worth noticing is Milton's introduction into the language of the forms *azurn* and *cedarn*.

Lycidas, one of the most beautiful poems in the world, has been undervalued by a few critics who have failed to grasp its character. It is lyrical and ideal, not descriptive and realistic. Johnson condemned the unreality of the pastoral form, and found the diction "harsh." Ruskin, who praised the great speech of St. Peter, objected to some of the flower epithets in the passage which follows. Neither critic seems to have come under the spell of the entire poem, or to have had ears for its unrivalled verbal music. The words are subordinate to the melodious surge of the great paragraphs. Phrases of great energy stand out here and there, like the "blind mouths" praised by Ruskin, but there is no just reason to condemn the epithets of the flowers because they are fanciful rather than true. Associations, not facts, are the material of the poem. It is a fabric of memories varied by visions, but what Milton has conveyed is not the dry record of his studies, but his impassioned delight in poetry and learning. Here and there one of the innumerable sources of the poem appears in the diction, as in the Virgilian "*meditate* the thankles Muse," but in general Milton has not displayed his reading—he has given only its finest essence. He does not describe, but *name*. In description, language should appear fresh and new; in naming, it should appear old and mellow. *Hippotades, Deva,* and *Mona* are legends in themselves, so is "the fable of *Bellerus* old." The character of the diction is significantly revealed by the fate of the word *freak'd* (with jet). It is new; and had it been in a truly descriptive context, it would, like Shakespeare's *gnarled,* have entered the common language. But in spite of its familiarity it is little used except as in echo of Milton.[6] The whole poem, in spite of the apparent disavowal of the opening lines, is one of maturity—the maturity of Milton's youth.

L'Allegro and *Il Penseroso* are largely descriptive. They appealed to the acute but limited taste of Johnson, who saw that they are faithful to real life. It is true that *L'Allegro* begins with mere names—the Stygian cave, and ebon shades—but it passes rapidly to things. Each poem gives the essence of a day such as Milton actually lived in the most favoured period of his life. A little of the diction is literally new; the rest appears new by its arresting fitness. Some of the words, for instance *cynosure,* though not introduced by Milton, have survived chiefly as a reminiscence of the context in which he placed them.[7] *Chequer'd,* as we have seen, was not a new epithet in description, but its classic use is in Milton's line (*L'All.,* 96),

> Dancing in the Chequer'd shade.

Who can add to or improve the description of a wet morning in an English summer (*Il Pens.,* 125–30)?

> Cherchef't in a comly Cloud,
> While rocking Winds are Piping loud,
> Or usher'd with a shower still,
> When the gust hath blown his fill,
> Ending on the russling Leaves,
> With minute drops from off the Eaves.

To praise the language of the two poems any further is superfluous. The compactness of the diction is a model for descriptive writing. Macaulay merely found a simile for what everyone has felt when he compared it to "attar of roses."

The long interval in which Milton wrote no poetry except a few sonnets and translations of Psalms was the season for the gradual maturing of the style of *Paradise Lost.* Hints of the direction in which he was moving appear in certain of the sonnets which break down the barrier

---

[6]Robert Bridges, a close student of Milton, used it frequently. It is also found in *The Seasons* (*Winter,* 813), a poem saturated by Milton's influence; see p. 135.

[7]Cf. Carlyle, *French Revolution*: "The Fair young Queen . . . the cynosure of all eyes."

between octave and sestet and foreshadow the sustained periodic structure of the epic verse paragraph. Though little indication is given of the
new style and diction which he was preparing, in some of the sonnets
there is a grander and graver note than has been heard before, and the
vigorous use of periphrasis—"the triple Tyrant," "Jove's great son"—
forms a link between past and future. The confidence of tone with
which *Paradise Lost* opens, and the consistency which continues,
through all the necessary variations, to the last book, show that Milton
had completely formed in his mind the principles of his style before he
began the composition of the poem.

The task of finding the right diction for the "unattempted" theme of
Paradise Lost was extremely delicate and complex. Milton had left the
realm of reality which he described so exquisitely in some of his minor
poems, and was again in the region of pure imagination. The action of
the epic was to take place between Hell, Heaven, and the Earthly Paradise. It was to include journeys through immeasurable space; to record
the War in Heaven, the expulsion of the rebel angels, and the creation
of the world; and finally, to contain extended visions into the future of
the human race up to the final overthrow of Satan and the creation of
new Heavens and a new Earth. Two main problems presented themselves: one was to raise and universalize the style to make it fit to cope
with a theme so elevated and so vast; the other, to give the illusion of
reality to unimaginable scenes. For both tasks, the utmost stretch of art
was necessary, and of the two, the former was the more practicable.
In its sublimity, the style of *Paradise Lost* remains unsurpassed in literature: there, Milton succeeded to a miracle. But to describe a Heaven of
absolute Good was a task beyond him or any man. The Paradise of
Dante is peopled by inhabitants who were, once, human beings; the
Heaven of Milton is peopled by theological abstractions, who are like
neither gods nor men, and are far less real than their antagonists in the
Palace of Pandæmonium. The conception breaks down, yet the scenes
in Heaven are saved from total failure by the sustained assurance of the
poet's tone. The question which Coleridge asked about Virgil's *Aeneid*
is more relevant to Milton's Heaven: take away his style and diction
and what is left? But in describing the ideal landscape of Eden and
devising dialogues suitable to Adam and Eve in their sinless state, Milton's imagination and style are both at their greatest.

It will be necessary to consider the diction of *Paradise Lost* from two
points of view: first, as to its general character; secondly, as to its
functions in different parts of the poem.

II

The most conspicuous general feature of Milton's diction is the large Latin element, and for this he is apt to be blamed, especially by certain recent critics. It must be remembered, however, that there was a difference between the practice of his time and of ours. Many of the words derived from Latin in *Paradise Lost* are simply part of the literary diction of the sixteenth and seventeenth centuries; and indeed some of those which strike the modern reader may be found lingering into the age of Victoria. Various words supposed to be examples of Milton's tendency to "Latinism" will in fact be found in the writings of Spenser, Sylvester, Donne, Dryden, Wordsworth, Shelley, Tennyson, and even Dickens. Nor was Milton by any means alone in coining words from Latin for his own use: even so domestic a writer as Herrick, as we have seen, frequently did the same thing. It is impossible, without reference to the authorities, to distinguish between the words which Milton coined and those which were in general currency. For example, *effulgence* and *divulg'd* ("made common") were apparently introduced in *Paradise Lost* (III.388; VIII.583); but *circumfluous* and *transpicuous* (VII.270; VIII.141), which might seem to be in the same class, were already in use. In the following paragraphs the reader is referred to the footnotes which distinguish between the Latinisms which Milton introduced and those which independently belong to literary English.

Derivatives from Latin are most apt to attract attention when they are used in their literal, rather than in their acquired English sense. Latinisms of this kind are so frequent in *Paradise Lost* that in any discussion of Milton's diction an ample list of specimens must be given. Examples are : "while Night *invests*[8] the sea" (I.207–8); "There went a *fame* [i.e., rumour][9] in Heaven" (I.651); "Let none *admire*[10] that riches grow in Hell" (I.690–1); "[bees] . . . *expatiate*[11] and confer Thir State affairs" (I.774–5); "by *success* [i.e., the issue][12] untaught" (II.9); "his look *denounc'd* [i.e., proclaimed][13] Desperate revenge" (II.106–7); "Will he, so wise, let loose at one his ire, Belike through *impotence* [i.e., lack of self-restraint][14]" (II.155–6); "like a Furnace

[8]The original sense in literary English.
[9]"Now *rare*" (*O.E.D.*), but an established literary word in Milton's time.
[10]Archaic now, but found even as late as Dickens.
[11]"Now somewhat rare in the literal sense" (*O.E.D.*).
[12]Obsolete, but found between 1537 and 1733.
[13]"Obsolete" (*O.E.D.*). The last example given is from *The Rambler*.
[14]A common seventeenth-century sense, but the usual form is "impotency."

mouth cast forth *redounding*[15] smoak" (II.888–9); "the sacred *influence*[16] Of light" (II.1034–5); "His habit fit for speed *succinct*[17]" (III. 643); "mazie *error* [i.e., wandering][18] under pendent shades" (IV.239); "Or if, *inspiring*[19] venom, he might taint Th' animal Spirits that from pure blood arise" (IV.804–5); "warne him to beware He swerve not too *secure* [i.e., confident][20]" (V.237–8); "in fight they stood Unwearied, *unobnoxious*[21] to be pain'd" (VI.403–4); "Night her course began . . . *Inducing*[22] darkness" (VI.406–7); "Heav'n *ruining* [i.e., falling headlong][23] from Heav'n" (VI.868); (of rivers) "with *Serpent*[24] errour wandring" (VII.302); "Bush with frizl'd hair *implicit*[25]" (VII. 323); "some of Serpent kinde . . . *involv'd*[26] Thir Snakie foulds" (VII. 482–4); "his circling Spires, that on the grass Floted *redundant*[27]" (IX.502–3); *pontifical*, i.e., bridge-making[28] (X.313); "A monstrous Serpent on his Belly prone, *Reluctant* [i.e., writhing][29]" (X.514–15); "Who can *extenuate* [i.e., diminish][30] thee?" (X.645); "by envious windes Blow'n *vagabond*[31]" (XI.15–16); "his taste of that *defended* [i.e., forbidden][32] Fruit" (XI.85–6); "to the evil turne My *obvious*[33] breast" (XI.373–4); "what thou livst Live well, how long or short *permit*[34] to Heav'n" (XI.549–50); "Led them direct, and down the Cliff as fast To the *subjected*[35] plaine" (XII.639–40).

[15]Also used in this sense by Spenser.
[16]Established in literary English since the time of Chaucer.
[17]"Archaic or poetic" (*O.E.D.*). This example is the first given.
[18]"Now only poetic—in French and English it occurs only as a conscious imitation of Latin usage" (*O.E.D.*).
[19]Also in Spenser and Dryden.
[20]Formerly common in literary English.
[21]Also in Donne and Wordsworth.
[22]A little unusual with such a word as "darkness."
[23]Found before Milton, also in Shelley, Tennyson, etc.
[24]Used by Sylvester.
[25]"Obsolete" (*O.E.D.*). The sense is unusual, though not confined to Milton.
[26]Unusual, but an author in 1555 writes: "involved after the manner of a sleeping snake."
[27]"Obsolete" (*O.E.D.*). First example quoted, and only one other given (from Pope's *Odyssey*).
[28]The first example given by the *O.E.D.* of the word as used in this "reputed etymological sense."
[29]"Rare" (*O.E.D.*). First example quoted, and only one other given (from Shelley).
[30]This sense is "obsolete" (*O.E.D.*).
[31]Quoted by the *O.E.D.* as a figurative use of the word.
[32]"Obsolete" (*O.E.D.*); "fruyt defendid" is in Chaucer. Milton's use is the last quoted.
[33]"Obsolete or archaic" (*O.E.D.*). Examples from literary use between 1603 and 1814 are quoted.
[34]"Obsolete" (*O.E.D.*).
[35]"Obsolete or archaic" (*O.E.D.*).

Secondly, there are the Latin derivatives which attract attention by some unusual feature in their form; for instance, the passive participial forms without the English inflexion. Examples are: "thoughts more *elevate*[36]" (II.558); "Bright effluence of bright essence *increate*[37] [uncreated]" (III.6); "the main Abyss Wide *interrupt*[38]" (III.83–4); "with *submiss*[39] approach" (V.359); "*alienate*[40] from God" (V.877). Some of the present participles from Latin have a distinctly foreign air, e.g., *nocent*[41] (IX.186); "*Ponent*[42] Windes" (X.704); *plenipotent*[43] (X.404); *fulgent*[44] (X.449); *peccant*[45] (XI.70); "his *volant*[46] touch" (XI.561). Among the rarer words of Latin origin are *opacous* (III.418); "*magnific* Titles" (V.773); "warr in *procinct*"[47] (VI.19; Latin "in procinctu"); *petrific*[48] (X.294); *appetence*[49] (XI.619). Lastly, certain of his English words are suggestive of Latin usage rather than native idiom. *Shade* for "umbra" and *grove* for "nemus" are common. Other instances are the use of *strive* for "certare": "nor that sweet Grove . . . might with this Paradise of Eden *strive*[50]" (IV.275), and of *kind* for "genus": "the total *kind* of Birds" (VI.73–4).

Milton's Latinism is in some measure his deliberate choice, and it is natural to ask what reasons there are for this pronounced feature of his style. The question cannot be answered simply, for the reasons are numerous and complex. One motive is variety. Milton's theme is a vast one, but without the help of art it would be dangerously void. The use of elaborate language helps to fill the vacuity and to disguise the uniformity. Many things in his unfilled Universe have to be mentioned more than once, and Latinisms, like periphrases, may conceal the repetition. The central act of *Paradise Lost*, on which such enormous issues

[36]"From 18th c. only poetic." The earliest example in *O.E.D.* is from Chaucer.
[37]Lydgate has "Myghty Ioue eterne and increat" (*O.E.D.*), which is almost Miltonic.
[38]*O.E.D.* gives examples from Lydgate and others. Milton is the latest author quoted.
[39]"Obsolete or archaic" (*O.E.D.*). Examples in literary use between 1570 and 1904 are quoted.
[40]The earliest *O.E.D.* example is from Lydgate, 1430.
[41]"Now rare" (*O.E.D.*).
[42]"Obsolete or archaic" (*O.E.D.*). Used in descriptive writing before Milton.
[43]*O.E.D.*, "rare." First example 1658.
[44]"Now poetic or rhetorical" (*O.E.D.*).
[45]Used by G. Fletcher (1610).
[46]Milton's figurative use has been sometimes copied.
[47]"Obsolete. Only in *In procinct*, ready, prepared" (*O.E.D.*). The first example given is from Chapman's *Iliad*.
[48]The first example in *O.E.D.*
[49]The first example in *O.E.D.* is from G. Fletcher (1610).
[50]The use of *strive* in this sense is found in Chaucer, and even earlier, but I find it hard not to believe that in Milton the word is based on the Latin idiom.

depend, is the eating of an apple. Even in an age of Bible-worship the use of a word so simple as *apple* in a style so magnificent as Milton's was dangerous. Satan scornfully mentions the "apple" by name when he is boasting of his success in Hell (X.487); but in Milton's lofty invocation it is called "the fruit of that forbidden tree" (I.1-2). It cannot be so named again, and when there is need for another periphrasis, Milton takes refuge in a Latinism and calls it "that *defended* Fruit" (XI.86). A second motive is the desire to give reality to actions and scenes outside experience, and almost beyond imagination. Milton's memory for the historical and fabulous analogies which bear on the course of his narrative is the chief solution for this difficulty, but he is also helped by his profound knowledge of words. A technical term may sometimes seem to lend the sanction of science to a fiction of poetry. An example is the word *influence*, an astrological word for the effect of stars or planets on human destiny. It was not so rare as to seem pedantic, and it is a word with a solid core of thought. Milton uses it with fine effect at the end of Book II (1034-7). Satan, having escaped from Hell, has just passed through the wild confusion and "eternal anarchy" of Chaos, and looks up at last to the world of unalterable law:

> But now at last the *sacred influence*
> Of light appears, and from the walls of Heav'n
> Shoots farr into the bosom of dim Night
> A glimmering dawn.

A third motive for Latinisms was to create contrast. Milton's vast learning left intact his poetic love of native words, and no one has felt more keenly the beauty of biblical English. Such language loses its force by repetition or over-use; it must be blended with exotic words, or reserved for crucial moments. A striking instance of its effect, heightened by contrast, occurs in Book IX (182-7). Milton has first to describe the beauty of the serpent before the Fall, and as this is invention he weaves an elaborate tissue of artificial words:

> him fast sleeping soon he [Satan] found
> In Labyrinth of many a round self-rowld,
> His head the midst, well stor'd with suttle wiles:
> Not yet in horrid Shade or dismal Den,
> Not nocent yet, but on the grassie Herbe
> Fearless unfeard he slept.

In the awful moment of the temptation, Milton keeps close to the biblical account, altering its words only with the slightest touches for the sake of metre; but he inserts one phrase of his own (IX.659), introducing Eve's answer to the tempter, with the words:

> To whom thus Eve *yet sinless.*

The difference in effect between words like *nocent* (or *peccant*) and *sinless* suggests one main principle of Milton's diction. Latinisms are employed to give his style "material sublimity": they create grandeur of sound, and splendour of allusion; they are a "glistering foil": but for "moral sublimity" he depends on simpler means. Neither kind of diction would produce its full effect by itself; but, used in appropriate places, each enhances and enforces the other. The three main uses of Milton's Latinisms, then, are for variety, solidity, and contrast.

Latin is the main source of Milton's exotic words, but his style is also enriched by memories from other sources. His love of Italian poets gives a distinct colour to his diction. Tuscany supplies two of his most musical place names, *Valdarno* and *Vallombrosa*; and other words or forms of words may have been suggested by his Italian reading: for example, *harald*[51] (I.752), *Sovran*[52] (I.246 etc.), *sdein*[53] (IV.50), *imparadise*[54] (IV.506), and the adjective *adorn*[55] (VIII.576). Signs of Milton's reading in English poetry are frequent. He is in some measure a Spenserian, and *The Faerie Queene* may have suggested some of his archaisms: *nathless* (I.299), *grieslie*[56] (II.704), *maugre* (III.255), *clomb* (IV.192), *arreede*[57] (IV.962), *griding*[58] (VI.329), *wonns*[59] (VII.457), *unweeting*[60] (X.335), and from Spenser, as we have already shown, are derived some of his descriptive words, e.g., *finny, mazy, empurple*. Interesting traces of other Elizabethans appear elsewhere. For instance, *intestine broiles* (*P.L.*, II.1001) is perhaps from Marlowe's *Hero and Leander* (I.245); the verb *rowle*, used of thunder (X.666), from Sylvester; the *blasted Heath* (I.615) from *Macbeth*, and *this goodly Frame* (VIII.15) from *Hamlet*. Reminiscences of the 1611 Version of the Bible are naturally too numerous for record.

As a stylist, Milton had two general aims which frequently affected his choice and use of words: these aims were conciseness and euphony. Conciseness is largely a matter of syntax, and to obtain it Milton was often boldly elliptical, as in the phrase: "thus much what was askt"

---

[51]Ital. *araldo.*

[52]Milton's spelling of "Sovereign," after Ital. "Sovrano" (*O.E.D.*).

[53]Cf. Ital. *sdegnare*; but *sdeigne* is common in Spenser.

[54]Cf. *imparadisa* (*Par.*, XXVIII.3), but the word may have been formed independently.

[55]Ital. *adorno*, short for *adornato*. *Adorns* occurs in one of Milton's own Italian sonnets (IV).

[56]In both *Sheph. Cal.* and *F.Q.*

[57]In Spenser in the sense of "counsel."

[58]A very Spenserian word. The *Sheph. Cal.* Glosse says: "an olde word much used of Lidgate."

[59]In Spenser, P. Fletcher, etc.

[60]Both Spenser and Milton also use "unweetingly."

(IV.899) which means: "I reply thus much to what was asked." Conciseness in diction he often obtained by using intransitive as transitive verbs, thereby suppressing insignificant particles. Examples of verbs so used appear continually through *Paradise Lost,* e.g., "be *warnd* Thir sinful state" (III.185–6); "ere he *arrive* The happy Ile" (II.409–10); "The Trepidation *talkt*" (III.483); "Here matter new to *gaze* the Devil met" (III.613); "When God hath *showrd*[61] the earth (IV.52); "*wandring* many a famous Realme" (IV.234); "*Grasing* the tender herb" (IV.253); (the Devil) "*pin'd* His loss" (IV.848–9); "to *hymne* his Throne" (IV.944); "*soaring* th' air sublime (VII.421); "whatever *creeps* the ground" (VII.475); "Whom they [the devils] *triumph'd* once lapst" (X.572); "wilt thou enjoy the good, Then *cavil*[62] the conditions?" (X.758–9). Not only is Milton anxious to exclude the smaller parts of speech; he even shows a preference for aphetic forms of words, as if grudging an unnecessary syllable: thus *'scapt* for "escapéd"; *'swage* for "assuage" are characteristic. But this desire for compactness is balanced by an equal care for euphony. He sometimes prefers the rarer of two proper names, for example, *Ausonian* for "Italian," *Busiris* for "Pharaoh"; and he often chooses the more euphonious of two possible forms: for example, *Basan* for "Bashan" (I.398), *Chemos* for "Chemosh" (I.406), *Hesebon* for "Heshbon" (I.408), *Sittim* for "Shittim" (I.413), *Azotus* for "Ashdod" (I.464). He uses *Chineses* as a noun (III.438) but the more liquid *Sinaean* (XI.390) as an adjective.

Milton's conciseness is the reverse of Spenser's redundance, but he did not altogether discard the Elizabethan freedom of word-formation and word-transference. He used it with judgment and moderation. He did not form a great number of words but such as he did have often been adopted. The familiar noun *gloom* (in the sense of "darkness"), which he uses nine times, was possibly of his formation (*O.E.D.*). *Pandæmonium* (I.756) and *anarch* (II.988), derived from Greek, he introduced, also perhaps the word *serried*[63] (I.548). His new noun *gurge* (whirlpool, XII.41) has sometimes been revived in literary use. The language was still fluid enough for Milton to invent the words *disespous'd* (IX.17), in allusion to the breach of Lavinia's nuptials, and *inwoven* (IV.693), and he uses the following which were still comparatively rare or new: *disinthrone* (II.229), *inwreath'd* (III.361), *disrelish* (verb, V.305), *disincumberd* (V.697), *impearls* (V.744), *imborderd* (IX.438). Milton also practises with moderation the licence of using

---

[61]The first transitive use of the verb recorded in *O.E.D.*
[62]The same phenomenon occurs in the passive use. Cf. *P.L.*, VIII.502–3:
> Aire, Water, Earth,
> By Fowl, Fish, Beast, was flown, was swum, was walkt.
[63]The first two examples of the word in the *O.E.D.* are both from *P.L.*

nouns as verbs, and verbs as nouns, sometimes, like Shakespeare, as occasion for metaphor. Examples of the first are: "Into thir inmost bower *Handed*[64] they went" (IV.739), "*Hymning*[65] th' Eternal Father" (VI.96), "They *Lim*[66] themselves" (VI.352), shoals "*Bank* the mid sea" (VII.403); of verbs as nouns: *acclaime*[67] (III.397), *roam*[68] (IV. 538), "without *disturb*[69]" (VI.549), "the place of her *retire*[70]" (IX.267).

These instances are of historical interest as showing how large an amount of grammatical fluidity remained in the mid-seventeenth century; further, they help to dispose of the figment that Milton fastened the language in shackles of iron. Actually he stood for a rational use of freedom; but the personality of his style is so dominating that every word in it seems pre-ordained. Hence there has been a tendency to regard all his language as the result of his own will and choice, whereas much of it is simply the literary English of the period. The failure to distinguish between Milton's language and his style has caused many mistakes both in poetry and in criticism. Poets who have admired his language have sought to copy his style which (unless they can think as Milton thought) is inimitable; critics who have recognized that his style is inimitable have sometimes condemned his language as a vicious model. Had the relation between Milton's diction and the unique objects which he pursues in *Paradise Lost* been more carefully considered, both mistakes might have been avoided.

III

It has never been claimed that Milton is equally successful throughout *Paradise Lost*, and all admirers of the poem admit that they prefer some parts to others. *Paradise Lost* is a poem about Hell, Heaven, and Earth. It is commonly held that the first two Books—the portion concerned with Satan and his Angels—are Milton's masterpiece; but the description of the Earthly Paradise is certainly little inferior. No one, I think, places the books on Heaven above the rest, and critics who have attacked the poem have generally fallen upon those parts as its vulnerable places. In the first two Books, technical problems shrink under the magnificent conception of Satan and his Angels. But no sooner is the

---

[64]First example in *O.E.D.* from Milton's prose.
[65]First example in *O.E.D.*, often in later poetry.
[66]First example in *O.E.D.*
[67]"Mostly poetic" (*O.E.D.*). Four times in Milton's epics.
[68]First example in *O.E.D.*
[69]One earlier example in *O.E.D.*
[70]"Now rare" (*O.E.D.*). Examples are given from Spenser and Daniel.

invocation of Book III passed, than the difficulties begin—the difficulties and the miracles. Whereas Milton has a distinct and tremendous idea of Satan, his idea of Heaven and its inhabitants is not distinct and not wholly satisfying. It is here that the miracle of his style is shown: for the splendour of the execution half disguises the vagueness of the conception. But when Milton leaves the hymning choirs, and returning to Satan's voyage, describes the newly created world and its inhabitants, he is again a poet and an artist of the highest order. His conception of Eden and the words in which he conveys it combine to form a marvel of beauty. The style of this part of *Paradise Lost* fascinated poets for generations; and no wonder, for where else is there such a description of ideal existence? The scenes in Heaven and the scenes in Eden make the first claim on our attention, for it is in these places that Milton's command of diction is put to its most exacting test.

To illustrate the language of Milton's scenes in Heaven, I will take as typical the following lines on the Archangel Michael's mission to the Earth (V.246–53):

> So spake th' Eternal Father, and fulfilled
> All Justice: nor delaid the winged Saint
> After his charge receivd; but from among
> Thousand Celestial Ardors, where he stood
> Vaild with his gorgeous wings, up springing light
> Flew through the midst of Heav'n; th' angelic Quires
> On each hand parting, to his speed gave way
> Through all th' empyreal road.

There are finer things in Milton than writing of this kind, but such a passage is an extraordinary proof of the power of style to give the illusion of sublimity. Three qualities in the diction can be distinguished. First, there are the "celestial phrases" which are always at Milton's command: "vaild with his gorgeous wings," "angelic quires," "empyreal road." They have the quality of music and are almost "inarticulate poetry," being used for elevation rather than expression. The Graeco-Latin element is conspicuous in diction of this kind: *adamantine, myriads, amarant, asphodel, hyacinthine, ambrosia*; by contrast, words of pure Latin origin are needed for occasions of especial energy. Secondly, there is the outstanding phrase "thousand celestial ardors." Vague as the meaning is, the words are sanctioned by the force of Milton's aspiring personality. They are illuminated by the reflected memory of other passages, such as the lines *At a Solemn Musick*. Such phrases, unlike the words of the first class, are for single use, and do not bear repetition after one great occasion. Thirdly, there are the synonyms, which in Milton's style perform a most important function. For "God" and "Angel"—words which by frequent use would soon lose all effect—are substituted "th' Eternal Father" and "the winged Saint." Such phrases, slightly varied but always new, flow inexhaustibly from Milton's pen. By these diverse means, he fills the spaces of Heaven with the phantoms of glorious poetry.

But it is not only in Heaven that Milton's style is called upon to amplify and exalt. In other parts of the poem it continually fulfils the same functions. His unique feeling for the poetry of learning supplies him with the similes and allusions which are his chief form of elaboration, but in a humbler way, the choice of single words contributes much towards the same result. A few illustrations may be given. Sometimes a generalized place-name gives definiteness to a description. In Hell, a mountain is an "Alpe" (II.620) and a quicksand a "Syrtis" (II.939). Vast and shadowy conceptions are suggested, in the Latin manner, by adjectives: "the palpable *obscure*[71]" (II.406); "this huge *convex*[72] of Fire" (II.434); "the vast *abrupt*[73]" (II.409); "the *Void*[74] immense" (II.829); "the *vast*[75] of Heav'n" (VI.203); "the pure *Empyrean*[76]" (III.57); "one entire *globose*[77]" (V.753); "oft they quit The *Dank*[78]" (VII.441). The supernatural persons are named with a wealth of varying titles. Satan, in the eyes of his followers, is an "Emperor" (I.378); a "Sultan" (I.348); a "mighty Paramount" (II.508). To the fallen Angels, God is "the Potent Victor" (I.95); to Eve, after her fall, He is "Our great Forbidder" (IX.815). Throughout the poem, a rare name or synonymous phrase delights the imagination or the ear: the Dead Sea is "th' *Asphaltick* Pool" (I.411); the storm-swept coast of Sicily is "The hoarce *Trinacrian* shore" (II.661). Familiar things, not ignoble in themselves, receive new and magnificent titles: the trumpets of Satan's followers are "sonorous mettal" (I.540) or "sounding Alchymie" (II.517); a rainbow is "the showrie Arch" (VI.759); the sun, "this diurnal Starr" (X.1069). Occasionally, the re-naming is a poetic failure, and Milton's unlucky idea of materializing the War in Heaven involves a reference to cannon-balls as "Iron Globes" and "Balls of missive ruin" (VI.590; 518–19). Such flaws are not frequent enough to constitute a feature of the style.

[71]The first example of several in the *O.E.D.* Occurs twice in *P.L.*
[72]"By Milton stressed *conve.x*, which is not infrequent with later poets" (*O.E.D.*) Occurs three times in *P.L.*
[73]Only example in *O.E.D.* of this use.
[74]First example in *O.E.D.* of this use.
[75]"Chiefly poetic" (*O.E.D.*). Occurs earlier in seventeenth century.
[76]Occurs five times in *P.L.* No earlier example in *O.E.D.*
[77]Only example in *O.E.D.*
[78]"Obsolete" (*O.E.D.*). Two earlier examples quoted.

A more constant danger is that of lapsing into mere verbalism. But of this also the examples are extremely rare. One occurs in Book VI (664-5):

> So Hills amid the Air encounterd Hills
> Hurl'd to and fro with jaculation dire,

where "jaculation" merely repeats the idea of "hurling." As a rule Milton's periphrases and expansions add richly to the beauty of his style. For instance, the line on light in the Invocation of Book III:

> Bright effluence of bright essence increate

forms a glorious contrast to the biblical simplicity of "God is light" three lines before. Milton's style is a synthesis of austerity and splendour; so regarded, it is seen to reflect the highest type of mind in a great age of human culture. It is the expression of "plain living" and "high thinking."

There is no sharp formal difference between Milton's "celestial" style and his descriptive style, but there is a great difference of effect. If we attempt to imagine a "winged Hierarch," it is our picture, not Milton's; but the landscape of Eden has been mapped and plotted, and it is described with the passion of a lover. Milton seems to be surveying a fertile scene from a great height: he cannot discern the details, but delights in the vast extent and the rich variety of the general features. Language used naturally and simply is best adapted to describing scenes near at hand—the objects encountered in the day's work, for each of which there is a familiar name. Milton's Eden is surveyed in the mood of contemplation and the spirit of art: it has no associations with the toil of man, but is beautified by the lavish hand of the Creator. To describe such a scene, a diction is needed from which all local associations have been rooted out. The danger of enervation is obvious, but Milton's command of a mixed style here comes to his aid: what he loses in distinctness, he gains in elevation. The following lines (IV. 137-42) are a superb example of Anglo-Roman diction adapted to ideal description:

> over head up grew
> Insuperable highth of loftiest shade,
> Cedar, and Pine, and Firr, and branching Palm,
> A Silvan Scene,[79] and as the ranks ascend
> Shade above shade, a woodie Theatre
> Of stateliest view.

[79]"Silvis scaena coruscis," *Aen.,* I.164.

Where he can, Milton draws upon actual memories, whether English or Italian, though he artfully generalizes the language (IV.244–6):

> Both where the morning Sun first warmly smote
> The open field, and where *the unpierc't shade*
> *Imbround the noontide Bowrs,*

and he continues in a legendary strain of description (IV.246–50):

> Thus was this place
> A happy rural seat of various view:
> Groves whose rich Trees wept odorous Gumms and Balme,
> Others whose fruit burnisht with Golden Rinde
> Hung amiable, *Hesperian* Fables true. . . .

If the poet's affection for the sights and smells of an English spring tempts him for a moment, he quickly passes on to the vaguer music of Greek names (IX.1039–41):

> Flours were the Couch,
> Pansies, and Violets, and Asphodel,
> And Hyacinth. . . .

Milton's grasp of history and legend, his union of simplicity and grandeur, his incomparable sense of the drama of light and darkness, day and night—these together make *Paradise Lost* the greatest of all the hymns of Creation.

IV

So famous is Milton's command of elaborate diction that it seems paradoxical to praise him as a great master of simple English. Such, however, is the fact, though it appears more plainly in the latter part of *Paradise Lost* than in the better-known earlier books. It is, of course, obvious that some of Milton's most impressive lines come almost unchanged from the text of the Bible, such as the question of God to Eve after the Fall (X.158):

> Say Woman, what is this which thou hast done?

But much of Milton's simplicity of diction is due to other causes. The latter part of *Paradise Lost* is necessarily marked by a considerable change in tone and style. The bliss of innocence is forfeited; but the first step towards a Paradise regained has already been taken, and the departure of our Parents from the Garden is not made in despair. The words of Michael directing Adam to the path of virtue still sound in his ears (XII.585–7):

> then wilt thou not be loath
> To leave this Paradise, but shalt possess
> A Paradise within thee, happier farr.

From the moment when Adam and Eve fall prostrate and confess their fault, a change comes over the style of the poem. It is felt in the restrained and "inward" beauty of the lines in which the Archangel consoles Eve (XI.287–92):

> Lament not *Eve*, but patiently resigne
> What justly thou hast lost; nor set thy heart,
> Thus over fond, on that which is not thine;
> Thy going is not lonely, with thee goes
> Thy Husband, him to follow thou art bound;
> Where he abides, think there thy native soile.

This new quality is the main feature in the style of *Paradise Regained*, which is anticipated in the austere beauty of the passage just quoted. The shadow of the new poem is cast backward on the closing books of *Paradise Lost*.

The fundamental style of *Paradise Regained* is one of simplicity and restraint, or as I have called it "inwardness." It is the correspondence of this "inwardness" with the spiritual conception of the entire poem that constitutes the singular beauty which has been appreciated by the more poetic lovers of the work. That the restraint is self-imposed and deliberate Milton reminds us in two great passages of rich, elaborate, and ornate diction: the descriptions of the banquet in the wilderness and of the earthly kingdoms. Never did the music of Milton's syllables sound more winningly than in the first, or with greater pomp than in the second, e.g. (*P.R.*, III.286–7):

> *Ecbatana* her structure vast there shews,
> And *Hecatompylos* her hundred gates. . . .

Nevertheless, as Lamb perceived, there is a higher beauty in the passage on the "Divine Hungerer's" dream of simple fare than in the artistic allurements of the feast, and Milton's new style is equal to the task of expressing the contrast. Typical of one phase of Milton's verbal art is the line (II.361):

> *Lancelot* or *Pelleas*, or *Pellenore*,

but of a higher beauty is the subdued and concealed art of (II.268):

> Food to *Elijah* bringing Even and Morn.

Other passages harmonizing equally with what Lamb called "the deep, abstracted, holy" character of the poem occur at intervals, such as the episode which begins (I.294):

> So spake our Morning Star then in his rise,

or the description of night in the wilderness (I.499–502), which as poetry rivals the lines on night in Eden, though the later scene closes with nothing but darkness and its perils:

> for now began
> Night with her sullen wing to double-shade
> The Desert, Fowls in thir clay nests were couch't;
> And now wild Beasts came forth the woods to roam.

The last is one of the most beautiful lines of monosyllables in the language.

Paradise Regained is not eminently a Christian poem, save in so far as it records the solitary battle of a soul against the subtlest temptations. Its spirit rather is stoical; and it might appear that a theme of such austerity was impossible to treat in poetry. It would be, had not Milton attained an elevation of mood, a perfect metrical skill, and a mastery over the instrument of speech which make *Paradise Regained* one of the sublime poems of the world. The choice of words, undistinguished over long passages by any positive mark of poetry, is determined by the most rigid process of exclusion.

Samson Agonistes is a poem of a different order. The execution does not require the same vigilant care over every word. On the contrary, some admixture of ordinary language and ordinary passions is necessary for the dramatic effect. Milton has not excluded "poetic" turns of style, and here and there are lines which might have come straight from *Paradise Lost*, for instance (628):

> Nor breath of Vernal Air from snowy *Alp*.

But in general he has brought the diction some degrees nearer to contemporary usage. The licences of grammar which date from Elizabethan times and were soon to be discarded by scrupulous writers are used somewhat freely, as in *proverbd* (203), *harrass* (a noun, 257), *duell'd* (a transitive verb, 345), *blank* (a verb, 471), *enforce* (a noun, 1223), *dispose* (a noun, 1746): their effect is to give something of the roughness of ordinary speech. At moments, the diction recalls certain types of phrase current during the Commonwealth. For instance, the coining of compound words in which self- is the first element was common among the Puritans, and in *Samson Agonistes* there are *self-rigorous* (513), *self-displeas'd* (514), *self-severe* (827). Besides, there are plentiful touches of ordinary human emotion: phrases of bitterness, "avoided as a blab" (495); of angry resentment, "Witness when I was worried with thy peals" (906); of contempt, "Tongue-doubtie Giant" (1181), "Politician Lords" (1195); and at moments the language is almost homely (1350–1):

He's gone, and who knows how he may report
Thy words by adding fuel to the flame?

But throughout the tragedy, diction is subordinate to cadence, and it is on the masterly handling of metre and rhythm that Milton chiefly relies to produce the difference of effect between the despondency of the opening speeches and the exultation of the final mood.

Imitation of Milton's style plays an immense part in English poetry, and the results have not always been fortunate. The more obvious features of the diction and metre of *Paradise Lost* were parodied by John Philips, author of *The Splendid Shilling* and *Cyder*, poems of the early eighteenth century. But as knowledge and appreciation of Milton increased, his style pervaded literature more subtly, and his poetry entered deeply into the national consciousness. His theology was largely accepted in the eighteenth century; his cosmology harmonized sufficiently with the assumptions of Newtonian physics; and the epic form which he had used was still regarded by critics as giving the amplest scope to the highest human powers. An extensive poem on Nature like Thomson's *Seasons* was bound to base itself on the "Creation" passages of *Paradise Lost*; a blank verse epic like Glover's *Leonidas* could not escape the spell of Milton's general style. It was difficult to realize that *Paradise Lost* was the last word in a particular kind of poetry; that the secret of its style died with its author. *Paradise Lost* is not a classical model in the sense supposed. Men like Gray, Landor, Tennyson, and Bridges—great craftsmen and scholars in their art—regarded Milton as the nearest approach to perfection, and learned much of their own art in studying him. But the ideal of finish may be dangerous. It was not surprising that a young writer like Keats, who died too soon to understand his own powers, should come to feel Milton as an alien influence. Generations of poets have been too near to Milton to see his work in perspective, and perhaps it is only now that we can survey it in its proportions and its entirety. After all, Milton is not an author of one poem only, or of one style, and his example may act in various ways. His poems of real Nature, *L'Allegro* and *Il Penseroso*, have helped many poets to discover their own talent for description. His sonnets and his epic style helped to free Wordsworth from the spell of the ballad and showed him how to combine grandeur with simplicity. Shelley found Milton to be a liberating not a restricting influence. Milton was a poet whose consistent pursuit of perfection was accompanied by perpetual growth.

IT has always been the fate of Dryden to invite comparisons with other poets, and in the present survey it is impossible not to regard him in his relation to Milton on the one hand and to Pope on the other. Milton is the greatest among English poets in the art of select diction, but Dryden, his younger contemporary, stood too near to him in date to see his achievement in proper perspective. Nor had he the unworldly character which might have made him an apt pupil. In a moment of enthusiasm he could write of Milton "This man cuts us all out and the ancients too," yet he was capable of dramatizing *Paradise Lost* as *The State of Innocence, and Fall of Man*. It was characteristic that his praise should be sounder than his practice, for it is in the prose criticisms and the verse prologues and epilogues of Dryden that the most attractive side of his nature appears—his capacity for frank and generous admiration for work well done. The critic sometimes atones for the poet: his admission, for instance, that Virgil's diction "is never to be copied" makes some amends for the defects of his own translation. Nor is it fair to overlook his services to the English language in the direction of order and regularity, even while stressing the lack in his own work of the higher poetic beauties. Dryden was a great master of his own tongue, and without subscribing to Johnson's eulogy that he found it brick and left it marble, we may remember that Gray, a better critic of poetic style than Johnson, recognized him as a classic among English poets. No man in his generation had such a well-founded respect for our poetic traditions or so generous a breadth of taste as Dryden, and these qualities force themselves into view even when he appears most anxious to confine his style to the narrower taste of his time.

To regard Dryden's style as a mere preparation for the more perfect work of Pope is a great mistake. It is, however, an error against which it will always be necessary to protest, for it contains an element of truth. As a lyric poet, Dryden was clearly the superior of Pope: yet Pope was no less certainly the more finished writer in the main work of both—satire and translation. Johnson perhaps preferred Pope, yet he allowed Dryden certain points of superiority. Gray, Churchill, and Cowper all considered Dryden the better poet, and in the next generation, Wordsworth, Scott, and Keats apparently held the same view. None of these men dismissed him as a less correct Pope, and it may be that his very imperfection in details sometimes stood in his favour. Each writer, in fact, represents a particular mode of composition. One was a poet who refrained from retouching, the other was meticulous in polishing to the last syllable.

Dryden makes a characteristic defence of rapid writing: "Let me assure the Reader, that, in hasty productions, he is sure to meet with an Author's present sence, which cooler thoughts would possibly have disguisd." And he expresses the same view with greater distinctness in the couplet:

> Poets, like lovers, should be bold and dare,
> They spoil their business with an over-care.[1]

The lines are from the Prologue to *Tyrannic Love*: they are not the excuse of a lazy man, but the considered opinion of a practical playwright.[2] Dryden's couplets succeeded in the theatre of his own time, and the tragedy in blank verse which he wrote to please himself, *All for Love*, is still an actable work. The finish of Pope's couplets would have disqualified them on the stage, even when the vogue for rhyming drama was at its height. There are other contrasts as striking. The satires of Dryden had a practical aim in view: he did not "keep a piece nine years" but threw it into the heat of a controversy: *Absalom and Achitophel* and *The Medal* are historical events in a political struggle. *The Dunciad*—which is mainly a personal attack on literary rivals—was only published after the most careful preparations for the maximum effect. Dryden was a party man; Pope stood aloof with boasted "moderation." Dryden discovered the extent of his powers by adapting them to circumstance: his career was an evolution. Pope knew his aims at an early age and realized them: his career was a development. Like Shakespeare, Dryden was a great improviser: he survives through his vitality. Pope had the leisure to cultivate the finish at which he aimed, and by which he survives.

I

Much of Dryden's success lay in his style. "The proprieties and delicacies of English," he wrote, "are known to few."[3] He does not add,

---

[1]Quotations are from *The Poems of John Dryden*, ed. J. Sargeaunt (Oxford, 1935).

[2]He repeats the point, with special reference to the drama, in the Preface to *Annus Mirabilis*; see *Essays of John Dryden*, ed. W. P. Ker (Oxford, 1900), I, 15.

[3]In the original, "the English"; Preface to *Sylvae*, *ibid.*, p. 253.

what he had the right to imply, that they were known to him. His mastery of English and his mastery of metre made him what he was, and still is, a most animated writer. "Dryden's style," says Mr. Van Doren, "was a constant delight to his contemporaries because it was unfailingly fresh; new poems by Mr. Dryden meant in all likelihood new cadences, new airs."[4] His powers of invention were indeed limited. The scenes of friendship and the quarrels of friends in his dramas are deservedly famous and the character portraits in his satires, especially the portraits of forceful men of action, are unsurpassed. But he has no deep insight into general human nature, little sense of the relation between man and nature, little sense of the mysteries of being. He appreciated these qualities in other poets, but for himself literature is above all things the art of transmitting. He was a tireless adapter and translator. He adapted Shakespeare, Milton, and Molière; he modernized Chaucer, and he translated from more than half-a-dozen classical poets. In all this work Dryden is an independent man of letters, more desirous to please himself and his readers than to display his scholarship. Some of his translations are indeed almost original works, and of one of them, his version of Horace's Ode on Fortune (III.29), he goes as far as to say: "I have taken some pains to make it my master-piece in English."[5]

To modern ears, Johnson's saying that Dryden found the English language brick and left it marble sounds, at first, like a curious historical error. Scholarship and criticism have now done justice to Elizabethan English; yet had not a lexicographer, critic, and Latinist, some special cause of enthusiasm for the reforms of the Restoration? The language of Shakespeare is a marvellous instrument for drama and lyric; but for definition, statement, and argument, who would not prefer the more sober and even English of Dryden? Almost every book published around 1645 suggests that poets and enthusiasts have had their way with style for too long. The prose of Milton and Browne belongs to an age of scholars and visionaries, and the speeches of Cromwell cry aloud for the discipline of a social standard. It was from the poets themselves that reform came. In his volume of 1645, Waller's trivial but easy vein suggested that there was a future in literature for the man of the world, and the years which preceded the Restoration showed that several poets were of the same mind as to the reform they desired. The epic *Gondibert*, published by Sir William Davenant in 1651, was regarded by some leading writers as the prelude to a rational and civilized order of poetry. Hobbes in a prose essay, Waller and Cowley in verse, wrote to com-

---

[4]Mark Van Doren, *The Poetry of John Dryden* (New York, 1920), p. 93.
[5]*Essays*, ed. Ker, I, 267.

mend the theme and style of the new poem. The two poets praised Davenant for writing on "men and manners" instead of "some fantastic fairy-land." Hobbes in the following passage commended its language for steering a middle path between the dilated and the condensed:

There be so many words in use at this day in the English Tongue, that, though of magnifick sound, yet (like the windy blisters of a troubled water) have no sense at all; and so many others that lose their meaning, by being ill coupled. . . . To this palpable darkness, I may also adde the ambitious obscurity of expressing more than is perfectly conceived; or perfect conception in fewer words than it requires. Which Expressions, though they have had the honour to be called strong lines, are indeed no better than Riddles, and not onely to the Reader, but also (after a little time) to the Writer himself dark and troublesom.[6]

Hobbes does more than praise Davenant's style; he denies the existence of any such power as the Imagination, as conceived by critics of the school of Wordsworth and Coleridge. To him, poetry is simply the art of recording facts: "the Ancients therefore fabled not absurdly, in making Memory the Mother of the Muses." Memory and Judgment gather and classify the "parts of Nature" "whereby the Fancie, when any work of Art is to be performed, finding her materials at hand and prepared for use, needs no more than a swift motion over them, that what she wants, and is there to be had, may not lie too long unespied."

It was not in Dryden's nature to adopt any hard-and-fast theory of poetry, and of all great writers he, less than any, would have concerned himself with the metaphysics of Imagination. Yet he seems almost the living realization of Hobbes's ideal. The image of Fancy finding the materials of poetry ready prepared by Memory and Judgment, and needing "no more than a swift motion over them" gives a wonderfully exact picture of Dryden's mental action in his most happily conceived poems: abundance of facts, orderliness of arrangement, gusto of style— all are present, and they are enough. So, too, Hobbes's ideal of language is closely followed by Dryden. He had the art of making his poems the right length, stimulating without fatiguing the reader. He had little need for words of "magnifick sound" which were associated with a bygone age, and carried memories of the Presbyterian pedantry laughed at in Butler's *Hudibras*. Equal dislike was felt by Dryden for the crabbed manner of the metaphysicals. He tried it himself in his earliest work, but gave it up for the "strong lines" of his mature style—strength attained by vigour of statement and clearness of meaning.

But when did Dryden attain his mature style? Certainly not before

[6]*The Answer of Mr. Hobbes to Sr. Will. Davenant's Preface before Gondibert.* (*Gondibert: an Heroick Poem*; written by Sir William D'avenant.) London, 1651.

he was well into middle age. His early poems are so imperfect—tame in some parts, violent in others—that they do not deserve here more than a passing mention. The lines *Upon the Death of the Lord Hastings* (1650) are disfigured by the untidy metre and scholastic diction which often marked the verse of the Commonwealth. The *Heroic Stanzas* on the death of Cromwell (1659) have scarcely any of the concise vigour which Dryden attained later, and the use of a word like the Spenserian *designment* (*F.Q.*, II.xi.10) for "design" contrasts with the strict economy of syllables which marks his style in its full strength. The *Annus Mirabilis* (1666), often blamed for its conceits, has another defect at least as prominent: the want of what the author himself called "significant" expressions and cadences. For instance, his simile of the "trodden" snake unluckily recalls a well-known "significant" line in the *Æneid*,[7] for the word *volume* is an echo of the Virgilian "volumine." Dryden's lines (stanza 123) are:

> So glides some trodden Serpent on the Grass,
> And long behind his wounded Volume trails.

How much more "significant" the second line might have been is shown in Pope's well-known re-cast of it:

> That, like a wounded snake, drags its slow length along.

It is true that Dryden's metre did not admit the use of an Alexandrine, but the comparison fairly brings out a flatness of execution in the poem as a whole. Nor does the diction exert its full effect. For instance, in the following stanza (98):

> Amidst these Toils succeeds the balmy night;
> Now hissing waters the quench'd Guns restore;
> And weary waves, withdrawing from the Fight,
> Lie lull'd and panting on the silent Shore,

the phrases "balmy night," "hissing waters," and "weary waves" are the raw material of a style not yet matured. They are selected phrases obviously—the poet himself informs us that "weary waves" is a reminiscence from Statius—but they are not animated by an assured mastery of metrical effect.

The greater part of Dryden's work for the theatre was done during the next fifteen years. In the drama, where the standard of expression is relative, not absolute, the scope for poetic language is clearly restricted, for the author must not let his own taste conflict to any startling

---

[7]Dryden's own note calls attention to the "imitation," referring the reader to *Georgics*, III.423–4. The "volumine" passage is *Æn.* II.207–8.

extent with the exhibition of character. Dryden at his best (as in *All for Love*) is an excellent dramatist, but perhaps the importance of his plays, in the long run, lies simply in the fact that they taught him to write effectively. The couplets of *The Conquest of Granada* at least roll off the tongue, and must have sounded very fine to an audience which loved rhyme and rhetoric. The management of the metre is less rigid than in the earliest plays, though not as flexible as it became six years later in *Aureng-Zebe* (1676). It is in this play that Dryden makes his well-known protest against the use of rhyme on the stage. "Our Author," says the Prologue,

> has now another taste of Wit;
> And, to confess a Truth (though out of Time,)
> Grows weary of his long-loved Mistris Rhyme.
> Passion's too fierce to be in Fetters bound,
> And Nature flies him like Enchanted Ground.

That the dialogue presented to them was not natural did not greatly disturb a Restoration audience. Dryden's dramatic diction is often turgid—a defect inherent in the heroic play—but it is animated, it is lucid, and it is often witty. These merits he acquired because they were demanded. He had no pretensions to be the equal of Shakespeare, but he was certain he belonged to a much cleverer generation. He paid his audience a handsome compliment in the Epilogue to the Second Part of *The Conquest of Granada* where he draws a contrast with the age of Jonson:

> If Love and Honour now are higher rais'd,
> 'Tis not the Poet, but the Age is prais'd.
> Wit's now arriv'd to a more high degree;
> Our native Language more refin'd and free;
> Our Ladies and our men now speak more wit
> In conversation, than those Poets writ.

He also knew, as a practical dramatist, that he must base his work on the capacities of his audience:

> They who have best succeeded on the Stage,
> Have still conform'd their Genius to their Age.
> Thus *Jonson* did Mechanique humour show
> When men were dull, and conversation low.

It may seem strange that Dryden did not more often attempt the pure comedy of manners. He perhaps felt that this kind of work demanded a greater concentration of effort and a lighter touch than he naturally possessed.

What he really enjoyed writing was the Prologues and Epilogues. In these he could be witty, satirical, instructive, critical as he pleased, and he could enjoy his increasing success in making the couplets flexible, the rhythms expressive, the language incisive. In these small compositions he discovered a form of literature which he both invented and perfected. On this subject Mr. Van Doren must again be quoted. "Spectators," he writes, "relished his confidences and his innuendoes; often there was more real meat in his forty lines of introduction than the whole ensuing tragedy or comedy could furnish forth. The secret of his success lay in the intimacy yet dignity of his harangue. He was both easy and important; he was fluent, but he was always condensed. There was something peculiarly satisfying in his form; he rounded off his little speeches as though they were clay and his brain was a potter's wheel. The final impression was one of many riches casually summoned but faultlessly disposed."[8] In these Prologues and Epilogues we certainly see Dryden's mature style, and there could not be a better general description of that style than the words which I have just quoted.

These small compositions, however, could not be more than minor works for Dryden, who had larger powers to use than their limits could contain. It was not until 1681, when he was fifty, that he found the subject which called forth the whole of his original powers. *Absalom and Achitophel* belongs to that date: but the year before he had done a piece of work equally congenial. This was the translation of three epistles of Ovid. In taking at last to translation and satire, Dryden discovered his true vocation. The business of rendering the classics into English was about to become a task of high importance, for critical opinion was moving towards the position that to copy the Ancients and to copy Nature were one and the same thing. There had, it is true, been earlier translations of note: Chapman's *Homer*, Ogilby's *Virgil*, Sandys's *Ovid*; but these and the rest were felt to be old-fashioned or inadequate. Dryden did not underestimate the merits of Elizabethan and Jacobean English: he praised it eloquently in his *Essay of Dramatic Poesy*, but he saw that the language had long been in a state of anarchy through want of critical standards. Since 1660, the tendency had been towards stability and some measure of "refinement": the language, therefore, was ripe for the labours of the translator. The veneration for the classics all over Western Europe, the brilliance of letters at the court of Louis XIV, the production of critical poems by men of rank, like the Earl of Mulgrave's *Essay upon Poetry* (1682) and the Earl of Roscommon's

[8]*The Poetry of John Dryden*, pp. 163–4.

Essay on Translated Verse (1684), combined to create the promise of a permanent civilized order in which literature would perform a high function. There was therefore an encouragement to translate from the classics such as had never before existed. Dryden grasped the situation, and derived from translation a sense of importance and power. It is the feeling that his work will carry weight that gives his style in translation its ease and assurance.

Absalom and Achitophel is commonly called a political satire (on the title-page it is described as "a poem"), but there are many moods in it besides the Juvenalian "indignatio." It is executed rather with an artist's gusto than a moralist's passion. It is true that in drawing the character of Buckingham, Dryden had old scores to pay off against the author of *The Rehearsal*: but he had the wisdom to let wit hold the reins of his resentment. "The character of Zimri in my *Absalom*," he wrote, "is, in my opinion, worth the whole poem: it is not bloody, but it is ridiculous enough. . . . I avoided the mention of great crimes, and applied myself to the representing of blindsides, and little extravagancies; to which, the wittier a man is, he is generally the more obnoxious. It succeeded as I wished; the jest went round, and he was laught at in his turn who began the frolic."[9] The poem gave scope for other things which Dryden could do superlatively well. The temptation of Absalom by Achitophel, for instance, is admirable in its artfulness and cogency. Dryden's long, connected arguments cannot be properly illustrated by quotation, but a few couplets (408–18) will recall to the reader the vigorous current of life which flows through this passage. Absalom's doubtful title, says the tempter, may be passed by David into law:

> If not; the People have a Right Supreme
> To make their Kings; for Kings are made for them.
> All Empire is no more than Pow'r in Trust,
> Which, when resum'd, can be no longer Just.
> Succession, for the general Good design'd,
> In its own wrong a Nation cannot bind:
> If altering that, the People can relieve,
> Better one suffer, than a Nation grieve.
> The *Jews* well know their pow'r: e'r *Saul* they chose,
> God was their King, and God they durst Depose.

Fusing the force of reason with the emotion of angry partisanship, Dryden produces some of his most powerful verse. This sinewy, athletic English, stripped for labour, reappears in *Religio Laici*, "unpolish'd, rugged Verse . . . fittest for Discourse, and nearest prose." Dryden has now attained his mature style.

[9]*Discourse of Satire*; see *Essays*, ed. Ker, II, 93–4.

II

Dryden's "rugged verse," though addressed to the intellect, makes some appeal to the emotions and the imagination. The failure to give enough relief to the argument in *Religio Laici* is the main fault of that poem: *Absalom and Achitophel* succeeds better by providing more variety. It is true that the voice of the satirist never attempts song; it breaks off at the prospect of a lofty subject (854–5):

> Here stop my Muse, here cease thy painful flight;
> No pinions can pursue Immortal height;

but it has noticeable modulations of tone. Achitophel is not simply logical: he is eloquent, and quotes Scripture for his purpose (232–3):

> Thy longing Country's Darling and Desire;
> Their cloudy Pillar, and their guardian Fire,

he calls Absalom, and again in biblical phrase (239):

> The Young mens Vision and the Old mens Dream!

Absalom, too, feels a generous emotion when he alludes to David (349–50):

> For when my Father from his Toyls shall Rest,
> And late Augment the Number of the Blest,

and another emotion, one of bitter disdain, is heard when the thought of the religious visionaries enters the poet's mind (529–30):

> A numerous Host of dreaming Saints succeed;
> Of the true old Enthusiastick Breed.

Thus, even in his political satires Dryden's style is sparingly touched with colour, and in his other writings he had various further motives for departing from the severity of discourse and the plainness of prose.

In addition, he was often concerned to give his work a contemporary character: hence he uses recent slang words like *sham* and *bore*, and also a number of new or recent gallicisms such as *reprise*,[10] *parterre*, *gridelin*, *simagres*, *surtout*, some of which are a good deal more far-fetched than the French flowers of speech with which he satirically decks the conversation of Melantha, in his comedy, *Marriage a la Mode*.[11] Though Dryden mostly uses the couplet in the "public" poetry of his satires and prologues, that metre could still allow a few strokes of genial vulgarity, and the poet uses certain phrases which are below the urbane standards of its later career. Thus in one prologue he speaks

---

[10]Dryden seems to have introduced two new senses of this word. See *O.E.D.*
[11]See also E. A. Horsman, "Dryden's French Borrowings" (*Review of English Studies*, N.S., I, Oct., 1950).

of poets compelled to labour "for some small snip of gain"; in another, of a butcher's tearful wife who "dribs her part"; in a third, Thomas Aquinas is dubbed "Tom of Aquin," and in a fourth, Ireland is called "Bogland." But he is formal enough when it suits him. Addressing the Duchess of Ormond he calls Ireland "Hibernia," thus setting the tone for much complimentary verse in which England is "Albion" or "Britannia," Scotland "Scotia" or "Caledonia," and so on.

Above all, Dryden is the chief artificer in the mechanics of the heroic couplet. He studied to produce the effect then known as "harmony of numbers," that is, the euphony of vowel and consonantal sounds in succession, and the right proportion of longer and shorter words. Unfortunately, the closed couplet is so small a unit that any felicity of phrase is bound to be remembered and repeated. Certain Latinisms became associated with the craft of the couplet, and Dryden's diction contains many early uses of terms which formed the "gradus" vocabulary of the next century: *expect* for "await"; *conspire* for "combine"; *tempt* for "explore." So too we find him repeating again and again a certain limited number of words, whether as synonyms or as elements in periphrasis. Thus, *care* (corresponding to Latin "cura") may be a "brood of nestlings" as when a bird "hovers round her *care*" or it may form part of a phrase like *woolly care* for "sheep." Earlier parallels to this kind of diction may be found in Spenser, but in Dryden the significant thing is not so much the use of such words as their frequent repetition. There was a special reason why such diction appealed to the age, as we shall see later,[12] but it was also convenient as part of what I have called "the mechanics of the couplet." The words most used for synonym and periphrasis were, like *care* itself, useful rhyme-words, and in regularizing the couplet nothing was more necessary than a collection of varied and suitable rhymes. The point may be illustrated from the early part of *Palamon and Arcite*. Dryden there uses within a short space three titles for the group of forlorn women who were awaiting Theseus: they are a "mourning Train," a "helpless Kind," and a "suppliant Crew" (I.89,92,98); each of these phrases occurs at the end of a line, and it will be noticed that *train, kind,* and *crew* are all convenient rhyme-words. In all this, Dryden is systematizing and extending a form of Spenserian diction. He was preparing the way for the writers who converted poetry into the "mechanic art" described by Cowper.[13]

Dryden's periphrases cannot be too closely studied by anyone who wishes to understand the complex character of eighteenth-century

[12]See pp. 115–16.
[13]See also p. 156.

"poetic diction." Dryden is principally responsible for the vogue of the word *honours* which invariably introduces a note of artifice and unreality when used in periphrases: "the sacred honours of his head" for "hair"; "the woods their honours cast" for "leaves," and so on. He is equally responsible for the extended use of "war": a flood is "the wat'ry war," thunder is "the rowling war." The form of periphrasis which fills an entire line is one of the most copiable and copied features of Dryden's style: his phrase for the nightingale in *The Flower and the Leaf*,

> The rural Poet of the Melody,

and his phrase for barley in the *Georgics*,

> The bearded product of the golden year,

are early examples of a series which extends at least as far as the nineteenth century.[14]

Dryden praises English for its wealth of "significant" words, but he can hardly rank among the chief masters of imitative language: his instincts led him along other lines. Yet it is interesting to note that the first known use of the verb *coo* occurs in his verse, and he may perhaps be credited with supplying the noun *caw* which only existed before as a verb. His taste in expressive and echoic words was rather narrow and he had an undue preference for the noisy variety. In four lines of *Palamon and Arcite* (III.445-8), we hear of the *rattling* of a shield, the *clattering* of armour, and the *battering* of horses' feet on the pavement. This is the kind of imitative language which Dryden most likes, and the number of objects which he finds capable of "rattling" is a revelation.[15] In his last two odes on music, *St. Cecilia's Day* and *Alexander's Feast*, he experiments in the effect of iterated words, and he produces some vigorous "significant" lines, like:

> The double, double, double beat
> Of the thund'ring drum.

But to later generations such effects have appeared somewhat childish.

A pleasing feature of Dryden's work is his use of names hallowed by their association with art and literature. He does not possess Milton's vast sense of the poetry of learning, but he has a genuine reverence for the nobler works of man. Painting he regarded as one of the chief fruits

---

[14]Cf. Wordsworth: "The pensive warbler of the ruddy breast" (sonnet, *The Trosachs*).

[15]Chatterton in a prose letter parodying "heroics" writes of "clouds, teeming with the rattling hail." Quoted by E. H. W. Meyerstein, *A Life of Thomas Chatterton* (London, 1930), p. 80.

of civilization, and the names of great painters had the same music for his ear as those of certain cities—Athens or Oxford—or of poets— "mighty Homer" or "sacred Virgil." But how, he asks in the *Epistle to Mr. Lee* (51–2):

> . . . shou'd any Sign-post-dawber know
> The worth of *Titian*, or of *Angelo*?

And in the lines *To my Dear Friend, Mr. Congreve*, he draws a parallel between himself and the younger poet on the one hand, and two Italian painters on the other (39–40):

> Thus old *Romano* bow'd to *Raphael*'s Fame,
> And Scholar to the Youth he taught, became.

The same poem contains a beautiful and characteristic illustration drawn from architecture. Congreve is addressed as the poet who for the first time unites the opposite merits of two ages (15–19):

> Till you, the best *Vitruvius*, come at length,
> Our Beauties equal, but excel our Strength.
> Firm *Dorique* Pillars found Your solid Base,
> The fair *Corinthian* crowns the higher Space;
> Thus all below is Strength, and all above is Grace.

Equally true is the poetic feeling for music which is shown in *St. Cecilia's Day*.

Dryden wrote effectively in the grandiose style whenever he tried, but his real desire was for sublimity. His taste inclined to the heroic, and the study of Longinus heightened his ambition. The sustained loftiness of the sublime ode was beyond his reach, but occasional grandeur of phrase and passages of lofty beauty do occur in his odes, and they constitute one of his clearest claims to the title of poet. In the first stanza of the Killigrew Ode he uses, and proves himself worthy to use, some lofty phrases of the Miltonic order. The slow grave expansion and the solemn close of the great stanza revolve on the words *immortal, majestic, celestial, eternal*. Equally fine, in a different way, are the first eleven lines of *Religio Laici*, which constitute a poem not indeed equal to Milton's *At a Solemn Musick*, but of the same high order. The phrases "nightly tapers" and "day's bright lord" are faultless in their setting, and are perhaps the most beautiful things ever done by Dryden in poetic wording.

III

Dryden was most at home with literature, art, politics, and general ideas. In writing of civilization and social forces his interest and enthusiasm are especially aroused, but in writing of Nature he is not truly natural. His mind is kindled by the contemplation of the grand system of Creation, but its details pass with little notice and little love. Such at least is the impression conveyed by his language, and also by the balance of his couplets, which are themselves an implied denial of the freedom and variety of Nature. The generalized diction we have noticed is more than a stylistic device adopted to aid the mechanics of the couplet: it is an early expression of that neo-classical preference for general to particular truths which was expounded by Sir Joshua Reynolds in his *Discourses* to the Royal Academy. Phrases in Dryden's verse like "the bounteous year," "the yellow year," "the winter year" tend to merge "the seasons' difference" into a vaguer and more general conception, and such is the usual effect of his periphrases. Thus any beauty there may be in the precise name or the concrete idea disappears when blossoms are called "the flowery pride of meads," honey "the golden flood," or young birds "the unfeathered innocence." One would have supposed that this principle had been sufficiently established by the Romantic critics of the nineteenth century, but the exaggerated praise which Dryden's poetry has recently received in some quarters reminds us that certain principles have to be constantly re-stated. The plain fact is that Dryden did not feel the poetry of Nature deeply enough to describe it in natural language. He had glimpses of the sublimity of the universe and a habitual sense of its general laws: apart from that, he is most affected by images of gloom and destruction. He likes sensational and theatrical effects. One remembers the high esteem in which Salvator Rosa—the "savage Rosa" of Thomson—was held at this time, and Dryden shares with contemporary portrait-painters the taste for a background of dark shades and sombre tints. He delights in a "brown horror" and "brown shadows," and convulsions of Nature like that which precedes the apparition in *Theodore and Honoria* (90–5):

> At once the Wind was laid; the whisp'ring sound
> Was dumb; a rising Earthquake rocked the Ground:
> With deeper Brown the Grove was overspred,
> A sudden Horror seiz'd his giddy Head,
> And his Ears tinckled, and his Colour fled.
> Nature was in alarm.

For Dryden, Nature is a system which alternates between order and convulsion, and his diction communicates the excitement aroused by these contrasted aspects.

IV

It is in its latest phase that Dryden's diction assumes most of its Spenserian qualities. The work of his middle period when he was strengthening the heroic line as a weapon of debate, in stage declamation or satirical attack, left little room for the finer kind of ornament. But in his later years he wrote more to please himself, finding a particular satisfaction in translation. More than once he defended his departure from diction of the strictly "useful" kind. He had long sought "significant" words, but in his later works he felt justified in choosing them outside the range of contemporary usage. "When an ancient word for its sound and significancy deserves to be revived," he writes in 1699, "I have that reasonable veneration for antiquity to restore it."[16] Dryden followed his own recommendation so well that an examination of his practice impelled Thomas Gray to write in his celebrated letter to Richard West (April, 1742):

> The language of the age is never the language of poetry; except among the French, whose verse, where the thought or image does not support it, differs in nothing from prose. Our poetry, on the contrary, has a language peculiar to itself; to which almost every one that has written, has added something by enriching it with foreign idioms and derivatives: Nay, sometimes words of their own composition or invention. Shakespeare and Milton have been great creators this way; and no one more licentious than Pope or Dryden, who perpetually borrow expressions from the former. . . .[17]

He then quotes some of Dryden's old-fashioned expressions e.g., "Full of *museful mopeings*—a *roundelay* of love—stood silent in his *mood*— his *boon* was granted—the *foiled dodderd* oaks—the *beldam* at his side."

It is in his translations that the two extremes of Dryden's diction, the plain and the adorned, appear in the greatest contrast. As we have said, Dryden's heart was in the work of translation. Mr. Van Doren justly says, "Expression, elocution, diction, were cardinal points with Dryden; they absorbed the greater part of his effort in virtuoso-works like the *Virgil* and the *Fables*."[18] But many of Dryden's translations needed little or none of the verbal colouring which makes the *Virgil* a virtuoso-work. Dryden's manner varies with his original. He translated from Homer, Theocritus, Virgil, Lucretius, Horace, Ovid, Persius, and Juvenal. It is not necessary to examine all the varieties of diction employed in so many renderings: but the two opposite extremes of the plain and the ornate, and the style of the *Homer* are important. In the translations from Juvenal, Dryden keeps close to the unpolished verse

---

[16]Preface to the *Fables*; see *Essays*, ed. Ker, II, 266–7.
[17]*Works of Thomas Gray*, ed. W. Mason, 2 vols. (London, 1807), I, 302–3.
[18]*The Poetry of John Dryden*, p. 68.

which is nearest prose. His author's text gave him ample opportunity for the use of that blunt satirical style which he had perfected in the portraits of MacFlecknoe, Doeg, and Og. Johnson considers that he misses the dignity of the original, and certainly his style and diction are most forcible in those passages which mock at misfortune. There is no question of his success in producing a caustic and almost cruel effect in passages like the following from the Third Satire (332–45):

> *Codrus* had but one Bed, so short to boot,
> That his short Wife's short Legs hung dangling out;
> His Cup-board's Head six Earthern Pitchers grac'd,
> Beneath 'em was his Trusty Tankard plac'd;
> And, to support this Noble Plate, there lay
> A bending Chiron cast from honest Clay:
> His few Greek Books a rotten Chest contain'd,
> Whose Covers much of mouldiness complain'd;
> Where Mice and Rats devour'd Poetick Bread,
> And with Heroick Verse luxuriously were fed.
> 'Tis true, poor *Codrus* nothing had to boast,
> And yet poor *Codrus* all that Nothing lost;
> Beg'd naked through the streets of wealthy *Rome*;
> And found not one to feed, or take him home.

Here everything is effective, except the moral in the last couplet which needs more weight and gravity of language than Dryden gives it. Had Johnson translated the lines his whole force would have been put into the sombre reflection on the inhumanity of the rich: but Dryden's strength is put into the ludicrous description of the poor. He has succeeded powerfully in the passages requiring animation and wit. The language could not have had more life if Dryden had invented the matter, or Juvenal had written in English.

At the other end of the scale is the translation of Virgil. Here Dryden had a more difficult task, for instead of merely applying a style of his own which he had brought near to perfection, he had to exert his ingenuity in a "virtuoso-task." "Recognising clearly enough," says Mr. Van Doren, "that Virgil's haunting melody was well beyond his reach, he endeavoured to compensate the readers of his translation with obvious and rather sensational substitutes."[19] An interesting comparison is made between a prose rendering of *Æneid* I.159 ff. and Dryden's version, I.228–38, showing how Virgil's language is embroidered with phrases like "briny waters," "sylvan scenes," and "crystal streams." Perhaps the *Georgics* show even more clearly Dryden's artifices, for there the purpose of Virgil himself is, as he says, to make poetry out of diction:

[19]*Ibid.*, p. 79.

the mean matter which my theme affords
T' embellish with magnificence of words.[20]

All the artifices of Dryden's style, previously mentioned, are here brought to a focus. Instances are thick on every page, and the reader has only to open the poem at random to see how numerous they are. I will give a few illustrations. Bees are "the winged nation"; their progeny are "their young succession"; when they swarm, they "make a large dependence." Water is a "watery store," and milk is a "milky store." *Cheerful, awful,* and *rattling* supply gaps in the metre; and favourite Latinisms, such as *involve, erring, conspire, confess'd, liquid*[21] are frequent. A special feature of Dryden's decorative style is here most conspicuous. Mr. Van Doren notes the large number of epithets ending in *-y* which he employs, having failed to find "a sufficient stock of disyllabic adjectives in the language." Of the eighteen specimens which he quotes, seven are found in the *Georgics,* viz. *chinky, pory, sweepy, fainty, spumy, roofy, ropy,* to which might be added three more: *snary, steepy,* and *bleaky.* The general result is a strong impression that Dryden's style is not adapted to the task which it attempts. His admiration for Virgil was sincere and deep, but he had no close affinity with the Roman poet's love of Nature, profound humanity or stately diction. He might well admire these qualities, and remain wholly unable to reproduce them. That this was the fact he frankly admits: "There is an inimitable grace in Virgil's words, and in them principally consists that beauty, which gives so unexpressible a pleasure to him who best understands their force. This diction of his, I must once again say, is never to be copied; and, since it cannot, he will appear but lame in the best translation."[22]

In the last years of his life Dryden made the belated discovery that Homer's impetuous and rapid style was more akin to his own genius than Virgil's greater deliberation. "This vehemence of his, I confess, is more suitable to my temper; and therefore I have translated his First Book with greater pleasure than any part of Virgil."[23] This admission suggests some curious reflections. Dryden's *Virgil* was the chief model for Pope's *Homer;* and those two translations together were largely responsible for the great vogue of "false" or artificial diction in the poetry of the eighteenth century. Supposing Dryden had earlier discovered his affinity with Homer, and translated the whole of the *Iliad*

[20]*Georgics* III.455–6 (Dryden's translation).
[21]Meaning "wrap," "wandering," "co-operate," "acknowledg'd or revealed," "penetrable."
[22]Preface to *Sylvae;* see *Essays,* ed. Ker, I, 258.
[23]Preface to the *Fables; ibid.,* II, 254.

instead of the *Æneid*, what would have happened? That the version would have been truly Homeric is not likely, for the single book which Dryden translates contains many of the mannerisms of the *Virgil*. On the other hand, the translation is a spirited piece of work, and Dryden's diction is more Homeric than Pope's. The compound epithets which he translates from the Greek fit more easily into his freer verse than Pope's, and his *far-shooting King, hoarse-resounding shore, cloud-compelling Jove*, etc., cannot be bettered. It really seems that if Dryden had given his time to Homer instead of to Virgil, the resulting translation would have offered to the eighteenth century the model of a freer, more Spenserian type of diction—with some interesting consequences in the history of English poetry.

We may now attempt to summarize Dryden's achievement in the diction of poetry. He belonged to an age which regarded verse as the natural medium for political polemics and the diffusion of culture. The work of his prime, therefore, was to fit poetry for satire and intellectual discussion, and for translation. For such purposes it was necessary to stiffen the sinews of verse and to fashion an idiom at once strong and supple. Such a task could not produce an instrument of great beauty, and much of Dryden's work is, as he himself said, near to prose. But his mind was fired by an unflagging admiration for great poetry, and this feeling finds expression in his translations and odes, as well as in his later cult of ornament in diction. An element of Spenserian elaboration, archaism, and adornment enters into his later verse; and though the phrases lose some of their finer tone and colour when forced into the mould of the couplet, they retain enough of their original freedom both there and in the lyric measures to give Dryden a place in the Spenserian as well as in the neo-classical tradition. The diction of Dryden, therefore, has a twofold aspect. In satire it has the quality signified in the couplet of Young (*Universal Passion*, II):

> Heroes and gods make other poems fine:
> Plain satire calls for sense in every line.

The "plainness" of Dryden was a model for many succeeding writers and his influence is as evident in prose as in verse. On the other hand, his place in the Spenserian tradition gave his work a special value in the eyes of Gray, Cowper, and others whose sense of poetry could not be satisfied by the neo-classical standards of their day. The full merit of Dryden can only be appreciated in the light of his long line of admirers.

COMPARISONS between Dryden and Pope began to be made well before the death of the younger poet. It is not necessary that another should be added now, but seeing how much of his style and diction Pope derived from Dryden, a few outstanding features of similarity and difference between the two poets may profitably be recalled. First, Pope was more than half a century younger than Dryden, and passed his youth, not in a period of political upheaval like the Commonwealth, but amid the military glory and economic strength which ushered in the calm of the eighteenth century. By temperament Pope was in many ways a contrast to Dryden, but they had one strong resemblance. The genius of both men was active rather than contemplative: both flourished in congenial society, and would have withered in solitude. Pope's early ambition, directed by his friend Walsh, was characteristic. "He used to encourage me much," Pope told Spence, "and used to tell me, that there was one way left of excelling; for though we had several great poets, we never had any one great poet that was correct; and desired me to make that my study and aim." Walsh of course discerned that Pope's powers were fine rather than robust, and that his bent was towards the critical. Pope was always anxious to profit from the experience of others, and, as Johnson informs us, "consulted his friends, and listened with great willingness to criticism." His method of composition might be inferred from the nature of his poetry: it was the opposite of Dryden's impetuosity, being, as Johnson says, "to write his first thoughts in his first words, and gradually to amplify, decorate, rectify, and refine them." Lastly, the abundance of poetic models in English made his chief task one of selection rather than of invention. Being an improver more than an originator, he gave his energy to intense selective reading, and when on the point of writing *The Rape of the Lock*, he had, as Johnson remarks, "all the gay varieties of diction . . . already at his hand."

Although Pope attained skill in versification at an early age, and although he used rhyming couplets in the vast majority of his writings, the quality of his poetry varies considerably at different periods of his life. A study of his diction makes this fact especially evident. In the first group of his poems, the *Pastorals, Windsor Forest,* and *The Messiah,* the content is nothing, the technique is everything, and often the author has more words at command than he knows how to use. In *The Rape of the Lock,* the "gay varieties of diction" are mostly adapted to purposes of parody. In the translations of Homer, the diction is, as Johnson remarked, "artificial." Not until we come to the group consisting of the *Essay on Man,*[1] the *Moral Essays,* the *Satires,* and the *Epistles* do we find that characteristic diction of Pope of which the predominant features are economy of means and pungency of effect. In *The Dunciad,* Pope returns to his heroi-comical vein and indulges in a good deal of humorous extravagance. Parody is not of primary importance in our present study, but the other types of poem and their diction must be considered separately.

I

The earliest group of Pope's poems—the *Pastorals* and *Windsor Forest* in particular—were warmly praised in his own day, but their reputation did not survive the rise of a new and great poetry of Nature at the end of the century. The recent popularity of Pope has brought about a reaction in favour of these early poems, and they have received what is, in my opinion, some indiscriminate praise. The matter deserves special attention: for if the *Pastorals* and *Windsor Forest* are models of their kind, most descriptive poetry since written has been conceived on false lines. It is possible to think lightly of these early poems without any disparagement to Pope's later work, and he himself outgrew his taste for pastoral description. He boasts in a later poem (*Epistle to Dr. Arbuthnot*) that

> not in fancy's maze he wander'd long,
> But stoop'd to truth and moralized his song.

The conventional "fancy" and the misplaced beauties—disfigurements, therefore—of the style are the two chief faults in these early poems.

The *Pastorals* of Pope (Spring, Summer, Autumn, and Winter) are a marvel of elegant versification: each contains a situation suitable to the season, and the diction abounds in reminiscences from the best pastoral poetry. Such, in my view, is the full extent of the praise to which this early composition is entitled. But some contemporary criticism has gone further, and by an excess of praise has brought to light faults which

---

[1]This, however, is the least characteristc member of the group. Johnson considers that the *Essay* "contains . . . more harshness of diction, more thoughts imperfectly expressed . . . than will easily be found in all his other works."

otherwise might have passed unnoticed. An article entitled "Eighteenth-Century Poetic Diction," by Professor Tillotson,[2] is of great interest. As a general analytical explanation of that diction, it could not be bettered, but on one or two particular points it is not wholly convincing. An important issue may hang on a single word, and Professor Tillotson's remarks on Pope's use of the epithet *whitening* appear to raise a fundamental question of criticism. The word occurs in the following lines from the first Pastoral (17–19):

> Soon as the flocks shook off the nightly dews,
> Two swains, whom Love kept wakeful, and the Muse,
> Pour'd o'er the whitening vale their fleecy care.[3]

With the critic's remarks on *fleecy care, vale, pour'd,* and *shook off* every reader, I think, must agree: but the following views are more controversial: "*Whitening* is old, but also new. It goes back to Virgil where it is used of the light of dawn (*ut prium albescere lucem Vidit*).[4] Pope, indeed, appears to count on our knowing this, otherwise we might take his phrase to mean that the valley was whitening with daisies, or by being spread with lime, or whitening by the fleeces of the sheep themselves—a flock of sheep can appreciably alter the general colour of a field. But *whitening* is not merely a quotation from Virgil, since it is applied to *vale* and not to *light*. Pope counts on the reader's remembering Virgil's phrase and so not applying the word literally. A valley cannot whiten in the light of dawn except in the sense that the light of dawn itself can whiten." The reasoning in these last two sentences is not easy to follow. No doubt Pope's epithet was suggested by Virgil's verb, but in transferring the word from the light of dawn to a valley he has surely committed a blunder in description. That the valley is not in process of being whitened by daisies, etc., is obviously true; but why does a Virgilian reminiscence exempt the word from being applied literally? Pope does not indicate the precise sense of "whitening" in its new setting. The assumption that words are redeemed by literary reminiscence when they are not appropriate in themselves is the fundamental error of "false poetic diction," and it is an error which Pope, in his early work, not infrequently commits.

Another example of ill-judged transference occurs in *Windsor Forest*. Pope was a great reader of Milton and often adopts his language. Like everyone else, he had enjoyed reading the lines in *L'Allegro* (93–6):

[2]*Essays and Studies by Members of the English Association*, XXV (1939), 68.
[3]Line-references are to *Pope*, ed. Henry W. Boynton (Cambridge Edition of the Poets, Boston and New York, 1903).
[4]*Æneid*, IV.586f.

> When the merry Bells ring round,
> And the jocond rebecks sound
> To many a youth, and many a maid,
> Dancing in the Chequer'd shade. . . .

The beauty of "chequer'd" lies in its immediate evocation of an image: the reader sees instantly the variegation of light and shadow on the ground. To borrow a word so closely linked with its context is a delicate task, for by itself "chequer'd" does not convey the sense which it has in the entire passage. Pope, however, makes the venture, and puts the word into an early couplet of *Windsor Forest* (17–18):

> Here waving groves a chequer'd scene display,
> And part admit, and part exclude the day.

By the time the whole couplet has been read, one perceives that "chequer'd" has the same meaning as in *L'Allegro*. But this time the word, instead of illuminating the whole passage, has itself required an explanation. In isolation the first line is unintelligible: the possibilities of "chequer'd" without "shade" are too vague to convey any sense; it is only from the second line that one gathers the nature of the "chequer'd scene." The difference in descriptive poetry between the word which suggests a picture and the word which produces a problem is the difference between mastery and muddle. Whether the versification of *Windsor Forest* can make amends for the bad diction—for such it is—may admit of discussion, but nothing can justify the mechanical use of this particular word.

Windsor Forest may be a well-designed poem, but the form is dressed in borrowed plumes. It is one of those works which accentuate the difference between the author's strength and his weakness. Pope's skill in versification only brings into sharper relief the faults of his diction. An ingenious defence is offered by Professor Tillotson of the well-known type of phrase *scaly breed, feather'd race*, etc. "It helps," he says, "to express some part of the contemporary interest in the theological and scientific side of natural phenomena. . . . The creatures were a continual proof of the wisdom and variety in the mind of the Creator and a continual invitation for man to marvel and understand." He alludes to the Boyle Lectures of 1713, of which "one chapter concerns the *Clothing of Animals* 'in which we have plain Tokens of the Creator's Art, manifested in these two Particulars; the *Suitableness of Animals Cloathing to their Place and Occasions*, and the *Garniture and Beauty thereof.*' " "The poetic diction," he continues, 'is obviously a means of differentiating the creatures in this way: *the scaly breed, the feather'd race*, and so on." As a general statement, this is most valuable. There was a widespread disposition at the time fostered by theology, poetry, and science, to admire the scheme of Creation. It is evident alike in *Paradise Lost*—which supplied the unsurpassable diction for celebrating the words of God, in Addison's hymn "The spacious firmament," in Thomson's *Seasons*, and in Blackmore's *Creation*. But marvelling is an exceptional mood: even the contemplative man is sometimes off duty. *Scaly breed* is legitimate, no doubt, when the context invites the reader to admire the "Tokens of the Creator's Art." In other settings such language sounds facetious, as it is meant to do in *The Rape of the Lock* (II.26), where the poet enumerates the destructive powers of hair:

> Slight lines of hair surprise the *finny prey*.

But *Windsor Forest* is not comic in intention, nor is its author in the contemplative mood of the poets who invented his diction. In the animated description of the angler (139–40):

> With looks unmov'd, he hopes[5] the *scaly breed*,
> And eyes the dancing cork, and bending reed,

fish are not "Tokens of the Creator's Art" but the prey of the sportsman. On any large view of style and diction *scaly breed* is clearly a phrase misplaced.

Much the same may be said of the mythology. To some poets the gods of Greece and Rome are living beings. They may take a wondering delight in the fresh discovery of the stories, as in the Renaissance; or they may feel an imaginative sympathy with the myths as interpretations of Nature. Spenser, Drayton, Milton, and Keats delighted in the myths as wholly poetic and partly true. In the large spaces of *Paradise Lost* there is full room for the latent poetry of the names to expand, as in the comparison (V.15–17):

> then with voice
> Milde, as when *Zephyrus* on *Flora* breathes,
> Her hand soft touching, whisper'd thus.

Pope was more sophisticated. His admiration for Homer and Virgil is beyond question, but it was hardening into a dogma. He enjoyed transferring the names of the deities to the pages of a translation, and he used them, in his early work, as a safe convention; but he had no vestige of feeling that the gods and goddesses still lived in the reign of Queen Anne. His own "epic" poems—*The Rape of the Lock* and *The*

---

[5]"The active use of the word hope, though authorised by Dryden, appears to my taste intolerably harsh and affected.—Wakefield." See Elwin's ed. of *Pope*, I (London, 1871), 348n.

Dunciad—are parodies; his "receipt to make an epic poem" is a jest at the expense of the belated epic bards. The right place in his verse for Jove and Neptune was in the battle at Hampton Court for Belinda's lock, and there he puts them. Deities have no business in his Windsor Forest, where they are nothing but diction (37–8):

> See Pan with flocks, with fruits Pomona crown'd,
> Here blushing Flora paints th' enamell'd ground.

Had Pope felt what these names had once been and might still be, he could not have packed them as he does here into a crowded couplet. *Pan, Pomona, crown'd, blushing, Flora, paints*, and *enamell'd* are old poetry and he does not love it. It is true that good words, however hackneyed, may be restored. But Pope was not one of the redemptive poets: his instinct was to give bad poetry and dying words the *coup de grâce*.

Yet there are some things in *Windsor Forest* which Pope does excellently. Like many men who are not contemplative, he was keenly observant. Even in the *Essay on Man* where he invites the reader to survey the whole Creation, it is the separate couplets and the single details that are effective. He is less inclined to wonder at the regular course of being than to feel active surprise at some *lusus naturae*. In picturing a scene which has not been described too often before, he finds a ready flow of expressive phrases. This is how he sees a reflection in the still water of a stream (211–16):

> Oft in her glass the musing shepherd spies
> The headlong mountains and the downward skies;
> The wat'ry landscape of the pendent woods,
> And absent trees that tremble in the floods:
> In the clear azure gleam the flocks are seen,
> And floating forests paint the waves with green.

How much fresher are the "headlong mountains" and the "downward skies" than "blushing Flora" and "the enamell'd ground." Even better are the descriptions of spirited action. All the verbs—words not gathered from books, but drawn from life—are exactly right in the animated hunting scene (155–8):

> See the bold youth *strain* up the threat'ning steep,
> *Rush* thro' the thickets, down the valleys *sweep*,
> *Hang* o'er their coursers' heads with eager speed,
> And earth *rolls back* beneath the flying steed.

These remarks on *Windsor Forest* which serve to indicate the limits of Pope's early descriptive powers[6] and the connection of a conventional

---

[6]Pope did, however, originate the use of a few descriptive epithets in poetry. His "spiry fir" in *The Messiah* is perhaps the source of similar uses, e.g., Dyer's "*spiry* cypress" and Cowper's "*spiry* myrtle." See also p. 126.

diction with the prevalent couplet also suggest a point of resemblance between Dryden and Pope. In spite of many differences both poets were more akin in spirit to Homer than to Virgil, even though Pope's practice of laboriously correcting his verses is also ascribed to Virgil. Two of Virgil's essential qualities—meditative pathos and the lingering love of beauty—were far from Pope's nature, even if he had possessed the metre in which to convey them. It was fortunate for him that Dryden had left the field open for a complete translation of the *Iliad* and the *Odyssey*.

II

Pope's *Iliad* is a work of the highest importance in our literature from several points of view. In spite of its shortcomings—which have perhaps been exaggerated—it is the principal translation of Homer in English, and, after the 1611 Version of the Bible, the principal translation of any foreign text. Notwithstanding Bentley's adverse verdict, it has been the chief means of transmitting Homer's poetry to the English reader. Its style has a twofold importance: historical, from the fame of the translation; essential, from the accomplishment and finish of the execution. Enough has already been said of the faults of Pope's diction: we have now to consider its other aspects. In the mechanics of the artificial style, Pope attained perfection in the *Iliad*—a fact he obviously realized when he handed over large portions of the *Odyssey* to be translated by his collaborators, Broome and Fenton. In Pope's *Homer*, the end and culmination of an experiment in verse are reached. The canons of a poetic idiom are settled and concluded. Imitators there were in abundance; improvers there could not be. For Pope, the inheritor of Dryden's style, there had been some work of refinement and enrichment still to be done; for Pope's successors there was no way but imitation. Some detailed attention is obviously due to the chief work in a style which some critics supposed would never grow obsolete as a model in English poetry.

The qualities of Pope's translation were pretty well understood in his own century, and though scholarship, in the person of Bentley, slighted the work, criticism warmly applauded. Homer was not rendered literally, but he was made available for English readers in the most polite and elegant form that our language seemed likely to attain. "It is remarked," says Johnson, "by Dr. Watts, that there is scarcely a happy combination of words, or a phrase poetically elegant in the English language which Pope has not inserted into his version of Homer." To Johnson himself, it was a unique poem, "a poetical wonder . . . a

performance which no age or nation can pretend to equal." Johnson
had no nice scruples about fidelity: if Homer was to be read, he must be
improved: Pope "knew that it was necessary to colour the images and
point the sentiments of his author." "Knowledge finds no willing recep-
tion till it is recommended by artificial diction. . . . First writers are
simple, and . . . every age improves in elegance." Johnson's love for
rhyming couplets leads him to condone the freedoms which they frequently compelled Pope to take: "he now and then admits an epithet
rather commodious than important." He also knew that the English
Iliad owed much to the English *Æneid*, and he is perhaps just to both
poets when he remarks: "Pope searched the pages of Dryden for happy
combinations of heroick diction, but it will not be denied that he added
much to what he found."

It should be remembered that Pope's *Homer* is the product of an age
as well as of its translator's own preferences. The taste of the time demanded that the final result should be an Anglo-Roman, not an Anglo-
Hellenic poem. There could be no question of leaving names like Ares,
Poseidon, and Aphrodite in their Greek form: they must be translated
into their Latin equivalents. Again, there was a general prejudice
against an excess of "Saxon monosyllables," and to supply their place
or vary their monotony Pope was compelled to draw largely on the
vocabulary of artificial elegance. Further, the code of the heroic line
required the due mingling of longer and shorter words, and if certain
of the most admired types were to be much used, such as

> The graceful husband of the Spartan bride

(*Il.*, VII.429), disyllabic adjectives would be in demand. Though Pope's
work was by far the greatest expression of the taste of his age, that taste
existed as an independent force, and it made the most exacting demands upon him.

It will be convenient to make a short classification of the chief features of Pope's Homeric diction. A few remarks will be made on each
point, especially by way of comparison with Dryden's example.

1. A considerable number of special words are about equally common in Dryden and Pope. For instance, the characteristic *expect* (await),
conspire (combine), and *involve* (wrap, enclose) are frequent in both
poets: to these words may be added (*un*)*erring* and *awful*. The following are probably more common in Pope than in Dryden: *grateful, resist-
less, doubtful, refulgent, indignant, cheerful, conscious, various.* These
adjectives are sometimes introduced as additions to the Greek text.

2. Pope's style is somewhat less Latinized than Dryden's, but he introduces a fair sprinkling of rare Latin derivatives, of which the following are examples: *protended, fulgid, ignipotent,*[7] *circumfused,*[8] *retorted,*[9] *infrangible, extant* (prominent),[10] *resulting* (leaping back),[11] *irremeable,*[12] *manes* (departed spirits).[13]

3. Short periphrases, some of them incorporating abstract for concrete words, occur frequently in both poets. Like Dryden, Pope uses many locutions for "sea," e.g. *watery plains, liquid road, briny wave, briny main, watery reign, watery deep, liquid element, watery way.* There are also frequent phrases for persons, e.g. *venerable sage* (Calchas), the *Pylian sage* (Nestor). Arrows or other missiles are *feather'd deaths*, the *pointed death*, the *feather'd vengeance*, the *flying death*, the *winged death*. Insects are the *wandering nation*; the sky is the *ethereal plain*, etc.

4. The whole-line periphrasis, noted already as occurring in Dryden, is commoner in Pope, and is a distinct feature of his style. Of the four following examples (*Il.*, V.482; VIII.114; XI.639; XIII.68), it will be observed that three constitute the same syllabic type of line:

> Th' imperial partner of the heav'nly reign [Juno]
>
> The hoary Monarch of the Pylian band [Nestor]
>
> The wounded offspring of the healing God [Machaon]
>
> The God whose earthquakes rock the solid ground [Neptune].

5. A small number of special words are widely generalized by Pope. For example, like Dryden he made *war* perform the office of various kindred words. *War*[14] is a favourite rhyme-word, occurring in the *Iliad*, Book XVI fifteen times in rhyme, with such different senses as "troops," "attack," "tumult," "fighting," "battle." Elsewhere, phrases like the following occur: "provoke the *war*," "all the *war* be mine," "wait the growing *war*," "shepherds gall him with an *iron war*," "the *sylvan war*" (wood-cutting).

Day is frequently generalized: it is particularly common as a synonym for "light" (as in Virgil, Ovid, etc.), for instance in Book XXI (484–5):

[7]These three are in Blount's *Glossographica* (1656).
[8]In Herrick, 1648.
[9]First example in *O.E.D.* with "eyes."
[10]"Archaic" (*O.E.D.*).
[11]In Bullokar, *An English Expositor* (1616).
[12]In Dryden's *Æneid*, VI.575.
[13]In Dryden's *Conquest of Granada*, Part I, IV.ii.
[14]The word developed new senses in poetry and rhetoric in medieval times. Milton is quoted in the *O.E.D.* as the earliest known source for two uses, viz.: "instruments of war" and "soldiers in fighting array."

> The goddess spoke, and turn'd her eyes away,
> That, beaming round, diffused celestial day.

6. Pope uses as many adjectives ending in -*y* as Dryden, usually of course with a descriptive purpose, but at times simply as useful disyllables in the gaps of the heroic line. The following is a select list from the *Iliad*: *fleecy, gleamy, plumy, gulfy, scaly, beamy, heapy, steepy, towery, forky, streamy* (i.e. having the appearance of a stream), *tusky, moony, spiry, flamy, beaky,*[15] *sweepy*. In a less degree, Pope also affects the disyllabic adjective terminating in -*ful*. Some of the following are common: *grateful, lengthful, fountful, deathful, foodful, spleenful.* (*Cheerful* and *doubtful*, the most frequent perhaps, have been mentioned already.)

7. Like Dryden, Pope applies various abstract words to concrete objects, using especially words of Latin origin, e.g. "the ponderous ruin" for a heavy falling rock. Pope copies Dryden's use of *honours* in similar phrases, e.g. "his brow's large honours" (of a goat's horns), "the grove's old honours fall" (of leaves), "the purple honours glow" (of plumes).[16]

8. Unlike Dryden, Pope is somewhat reluctant to render Homer's compound epithets by similar formations of his own. He considered them a danger to "the purity of our language." When Homer's meaning, he says, "can be as fully and significantly expressed in a single word as in a compound one, the course to be taken is obvious" (Pope's Preface). He does, in fact, use Spenser's *rosy-finger'd* (*Il.*, XXIII.131) but he prefers to distribute the sense over the whole line, instead of concentrating it in a single word, as in (I.623):

> Till rosy morn had purpled o'er the sky.

He also adopts Waller's epithet *cloud-compelling* (*Il.*, I.517; V.787); but sometimes he prefers to render a word like πολυπῖδαξ not in Tennyson's literal form "many-fountain'd" but in the disyllable *fountful*.[17] In this respect, therefore, Dryden is more Spenserian than Pope.

9. Like Dryden, Pope seeks out the "significant" words of the language, true to his own precept that "the sound must seem an echo to the sense," but he remembers his own warning against singularity: "Be not the first by whom the new are tried." The following passage (*Il.*, XXIII.147-9) is in the best style of "significant" diction approved by Dryden:

---

[15]I.e., "furnished with a beak," of ships: "beaky prores," *Iliad*, XV.834, the earliest example in *O.E.D.*

[16]*O.E.D.* quotes Shakespeare, *Henry VIII*, III.ii.35, "blushing honours," as the first example of this "poetic" use.

[17]Following Chapman and Sandys who both use this word in translation.

> On all sides round the forest hurls her oaks
> Headlong. Deep-echoing groan the thickets brown;
> Then rustling, crackling, crashing, thunder down.

10. A minor but characteristic feature of Pope's diction is the use of expressive and often metaphorical verbs. He shows some preference for those which are monosyllabic. We have already noticed examples in *Windsor Forest*; in the *Iliad* (XVI.453) "affrighted steeds"

> *Scour* o'er the fields, and *stretch* to reach the town.

Several times the verb "smoke" occurs to suggest rapid movement over a dusty surface: e.g. "the chariot *smokes* along"[18] (VIII.191); "the whirling car *Smokes* through the ranks" (XVI.460–1). Such words help to give the style of Pope's translation its great animation.

III

Pope's *Iliad*, excellent though it is, was a piece of task-work. It occupied some five years of his life, and though he at last found the toil an amusement, in its early stages it was irksome and anxious. He naturally wished to return to original work. He had already discovered, in *The Rape of the Lock* and the *Essay on Criticism*, the types of poetry in which he was to excel. After his *Iliad* was finished, he settled down to composing that great series of moral, critical, and satirical poems which are the successors of the didactic *Essay on Criticism*. In the middle of his later career, he returned to the mock-epic style and produced *The Dunciad* in succession to *The Rape of the Lock*.

It is in these later works that Pope discovers his natural voice and true style. In his earliest work he had been descriptive, decorative, and fanciful. Next, he had laboured to perfect the code of the conventional diction, and the use of the couplet. In his last phase, he limited and almost discarded his use of decoration and realized the ideal of an elegant diction designed to express the triumph of "good sense" (*M.E.*, IV.43–4) in the fields of manners and morals:

> Good Sense, which only is the gift of Heaven,
> And though no science, fairly worth the seven.[19]

Pope was even in some measure to anticipate the work of Wordsworth in disposing of diction which had outlived its day. He did not turn

---

[18]Borrowed from Dryden's *Æneid*, VII.909: "Proud of his steeds he smokes along the field."

[19]Pope's Epistles, "Of the Use of Riches," etc. will be given their familiar name *Moral Essays* in order to keep the line-references in the text as short as possible.

against the newer conventions of his own *Iliad*, but he dismisses the "crystal" and "purling" streams which still lingered as a memory from Elizabethan days. He already ridicules this language in the *Essay on Criticism* (II.150–3):

> Where'er you find "the cooling western breeze,"
> In the next line, it "whispers thro' the trees":
> If crystal streams "with pleasing murmurs creep,"
> The reader's threat'n'd (not in vain) with "sleep."

This insipid style is, for him, a relic of his own immature taste described in the *Epistle to Dr. Arbuthnot* (149–50):

> Like gentle Fanny's was my flow'ry theme,
> A painted mistress, or a purling stream,

and in the same poem he gives this kind of diction a ludicrous turn in the line on the Grub Street author (42):

> Lull'd by *soft Zephyrs* thro' the broken pane.

He had disposed of amorous diction some years earlier in *The Rape of the Lock*, in the summary phrase "Wounds, Charms, and Ardours" (I.119) and in the line sung by the dying Wit (V.61): "O cruel Nymph! a living death I bear."

In Pope's verse, the place of impulse is supplied by the most studied art. Occasionally, the poet nods, and a phrase slips through the meshes of his net which lacks the note of distinction, as in the couplet (Horace, *Ep.* I.vi.48–9):

> Graced as thou art with all the power of words,
> So known, so honour'd, at the *House of Lords*,

where the last phrase suggests the bathos of Crabbe; or in a line which gives "ten low words" in all their bareness (Horace, *Ep.* II.ii.15):

> But, Sir, to you with what would I not part?

Yet page after page of the *Satires*, *Epistles*, and *Moral Essays* may be read without yielding a single instance of failure. Choosing subjects in the purely didactic or critical line such as "The Use of Riches" or "The Knowledge and Characters of Men," he none the less realizes, as well as any poet in the language, the principle of Aristotle: "the perfection of diction is to be clear without being mean." The union of clarity with distinction is the characteristic of Pope's style.

But clarity and distinction alone do not make living poetry. Within the limits of satire, Pope finds scope both for beauty of phrase and for variety of diction. His choice of subject often brings into view defects rather than beauties in what he describes. His business is less with Nature than with the unnatural. The subject of false taste and bad art calls forth his neatest skill in phrasing—a skill which often rises above aptness to beauty. In the Epistle "Of the Use of Riches," he tells how Sabinus had loved to watch "the stretching branches" and "the thickening shade" of his woods. The next generation follows a different mode (*M.E.*, IV.93–6):

> His son's fine taste an opener vista loves,
> Foe to the dryads of his father's groves;
> One boundless green, or flourish'd carpet views,
> *With all the mournful family of yews.*

Scarcely less good is the couplet (*M.E.*, III.295–6) on the bad taste in church monuments:

> That livelong wig, which Gorgon's self might own,
> Eternal buckle takes in Parian stone.

By a contrast in diction, not overdone, but perfectly evident to the attentive reader, he punctures the absurdity of the landowner, Villario, turned landscape-gardener (*M.E.*, IV.83–8):

> A waving glow the bloomy beds display,
> Blushing in bright diversities of day,
> With silver quiv'ring rills meander'd o'er—
> Enjoy them, you! Villario can no more;
> Tired of the scene parterres and fountains yield,
> *He finds at last he better likes a field.*

Names play a large part in Pope's style, as in Milton's. Those which he delights to mention, in the pride of friendship, were among the most illustrious of the time. Pope knew the position which his talents had given him, and that by introducing the most famous names of his day, his verse conferred as well as received distinction. The following passage of reminiscence in the *Epistle to Dr. Arbuthnot* (135–42) is little more than what Pope himself called "a muster-roll of names," but it certainly has a poetry of its own:

> Granville the polite,
> And knowing Walsh, would tell me I could write;
> Well-natur'd Garth inflam'd with early praise,
> And Congreve lov'd, and Swift endur'd, my lays;
> The courtly Talbot, Somers, Sheffield, read,
> E'vn mitred Rochester would nod the head,
> And St. John's self (great Dryden's friends before)
> With open arms receiv'd one Poet more.

The effect of these lines is repeated in the *Epilogue to the Satires* (Dialogue II), where a list beginning with Somers and Halifax and ending with Argyle and Wyndham is concluded with Pope's comment (90-1):

> Names which I long have lov'd, nor lov'd in vain,
> Rank'd with their friends, not number'd with their train.

It is true: he *has* loved these names, and they make one of the high lights of his style.

The use of proper names in verse was a matter of considerable importance to eighteenth-century writers. Poetry had to be at once actual and elegant. There was a strong preference for contemporary subjects, and at no period does poetry approach so near to being a political and social record. The Low Countries cause Matthew Prior, the chronicler in verse of Marlborough's wars, many a humorous sigh, and he is especially uneasy over a name like "Cutts," unmusical in itself, and not quite famous enough to cause its plainness to be forgotten. In the next generation Cowper does not allude by name to so "low" a man as the Methodist Whitefield, but calls him "beneath well-sounding Greek" Leuconomus (*Hope*, 554-5).[20] Pope's names never provoke a smile, except when he means that they should, for they belong, in large measure, to the ranks of the famous or fortunate; and, moreover, in selecting them, he exercised his subtle sense of verbal euphony. Choice of subject for him involved choice of names, and in one of his Satires (Horace, II.i.23) he answers the proposal that he should "write Caesar's praise" with a typical objection on the score of style:

> What? like Sir Richard,[21] rumbling, rough, and fierce,
> With ARMS, and GEORGE, and BRUNSWICK, crowd the verse?

His friend therefore recommends a gentler theme (29-32):

> Then all your Muse's softer art display,
> Let Carolina smooth the tuneful lay;
> Lull with Amelia's liquid name the Nine,
> And sweetly flow thro' all the royal line.

Taste demanded that a name should be dignified in its associations, and euphonious in its syllables: of two available names, the less common was to be preferred. Thus, Aristotle is usually *the Stagyrite*; Virgil is *Maro*; Ovid, *Naso*; Cicero, *Tully*; England, *Britannia*; London, *Augusta*. The Latinization of style which this practice tends to produce is avoided

---

[20]See p. 156.
[21]I.e., Blackmore.

by Pope, whose choice between the rare and the familiar name is, to borrow Professor Tillotson's word, "unpredictable." Many readers of Pope must have enjoyed the skill in names which enables him to link together in a single line (*Essay on Man*, IV.245) ancient and modern history:

> Or on the Rubicon or on the Rhine,

or Roman culture and English wit (*M.E.*, I.187):

> He'll shine a Tully and a Wilmot too.

IV

Pope was reluctant to leave the safe limits of the couplet and was apt to despise the language of the past. He understood the true theory of poetic diction, and no one has given better directions on this subject. The poet, he said (Horace, *Ep.* II.ii.165–70), should

> Mark where a bold expressive phrase appears,
> Bright thro' the rubbish of some hundred years;
> Command old words, that long have slept, to wake,
> Words that wise Bacon or brave Raleigh spake;
> Or bid the new be English ages hence;
> (For Use will father what's begot by Sense).

Coleridge himself could not have written more wisely, but Pope does little towards putting his theories into practice. It is doubtful whether he has revived, except by way of parody, any old words, and he is less of a word-maker than Dryden. *Casuistry* is perhaps his most notable contribution to the language.[22] More important is the sterility of his example to future poets. In this respect, he is a great contrast to Dryden, whose work had a strong power of germination. Pope's easily imitated manner enabled scores of poets to be like him, but very few to be themselves.

For "genial" descriptions of Nature, which more than any other kind of writing demand free and fresh effects of style, Pope cared little. But he had certain special tastes in description and sentiment. His feelings, when he yielded to them, were for "gothic" effects, and he even anticipates the peculiar sensationalism of the later century. The vagueness and gloom of the following description of the afflicted Eloïsa's imaginings are worthy of the romantic pages of Mrs. Radcliffe (163–70):

[22]His use of *lone* applied to places ("lone isle," *Rape of the Lock*; "lone walls," *Eloïsa*) perhaps introduced the poetic use of the word.

> But o'er the twilight groves and dusky caves,
> Long-sounding aisles and intermingled graves,
> Black Melancholy sits, and round her throws
> A death-like silence, and a dread repose:
> Her gloomy presence saddens all the scene,
> Shades ev'ry flow'r, and darkens ev'ry green,
> Deepens the murmur of the falling floods,
> And breathes a browner horror on the woods.

Here the diction is a mixture of the sombre and the indefinite—the items of the scene are in the plural. As a contrast, except in its gothic gloom, may be quoted the passage admired by Joseph Warton (*M.E.*, III.187–96), in which the descriptive words could not be more clear and precise:

> Like some lone Chartreux stands the good old hall,
> Silence without, and fasts within the wall:
> No rafter'd roofs with dance and tabor sound,
> No noontide bell invites the country round;
> Tenants with sighs the smokeless tow'rs survey,
> And turn th'unwilling steeds another way:
> Benighted wanderers, the forest o'er,
> Curse the sav'd candle and unop'ning door;
> While the gaunt mastiff, growling at the gate,
> Affrights the beggar, whom he longs to eat.

Here Pope neither revives old words nor invents new ones, though he has escaped, as in the famous passage in the same Epistle, "In the worst inn's worst room" (299–314), from self-imposed limitations. One wishes that his poetry contained more such descriptions, but he has not the large contemplative power of passing frequently beyond his habitual self. It is this that prevents him from being or from deserving to be, a poet of Nature. As one would have expected, he likes moonlight, but the lines in which he tells us so (*M.E.*, II.253–6) suggest the invalid rather than the poet:

> So when the sun's broad beam has tired the sight,
> All mild ascends the moon's more sober light,
> Serene in virgin majesty she shines,
> And unobserv'd the glaring orb declines.

England is not a country of intolerable sunlight or of unlovely sunsets. Pope is here writing out of mere irritated sensibility; but it is better to do this than to describe scenes which he has scarcely looked at, in the misappropriated diction of other poets.

Pope's proper study was the study of man. He was not, in the largest sense, a student of humanity: he was too much engrossed in personal friendships and personal enmities. But compliment and ridicule did not make up the whole of his life. He always claimed to be the disinterested lover of Virtue and to prize, beyond all else, an honest man. His passion for obscure worth is perhaps doubtful, but he certainly cherished an enthusiasm, rather poetic than moral, for Virtue in the abstract. Such a feeling was in the air, and is expressed in the universal taste for personified qualities, like Goodness and Innocence. Besides this, ordinary Englishmen of the time felt a righteous horror of "bribery and corruption," an emotion fostered by the eloquence of the "statesmen out of place" among whom Pope lived. On this theme he can write with truly fervid eloquence. He has none of the cant of Liberty, but he clearly delights, like all his countrymen, in the freedom of speech which the laws of the land assured him:

> When black Ambition stains a public cause,
> A Monarch's sword when mad Vainglory draws,
> Not Waller's wreath can hide the nation's scar,
> Nor Boileau turn the feather to a star.

> Not so, when diadem'd with rays divine,
> Touch'd with the flame that breaks from Virtue's shrine,
> Her priestess Muse forbids the good to die,
> And opes the Temple of Eternity. . . .
> Let Envy howl, while heav'n's whole chorus sings,
> And bark an honour not conferr'd by Kings;
> Let Flatt'ry sick'ning see the incense rise,
> Sweet to the world, and grateful to the skies:
> Truth guards the Poet, sanctifies the line,
> And makes immortal, verse as mean as mine.

Here (*Epilogue to the Satires*, Dialogue II) Pope is inspired by a genuine enthusiasm, and the diction is, in no ignoble sense, "poetic." But at times it can assume a still finer quality, without recourse to abstractions like "Vainglory" and "Virtue." It has already been said that Pope seldom forgets himself in his theme and therefore seldom loses his Augustan manner. When he does so, he rises to a purity of language which is almost undateable. His style and diction are at their best in such a passage as the following lines of grave wisdom (Horace, *Ep.* I.i.35–46):

> Long, as to him who works for debt, the day,
> Long as the night to her whose love's away,
> Long as the year's dull circle seems to run
> When the brisk minor pants for twenty-one;
> So slow th'unprofitable moments roll
> That lock up all the functions of my soul,

That keep me from myself, and still delay
Life's instant business to a future day;
That task which, as we follow or despise,
The eldest is a fool, the youngest wise;
Which done, the poorest can no wants endure;
And which not done, the richest must be poor.

In conclusion, it is natural to attempt some general estimate of the diction in Pope's poetry. We must begin by recognizing the opposing attitudes in his career which he associated with the names of Fancy and Truth. As the poet of Fancy he parades all the "gay varieties of diction" which he collected from other writers for his mock-heroic and descriptive styles. But the best passages in these early poems are those which are expressed in original words embodying his own observations: the second-hand language is liveliest when used for parody or ridicule. For conveying the various shades of sensibility then in vogue Pope had all the requisite powers, and he is at no loss to supply the "gothic" diction for *Eloïsa to Abelard*. He is more sensitive to contemporary artifices than to enduring simplicities, and this feature of his temperament is reflected in his diction. The *Homer* deserves the highest praise which is due to an "artificial" version, but Pope's diction in this work lacked the Spenserian quality of being "susceptible of adaptation." It was only susceptible of imitation; and later in the century, when its spell was still strong, it provoked that feeling which denounced Pope's art as "mechanic." In the second style, devoted to "Truth," there is no want of colour, though it is a colour often derived from incidental and private emotions, so that full critical appreciation of it is impossible without the historical attitude. None the less it is this second phase which includes Pope's most enduring work, that in which he transcends himself most completely. After all, Pope is and deserves to be one of the most quoted of poets. He is altogether at his best when his "truth" passes out of the narrow bounds of satire into the wider region of wisdom.

THE PURPOSE of the present chapter is to illustrate the continuity in the diction of poetry during a period dominated by the genius of Pope. The three poets whose diction we are to consider had neither the original force nor the perfected art of Pope, but each developed an interesting and largely independent style of his own. Two of them (Prior and Young) were born before Pope; Thomson was his junior by twelve years, but died only four years later; Young was the last survivor of the four: they were all therefore roughly contemporary. Several minor writers of the time, such as Tickell and Parnell, would deserve attention in a more detailed study.

PRIOR

Matthew Prior (1664–1721) has long excited most interest by his familiar verse, and when Pope includes him with Swift among the "authorities for poetic language" it is no doubt on account of this aspect of his work. Familiar verse is by its very nature excluded from our scope, for its essence is to be as close as possible to common contemporary usage, to allow only the lighter touches of emotion and fancy, and to be detached in its attitude towards the ritual of serious poetry. Swift is as sparing of "colour" in his verse as in the ironical restraint and studied understatement of his prose. Prior, in such pieces as the lines *Written in the Beginning of Mezeray's History of France* or those *For My Own Monument*, has the charm of seriousness without gravity and is a model for the familiar style in poetry. In its author's own phrase, the verse is "little polish'd, tho' mighty sincere." Prior's tales and Anacreontic verse, equally fluent and easy, are more trivial and do not strike the same serious note. In all this work Prior is, as he should be, as nearly "contemporary" as possible.

But Prior has a great deal of variety: even his familiar verse is not all after one pattern, and in his philosophical and complimentary poetry he often digresses far from contemporary usage. The Butler-like couplets used in his sceptical poem *Alma* and in some of his occasional verse are less saturnine than their model and more urbane. Like his original, he affects a somewhat scholastic diction, with bits of Latin and French, and he likes a kind of academic slang:

> Criticks I read on other Men,
> And *Hypers* upon Them again.[1]

There is a jocular pedantry in phrases like *"vimineous* dome" (of a beehive), and in words like *paneity* ("breadness"),[2] also in his occasional archaisms like *leasing* and *weet*. With his love of variety and experiment, it was natural that he should try the elaborate style. His panegyrical poem, the *Carmen Saeculare*, is an early model of laureate verse, distantly prophetic in its lavish praise of William III of Tennyson's loftier strain in his *Ode on the Death of the Duke of Wellington*. Artifice in the *Carmen Saeculare* is unconcealed, and it is equally evident in *Henry and Emma*, a modernization and elaboration of *The Nut-brown Maid*. Prior's diction makes no very pleasant contrast with the naivety of the original, and the reader naturally apprehends a total failure when he finds Emma protesting to Henry in such terms as these:

> And potent VENUS shall exalt my Name,
> Above the Rumors of censorious Fame.

But Prior was of too complex a nature to be the dupe of a single style: for instance, he will call the conqueror of Louis in one place "great Nassau" and in another "little Will, the scourge of France." His most ambitious poem, *Solomon*, is a translation into narrative and imagery of the dark broodings of *Ecclesiastes*. He apologizes in his Preface for the want of finish in his style by alluding to the frequent interruptions of his private studies by public duties: "my thoughts (such as they are) having generally been expressed in foreign language, and even formed by a habitude very different from what the beauty and elegance of English poetry requires." It is true that there are some gallicisms in his diction: *luxe*, for instance, for "luxury" and the verb *elance*. Some of his adjectives, such as *genial, awful, gleby*, and of his nouns, such as *nod, dome*, and *convex* ("to the large convex of yon azure sky"), give *Solomon* a superficial appearance of conventionality. But Prior is more of a leader than a follower. His criticisms of the rhyming couplet are as independent as they are sensible. Though he found the verse of Donne "too dissolute and wild" he considered that the reformers had gone too far. "As Davenant and Waller corrected, and Dryden per-

---

[1] *An Epistle to Fleetwood Shepherd, Esq.* Quotations from Prior are from *Poems on Several Occasions*, ed. A. R. Waller (Cambridge, 1905).

[2] *Alma*, III; *Epistle to Shepherd*.

fected it [i.e. verse], it is too confined: it cuts off the sense at the end
of every first line . . . and brings every couplet to the point of an epigram." Prior is a poet who makes his knowledge of the human passions
powerfully felt. This is especially so in Book II of *Solomon* entitled
"Pleasure." He has indeed a deeper experience of life than either Pope
or Dryden.

The freedom and adaptability of Prior atone for much and make
even his less successful experiments worth some attention. Besides the
forms already mentioned, he uses blank verse in his translations from
Callimachus, and adopts several of the older styles of poetry. His slight
imitations of Chaucer contain little more than a sprinkling of old words,
but his *Ode to the Queen* (Anne) "written in imitation of Spenser's
style" is noteworthy though not wholly successful. He uses a ten-lined
stanza roughly modelled on Spenser's and he avoids the more obsolete
words of his master. "I have, however, retained some few of them," he
says in the Preface to the *Ode*, "to make the colouring look more like
Spenser's. *Behest*, command; *band*, army; *prowess*, strength; I *weet*,
I know; I *ween*, I think; *whilom*, heretofore; and two or more of that
kind, which I hope the ladies will pardon me, and not judge my Muse
less handsome, though for once she appears in a farthingale. I have
also, in Spenser's manner, used *Caesar* for the emperor, *Boya* for
Bavaria, *Bavar* for that Prince, *Ister* for Danube, *Iberia* for Spain, etc."
Neither these remarks nor the *Ode* itself show a profound acquaintance
with Spenser's language. Prior uses few old words beyond those which
he mentions, and his proper names suggest Waller or Dryden rather
than *The Faerie Queene*. Still, the experiments are interesting, and
Prior at least shows that the older sources and models of poetic diction
were not forgotten even at the height of the neo-classical age. For our
present purpose the following remarks from Prior's Preface are perhaps
as instructive as the poem itself: they do not command the full assent
of the modern critic, but they show the strength of the Spenserian tradition in an unfavourable period: "My two great examples, Horace and
Spenser, in many things resemble each other: both have a height of
imagination, and a majesty of expression in describing the sublime; and
both know to temper those talents, and sweeten the description, so as
to make it lovely as well as pompous: both have equally that agreeable
manner of mixing morality with their story, and that *curiosa felicitas* in
the choice of their diction, which every writer aims at, and so very few
have reach'd: both are particularly fine in their images, and knowing in
their numbers."

THOMSON

John Philips (1676–1709) is in some respects Thomson's predecessor in the reign of Queen Anne: his work is at least equal evidence of the familiarity of his generation with the style and diction of *Paradise Lost*. In *The Splendid Shilling*, Philips undertook, as Johnson says, "to degrade the sounding words and stately construction of Milton by an application to the lowest and most trivial things." This burlesque poem enumerates among the subjects of "mournful verse"

> Groves and Myrtle Shades,
> Of desperate Lady near a purling Stream,
> Or Lover pendent on a Willow-tree.[3]

Later, Philips turned his adopted style to more serious account, and produced some of the earliest examples of "false" Miltonic diction. His *Blenheim* is a standard warning against applying a highly individualized diction to a purpose for which it was not intended. The following passage was of course suggested by the war in Heaven: it is hard to believe it is a serious description of an earthly conflict:

> Now from each Van
> The brazen Instruments of Death discharge
> Horrific Flames, and turbid streaming Clouds
> Of Smoak sulphureous; intermix't with these
> Large globous Irons fly.

In the same style the Danube is called "th' outragious Fluent."

To James Thomson (1700–1748) Milton's style was less curious than natural: it was a liberating influence which enabled him to discover himself. This is the truth behind Johnson's apparently paradoxical statement that "his numbers, his pauses, his diction are of his own growth, without transcription, without imitation." For the moment we are concerned not with *Liberty*, which has less original character than Thomson's other work, or with *The Castle of Indolence*, which will be discussed among the Spenserian poems in the next chapter, but with *The Seasons* only. This poem is a work of truly original feeling and perception. Thomson's imaginings are extensive, if sometimes vague, and Miltonic blank verse allowed him freedom and movement not to be found elsewhere. It was Milton's "ample spaces" that attracted him. We will first consider Thomson's indebtedness to other poets and then his originality.

Though Milton is the principal source of Thomson's diction, it is

[3]*Poems of John Philips*, ed. M. G. Lloyd Thomas (Oxford, 1927).

clear that he had studied and absorbed much of the work of Spenser, Dryden, and Pope. In view of his known admiration for *The Faerie Queene* we may conjecture that he borrowed for *The Seasons* such words as *attuned* (*Sum.*, 1385),[4] *dispreading* (*Sum.*, 209), and *empurpled* (*Aut.*, 674) from the fountain-head; and *attempered* (*Aut.*, 28), though not one of Spenser's inventions, was perhaps drawn from the same source. The type of periphrasis which grew in favour all through the seventeenth century and was approved by Dryden is frequent, and it is nowhere more appropriate than in a poem which so frequently extols birds, beasts, and fish as "Tokens of the Creator's Art."[5] Thomson felt strongly the poetic aspect of Deism. Thus he brings to our contemplation "the plumy people" (*Sp.*, 165), "the finny race" (*Sp.*, 395), "the busy nations" (bees; *Sp.*, 510), "the tuneful nations" (birds; *Sp.*, 594)—phrases indicative of the various "types." In conception, such expressions are similar to many more extended descriptions like the well-known passage in *Winter* (256–7) beginning:

> The foodless wilds
> Pour forth their brown inhabitants.

In the Dryden-Pope manner, Thomson uses many epithets terminating in -y, e.g. *spiry, vapoury, dimply, piny*, and he has in strong measure the taste of his time for the -*id* ending: *humid, horrid, turbid, liquid, torpid, gelid, sordid, placid, torrid*, and *lucid* and others of the class being in evidence everywhere. There are too, as in Pope's *Homer*, many epithets ending in -*ful*: in *Summer* alone, for instance, we find *refreshful, blushful, foodful, forceful, direful, vengeful*, and *formful*. Of the Miltonic features which have rather a grammatical than a critical interest may be noted the practice of using intransitive verbs transitively, e.g., "listening every noise" (*Sum.*, 497) and "gazing the inverted landscape" (*Sum.*, 1247). In addition to a large Latin element in the vocabulary is the occasional reduplication such as is found in Milton's line (*P.L.*, VI.665):

> *Hurl'd* to and fro with *jaculation* dire;

for instance, Thomson writes (*Sp.*, 314):

> Wide-dashed the *waves* in *undulation* vast.

The most interesting traces of Milton's diction in *The Seasons* are those which have been suggested by descriptive passages. Thomson had evidently read Milton's early poems to much purpose. For instance, the participle *shagged*, "Shagged o'er with wavy rocks" (*Win.*, 918),

---

[4]Quotations from *Poetical Works of James Thomson*, ed. J. Logie Robertson (Oxford, 1908).
[5]See p. 115.

is evidently borrowed from *Comus*: "*shag'd* with horrid shades" (429);
"Sighs the sad genius of the coming storm" (*Win.*, 67) is perhaps an
echo of the *Nativity Ode*: "The parting Genius is with sighing sent";
the line on the moon in *Autumn* (1096), "Now through the passing
cloud she seems to stoop," recalls *Il Penseroso*:

> And oft, as if her head she bow'd,
> Stooping through a fleecy cloud;

"freakt with many a mingled hue" (*Win.*, 813) suggests *Lycidas* (144):
"the Pansie freakt with jeat"; "villages embosomed soft in trees" (*Sp.*,
954) reminds one of *L'Allegro*'s "Bosom'd high in tufted Trees," and
the list could be much extended. That Thomson should have drawn
largely on *Paradise Lost* is entirely natural, for the whole of *The Seasons* is an expanded "Hymn of Creation":

> See where the winding vale its lavish stores,
> Irriguous, spreads

is suggested by

> the flourie lap
> Of som irriguous Valley spread her store;[6]

Thomson's

> blackening woods,
> High-raised in solemn theatre around

by Milton's

> woodie Theatre
> Of stateliest view;[7]

Thomson's woods,

> Shade deepening over shade, the country round
> Imbrown,

by Milton's lines:

> where the unpierc't shade
> Imbround the noontide Bowrs.[8]

The transitive sense of the verb *roll* applied to the action of a river flowing onward "with a sweeping motion" (*O.E.D.*) dates from Milton's
lines (*P.L.*, II.583–4):

> *Lethe* the River of Oblivion roules
> Her watrie Labyrinth,

and this sense is repeated by Thomson in a similar passage (*Sum.*, 718):

> And where the Ganges rolls his sacred wave.

[6]*Sp.*, 494–5; *P.L.*, IV.254–5.
[7]*Sum.*, 719–20; *P.L.*, IV.141–2.
[8]*Aut.*, 951–2; *P.L.*, IV.245–6.

The Miltonic origin of numerous other phrases, such as "grotesque and wild" and "uncreated light," will be easily recognized.

As has been said, Thomson's feelings and perceptions were very much his own. The diction of Milton did not suppress but stimulated his originality. Thomson's own diction, in spite of its indebtedness, is vital and expressive: it was also a fruitful source of suggestion to later poets. His tastes in natural description are graphically expressed in a few sentences of praise which he wrote on some lines in Mallet's *Excursion* beginning with an image of Night:

> Onward she comes with silent steps and slow,
> In her BROWN mantle wrapt:

"This equals any image our Milton gave us of the evening—You paint Ruin with a masterly hand—This is a fine, extensive, lively, just simile —where learned you this ancient simplicity of expression!—This is a very full, natural, dismal picture—This is Poetry–this is arousing fancy-enthusiasm–rapturous terror." To point the contrast with Pope, let it be noticed how superior is Thomson's use of the word *whiten*.[9] It occurs, for instance, in a picture of moonlight extending over a night sky (*Aut.*, 1101–2):

> The whole air whitens with a boundless tide
> Of silver radiance,

and again as one of the changing colours in a cataract (*Sum.*, 594–8):

> At first, an azure sheet, it rushes broad;
> Then, whitening by degrees as prone it falls,
> And from the loud-resounding rocks below
> Dashed in a cloud of foam, it sends aloft
> A hoary mist and forms a ceaseless shower.

His love of "extensive" effects is evident in the many phrases suggesting multitude, such as "innumerous songsters" (*Sp.*, 608), "unnumbered wings" (*Sp.*, 654), and still more in his phrases and pictures of great distance, like "the illimitable void" (*Sum.*, 34) or (*Sum.*, 691–2)

> interminable meads
> And vast savannas.

It is also apparent in some of his compound epithets, e.g. "the many-twinkling leaves of aspen tall" (*Sp.*, 158–9); "his many-bleating flock" (*Sp.*, 835). Thomson in fact appears to have introduced into English poetry this quasi-adverbial use of "many" in the sense of "in many ways, many times" as the first element of compound epithets. The practice has been blamed by the severely grammatical critics, but it has been

[9]See p. 114.

followed by various poets including Byron, Shelley, and Tennyson, often with fine effect. The compound epithets, which are one of the chief beauties of Thomson's diction, have been delightfully discussed in an article by Dr. J. W. Mackail.[10] It is enough to quote a few examples: "ships, dim-discovered" (*Sum.*, 946), "prone-descending rain" (*Sum.*, 1146), "close-embowering woods" (*Aut.*, 208), "the plume-dark air" (*Aut.*, 869). A new and brilliant turn is given to a conventional epic epithet in the phrase "Abyssinia's cloud-compelling cliffs" (*Aut.*, 801). Thomson's love for the "dismal" appears in the frequency of phrases like "brown night" and "gloomy woods," and in sombre and even tragic descriptions like that of the autumnal flood (*Aut.*, 337–8):

> Red from the hills, innumerable streams
> Tumultuous roar.

His imagination of the foliage in the Asian Taurus paints it as a "huge incumbrance of horrific woods" (*Aut.*, 782). The emotional effect intended by these dim shapes and sombre hues of forested hills is explicitly stated in *The Castle of Indolence* where "blackening pines . . . Sent forth a sleepy horror through the blood."

Thomson's diction gave many suggestions to writers of his own age, such as Gray and Collins, and to those of the next, such as Wordsworth and De Quincey. His style, compared with that of the later masters, has something of the heaviness which a Constable landscape appears to wear by the side of a Turner. A lover of strong effects, Thomson is most impressive in the extreme seasons, Summer and Winter. Wordsworth spiritualized Nature, and the poets who followed him at least suffused their descriptions with their own emotions. Thomson is content to give the poetry of material nature, for his Deism is far from being deeply interfused. To enjoy him, one needs only to take a contemplative pleasure in the changes of the seasons, and to assimilate a poetic idiom two centuries old in which much beauty survives.

YOUNG

Though there is far less originality of style in Edward Young (1683–1765) than in Thomson, he succeeded in one important point where Thomson failed. Thomson had applied Miltonic blank verse to a didactic subject in his *Liberty*, which most readers have found a dreary poem, despite its historic interest. Young came to the task with a very different training. He had already succeeded brilliantly as a satirist in his *Universal Passion*. The sudden loss, within a short space, of three

[10]"The Poet of *The Seasons*," *Studies of English Poets* (London, 1926).

near relatives turned his thoughts in a sombre direction: the result of which was *The Complaint, or Night Thoughts* (1742–5). In the course of the poem he compares himself to Homer, Milton, and Pope (I.451–3):

> Dark, tho' not blind, like thee, *Maeonides!*
> Or, *Milton!* thee; ah! could I reach your Strain!
> Or *His*, who made *Maeonides* our *Own*.[11]

There is little of Pope's diction in *Night Thoughts*, though the traces of his manner are visible in the detachment of the end-stopped lines. The general tone of Young is epigrammatic and hortatory: he is a poet of short passages and single lines. Echoes of Milton are heard constantly, but more in some parts than in others. The anti-Lucretian Seventh "Night"—the best book in the poem—urges the proofs of immortality in an unadorned style which is scarcely Miltonic at all. The Ninth "Night," however, is imaginative and rhapsodical: it contains a vision of the Last Judgment, with "a moral survey of the nocturnal heavens," and abounds in phrases from *Paradise Lost*. *Night Thoughts* has been one of the most read and most translated of English poems, and the style of so famous a work naturally deserves some attention.

The *general* Miltonic features of Young's diction are the new or rare derivatives from Latin such as *terraqueous*[12] (I.286), *solute* ("a brow solute," II.585), *antemundane*[13] (V.93), *tenebrious*[14] (IX.963), and the use of adjectives as nouns, for instance: "the opaque of nature," "the sublime of Life," "their sweet serene," "the grand of nature," "the fathomless of thought." The *particular* echoes do not, like those in *The Seasons*, come principally from the descriptive parts of *Paradise Lost*, but indifferently from the whole poem. Many parallels occur, such as the following—*Paradise Lost* being the first in each pair:

> the Sons
> Of *Belial*, flown with insolence and wine.
> Ere-while high-flusht, with Insolence and Wine.[15]

> Dark with excessive bright thy skirts appear.
> The great *First-Last!* pavilion'd high he sits
> In Darkness, from excessive Splendor born.[16]

The reminiscences appear most closely in the early part of "Night" IX, which for a time is little more than a tissue of Milton's phrases. As

---

[11]*The Complaint: or, Night-Thoughts on Life, Death, and Immortality* (London, 1765).
[12]In Phillips's Dictionary, 1658.   [13]In Bailey's Dictionary, 1731.
[14]"Apparently altered from tenebrous" (*O.E.D.*).
[15]*P.L.*, I.501–2; *N.T.*, II.409.   [16]*P.L.*, III.380; *N.T.*, IV.412–13.

mentioned, this is the eschatological part of Young's poem. Here are two of the parallels occurring within a short space—the lines from Milton again precede:

> Patron or Intercessor none appeerd.
>
> No Patron! Intercessor none.[17]

> his face
> Deep scars of Thunder had intrencht.

> the Foe of God and Man
> . . . his brazen Front, with Thunder scarr'd.[18]

And so it continues. But all these echoes do not suffice to give Young anything of Milton's sustained grandeur of language. The effect is at once strained, irregular, and spasmodic. Young is often quite informal: it is curious to find amid so much intended sublimity lines such as (I.89–90):

> An Angel's Arm can't snatch me from the Grave;
> Legions of Angels can't confine me here.

The frequency of iterative verbs, such as *regive, re-inthrone, re-thunder, re-embrace, re-resolve,* is one of several features not tending to raise the style. The sudden changes in tone from the "sublime" to the collo-quial give it something of the effect of hysteria.

Night Thoughts, however, is an interesting poem from our point of view. Taken with the work of Philips and Thomson, it illustrates how variously Milton could affect his followers in the eighteenth century. In Young there is nothing of Philips's vein of parody, or of Thomson's absorption in description. Young assimilated from Milton what he wanted in his own way. He carried his Miltonic learning lightly, and his style loses none of its individuality in showing so many traces of its principal source.

[17]*P.L.,* III.219; *N.T.,* IX.266.
[18]*P.L.,* I.601–2; *N.T.,* IX.270–2.

IF the word "Spenserian" be allowed to bear the wide connotation which we have hitherto given it in this study, it will be found to cover many of the principal changes in poetic style and diction from the middle of the eighteenth century to the appearance of *Lyrical Ballads*. The new archaism in poetry was of course inspired by other writings besides those of Spenser: by ballads, by the early work of Milton, by Percy's *Reliques*, and by the poetry of Chaucer. But in view of Spenser's peculiar place in English poetry, of the strongly traditional character of his work, of the association of his diction with the past, as well as of the direct imitation of him by several poets of the period, it seems natural to give his name the representative significance which is here suggested. The new Spenserianism was a movement towards that greater freedom of word-usage which was included among the features of the Spenserian style enumerated at the beginning of this work.

The prevalence of "poetic diction" was of course one of the main features of eighteenth-century verse. But the emphasis in this chapter, as throughout the book, is on the diction of poetry rather than on "poetic diction." That once abused body of language has recently had its able defenders, and it is well that the use of "gradus" phrases should not be indiscriminately condemned by a mechanical criticism. So far the change of attitude is a gain. But to go to the other extreme and defend much second-rate writing on historical grounds as one form or another of the idiom of the age is a serious error. Many of the old charges against the use of the "gradus" language are true and cannot be reversed. The task of criticism in this sphere is to distinguish between the fresh and the stale, and it is a task which any reader with a healthy taste in language and an alert sense of poetic rhythm can often perform. Even if we do not denounce "poetic diction" as unnatural in itself, we must in fairness admit that mechanical repetition often robs it of all force and freshness. It is to this aspect of "poetic diction" that the remarks to be made later in this chapter will be chiefly directed.

There is, however, an important corollary to the change of attitude about the eighteenth century which must be mentioned first. The older critics of "poetic diction" had a professional interest in bad verse, which held for them the attraction of a disease for the pathologist. For the reader whose taste inclines to the analysis of "falseness" in diction—triteness, insincerity, pomposity, and the like—much amusement is still to be found in the double columns of Chalmers's *English Poets*. He may, for instance, find diversion in a poem like *The Contemplatist* by John Cunningham, called by Chalmers "the worst of his compositions." Or he might turn to Glover's *Leonidas,* or for that matter to the weaker passages of Thomson, Shenstone, or Joseph Warton. But for criticism, the interest of such work has been well-nigh exhausted: it is more profitable to consider the good work of the period and its relation to the entire history of English poetry. Fortunately this has now for some time been the object of many good critics, and one may warmly agree with Dr. Nichol Smith in regarding the eighteenth century not so much as "a period of decadence" or "a period of preparation" but as "a period of definite achievement." This view is expressed in the Preface to *The Oxford Book of Eighteenth Century Verse,* the best anthology of its kind, and the source of many quotations in the present chapter. We shall be dealing with a bygone age, but one with some enduring traditions and much sound sensibility.

I

The new taste which became so evident about the middle of the century was marked by a revival of old metres no less than of old diction. *The Schoolmistress* of Shenstone was published in 1742, Thomson's *Castle of Indolence* in 1748, Thomas Warton's *Observations on the Faerie Queene of Spenser* in 1754. In the same period were composed most of the odes of Gray. The whole movement was distasteful to Johnson, who (*In Ridicule of Thomas Warton's Poems*) deplored both the language and the measures which these poets and their associates were reviving:

> Phrase that Time has flung away,
> Uncouth Words in Disarray:
> Trickt with Antique Ruff and Bonnet,
> Ode, and Elegy, and Sonnet.

But to the critic of today as to Cowper in 1781 it was clear that a reaction against the style of Pope was bound to occur if the art of poetry was to survive, for nothing is so fatal as the prevalence of a style in verse in which mechanical perfection is attainable. Pope had taught his followers to avoid the open vowels, the ten low words, the needless Alexandrine, and all the other mechanical imperfections of the couplet. At no other time do so many English poets seem to count their syllables, or to be so unwilling to vary their rhythms by substitution of alternative metrical feet. This regularity is of course most observable in the heroic couplet, but it extends equally to octosyllabics and the commoner stanzas of iambic lines, and it also affects the writing of blank verse. The cult of metrical regularity naturally influences diction, for a polished smoothness within the limits of the single line is unattainable without an abundant supply of "poetic" synonyms and expletive epithets. No one united elegance of versification and significance of diction with the brilliance achieved by Pope in his best passages. Others, including Pope himself in his weaker moments, sacrificed significance to polish, falling back upon the stock epithets and synonyms which smoothed the way. The words in greatest request were the disyllabic epithets, and a couple of these with a familiar rhyme-word at the end might virtually produce a complete line. Hence on words such as *conscious, various, genial, secret,* a large part of the "mechanic art" of verse depended. A line like

> And secret transport warmed the conscious swain

is an epitome of the process. The number of disyllabic epithets was increased by participles in indefinite numbers, though certain of them are repeated conspicuously, such as *warbling, purling, smiling, breathing, blooming.* Other groups are classes we have already noticed, consisting of words like *mazy, sedgy, lawny, thymy, plumy, beamy, bloomy,*[1] and the group *tepid, humid, florid, gelid, torrid,* and so forth. In addition there are *tuneful* and *artful* (later replaced by *artless*) and many others. *Swain* is not only a conventional synonym, it is also a convenient rhyme, and with it may be classed other words such as *groves, crowned,* and *dome* ("dwelling") which fit neatly into a neo-classical context. The last word is one of the most typical, and is used throughout the century. Thus we find "faery domes" (Tickell), "dome and farm" (Dyer), "the spacious dome" (Shenstone), "the vaulted dome" (T. Warton), "the princely dome" (Akenside), "the lordly dome" (Cunningham). Finally, there are the generalized words useful for the wide survey of Nature, in which there was often an element of half religious, half deistic Creation-worship. Examples of this class are *day* (for "light"), *gales* (for "breezes"), *meads* (for "fields"), *clime* (for "region"); also *rage* (for "passion"), *tube* (for "telescope," "gun," etc.). It will be noticed that all of these monosyllabic synonyms except the last are convenient rhyme-words.

---

[1] In the next century, diction of this kind is found in its decadence, for example in the slang use of *blooming,* and in passages like the following speech of Dick Swiveller: "I shall wear the emblem of woman's perfidy, in remembrance of her with whom I shall never thread again the windings of the mazy; whom I shall never more pledge in the rosy; who during the short remainder of my existence, will murder the balmy." *Old Curiosity Shop,* chap. lvi.

There is, however, a large element of repeated diction which has no obvious connection with the mechanics of verse. Many words and phrases were cherished purely for their literary associations, whether vague or definite. No English poet was more widely admired or esteemed more worthy of imitation than Milton, and Miltonic diction is the richest single source for literary phrases of this kind. We have already noticed the prevalence of the periphrasis-type "finny droves" in the early work of Pope. The phrase itself occurs in Spenser: it was Milton who gave such expressions their literary vogue, and their congeniality with Deism which recommended them to the eighteenth-century outlook.[2] The cult of such expressions continued in the generation after Pope. As fish are distinguished in the Creator's scheme by fins, so birds are distinguished by feathers: hence we find "feather'd choirs" (Shenstone), "feather'd songsters" (Mallet), "feath'ry tribes" (Collins). And the decadence of the fashion is marked by its jocose appearance, in the next century, in the prose of Thackeray: "She could climb a tree to rob the nests of the feathered songsters of their speckled spoils."[3] The diffusion of Miltonic expressions was extremely wide, though their origin was not always remembered. It is possible that the "amorous Descant" of Gray's *Sonnet on the Death of Richard West* is, as Raleigh thinks,[4] borrowed direct from *Paradise Lost*, yet we also find the phrase echoed, though more vaguely, in Shenstone's line (*Elegy* VI):

> Hear linnets argue, larks descant of love.

So, too, we may ask whether the generalized use in verse of words like *error* and *tube* is Miltonic or vaguely literary: probably by about 1750, the distinction is merely academic. What is more to the purpose is the fact that the poets of the mid-century were far more like each other than like the author of *Paradise Lost*. In the lines written by John Dyer (*The Fleece*, IV)[5]:

> Wide, o'er
> The globe terraqueous, let Britannia pour
> The fruits of plenty from her copious horn,

and those written by Robert Blair (*The Grave*, 98-9):

> Where the pure limpid Stream has slid along
> In grateful Errors thro' the Under-wood,

[2]Cf. p. 115.
[3]*Vanity Fair*, chap. x.
[4]*Milton* (1900), chap. vi.
[5]*Oxford Book of Eighteenth Century Verse*, no. 186. Further citation of numbers in the text will refer to this collection.

we see a pseudo-Miltonic diction of the same type, though "terraqueous" is not in fact one of Milton's words, while "error" is. We are reminded that, strictly speaking, style is a unit, and that the elements, rhythm and diction, are inseparable. Hence the true effect of Milton's diction is not reproduced until a poet recaptures something of the effect of his living style. This can only be done by an energy of inspiration which sustains itself continuously through line after line, making the unit of composition the entire verse-paragraph. Wordsworth, who at certain times emulated Milton, occasionally possessed this sustained energy, and in some of his grander blank-verse passages, such as *Yew Trees* and the lines on the Simplon Pass from *The Prelude*, there is a closer approach to the true effect and spirit of Milton's diction than in the work of any "Miltonic" poet who simply borrowed or adapted select phrases from his model.

II

The chief means of deliverance from the "mechanical" writing of verse lay in a free admiration for the more "artless" kinds of poetry and the cult of a new sensibility, later to be called "Romantic." These movements are represented by some of the greater poets of the century, whose work will later be considered separately. But it is necessary first to give some brief consideration to the movements in themselves, for the study of style suggests that they were led as much by minor and anonymous writers as by any one or two poets of outstanding originality.

Although the antiquarian movement in diction is usually dated at about the middle of the century, its origins are considerably earlier. The Spenserianism of Prior has already been briefly noticed. Not less significant is the early cult of ballad diction. Addison's praise of the ballads in the *Spectator* was notable as a criticism on general lines, but it is surprising to find a close reproduction of stylistic details in a work so early as David Mallet's ballad *William and Margaret* (1724). Among the clearest marks of ballad diction are epithets like *grass-green, clay-cold, blood-red*, and of these, the first two do in fact appear in *William and Margaret* together with other marks of the ballad style. One is led to conjecture that this "correct" specimen of the ballad is perhaps not the result of any revival so much as a literary handling of a surviving popular tradition. If popular ballad-writing persisted more widely than is generally believed, one must somewhat discount the importance attached to the publication of Percy's *Reliques* in 1765.

The view which associates the beginnings of the Romantic revival with the early poems of Milton is certainly sound. The popularity of *Il Penseroso* is especially significant: it coincides with that taste for pensiveness, contemplation, solitude, and melancholy which distinguishes the middle of the century from its opening decades. And yet the beginnings of a new Romanticism nourished on the spirit and imagery of Milton's earlier poems are clearly apparent before 1720. The new sensibility is plainly announced in the opening three lines of Pope's *Eloïsa to Abelard* (1717):

> In these deep solitudes and awful cells,
> Where heav'nly-pensive Contemplation dwells,
> And ever-musing Melancholy reigns . . .;

and that Pope had partly drawn his inspiration from the early poems of Milton—in particular from *Comus*—is certain. Two quotations will be enough to establish this point. A characteristic phrase from the Masque, "low-thoughted care," reappears in Pope's line (298):

> Divine oblivion of low-thoughted care!

and Milton's line (429):

> By grots, and caverns shag'd with horrid shades

is repeated with variations in Pope's (20):

> Ye grots and caverns shagg'd with horrid thorn!

But it must be admitted that Pope anticipates. Poetry in the reign of Queen Anne and the earlier years of George I does not show that decided preference of the *adagio* to the *allegro* mood—of the browner shades to the brighter hues—which is so apparent in the middle of the century. It is then that the new sensibility begins to prevail in new tones of diction. Thomson in his later years, Gray, Shenstone, the Wartons, Young, and Blair, all alike are susceptible to the charm of pensive (and, at times, funereal) melancholy. Even Collins, more lyrical than the rest, shares the prevailing mood in some of his odes. *Il Penseroso* is a poem in such perfect harmony with this phase of the new sensibility, and its phrases are so pregnant with suggestion, that it is natural to find the diction of the age deeply tinged with dyes of Milton's invention.

A typical word in the new romanticism is *pensive*, and "pensiveness" is a choicer thing than its sprightly counterpart. For Milton, the "pensive nun" is matched by the gay Euphrosyne, but it was not in the Romantic program that cheerfulness should be allowed to break in. At first pensiveness may accompany a wise content, as in the anonymous poem *The Retirement* (1730, no. 124); it is more wistful in

Shenstone's "Pastoral Ballad" *Absence* (1743, no. 213); and it is self-sufficing in Grainger's *Solitude* (1755, no. 262). By degrees it is identified with a gentle, but superior pessimism. Thus, John Langhorne in *The Evening Primrose* (1771, no. 321) asks—sure, no doubt, of an affirmative answer—

> Didst thou, shepherd, never find,
> Pleasure is of pensive kind?

Finally in 1790, Mrs. H. M. Williams renounces Hope as a "sweet flatterer" (*To Hope*, no. 380) and is content to be denied her "dear illusions":

> Visions less fair will soothe my pensive breast,
> That asks not happiness, but longs for rest.

Meantime, Thomas Warton had changed his mind about the new Romantic sensibility and was returning to a more cheerful and strenuous classicism. But his conversion costs him a pang. As he gazes on Sir Joshua Reynolds's "Painted Window" at New College, Oxford, he exhorts that master of the classical style to be lenient to a long cherished taste:

> From bliss long felt unwillingly we part:
> Ah, spare the weakness of a lover's heart!
> Chase not the phantoms of my fairy dream,
> Phantoms that shrink at Reason's painful gleam!

But the "chaste design" and "just proportion" of the window prevail, and the weak prayer is set aside as "a pensive bard's mistaken strain" (1782, no. 314).

Pensive is more than a word: it is the symbol of a mood, an attitude in miniature. But *Il Penseroso* is the source of many other repeated words and phrases which lie somewhere between pure diction and poetic imagery. A complete examination of this subject would be a lengthy work, and a few instances must suffice here. Thus, "the pealing organ" of *Il Penseroso* is repeated in Tickell's lines *On the Death of Mr. Addison* (no. 110):

> The pealing organ, and the pausing choir;

"storied windows" suggests the phrase "storied urn" in Gray's *Elegy*; the "mossy cell" of Milton's "peacefull hermitage" changes into a metaphor in Dyer's Nature-poem *Grongar Hill* (no. 180):

> *Grongar*, in whose Mossie Cells
> Sweetly-musing Quiet dwells;

"religious light" is repeated in Thos. Warton's *Verses on Sir Joshua Reynolds's Painted Window at New College, Oxford* (no. 314):

> Reynolds, 'tis thine, from the broad window's height,
> To add new lustre to religious light.

Again, the lines on the "far-off curfew" "Swinging slow with sullen roar" are turned, with variations, into a passage in an extremely "pensive" sonnet *To Oxford* by Thomas Russell (1789, no. 372):

> thy varying bells, which hourly sound
> In pensive chime, or ring in lively round,
> Or toll in the slow Curfeu's solemn roar.

More than one phase of eighteenth-century verse terminates in Victorian prose, and the last incident we need record in the history of these echoes from *Il Penseroso* is Dickens's choice of a title for a Christmas book, *The Cricket on the Hearth*.

With the "mossy cell' of *Il Penseroso* was associated the "hermitage" of the previous line, and the notion of a hermit's wise and solitary old age was one of the most popular fancies of the eighteenth century. All the details of the picture are to be found in the opening lines of Parnell's poem, *The Hermit*:

> Far in a wild, unknown to public view,
> From youth to age a reverend hermit grew;
> The moss his bed, the cave his humble cell,
> His food the fruits, his drink the crystal well.

No one can say how often the hermit-image was employed: it was not wholly exhausted even in the time of Charles Churchill, who could still write (*The Duellist*, II.247–8):

> Exiled by grief, self-doomed to dwell
> With some poor hermit in a cell. . . .

But Cowper had no longer the heart to use the image, and it is finally dismissed in the opening lines of *The Moralizer Corrected*:

> A hermit (or if 'chance you hold
> That title now too trite and old),
> A man, once young. . . .

A hermit was, as Cowper noted, no more than a "poetic" synonym for a grave elderly man: and a kindred title "pilgrim" was put to a similar use. The "pilgrim" like the "hermit" was a serious man in a contemplative mood. This fact is noted rather more severely by H. W. Garrod, who in a comment on the use of the word by Collins speaks of "the tiresome 'Pilgrim' . . . who is only, in plain English, a man out for a walk."[6]

The "pensive" shades off into the elegiac, and the elegiac into the funereal. It was fitting that the most popular as well as the most consummate poem of the age should have been an "Elegy Written in a Country Church-yard." Gray's work is the epitome and expression of a mood which had long been haunting the more sensitive minds of the century. A select vocabulary in honour of the dead had been for some time in process of formation, and now the *urn* and the *narrow cell*, the *sable weeds* and the *watery grave* (appropriate to a sea-faring race) were the common property of those who wrote in verse. Somewhat rarer phrases, such as *hallow'd mold*, passed from Tickell's elegy *On the Death of Mr. Addison* (1721) to Collins's *Ode* "How sleep the Brave," "written in the beginning of the Year 1746." In Gray's poem (no. 248), the diction of elegy is blended with that which belongs to the solemn meditation among ruins or tombs. To be deeply affected by the spectacle of "nodding towers" was a sign of true sensibility: "for Fancy is the friend of Woe." This mood, says William Mason (*Ode to a Friend*, 1746, no. 307), is the distinction of "pensive" Gray's "lofty Genius" which

> Roves thro' the glimmering, twilight gloom,
> And warbles round each rustic tomb.

There was a tender sadness to be drawn from the sight of damp and decay, and finer spirits might contemplate with Gray the "mould'ring heap" under the yew-tree; or with Mason "Some mouldring abbey's ivy-vested wall" (*The English Garden*, no. 308) or with Thomas Warton "the mould'ring caverns dark and damp" of a similar ruin (*Pleasures of Melancholy*, no. 310). In such meditative descriptions there is, perhaps, no epithet which is more fondly repeated than *moss-grown*. Pope had used it in the lines in which Eloïsa describes the seclusion of her monastery (142):

> These moss-grown domes with spiry turrets crown'd;

Mason contemplates a little stream at evening (*Ode to a Friend*, no. 307),

> Soft tinkling down the moss-grown hill;

the piles of Warton's ruined abbey are "moss-grown" (*Pleasures of Melancholy*, no. 310) and an "antient mossgrowne walle" marks the desolation of Cumnor Hall in Mickle's ballad (no. 329). This epithet

---

[6]*Collins* (Clarendon Press, 1928), p. 78.

of the melancholy mood survives all the changes of a crowded century, and the graves of Bridges's *Elegy among the Tombs* are "mossgrown" just as they would have been in the days of William Mason or Thomas Warton. Behind this pensive melancholy are gloomier figures and forms, each with its associated verb or epithet. In the *Mynstrelles Songe* (no. 325) of Chatterton's *Ælla* is a phrase, "the ravenne flappes hys wynge," which Mr. E. H. W. Meyerstein has traced back to "The raven flap'd his wing" of Tickell's *Colin and Lucy* (no. 113); one remembers too the second half of a stanza in Mickle's ballad:

> And thrice the raven flapp'd its wyng
> Arounde the tow'rs of Cumnor Hall,

lines which captivated the youthful Kipling.[7] Darker still is the vision of Night which haunted the imagination of the age and is perhaps the origin of the mysterious Queen in *The Magic Flute*. A similarity of wording marks the persistence of this image through several generations of poets. Thus, Young in 1742 draws the outline (*N.T.*, I.18):

> *Night*, sable Goddess! from her *Ebon* Throne. . . .

In 1780, Cowper repeats the words as something familiar (*Progress of Error*, l. 177):

> night, down-stooping from her ebon throne,

while Coleridge in 1796 in his *Songs of the Pixies*[8] apostrophizes Night as

> Sorceress of the ebon throne!

The spirit of the phrase varies: at one moment, we seem to be tracking down the mythology of the Age of Reason, the next, to be dealing with the merest affair of words.

III

The influence of Shakespeare on the diction of the age is less marked than that of Milton or Spenser. In them there was a well-defined idiosyncrasy to be imitated: in Shakespeare there was an incessant power of living description, but no single descriptive manner. Moreover, the

---

[7] Meyerstein, *A Life of Thomas Chatterton* (London, 1930), p. 57. Kipling: "But how or where I first heard the lines that cast the shadow is beyond me"; *Something of Myself* (1937), p. 9.

[8] *Poems on Various Subjects*. Cf. also Thos. Warton, *The Pleasures of Melancholy*:

> Hail, sacred Night! thou too shalt share my song!
> Sister of ebon-sceptr'd Hecat, hail!

Cf. also *Comus*, 134–5.

theories of the critics did not particularly recommend his style: it was "natural" but (in the bad sense) "artless." A phrase here and there, especially harmonious with the style of the time, is repeated, such as the "terrestrial ball" of *Richard II* which suits exactly the manner of Addison's ode or hymn, "The Spacious Firmament on high" (no. 25). Occasionally a picturesque phrase is remembered, like the "nodding violet" of *A Midsummer Night's Dream* which reappears, amid much verbal tinsel, in some lines of Joseph Warton's *To Evening*:

> When Phoebus sinks beneath the gilded hills,
> You lightly o'er the misty meadows walk.
> The drooping daisies bathe in dulcet dews,
> And nurse the nodding violet's slender stalk.

Robert Blair in *The Grave* very naturally borrows the phrase "Witching Time of Night" (no. 206) from *Hamlet*; Collins in his *Ode on the Popular Superstitions of the Highlands of Scotland* alludes expressly to Shakespeare's "wayward sisters"[9]; while Mrs. Greville, in a poem in *The Annual Register*, 1762 (no. 276), in which she begs Oberon for the gift of the nymph, Indifference, invokes "the glow-worm's glimmering light" in Shakespeare's own words. Such borrowings were in fact *quotations*, natural at a time when Shakespeare's lines were more popularly remembered than they have perhaps been in any other age.

The attitude of Gray to the diction of Shakespeare is a different matter. Gray admired it as a critic, and imitated from it consciously as a poet. "In truth," he wrote, "Shakespeare's language is one of his principal beauties. . . . Every word in him is a picture."[10] Being much of a precisian in his practice as a metrist—even though he neglected the couplet and wrote "Ode, and Elegy, and Sonnet"—he had none of the Elizabethan freedom which enabled some later poets not only to borrow largely from Shakespeare's language but to handle words with something of Shakespeare's creativeness, and his total borrowings form but a scanty group. But for the time they are significant. Gray's own term for borrowed phrases, often acknowledged in a footnote, is "imitations." Thus, in *Agrippina* (I.i), an unfinished tragedy, there is an "imitation" of Shakespeare's "silken dalliance in the wardrobe lies" (*Henry V*, II.chorus):

> Is he not
> The silken son of dalliance?

---

[9]"Weyward Sisters" of F. 1.
[10]Letter to Richard West, April, 1742. *Works of Thomas Gray*, ed. W. Mason, 2 vols. (London, 1807), I, 304.

Shakespeare's verb in "over-canopied with luscious woodbine" (*M.N.D.*, II.i.251) supplies the verb used in Gray's description of a beech which "o'er-canopies the glade" (*Ode on the Spring*); the line (*King John*, V.i.72)

> Mocking the air with colours idly spread

is half repeated in *The Bard* (no. 250):

> They mock the air with idle state;

the words of Brutus to Portia (*J.C.*, II.i.289–90):

> As dear to me as are the ruddy drops
> That visit my sad heart

are the source of another line from *The Bard*:

> Dear, as the ruddy drops that warm my heart;[11]

and the verb from the line (*J.C.*, II.ii.22),

> The noise of battle hurtled in the air

is imitated in *The Fatal Sisters*, where "iron-sleet"

> Hurtles in the darken'd air.

IV

The four principal Spenserian poems of the eighteenth century were: *The Schoolmistress* (Shenstone), 1742; *The Castle of Indolence* (Thomson), 1748; *The Minstrel* (Beattie), 1771; *The Cotter's Saturday Night* (Burns), 1786. Of these, *The Schoolmistress* is a burlesque, and the antiquated language is an amusing caricature of Spenser's style. *The Cotter's Saturday Night* is a blending of the Scots dialect with two strains of English—a homely, unaffected strain and a highly literary and artificial one, the element of dialect producing an effect somewhat like that of the archaic words in Spenser's style. *The Castle of Indolence* and *The Minstrel* are serious attempts to write contemporary poetry in the idiom of the past, the former—at least, in the first of its two cantos —being a finely executed work, the product of long and deliberate care. It is in Canto I which describes the charms of the wizard Indolence and his willing but deluded victims that the best poetry is found; though justice demanded that in Canto II, the Castle should be overthrown by the Knight of Arms and Industry. In the dreamy, languorous pictures of Canto I, with their seasoning of gentle wit and mild morality, Thomson's best stanzas have a melody not far below the best Spenserian

[11]See p. 36.

level, for they are composed as a single metrical unit, due regard being given to the effect of the final Alexandrine. The diction is not wholly free from the expletive epithets incident to a line-by-line structure, yet it is sifted with a watchfulness both rare and difficult at that time. An apology was offered by Thomson in his "Advertisement" for his simple and archaic expressions: "This Poem," he wrote, "being writ in the manner of Spenser, the obsolete words, and a simplicity of diction in some of the lines which borders on the ludicrous, were necessary to make the imitation more perfect." So sensitive was Thomson's age to the dignity required by verse that the modern reader has some difficulty in detecting these passages of ludicrous simplicity. As for the archaic words—*eftsoons, glaive, louting, muchel, noyance, sicker, yblent, yode* —they are frequent enough to colour the diction. Their strangeness was, of course, a welcome feature, and they are explained in a glossary added to the second edition.

Of Beattie's poem, *The Minstrel*, it will suffice to say that it contains, along with some Spenserian words which were now growing familiar, various "imitations" from Shakespeare and other writers, acknowledged in the fashion of Gray. The poem was, in fact, submitted to Gray's criticism. It is a good illustration of the manner in which the language of poetry was being enriched by words from the past chosen by artistic instinct and sound learning.

In its broader sense, the term "Spenserian revival" includes the novelties of diction found in Collins's *Ode on the Popular Superstitions of the Highlands of Scotland* "written about 1749" (no. 240). Though not so carefully "sifted" in style as *The Castle of Indolence*, the ode makes a similar attempt to launch a flight of imagination on the wings of rare words. Indeed, Spenser is himself mentioned as one who would have rejoiced to hear the "strange lays" of the North "taught by the father to his list'ning son." The novel feature is the number of Northern words, little known in Southern English. *Moss* ("a boggy heath"), *shiel, strath*, and *solan* were then almost unheard of outside their native limits. *Glen* was slightly more familiar as a word used in the pastoral verse of Spenser[12] and Philips, though even as late as 1773, Dr. Johnson thought it needed an explanatory note, when writing to Mrs. Thrale (Sept. 21): "about noon, we came to a small glen, so they call a valley." Collins's "to-fall of the day" is perhaps one of the earliest uses in verse of the expression, though "toofall" occurs in *The Braes of Yarrow* by Wm. Hamilton of Bangour (1724, no. 122). *Kelpie* (spelt by Collins "Kaelpie") is the first example quoted by the *Oxford Dictionary*.

---

[12]The "Glosse" to *The Shepheardes Calender* explains "glen" as "a country hamlet or borough."

V

The new sensibility and the reaction against the "mechanical" regularity of Pope leave certain traces in the style and diction of Goldsmith (1730–1774), Churchill (1731–1764), and Cowper (1731–1800). Churchill was an avowed adherent of Dryden as against Pope, and his truculent manner leaves no doubt as to his preference. Goldsmith and Cowper, being men of far finer nature, and on the whole conservative in their literary tastes, do not declare themselves so openly, and the significant features of their diction are not on the surface. The little that need be said about them here, however, may be suggestive.

Goldsmith's occasional remarks on poetic language sometimes anticipate the sensitive criticism of De Quincey and Coleridge. But the prevailing features of his own style, especially in the didactic poems, are steadily conservative: in spite of his volatile nature he was content to accept a large measure of the Johnsonian reserve. In many passages, such as the couplet on Holland (*The Traveller*, 293–4):

> The slow canal, the yellow-blossom'd vale,
> The willow-tufted bank, the gliding sail,

he contrives to be original and picturesque without breaking bounds. Many of the mechanical features of the couplet-diction, already discussed, are constantly repeated in his work. But he is also on the alert for fresh felicities. His vividly used verb—though the metaphor was not entirely new—in the couplet (*Traveller*, 185–6):

> Cheerful at morn, he wakes from short repose,
> *Breasts* the keen air, and carols as he goes

supplied Johnson with a quotation (under "Breast") for the second edition of his *Dictionary*. But perhaps the most striking thing in Goldsmith's diction is the implied heresy—from the neo-classical standpoint—in his use of the word "art":

> To me more dear, congenial to my heart,
> One native charm, than all the gloss of art,

he exclaims in *The Deserted Village* (253–4), repeating the word with the same disparaging implication thrice within the next sixty lines. Nothing is more significant of the new sensibility than the change in the associations of *art, artful,* and *artless.*

The historical interest of Charles Churchill's poetry gives it a claim to somewhat fuller treatment than its literary merit would seem to warrant. He was a poet in a hurry, and he made a virtue of his roughness: this is a basic fact of his importance, for it made him a spokesman of the reaction against Pope. He is in conscious revolt against the finished style: "E'en excellence unvaried tedious grows," he declares (*The Apology*, 369),[13] and he throws over the whole idea of art, adapting the words of Edmund in *King Lear* to his own case (*Prophecy of Famine*, 93–4):

> Thou, Nature, art *my* goddess—to thy law
> Myself I dedicate.

His model was Dryden, the "dearest name to all the tuneful nine" (*The Apology*, 377), but—according to his own testimony (*Gotham*, II. 171–8)—he composed with a headlong speed, compared with which Dryden's impetuosity was caution:

> Nothing of Books, and little known of men,
> When the mad fit comes on, I seize the pen,
> Rough as they run, the rapid thoughts set down,
> Rough as they run, discharge them on the Town.
> Hence rude, unfinish'd brats, before their time,
> Are born into this idle world of rime,
> And the poor *slattern* Muse is brought to bed
> With all her imperfections on her head.

Churchill's subjects, such as the contemporary stage viewed in a satirical light, or the candidature of the Earl of Sandwich for the Lord High Stewardship of Cambridge, were ill chosen for the survival of his work: its interest lies largely in his style, and his style is chiefly remarkable as a dissolvent force. To his stricter readers, his impetuous rhymes and long parentheses must have seemed grossly inelegant, and although he claims Dryden as his model, his couplets are more reminiscent of the careless fluency of Byron. He creates no new style in diction, but he is a keen and powerful critic of stale devices. His attack on the readers who accepted the outworn phrases of descriptive verse also hits the poets who offered them (*Gotham*, II.41–9):

> Let *liquid* Gold emblaze the Sun at noon,
> With *borrow'd* beams let silver *pale* the moon,
> Let surges *hoarse* lash the resounding shore,
> Let streams *Mæander*, and let torrents *roar*;
> Let them breed up the *melancholy* breeze,
> To *sigh with sighing, sob with sobbing trees*,
> Let Vales *embroid'ry* wear, let Flowers be *ting'd*
> With various *tints*; let Clouds be *lac'd* or fring'd,
> They have their wish.

Churchill does not sift his diction. He knew Shakespeare, and Shakespearian phrases crowd into his verse. But his realism gives him some

---

[13]Quotations are from *Poems by C. Churchill* (3rd ed., London, 1766).

originality, and like Crabbe after him, he likes to contrast the flowery diction of convention with harsh reality. Precisely in the manner of Crabbe[14] are his lines on the ruggedness of Scotland (*Prophecy of Famine*, 283–4):

> No streams as amber smooth, as amber clear,
> Were seen to glide, or heard to warble here.

This is an oblique satire on the *clichés* of descriptive verse. So too is his use of "amorous descant," a Miltonic phrase worn down to a meaningless counter by frequent repetition.[15] Churchill feels it as such, and makes it sound mockingly in his ludicrous picture of a Scottish peasant and his lass (*Prophecy of Famine*, 21–2):

> The youth, turn'd swain, and skill'd in rustic lays,
> Fast by her side his am'rous descant plays.

Johnson's hostility to Churchill is well known, but Cowper admired him. The two poets, so dissimilar in many ways, agreed in some of their dislikes, and Cowper evidently learned from Churchill's lines (*Prophecy of Famine*, 35–6),

> Then we discard the workings of the heart,
> And nature's banish'd by *mechanic art*,

a phrase which he incorporated in a famous passage of his own.[16] It was perhaps appropriate that this particular champion of nature should have drawn his manifesto from a speech by Edmund, son of Gloucester.

To read Cowper's poetry justly, one needs to exercise some discrimination, not to see it as more derivative than it really is. By instinct and education Cowper had no wish to oppose tradition: his originality was emotional and involuntary—the result of his acute sensibility. *The Task*, his best poem, is full of literary echoes. He borrowed, like the other "co-operative" poets of his time, but he gave a new life to some of the old diction. Even in his *Olney Hymns* there are traces of "polite" literature. For instance, in the hymn *Light shining out of Darkness* (no. 347) the line "Deep in unfathomable mines" is suggested by a phrase in *Night Thoughts*: "Heav'n's rich unfathomable Mines" (*N.T.*, VI.92). Cowper's hymns, like Charles Wesley's, remind us that their author was a man of letters.

[14]Crabbe's well-known line in *The Village* (Book I), "No; cast by Fortune on a frowning coast," was evidently suggested by a line in Churchill's *Gotham* (I.13), "Cast by a tempest on the savage coast."

[15]The phrase occurs in the sonnet by Gray quoted in Wordsworth's Preface to *Lyrical Ballads*. According to Wordsworth, Gray "was more than any other man curiously elaborate in the structure of his own poetic diction." See also p. 3.

[16]See p. 156.

Cowper's poetry could not flow forcefully within a confined channel, and that is one reason why his didactic poems, *Table Talk, The Progress of Error*, and the rest, are not a complete success. Pope and Young were his models, but in temper he was different from them both. Pope's exacting standards and deadly precision did not suit Cowper's inclination to make his moral satires evangelical tracts for the times. He chafes against the restraints of polite satire, and though his good breeding is on the side of propriety, his feelings tend towards certain unworldly "enthusiasms." He would like to name John Bunyan, but dare not (*Tirocinium*, 141–2[17]):

> I name thee not, lest so despis'd a name
> Should move a sneer at thy deserved fame;

he would like to mention the preacher George Whitefield, but dare not (*Hope*, 554–5):

> Leuconomus (beneath well-sounding Greek
> I slur a name a poet must not speak).

He does not criticize Pope directly, but the lines which he puts into the mouth of one of the speakers in the dialogue *Table Talk* (652–5) surely express an irritation which he felt himself, even while admitting that Pope "Gave virtue and morality a grace":

> But he (his musical finesse was such,
> So nice his ear, so delicate his touch)
> Made poetry a mere mechanic art;
> And ev'ry warbler has his tune by heart.

Cowper, however, was too perceptive a writer not to have read Pope to good purpose, and he characteristically profits from the most vital feature of Pope's descriptive style—his vivid verbs. The metaphorical *smoke*, for instance, common in the *Iliad*,[18] reappears in Cowper's description of a rain-storm (*Truth*, 238–9):

> See where it smokes along the sounding plain,
> Blown all aslant, a driving, dashing rain.

Didactic poetry in the style of Pope and Young did not offer Cowper the scope which his various gifts required. He needed a freer form in which his observant humour, now serious, now fanciful, could expatiate. It was a happy suggestion that prompted him to try blank verse—not in the high Miltonic style with its stately paragraphic structure, but on the

[17]Line references are from *The Poetical Works of William Cowper*, ed. H. S. Milford (Oxford, 1911).
[18]See p. 122.

lower levels accessible to a later age. This measure accommodated all that Cowper had to exercise: his talent for description, his sensitive feelings, his earnest conscience, his mild humour, his occasional energy. An ample diction was also needed, but this Cowper found in Milton himself, and the development of his style and vocabulary by his imitators of the eighteenth century. From earlier sources he borrowed little: Milton was his sufficing ideal, as he was his early admiration (*The Task,* IV.710–12):

> New to my taste, his Paradise surpass'd
> The struggling efforts of my boyish tongue
> To speak its excellence.

To enumerate the more formal features of Cowper's Miltonic diction would be profitless: the point is, that much of it is not mechanical. Rhetorical it sometimes is, in an idiom which is now obsolete:[19] at other times, it is vitally used as a medium of sensibility or observant description. Thus, the rare word *transverse* which Milton had used to describe the crossed position of an organist's hands as they "fled and pursu'd . . . the resonant fugue" (*P.L.*, XI.559) is revived by Cowper in a passage on an artless contrivance of gypsies (*Task*, I.560–2):

> A kettle, slung
> Between two poles upon a stick transverse,
> Receives the morsel.

The Miltonic *lapse* ("liquid lapse of murmuring streams," *P.L.*, VIII. 263) becomes visual in the setting which Cowper gives it in his lines on a snow-storm (*Task*, IV.326–9):

> Fast falls a fleecy show'r: the downy flakes,
> Descending, and with never-ceasing lapse,
> Softly alighting upon all below,
> Assimilate all objects.

The interesting epithet *arrowy*—a favourite word in picturesque descriptions of the earlier nineteenth century—is one of Cowper's happy borrowings from Milton. Remembering the phrase "sharp sleet of arrowie showers" in *Paradise Regained* (III.324), he adapted it to the warfare of the elements in a Russian winter (*Task*, V.139–40):

> his troops,
> The gloomy clouds, find weapons, arrowy sleet.

[19]See his strange use of the word *oscitancy* (*Task*, II.774) of the culpable yawning of a children's nurse: the passage, from its context, cannot be mock heroic.

Familiarity with Milton was so common among well-read persons in Cowper's time that he could appeal to it in some of his lighter sallies. Thus, a couplet in his verses *On Mrs. Montagu's Feather-Hangings*,

> The Peacock sends his heav'nly dyes,
> His *rainbows* and his *starry eyes*

is meant to recall the bird in *Paradise Lost* (VII.444–6)

> whose gay Traine
> Adorns him, colour'd with the Florid hue
> Of Rainbows and Starrie Eyes.

It was, I think, only with his favourite poets that Cowper took these liberties. He would hardly have borrowed the complete phrase "pregnant with celestial fire" (*Boadicea*) from Gray's *Elegy* had he not loved the poem. Gray did not offend his sensibility: whereas insensitive descriptions of nature and the mechanical use of "vogue-words" like *hermit*,[20] did. Against such things his critical sense and his humour were sufficiently alert.

VI

Any critic who writes on Chatterton (1752–1770)[21] today must acknowledge his obligations to Mr. E. H. W. Meyerstein, whose *Life* reasserts the half-forgotten merits of the "Rowley Poems." Mr. Meyerstein reminds us of what Coleridge, Keats, and Rossetti really thought of "the marvellous boy," and his praise of Chatterton is enforced with reasons and quotations which carry conviction. One effect of his book has been to revive a critical interest in Chatterton's style, the freshness and colour of which were in danger of disappearing under layers of philological comment.

Mr. Meyerstein makes little—perhaps too little—claim for Chatterton on the score of felicity in expression. "Seldom only, in Chatterton, does a verb or adjective force itself on the attention as a separate beauty."[22] And elsewhere: "His was an eager, impressionistic, unscholarly mind, alive to sound and colour; Kersey[23] was his paint-box, and he mixed the tints he found there with others of his own fancy."[24] But Chatterton's saturation in the language of the "purest" masters is

[20]See p. 147.
[21]Quotations are from *Poems, supposed to have been written at Bristol*, by Thomas Rowley, and Others (3rd ed., London, 1778).
[22]*Life of Chatterton*, p. 202.
[23]John Kersey, author of an English dictionary (1708), from which Chatterton obtained many of his rarer words.
[24]Meyerstein, *Life of Chatterton*, pp. 174–5.

also maintained: "It may fairly be said that a thorough self-education in Spenser, Shakespeare and Dryden is the core of Chatterton's poetic mystery, inspiration excepted."[25] This remark suggests that Chatterton may have helped to transmit certain types of poetic word-usage from earlier to more recent writers, seeing that Keats, Rossetti, and others read and admired the Rowley Poems.

Something of this we do, indeed, find. In some respects Chatterton is literally "Spenserian," especially in his use of the prefixes *a-* and *en-* in the formation of new "words." On a superficial glance, a select list of words beginning with *a-* from the Rowley Poems might easily appear to have been copied direct from a glossary to the poems of Spenser. Only on examination could it be pronounced that *agreme, accaie, agrote, adente, agylt, atturne* are in fact independent "discoveries" of Chatterton, while *awhape* is common to both poets. Between the old words which are rightly used, the old words which are wrongly used, and the "old words" which are spurious it is by no means easy to distinguish. No doubt the poets who read Chatterton cared little about such matters, and enjoyed him simply for the fresh bright colour of his descriptions. This, of course, is not to deny that his unusual words may have produced certain effects of their own. Formations such as *enshotynge, enyronn'd, enharme, enheped, enlowed, encheere* would, in their context, very likely contribute towards forming an impression in favour of the more fluid conventions of language, especially in free and fresh descriptions of Nature. Keats's praise of Chatterton as the most English of our poets may well have been due to some such perception as this, for it would agree with his intense approbation of a writer to whom so much was possible in the handling of words. In certain word formations and revivals Chatterton does in fact anticipate the earlier manner of Keats: for instance, *ardurous* and *emblaunched* might both have been used in *Endymion*.

The interest excited by the Rowley Poems was partly due to a love of antique spelling, which was one of the literary tastes of the time. But their enduring success has been largely due to Chatterton's remarkable skill in harmonizing the various elements of which his diction is composed. His skill in avoiding the wrong word may have been genius, or it may have been in part the ignorance of youth: it was not infallible, but it certainly served him in good stead. His sources were equally well chosen for the purpose he had in view—that of writing the best eighteenth-century Gothic. One notices for instance *noyance* (*Ælla*, 454), a Spenserian word revived by Thomson; *blatauntlie* (*Ælla*, 108),

[25]*Ibid.*, p. 198.

from Spenser's "blatant"; *swefte-fote* (tyme, *Ælla*, 996), an archaic spelling of an Elizabethan epithet used by Kyd and Sylvester. Ballad-phrases are present too: *claie-colde* (corse), *bloude-redde* (hue), *milkwhite* (breste).[26] He could not avoid the more picturesque elements of the "funeral" diction of his century, and accordingly in the *Myn-strelles Songe* of *Ælla*, "the ravenne flappes hys wynge"; nor could he wholly keep out such signs of his time as "the featherd songster" which has slipped into the first line of his *Bristowe Tragedie*. Yet if any other poet of the time had fabricated the Rowley Poems he would have passed scores of tell-tale expressions which were stopped by the fine meshes of Chatterton's net. His worst lapse is, I think, the word *leath-all*,[27] which he unfortunately uses again and again. The history of *slughorne*, another favourite, is well known: a form of "slogan" which Chatterton misused as "trumpet," it served the purpose of Browning in the same mistaken sense, and is likely to be long remembered, from its position in the dramatic conclusion of *Childe Roland to the Dark Tower Came*.

Many of Chatterton's words and phrases are of especial interest to the critic who is tracing the growth of that diction which enabled Nature-description to attain such extraordinary richness and veracity in the nineteenth century. The effects of "sound and colour" which Mr. Meyerstein notes in Chatterton's style could hardly have been attained without a true instinct for the technique of verbal description, nor, without this gift, would he have been so greatly admired by Keats. Chatterton's merits in this kind of word-use do not seem to have received full justice. It is true that much of his descriptive diction is not particularly original. Thus, a line like "Ynn daiseyd mantels ys the mountayne dyghte" (*Ælla*, 162) is simply the language of his genera-tion in pseudo-archaic disguise. But his word *enlefed* ("Lyche yonge enlefed trees," *Ælla*, 743) is an original touch, and it is much earlier in date than the relevant example quoted in the *Oxford Dictionary* (1837). The useful word *rain-storm* (*Oxford Dictionary*, 1816) is as early as Chatterton and perhaps his invention, though he spells it *rayne-storme* (*Ælla*, 675). He has as good a title to the descriptive word *treed* ("Ynn the treed forreste," *The Tournamente*, 49), attributed by the *Oxford Dictionary* to the middle of the nineteenth century. These few examples clearly suggest that this aspect of Chatterton's originality has been generally overlooked. He saw things in a vivid, fresh, colourful way, and he was poet enough to create the right diction to embody his

[26]*Elinoure and Juga*, 45; *Songe to Ælla*; *Battle of Hastings* (No. 1), 78.
[27]E.g. *Ælla*, 304: "ys leathall warre so deare?"

perceptions. He had, in fact, a purer and more vital talent for this kind of writing than any other Spenserian of the eighteenth century. One likes to imagine that this is one of the underlying reasons for the tributes to his memory paid by such poets as Wordsworth, Coleridge, Shelley, and Keats.

A word may be added on the cult of archaic or pseudo-archaic spelling, which is an offshoot of the Spenserian revival. The matter is hardly important enough to deserve detailed treatment, though the tendency to substitute -y- for -i-, -aunt for -ant, final -ie for -y, etc. is conspicuous enough. The preference of -y- to -i- is particularly noticeable. An editor of Blake once insisted that a "tyger" was not precisely the same to the imagination as a "tiger," and that an injustice was done to the spirit of Blake's poem when the spelling was normalized. However that may be, "tygers" certainly existed in the imagination, or at least in the dictionaries of poets long before the date of *Songs of Experience*. Mrs. Chapone, for example, had already declared Love to be "More fierce than tygers on the Libyan plain" (no. 261, "Written by 1755"), and in Christopher Smart's *Song to David* (1763, no. 282) there are "sleek tygers." Other "poetic" spellings of a similar kind are *blythesome* and *cloyster*: Chatterton's "*lyghtsome* sunne" is in the same class. W. J. Mickle affects spellings which are only a few degrees less "gothic" than those of "Rowley" himself, e.g. *bashfull, kist, lowlie, wilde* (and *wyld*), *rownd, towres, banck.* Apart from the pseudo-archaic tradition which was continued in *The Rime of the Ancyent Marinere*, the form *gulph* is a common specimen of "poetic" spelling (though it is not confined to verse): *lilly* (preferred by Keats) is another. One of the latest spellings of the "gothic" kind is *ghyll* for "gill," apparently introduced by Wordsworth, and from him extended into local use.[28]

[28]See *O.E.D.*

THE DICTION of Wordsworth has aroused more discussion than that of any other English poet. He began the controversy himself in the Preface to his *Lyrical Ballads* (2nd ed., 1801), and he returned to the charge in an Essay, Supplementary to the Preface. Coleridge took part in the contest, and in the middle chapters of his *Biographia Literaria* debated the theory of poetic diction in the most convincing and the most connected piece of argument that he ever wrote. It was on the weak places of Wordsworth's theory that Coleridge fastened, and he put the case for cultivating a special diction for poetry, against the view of Wordsworth that there could be no essential difference between the language of poetry and of prose, with an ingenuity and persuasiveness which are irresistible. The controversy was frequently alluded to in the nineteenth century, and it was reopened by Sir Walter Raleigh in his book, *Wordsworth*. The main new point brought forward by Raleigh is that word-order (taxis) is as important an element of style as vocabulary (lexis); and he showed that an artificiality of word-order may cause as bad a lapse from a true style in poetry as artificiality in the choice of words.

The issue has remained pretty much as Raleigh left it, though there are more critics friendly to the central point in Wordsworth's contention than there formerly were. But apart from the question of general principles, it seems that the interest of the discussion is now exhausted. One reason for this is that the debate is now seen to have relatively little bearing on Wordsworth's own practice. Wordsworth was writing verse for something like sixty years: he was writing great poetry for only a fraction of this period. In a large proportion of his best work the style is clearly inconsistent with the theories of the Preface, and if we consider the whole bulk of his verse—as we must—the discrepancy is of course much greater. For these reasons, I shall have little to say of the famous Preface, and will begin at once with Wordsworth's poetic style itself.[1]

---

[1] Quotations are from *The Poems of William Wordsworth*, ed. Thos. Hutchinson (Oxford, 1923), except in the instances specially noted.

I

Before coming to details, it will be as well to consider what general qualities of language are the peculiar note of Wordsworth's style. A remark of Matthew Arnold's, however, points to a difficulty. Wordsworth, he tells us, "has no style."[2] If Wordsworth has no style, it should be impossible to find anything consistent or characteristic in his choice of words. To a certain extent, this is really the case. A poem such as *Michael*—a work of nearly five hundred lines—seems from the point of view of style almost entirely negative. The story, though "homely and rude," appeals directly to our human feelings, or, as Wordsworth says, to "the affections." But this is all. It would be diffi- cult to name any poem in which the art is more self-effacing. The critic of style has exhausted his vocabulary in pronouncing the diction "pure" or "natural" or "simple." Nor is *Michael* by any means an exception. Many of Wordsworth's sonnets have this same negative quality. While other poets reveal the deepest qualities of their character in transform- ing language after the pattern of their soul, Wordsworth's diction is more impersonal than that of any other of our greater poets. Excep- tions to this statement will occur to many readers; yet such is certainly its general character. It would almost appear as if the critic of Words- worth's style has discharged his duty when he has repeated Arnold's well-known remark, or has adopted Bagehot's epithet "pure" from his famous comparison of Wordsworth, Tennyson, and Browning.

But this, after all, is not the whole truth. Some important facts emerge, both when we study the development of Wordsworth's style, its variations in different phases of his life and art, and also when we consider that style in relation to the special aim and quality of his poetic effort. The two inquiries cannot be kept wholly apart, but we may begin with the second. What is Wordsworth's peculiar position among English poets? He is still loosely classed as a poet of Nature, or a descriptive poet: but that which really distinguishes him from other poets is his philosophic character, which appears not only in *The Pre- lude* and *The Excursion*, but in almost every song or lyric that he ever penned. It is not mere fact that interests Wordsworth, but the relation of facts to the mind. The result is that description is not, with him, as it is with the "artistic" poets, an end in itself. No poet is more accurate in his record of details, but many poets are more intense in their ob-

---

[2]Preface to *Poems of Wordsworth*, chosen and edited by Arnold (1879): reprinted as "Wordsworth" in *Essays in Criticism*, Second Series.

servations and more vivid in their transmission of them. Instead of intensity, Wordsworth offers a large contemplative background. He gives the feeling suggested by the experience; and it is his object, as a poet, to humanize such feelings, however rare or novel they may be. He therefore endeavours to obliterate the literary origins of his style.[3] Everyone recognizes the beauty of passages like

> The music in my heart I bore,
> Long after it was heard no more

or

> Alas! the gratitude of men
> Hath oftener left me mourning.

This kind of writing is Wordsworth's speciality: it is to all appearances the poetry of unadorned statement. Wordsworth was most careful in his choice of language, constantly altering and improving: but it was his principal endeavour to bring his words into the closest possible agreement with the language of real life. His theory is the very antithesis of Pope's. For Wordsworth, poetry consists of thoughts (or feelings) which are new, and expressions which are not "dressed" at all, but as bare as the rocks and precipices of his own mountains.

Wordsworth, however, did not attain to his full conception of poetry at one bound, nor, having attained it, did he adhere to it for the remainder of his life. It is customary to say that he was a true poet for some dozen or fifteen years at most, and that his subsequent career produced only mediocre work. No critic contests the general truth of this statement, but no critic can allow it to pass in its naked crudity. The student of style who sees more clearly than the ordinary reader the eighteenth-century origins of Wordsworth's manner must of course admit that the more Wordsworth transcends his origins the greater he is. But it is not perhaps generally recognized that Wordsworth's memory was stored with a very wide knowledge of English poetry and that this influenced him throughout his career.[4] After all, he modernized Chaucer, imitated Spenser, borrowed from the Elizabethans, praised the language of Shakespeare, revered and studied Milton, and showed an acquaintance with almost the whole body of eighteenth-century verse. Wordsworth's inspiration came from Nature, but his language came from books: and his genius lay, not in selecting phrases from the real

[3]This statement is especially applicable to the poems written between 1798 and 1807. But throughout his career Wordsworth was scrupulous in acknowledging *conscious* literary debts by the use of quotation marks.

[4]This has become much clearer since the publication of E. de Selincourt and Helen Darbishire's edition of Wordsworth's *Poetical Works* (Clarendon Press, 1940–9).

language of men, but in giving an appearance of freshness and spontaneity to a style whose origins were literary. Coleridge speaks of Wordsworth's predilection for the dramatic; and there are well-known passages in *Resolution and Independence, The Idiot Boy,* and other poems in which he has apparently adopted some phrases really used by men. These passages, however, have received an exaggerated prominence from the controversy on "poetic diction." Wordsworth's habitual practice is more important than his occasional lapses, and even though he "had no style" he learned his diction from a wide and selective reading. His debts to other poets and the distinctive nature of his originality will be the chief themes in our discussion of his diction.

II

Not much attention need be paid to Wordsworth's two early poems, *An Evening Walk* (finished in 1789) and *Descriptive Sketches* (1792), but to the student of the evolution of a poetic style both pieces offer some points of interest. They are of a different quality, the execution of the later poem being much more confident and certain than that of its predecessor, but for convenience they may be considered together, as representative of the first phase of Wordsworth's poetry. The two poems are works of description, varied and modified by didactic touches—a type well known in the eighteenth century. They are full of minutely pictured scenes without any clear plan or unity; and when writing them, Wordsworth was obviously in that stage of his life when, in his own language, he was under the dominion of the eye, not of the imagination: content, as he says, "to observe and not to feel." Feeling is, indeed, not absent, but it is subordinte and diffused. Not having yet arrived at the maturity of his original power, Wordsworth is naturally more subject to the influence of other poets. The metre of the two poems is the heroic couplet, and Wordsworth uses many of the terms and devices of diction long associated with that measure. For example, the epithet with the added -*y* is fairly common: *spiry, paly, steamy, gleamy, piny.* Again, there are fairly frequent echoes from other descriptive poets, such as Milton, Gray, Thomson, and Greenwood (author of a *Poem on Shooting*). What is equally significant, Wordsworth shows himself a student of the Rev. William Gilpin, a writer on the picturesque, from whom he borrows the quoted phrase in the line (*D.S.,* 365; Quarto 1793):

And glad Dundee in "faint huzza's" expir'd.[5]

[5]See the note on this line *ibid.,* I, 327.

In the same spirit, as a student of the laws of the picturesque, he speaks of "the visto of the brook" (*E.W.*, 81; Quarto 1793). Some passages are quite startling in their imitative quality. Who, for instance, would suspect Wordsworth of having written such, lines as the following (*D.S.*, 60–3; Quarto 1793), which belong rather to the spirit of—let us say—Dyer's *Ruins of Rome*?

> The cloister startles at the gleam of arms,
> And Blasphemy the shuddering fane alarms;
> Nod the cloud-piercing pines their troubl'd heads,
> Spires, rocks, and lawns, a browner night o'erspreads.

It is, however, noteworthy that Wordsworth has already begun to use a few novel words such as the local *intake* and *ghyll* and the Scottish *sugh*. One line (*D.S.*, 130; Quarto 1793), of characteristic boldness,

> Thy torrents shooting from the clear-blue sky,

he incorporated in *The Prelude*.[6] But in general his early descriptive poems show him content to adapt, with variations, a well-worn style to subjects of his own choosing. "I had once given to these sketches the title of Picturesque" is a comment full of implications to a discerning reader of the poet.

III

In great contrast to these early descriptive works are the poems in ballad style which Wordsworth began to write soon after his meeting with Coleridge, and which formed a large and important part of his production about 1798–1800. In poems like those of the Lucy series, *The Fountain, The Two April Mornings, Simon Lee*, and many more, Wordsworth has clearly a definite manner: indeed, it is doubtful whether he ever came nearer to achieving a "style" than in the volume of *Lyrical Ballads* which he frankly called "an experiment" (Preface of 1801). Although other forms of verse soon rivalled the place which ballads occupied in his esteem, he long kept his affection for ballad simplicity and in *Peter Bell* he produced the last and culminating poem of the group.

There are few qualities in English poetry on which it is so hard to form a conclusive opinion as of Wordsworth's ballad simplicity. It is not the wholly novel thing that some of his critics seem to imagine. Cowper, Chatterton, Coleridge, and a score of other poets had revived the ballad, and they probably admired the artless pathos of poems like

---

[6]VI.629 (1850): "Thy" is altered to "the."

The Babes in the Wood little less than did Wordsworth himself. What distinguished Wordsworth from these other writers was his obstinate attempt to rebuild the art of poetry on a revolutionary democratic basis. Readers of A. C. Bradley's exposition of *Alice Fell* will know with what persuasiveness the case for Wordsworth's simplicity may be put by a great critic; yet it will still be possible to hold that the choice of style was mistaken, and that the execution does not come up to the conception. Paradoxical as the idea may seem, is it not true that Wordsworth's ballad style was too conventional to express the full strength of his radical reform in poetic outlook? "All good poetry," he said, "is the spontaneous overflow of powerful feelings": he will adopt "a selection of language really used by men." Those, and similar expressions seem to portend a change even more radical than that which Wordsworth did in effect attempt. He keeps metre; he keeps rhyme; he uses an artificial order of words; he even keeps part of the vocabulary current in the ballad style. His originality lies far more in the depth of his feelings; and it is this discrepancy between form and content that causes the unevenness in his style. As a narrative poet he has countless flaws and defects; as a reflective poet, he stands among the greatest. In such a poem as *Simon Lee*, for instance, the statement of facts is frequently quite laughable in style and diction. In the original version, the old man's age was announced in the lines:

> Of years he has upon his back,
> No doubt, a burthen weighty;
> He says he is three score and ten,
> But others say he's eighty.

This passage, like others more or less ludicrous, was afterwards altered; yet one is bound to admit that the lines are really characteristic: Wordsworth simply did not care how he reported a mere matter of fact. What he does care for is the opportunity of writing such lines as those already quoted:

> I've heard of hearts unkind, kind deeds
> With coldness still returning;
> Alas! the gratitude of men
> Hath oftener left me mourning.

There is no need to dwell on the more notorious of Wordsworth's lapses in diction. Most students of literature know the famous "measurement lines" in *The Thorn* (afterwards altered); equally familiar are the passage on the "goings on" of the stars in the 1807 version of *Gipsies* and perhaps some dozen more. There is a large number of passages on which opinions are divided. Some persons, for instance, consider that the last line spoils by its bathos one of the finest of the Lucy poems:

> But she is in her grave, and, oh,
> The difference to me!

Others regard the phrase as a fine example of effective understatement. There are certainly many passages on the borderline, and no less certainly, there are many poems (such as *Resolution and Independence*) which contain within a small compass some of the finest and some of the flattest passages in English poetry.

The important thing is that Wordsworth's "experiments" in the simplicity of the ballad style were on the whole justified. *We are Seven* and its companions may be an anomaly in our literature, but their "meditative pathos" (Coleridge's phrase) will always appeal to an important minority of readers, if not to a wider circle. As to the pieces in which the language is happily inspired, they strike with a depth and force which are unequalled. This is true not only of the Lucy poems but of passages scattered broadcast over Wordsworth's writings, in nearly every period of his life. We must admit that he is a writer of great poetry rather than of great poems; yet so characteristic are these occasional passages that we are after all compelled to question the dictum of Arnold that "he has no style." Where, for instance, shall we find words chosen with a surer instinct than in such a stanza as this from *The Fountain*?

> "And, Matthew, for thy children dead
> I'll be a son to thee!"
> At this he grasped my hand, and said,
> "Alas! that cannot be."

The same quality is present in the short poem of two stanzas which Coleridge called a "sublime epitaph." Wordsworth's practice is more significant than his theory; and though he did not revolutionize the style of poetry, he raised economy and simplicity of diction to a higher place in our poetry than they have ever had before or since.

IV

Wordsworth is famous not only for his experiments, but for his successes. He has written poems which are second to none in the depth of their appeal—poems which, if not exactly popular, are among the most universally loved and the most genuinely revered in the language. Chief among these is the *Ode on the Intimations of Immortality*, which is an undoubted triumph of style. With this may be classed some dozen or score of other poems, such as the *Ode to Duty*, the *Elegiac Stanzas*,

The Solitary Reaper, and the greatest of the sonnets. There are no poems in the language whose position in our literature is more unchallengeable than these.

It is obvious that the diction of these poems forms an important part of their beauty. One may even speak in connection with these pieces, of the "glamour" of Wordsworth's style. They are poetic alike in content and form, not experiments in simple language. One has only to recall phrases like

> The light that never was, on sea or land,
> The consecration, and the Poet's dream,

or,

> But trailing clouds of glory do we come
> From God, who is our home,

to realize that Wordsworth's magic is as unquestionable as his "purity." In these splendid poems, Wordsworth is often, in the most honest and the most genuine sense of the word, "romantic." There could hardly be a purer specimen of the romantic association of words than the phrase

> Of travellers in some shady haunt,
> Among Arabian sands,

nor could there be a finer example of the "golden phrase" than the concluding line of the sonnet *Mutability*:

> Or the unimaginable touch of Time.

But it is characteristic of Wordsworth that even in these poems there are moments when the diction betrays signs of a certain strain. The suggestive power of words, their tendency to lead the thought and determine their own claim to selection, is held under severe restraint. On the other hand, the poet's peculiar experience is constantly striving against the limits of language. This fact is clear, for instance, in such a passage as:

> But for those obstinate questionings
> Of sense and outward things,
> Fallings from us, vanishings—

where the obscurity of the thought has meant a palpable struggle with language, in which the poet is bound to resort to a series of verbal nouns.[7] It is the alternation of unerring phrases with mystical vision that makes Wordsworth, in his greatest poems, like the *Ode* and *Tintern Abbey*, the most impressive English poet of the last two centuries.[8]

[7] See also p. 175.

[8] Phrases from these poems, e.g. "the light of common day," "shades of the prison-house," "nameless, unremembered acts" were entering the literary language by the middle of the nineteenth century.

V

Description more than any other type of poetry calls forth the rarer resources of the poet's vocabulary. As we have already seen, Wordsworth abandoned the ordinary kind of descriptive or "picturesque" poetry after the first stage in his career. He no longer addressed the merely visual imagination of the reader; hence, he has created scarcely any of those pictorial epithets which were coined so freely by some of his contemporaries. The adjective *treeless* appears to have been his invention: if he has added any more words to our common descriptive vocabulary, they are certainly not numerous. But though Wordsworth abandoned the picturesque method of description, he remained through life a great descriptive poet. The difference is that in his maturity he sought to render not the external features of a scene but its *spirit*. In his description of *Glen Almain*, for instance, he seeks to convey an impression of tranquillity felt by the soul:

> It is not quiet, is not ease;
> But something deeper far than these.

For his purposes he needed not so much words conveying sense impressions, as the most accurate terms he could discover to indicate a special state of feeling. Of course Wordsworth in his vital passages never loses sight of the physical features of his scenes; he clings to "the language of the sense"; but his senses are, in a unique degree, spiritualized, and in his endeavour to make the reader share this sort of experience he finds it best to render the impressions of form and colour in the simplest, barest, most economical terms. There is a splendid example of this kind of language in an early passage in *The Prelude* (1850), where the poet recalls his sensations as a child in the dangerous sport of bird-nesting among the fells:

> While on the perilous ridge I hung alone,
> With what strange utterance did the *loud dry* wind
> Blow through my ear!

His descriptions abound in "rare epithets," not rare in themselves so much as in their power of giving a mental form to a sense-impression. One remembers, for instance, the "unrejoicing berries" of *Yew-Trees* and the perfect description of the wild fell-land about the source of the Duddon (Sonnet V):

> Sole listener, Duddon! to the breeze that played
> With thy clear voice, I caught the *fitful* sound
> Wafted o'er *sullen* moss and craggy mound.

One wonders what writer has ever equalled the poet of the English Lakeland in giving an articulate voice to his native region.

VI

Many of Wordsworth's critics have insisted on the originality of his best work, and have abandoned the rest to neglect. They have exaggerated the contrast and presented it as a conflict between light and darkness. Even from an entirely general standpoint this is a misrepresentation, as Edith C. Batho has shown in *The Later Wordsworth*, but the critic of style is especially aware of the inaccuracy. Wordsworth at his best does not write in a new language, as some writers seem to suggest: he simply writes the finest possible poetry in his particular vein of reflection, pathos, sublimity, or mysticism. Nor, at his second best, or even at his worst does he write without an intellectual self-respect. What he does is to rely on reminiscences from other poets, to reproduce qualities of style which his more vigorous judgment condemned. There is of course no need in a book of this kind to undertake a complete analysis of Wordsworth's style and diction. But the background of his work and the tokens of his reading are of some general interest, for Wordsworth, besides being the author of "a few fine lines," is a great figure in our literature. His use of language has both historical interest and importance. He was a great reader of English poetry, and he resembles the majority of poets in reproducing from time to time words and phrases from his favourite reading, and so forming a link in the long chain of tradition.

From about 1800 onwards, Wordsworth was a close student of Milton, and by degrees the Miltonic strain replaces the ballad simplicity which he admired so much during the time of his intimacy with Coleridge. At its best, Wordsworth's Miltonism belongs to the highest order of poetic discipleship: he reproduces something of the Miltonic grandeur in a form and style which are entirely his own. At no time, of course, did he copy the minor features of Milton's diction in the manner of those eighteenth-century poets who learned three-quarters of their art from the fourth and seventh books of *Paradise Lost*. He was clearly familiar with the whole range of Milton's work, which was a challenge to him to exert himself to the utmost. Originality of style is undeniable in lines like

<blockquote>
intertwisted fibres serpentine
Up-coiling, and inveterately convolved,
</blockquote>

yet the Miltonic foundation both in the choice and in the ordering of the words is patent. Again and again when Wordsworth writes in his most vigorous manner, some reminiscence from the language of Milton is traceable. I have just quoted from *Yew-Trees*, one of Wordsworth's most splendid pieces of description. Equally fine is the famous passage from *The Prelude* on crossing the Alps: here again there is a Miltonic echo—such at least I take to be the resemblance of the wording in the two lines:

Him first, him last, him midst, and without end.
Paradise Lost (V.165)

Of first, and last, and midst, and without end.
The Prelude (VI.640, 1850)

Two phrases from the *Ode to Duty* are clearly Miltonic: "Stern Daughter of the Voice of God" ("Sole Daughter of his voice," *P.L.*, IX.653) and "lowly wise" ("lowlie wise," *P.L.*, VIII.173). The blank verse of *The Prelude* contains many echoes, both faint and clear, of Miltonic wording, and it is sometimes impossible to say certainly how much is mere coincidence. For example, the expression "solemn and sublime" (*Prelude*, IV.441, 1850) occurs in *Paradise Lost* (XI.237). This is probably an echo rather than a coincidence and the same may be said of the phrase "prosperous or adverse" (*Happy Warrior*; *P.L.*, XI.364). "Liquid lapse serene" and "sinuous lapse" both occur in Wordsworth's *Duddon* series, and are not only genuinely Miltonic, but— applied to the Duddon in one of its smoother courses—very good description. About many of Wordsworth's Miltonisms, then, there can be no doubt whatever, and some are even avowed by quotation marks. "Parting Genius" (*Descriptive Sketches*), "rathe primrose" (*To May*), "trumpery" (*Ecclesiastical Sonnets*, II.xxviii) are obvious reminiscences duly acknowledged.

Milton is the chief contributor to Wordsworth's style and diction, but Shakespeare and many other poets of the seventeenth and eighteenth centuries are recalled by single words and phrases.[9] Curiously enough, it is really Wordsworth's chief failing that he is ready to borrow so much: for his borrowing is at times imperfect assimilation. Few English poets, if any, are so ready to incorporate into their verse whole phrases within quotation marks from other poets. These amount altogether to a considerable number: and they are characteristic. If, for instance, Wordsworth writes on Burns, he will incorporate various phrases from his original, such as "glinted" and "lonely heights and hows"—both of them quoted. If he writes on Yarrow, he will borrow from Hamilton of Bangour the phrase "winsome Marrow." In a poem to his infant daughter, Dora, he remembers a phrase from Dryden's Killigrew Ode ("heaven's eternal year") and again adopts it as a quotation. Not all

---

[9]Cf. "coignes of vantage" (from the sonnet "A volant Tribe of Bards") and "wooingly" (from the sonnet "Mine ear has rung"), both suggested by *Macbeth*, I.vi.3–10.

his borrowings are thus acknowledged, but he certainly had no wish to conceal any. Many are the traces of his reading in eighteenth-century verse. From Thomson's *Seasons*, for instance, he borrows, on two different occasions, the epithet *sole-sitting*.[10] From Young's *Night Thoughts* he takes the phrase "strenuous idleness"; from Gray's *Elegy* the epithet *incense-breathing*. Wordsworth was curiously susceptible to the influence of works which he had recently read. In his middle years he had occasion, when teaching Latin to one of his sons, to re-read Virgil: and the result was the majestic poem *Laodamia*, in which the diction, besides being heavily Latinized, clearly follows in one part the phrasing of the original (*Æneid*, VI.640–1):

> Largior hic campos aether et lumine vestit
> Purpureo.

> An ampler ether, a diviner air,
> And fields invested with purpureal gleams.

Such parallels show, what is not always admitted, that Wordsworth's work has its roots deeply fixed in the literature of the past.[11]

Imperfect assimilation is not a common defect of Wordsworth's diction. More serious are those examples of the pompous and over-literary which attended his moods of self-conscious dignity. Even *The Prelude* is not free from occasional lapses of this kind. But in some other poems a certain falsity seems to belong to the whole fabric and substance of the work, and this is true even of a few pieces of great merit. Thus, in the lines *Composed upon an Evening of Extraordinary Splendour and Beauty*, passages of vital power and melody appear fitfully in a style totally wanting in freshness and magic. The wrong note is struck in the first line: "Had this effulgence disappeared . . ." and it is repeated at intervals through the entire poem. It is unnecessary to dwell long on those more serious flaws—a favourite topic with some critics—which are due to a sense of the dignity of the poetic vocation. Even in the earlier *Prelude* (1805–6) Wordsworth had avoided direct mention of a children's parlour-game, calling it "strife too humble to be named in Verse" (I.540), but the prim euphemism of the *Ecclesiastical Sonnets* (I.xv) which calls the nose of Paulinus his "prominent feature" is almost ludicrous. The inequality of Wordsworth's poetry has of course never been in dispute. He lacked the saving sense of humour, and it is to be feared that he will continue to pay the penalty in over-measure.

[10]*Spring*, 725: *Poems on the Naming of Places*, iv.38; *To the Moon* (No. 1), 11.
[11]Wordsworth himself approved of the wider use of the word "Spenserian": e.g. he calls his lines *A Farewell* "Spenserian," though the poem contains no archaic words and does not use Spenser's stanza; see *Poetical Works*, ed. E. de Selincourt, II, 470.

VII

One feature of Wordsworth's diction already touched upon calls for somewhat fuller comment, and it is, next to "purity," the most interesting of all. Wordsworth is above all a serious and philosophic poet, and his steady purpose and constant preoccupation were the truthful expression of deep experience. His mind dwelt on the borderland of poetry and mysticism, and he is again and again impressed by the difficulty, amounting almost to hopelessness, of finding words to match his intuitions. Readers of *The Prelude* know how often, by the side of earnest professions of a love of language, there are expressions of a deep sense of its inadequacy. Often there is a feeling of frustration, as in the lines (V.45–7, 1850):

> Oh! why hath not the Mind
> Some element to stamp her image on
> In nature somewhat nearer to her own?

and there are many admissions like the line (III.184),

> It lies far hidden from the reach of words,

or (VI.593),

> Through sad incompetence of human speech.

He adds (XIII.273) that there is a class of contemplative men whose inarticulateness is a kind of spiritual distinction:

> Words are but under-agents in their souls.

His own experience frequently passes the bounds of even poetic speech, and we see him struggling to discover an adequate word, as in (I.393–5)

> O'er my thoughts
> There hung a darkness, call it solitude
> Or blank desertion,

and it is characteristic that he should write of "*nameless*, unremembered acts" (*Tintern Abbey*), or more impressively (*Prelude*, X.290), of

> A conflict of sensations *without name*.

The deficiency in language noted by Wordsworth is mainly one of nouns. In all ages, poets have felt the inadequacy of epithets, and it has been their pride to create them. As for nouns, they have revived them from the past, or borrowed them from other tongues; but poets have seldom felt with Wordsworth that much of their experience is "nameless." To find a parallel we must go to the prophets of the Old Testament, whose voices are unequal to the burden of utterance. Wordsworth does not have recourse to broken metaphors, but we find him in a more philosophic spirit creating new names for certain abstruse mental experiences. We have already noticed his use of verbal nouns—a process of "new naming"—in the passage (*Int. of Imm.*, 147-9):

> Fallings from us, vanishings;
> Blank misgivings of a Creature
> Moving about in worlds not realised.

Besides such words as these, there is a small but significant group of compound nouns. Some of these convey a subtlety of perception which penetrates below the surface, as in the lines (*Prelude*, VI.224-7, 1850):

> Another maid there was, who also shed
> A gladness o'er that season, then to me,
> By her exulting outside look of youth
> And placid *under-countenance*, first endeared.

A word of the same pattern is used (*Prelude*, VII.734-6) to express the twofold consciousness of the man

> who hath among least things
> An *under-sense* of greatest; sees the parts
> As parts, but with a feeling of the whole.

So, too, he recognizes a conflict between the superficial and the deeper qualities of his own adolescence (*Prelude*, VI.557-9):

> Yet still in me with those soft luxuries
> Mixed something of stern mood, an *under-thirst*
> Of vigour seldom utterly allayed.

Of a simpler kind, but of the same character, are the compounds which enrich the vocabulary of meditation and sentiment. Epithets like *heart-thrilling* and *heart-easing* are as old as Spenser and Shakespeare, but in Wordsworth's nouns there is an extension beyond the recorded experience of these poets. *Heart-humilities, heart-blessings, heart-experience*[12] indicate a habitual phase of Wordsworth's inward contemplations: *soul-illumination* and *after-meditation* (*Prelude*, VI.514; III.613) are words which may be added to the same group. *Master-bias* and *master-light* are two of his best-known compounds and are probably to be

---

[12]Sonnet: *On the Frith of Clyde*; *Descriptive Sketches*, 601 ("finally revised text"); *Prelude*, V.585.

regarded as contributions to the language.[13] He also creates from time to time compound nouns of a lighter kind, as when he calls the spring *primrose-time* (*Prelude*, VII.12), or in a charming fancy compares the graceful movements of an ash-tree to a visible melody (*Airey-Force Valley*):

> how sensitive
> Is the light ash! that, pendent from the brow
> Of yon dim cave, in seeming silence makes
> A soft *eye-music* of slow-waving boughs.

A recognition of the part played by these compound nouns in Wordsworth's style brings into view some of the subtler and rarer qualities of his work, just as a sense of his "purity" illustrates the passionate sincerity which is the chief mark of his greatness as a poet.

[13]*Happy Warrior; Intimations of Immortality.*

IT might appear at first sight as if Coleridge had no important place among the creators of poetic diction. The effects in his finest poems are, indeed, produced by subtleties of rhythm rather than by any transforming touch in the use of words. His position in the history of "gothic" diction is evident, but it is not of much significance to criticism. The first version of *The Rime of the Ancyent Marinere* contained many archaic words and spellings, but the number was much reduced on revision. Of the diction itself there seems but little to say, except of a curious word here and there. Yet Coleridge does have a significance in the history of poetic diction, less apparent in his three masterpieces than in his minor poems, a study of which reveals some points of considerable interest. Speaking generally, his diction is not original in the primary sense that he introduces many words or meanings not known before—though he is in fact a word-creator on a small scale; it is original rather in the sense that he revives words used once or twice by previous poets, giving them a more suggestive or individual effect. Coleridge was of course an omnivorous reader, and his poetic energy was seldom exerted to the full: the results of these facts are discernible in much of his diction, which has often the quality of creative reminiscence rather than of creativeness itself.

As an introduction to the more significant phases of Coleridge's poetic style, a brief mention may be made of his early *Songs of the Pixies* (1793).[1] Spenser is the presiding genius of this poem, which commemorates a rural expedition to the "Pixies' Parlour" in Devonshire, to which the author "conducted a party of young ladies; one of whom, of stature elegantly small, and of complexion colourless yet clear, was proclaimed the Faery Queen." The diction of the piece is luxuriant and full of reminiscence. There are words such as Spenser's *impurple*;[2] Shakespeare's *o'ercanopy*; Milton's *meek-eyed*; *fiery-tressed*,[3] perhaps a variant of Milton's *golden-tressed*; also *soul-subduing*, an epithet

---

[1]Quotations are from *The Poetical Works of Samuel Taylor Coleridge*, ed. J. Dykes Campbell (London, 1925).
[2]*Empurple* in Spenser.
[3]*Tressed* is dissyllabic, which the *O.E.D.* notes as a poetic peculiarity.

found in seventeenth-century poetry.[4] More recent expressions are the favourite *pensive* (twice) and a specimen of the "night-imagery" already mentioned: "Sorceress of the ebon throne." The whole poem, without being highly original, is an elegant piece of work in both fancy and style—perhaps the crowning poem of Coleridge's early youth.

About the same time signs of his mature style begin to appear in his more serious verse. His memory had stored up numerous felicities of the rarer kind encountered in his reading, and he could draw upon these for novel effects in his own compositions. Some of the distinctive elements in Coleridge's diction are "first-repeated" words: or if not literally "first-repeated," at least "semi-original." Such words are rarer than those already quoted from the *Songs of the Pixies*, and therefore finer. For instance, in the *Lines, on an Autumnal Evening* (?1793) we may see a result of Coleridge's selective reading in the line:

> Mine eye reverted views that cloudless day.

The first record in the *Oxford Dictionary* of this particular sense of "reverted" (applied to eyes, looks, etc.) is in the poetry of Gray, who uses it more than once. Coleridge uses it several times, most effectively in his lines *Time, Real and Imaginary* (?1815) in which he describes an "endless race" between "a sister and a brother," "two lovely children":

> This far outstript the other;
> Yet ever runs she with reverted face,

for the boy is blind: the epithet is strikingly felicitous in its context. A word which became characteristic in romantic description is *skiey*—a favourite with Shelley. Invented, apparently, by Shakespeare, who couples it with "influences," its descriptive value was discovered by Coleridge, who uses it in *Lines, on an Autumnal Evening*, and in more memorable contexts later. A special interest is attached to the word *undersong*. First recorded in *The Shepheardes Calender* (August) in the sense of a musical accompaniment, it became a traditional word in pastoral poetry, being used by Drayton, Browne, Dryden,[5] and Philips. When writing a set of Spenserian stanzas to Joseph Cottle, Coleridge revives this Spenserian word in a characteristic piece of romantic description, giving it a novel effect:

> But th' unceasing rill
> To the soft Wren or Lark's descending trill
> Murmurs sweet *undersong* 'mid jasmin bowers.

[4]E.g., in J. Beaumont's *Psyche*, 1648 (*O.E.D.*).
[5]In translating Virgil's Third Eclogue:
> incipe, Damoeta; tu deinde sequere, Menacla.
> alternis dicetis; amant alterna Camenae.

It even retained a trace of its origin when Wordsworth repeated it in his fireside fancy of the kettle's "undersong," for the phrase occurs in that set of four sonnets (*Personal Talk*) in which he pays special tribute to "heavenly Una with her milk-white Lamb." Among other words revived by Coleridge are *cedarn*;[6] *arborous*;[7] *jargoning*[8] (of birds' twittering). The current associations of *lonesome*, which, as the *Oxford Dictionary* notes, is now used "chiefly in emotional sense" are perhaps due to Coleridge. It is true that the word was so used by Nicholas Rowe in *The Fair Penitent* (1703), but the remembered and influential passage is from *The Ancient Mariner*, "Like one, that on a lonesome road." Wordsworth's similar use of the word in the next year (1799) in his *Influence of Natural Objects*, "A lonely scene more lonesome," confirms the impression that its modern emotional sense is due to the association of the two poets at this time, with a priority claim going to Coleridge.

We might expect that the writer who has added so many useful words to the vocabulary of philosophical exposition should have done something of the same kind for poetry. Coleridge's original additions to the poetic vocabulary are, however, more characteristic than numerous. He was, perhaps, too well aware of the existing wealth of the diction of English poetry to feel any strong impulse to add to it. Occasionally he invented compounds such as *ice-falls* and *sun-thaw*.[9] He was fond of diminutives, and apparently formed a new one, *cloudlet*.[10] The metaphorical use of *lidless*,[11] in the sense of "ever-watchful," is also his. Especially interesting is his descriptive formation *Cloudland*:[12] the word symbolizes that closer intimacy of the imagination with the vaster fields of Nature, which was one of the conquests of Romantic poetry.

SHELLEY

The poetry of Shelley does not fit easily into any historical sequence, and what is true of the essential spirit of his work is true also of much of the diction in which it is embodied. Shelley, at once impassioned and imaginative, a lover of philosophical abstractions and impatient of the slow processes of history, formed a diction largely of his own, which is exquisitely fitted to his finest conceptions and at the same time aloof from a great part of human life. It combines two contradictory qualities corresponding to the opposing elements in Shelley's poetic character,

[6]*Comus: Kubla Khan.*
[7]*Paradise Lost*, V.137: *To the Rev. George Coleridge.*
[8]*The Ancient Mariner*; "obs. from 15th to 19th Century" (*O.E.D.*).
[9]*Hymn before Sun-Rise, in the Vale of Chamouni* (1802).
[10]*First Advent of Love* (*O.E.D.*).   [11]*Ode on the Departing Year.*
[12]*Fancy in Nubibus* (1819).

recognized by Arnold's image of the "ineffectual angel." It is possible for the reader to respond to the "harmonious madness" which flows from his lips, and yet to experience a misgiving like that which Asia expresses to Panthea in *Prometheus Unbound* (II.i.108–9):

> Thou speakest, but thy words
> Are as the air.[13]

But the isolation of Shelley is only relative: it is not nearly so complete as that of Blake. In the genealogy of English poets, Shelley's ancestry may be semi-mythical, yet he has affinities with both Shakespeare and Milton, and his descendants are in the regular line—in Swinburne and Francis Thompson he has, himself, direct inheritors. Again, Shelley's diction appears differently in different aspects. In pure lyric, and in certain forms of imaginative description, it is sometimes perfection itself, but for the more realistic description of Nature, and of the passions, it is ethereally ineffective.

It is relevant to notice that Shelley was by far the least Spenserian of the five chief Romantic poets. Spenser, it is true, is an honoured name with him: he uses the historic stanza, and he was perhaps the first writer to revive the highly Spenserian word *faëry* in modern poetry.[14] But he writes nothing in the archaic Spenserian style, apart from a chance phrase in a moment of jest,[15] and in this respect he stands alone. Wordsworth wrote his *Stanzas* in the copy of Thomson's *Castle of Indolence*; Coleridge his *Lines in the Manner of Spenser*; Byron begins *Childe Harold's Pilgrimage* partly in the archaic Spenserian style; and Keats writes his *Imitation of Spenser*. One may see in each of these four compositions, even in Byron's, a mood of natural piety towards the common founder of four widely divergent poetic styles. In a more genial mood, such as that in which he wrote his *Letter to Maria Gisborne*, Shelley might have acknowledged that instinct of imitation which is a contributive source of originality. But his habitual preference was to emphasize the other side of the truth. To him, poets are the supreme originators—the creators of language itself (*Defence of Poetry*). It is, of course, obvious that in any poet's diction repetition must play a large part, and that originality consists largely in drawing on the right sources. This kind of originality Shelley is apt to disparage, and the result is that his style has the "tenuity" which all his readers notice. He repeats many words, it is true, but too often they are his own.

---

[13]References are to *The Poems of Shelley*, ed. Ingpen and Peck, 4 vols. (London and New York, 1927–8).

[14]*The Revolt of Islam*, Dedication, "To Mary—."

[15]See *Letter to Maria Gisborne*: "I'll leave, as Spenser says, 'with many mo,'" etc.

The foregoing remarks will indicate the line which will be followed in the criticism of Shelley's diction. Little need be said of certain passages in the unaccustomed field of drama in which he imitates speeches and parts of dialogue in almost the very words of *Lear* and *Macbeth*. He had little of the experience, and perhaps not much of the power, needed to create an individual style in tragedy. His own highly distinctive manner which is seen emerging even in the early *Queen Mab* is all that matters here. It may be viewed in two main aspects. There are the features which express the poetic temperament of Shelley—the emotional intensity, and the impatience of verbal artistry. There are other features—words and phrases—created in the exercise of his true imaginative function. "I am formed," he wrote in a letter to Godwin (Dec. 11, 1817), "to communicate the conceptions which result from considering either the moral or the material universe as a whole." It is when writing with this cosmic view, whether in brief passages or in entire poems, that Shelley creates his most vital words, those which give his style its keenest force and widest range of expressive power.

I

"When composition begins," Shelley tells us in the *Defence of Poetry*, "inspiration is already on the decline, and the most glorious poetry that has ever been communicated to the world is probably a feeble shadow of the original conception of the Poet." "The poem," says Shelley of his *Revolt of Islam*, "was produced by a series of thoughts which filled my mind with unbounded and sustained enthusiasm." This last statement, taken in conjunction with others of the same tenor, points to the intensity which is Shelley's general mood in composition: only at exceptional times does he write "in dejection." He is the poet of the infinite and the ideal, chafing against the limitations of his medium, and he writes in a mood of intense excitement or enthusiasm. The simplest way of expressing the infinite and the ideal—"the desire of the moth for the star"—is by the use of negatives; the simplest way of expressing enthusiasm is by superlatives. Shelley's ideal state for human beings is one of glorious negations (*Prom. Unbound*, III.iv.193–5):

> The loathsome mask has fallen, the Man remains—
> *Sceptreless*, free, *uncircumscribed*,—but man
> Equal, *unclassed*, *tribeless*, and *nationless*. . . .

He exults in the manifestations of liberty in nature: in "the *chainless* winds"; in the serenity of "*cloudless* skies and *windless* streams"; in "the deep, blue, *boundless* heaven" as a symbol of beauty; in the perfection of "*wordless* converse."[16] Negations also indicate the opposite of the ideal: as the Spirit of Beauty transforms "this dim vast vale of tears," so Emilia Viviani is the "veiled glory of this *lampless* universe" (*Epipsychidion*). In *Prometheus Unbound*, negative epithets form one of the conspicuous features of the style: he finds occasion for *sleepless, shapeless, moveless, tongueless, lidless, slumberless, printless, image- less, sunless, herbless, shoreless, bottomless, wingless.* "Unfathomable" is one of his most-used "infinite words": in *The Witch of Atlas* a lady's eyes are compared to "openings of *unfathomable* night"; in the same poem there are "*unfathomable* chasms" and caverns "yawning round *unfathomably*," also stars which "sparkled *unfathomably*." *Immeasur- able* is hardly less frequent in his poetry. To express the intensity of his conceptions, his favourite words are superlatives. "Serene" is not strong enough, he prefers "serenest": "*serenest* air," "*serenest* night," "*serenest* moon," "*serenest* sky."[17] So, too, we have "*profoundest* midnight," "*intensest* rime," even "*extremest* curve."[18] Every observant reader of Shelley will agree that such epithets are quite numerous enough to be regarded as a real characteristic of his style.

Shelley is not a minute observer, and his descriptions are often want- ing in distinctness. He is aware of this himself. "Once I was tremulously alive to tones and scenes," he wrote; "the habit of analyzing feelings . . . does not agree with this."[19] But though analysis may have weakened his power of observation, it did not conflict with his power of imagina- tion, and it is one of his rare qualities that in him passion and imagi- nation co-exist with an intense love of abstractions. It was, however, inevitable that being as he was, he should be apt to substitute an ideal beauty formed in his own mind for the real variety of Nature. The effect of this on his diction is to make it less finely discriminative than the language of good poetry usually is, and to encourage the repetition of certain typical words. He is, for instance, especially fond of the ambigu- ous word *purple*, and writes of *purple* waves, *purple* sky, *purple* clouds, the *purple* noon, *purple* seaweed, the *purple* sea, the "*purple* foun- tains" (*Revolt of Islam*, V.xxxviii) of the dawn. *Azure* is a rival of "purple." *Pavilion*, used metaphorically as a verb, appears in *Rosalind and Helen, The Cloud*, the *Ode to Liberty, Adonais, The Sensitive Plant, Hellas*, and no doubt elsewhere. Its frequency illustrates the fact that Shelley's poetic diction is a splendid but limited vocabulary, which is renewed from one poem to another, not so much by a natural growth

[16]*Mont Blanc; Prometheus Unbound*, I.i.681, II.i.114, II.i.52.
[17]*Prometheus Unbound*, I.i.64; *A Summer-Evening Churchyard, Lechlade, Gloucestershire; Ode to Liberty; Witch of Atlas*, lix.
[18]*Stanzas—April 1814; Witch of Atlas*, xliv; *Alastor*, 390.
[19]To Miss Hitchener, July 26, 1811; in Dowden's *Life of Shelley*, I, 167.

corresponding to the poet's expanding grasp of the sights and sounds of nature, as by fresh combinations within its own boundary, quickened into life by the increasing intensity of his inner experience. A deliberate search for new verbal effects was no part of Shelley's program. Since he liked compounds formed on the basis of the word "wingèd" (a taste strengthened no doubt by his reading of Aeschylus, who shared it with him), he repeats them in passage after passage: *spirit-wingèd, tempest-wingèd, seraph-wingèd, thought-wingèd, morning-wingèd, splendour-wingèd*, and the like. *Pyramids* and *pinnacles, aërial* and *tremulous* recur with a like frequency. Shelley's descriptions often have an effect of radiant unreality. It is as if mountains and forests were turned into a mirage, or the cloud-capped towers and gorgeous palaces into an insubstantial pageant.

II

This, however, is only the negative side of Shelley's diction. Taken on its own merits it has a unique beauty which certain minds, more or less akin to his own, perceive at once. To others, accustomed to the more concrete forms of poetic idealism, a certain amount of study may be necessary before its beauty is wholly revealed. To enter into its spirit it is necessary to grasp the full meaning of his words already quoted: "I am formed to communicate the conceptions which result from considering either the moral or the material universe as a whole." Shelley's poetry, in its most creative moments, entirely confirms this revealing piece of self-criticism. His strength as a descriptive poet lay in producing a sense of the interrelations of the various parts of the universe, especially of the solar and stellar heavens with the sublunar earth. In this respect his poetry has an analogy with the work of the great Romantic painter Turner in its latest phase, of which a critic has written: "He dissolved the foundations of nature—the concrete object—in veils of gold and white, of scarlet and emerald. . . . By the magic of light, Turner unites earth and sun and all heavenly bodies, and makes us feel that nature is . . . a part of the universe."[20] The comparison between Shelley's poetry in some of its most characteristic passages and the work of Turner here described is by no means fanciful or far-fetched. For example, the description of the sunrise in the *Lines written among the Euganean Hills* reads exactly like one of Turner's sunrises translated into the words and rhythms of poetry.

Our subject is the diction not the imagery of poetry, but in the style of any great poet the vital words are often compressed images, and it

[20]Thomas Craven, *The Story of Painting* (New York, 1943).

is instructive to examine in some of Shelley's work the fully expanded images which were at times—as a rule, subsequently—compressed into a narrower compass, often of single words. For example, in the early *Queen Mab* (240–3), written when the poet was only eighteen, he thus describes the downward view towards our earthly globe of a spirit conveyed through the upper regions of space:

> The sea no longer was distinguished; earth
> Appear'd a vast and shadowy sphere;
> The sun's unclouded orb
> Rolled through the black concave.

Such a passage explains Shelley's fondness for epithets like *spherèd* and *orbèd*—"the *spherèd* skies," "the *orbèd* world"[21]—which occur over and over again, for his mind is embracing the material world not indeed as an astronomical whole, but as a unit included within our ordinary imaginative vision. In the same manner, a simile in *The Revolt of Islam* (V.i),

> The City's moon-lit[22] spires and myriad lamps,
> Like stars in a sublunar sky did glow,

prepares us for the use of the word *star* as perhaps the most frequent of all the elements in Shelley's descriptive imagery. So, too, the beautiful lines in *Alastor* (435–8):

> Far below,
> *Like clouds suspended in an emerald sky,*
> The ash and the acacia floating hang,
> Tremulous and pale

prepare us for the single expressive words which symbolize the marriage of heaven and earth in the poet's imagination.

"Earth, ocean, air" are indeed a "beloved brotherhood." Just as the "sun *floats* up the sky," and the solid land of Lombardy is a "*waveless* plain" (*Euganean Hills*), so the things on earth that gleam and sparkle are "stars." "River-buds among the sedge" are *starry*; the drops dashed from breaking sea-waves are "*star*-showers"; there are "*stars*" of "golden dew" and blossoms which "*star* the winds with points of coloured light."[23] *Star-inwoven* and *star-wrought* are two of his favourite epithets; *starbeam* occurs over and over again. The moon and moonlight play a scarcely inferior part. His vocabulary is enriched with new or rare compounds such as *moonrise* (an early use) and *moon-glimpse*;

[21]*Adonais; Prometheus Unbound,* I.i.69.
[22]This is an earlier example of "moon-lit" than the earliest given by the *O.E.D.* (from Tennyson).
[23]*The Question; Stanzas, in Dejection; Prometheus Unbound,* II.i.130–1, III.iii.138.

and he forms the beautiful epithet *moonlight-coloured* for the white blossoms of the May tree.[24] His imaginative intercourse with Nature makes him a contributor to the vocabulary of description to which nineteenth-century writers were constantly adding. *Sun-fire, sun-gleam, sun-bow*[25] are apparently original formations of his. He is also credited by the *Oxford Dictionary* with the first use of *sunlit* after having already introduced the attributive use of *sunlight*.[26] *Sea-blooms, sea-buds, sea-murmur*[27] are perhaps no more than nonce-words, but they are typical of their creator.

Less decorative, but equally essential to the expression of the poet's conceptions are the words which suggest the interrelation of the forces of Nature. This principle may be asserted by plain statement as in *Love's Philosophy*:

> Nothing in the world is single:
>   All things by a law divine
> In one another's being mingle,

or it may be suggested in a single significant word, like the *interpenetrated* of the *Lines written among the Euganean Hills*: all things in vast panorama seen by the poet, land and sky, the Alps and the "dimly islanded" Apennines

> Interpenetrated lie
> By the glory of the sky.

So too the air is *ambient* or *world-surrounding*; darkness is *circumambient*; the ocean is *circumfluous*.[28] Such words, occurring frequently, are an indication of Shelley's consistent vision of the one in the many.

A few miscellaneous points of interest remain to be mentioned. No word in the English vocabulary bears so distinct a stamp of Shelley's imagination as the adjective *weird*. The only accepted sense before his time had been that which it has in "the weird sisters" (i.e., the "sisters of fate"). The current modern meaning emerges distinctly in passages like,

> Some said, I was a fiend from my *weird* cave,

or

> A tale more fit for the *weird* winter nights—
> Than for these garish summer days.[29]

[24]*Revolt of Islam*, II.x; *Hellas*, 633; *The Question*.
[25]*Ode to Liberty*; *Queen Mab*, III (the only earlier example in the *O.E.D.*, dated 1240, has a different sense); letter to Peacock (prose), July 22, 1816.
[26]*Triumph of Life*; *Euganean Hills*.
[27]*Ode to the West Wind*; *Prince Athanase*; *Euganean Hills*.
[28]*Alastor*; *To Constantia, Singing*; *Queen Mab*; *Witch of Atlas*, xxxiii.
[29]*Revolt of Islam*, IX.viii; *Witch of Atlas*, lxxviii.

This new "romantic" word quickly passed on to other writers.[30] In like manner, Shelley enriched his own style from the work of his contemporaries, especially from Wordsworth and Coleridge. However much he came to dislike Wordsworth as a "renegade" he was deeply influenced by some of his poetry. For instance, one notes in *Alastor* the phrase "natural piety" from the lines prefixed to the Immortality Ode, also "obstinate questionings" from the Ode itself, as well as the phrase "too deep for tears," which is printed as a quotation. Shelley, however, had none of Wordsworth's democratic tastes in language. His own vocabulary is in a large measure aristocratic: such "poetic" words as *main* for "sea," and *visage* for "face" are, on occasion, characteristically preferred to "the real language of men." Only in *The Cenci* does he modify his usual practice in accordance with the needs and nature of drama. "I have," he says, in the Preface to that work, "written more carelessly; that is, without an over-fastidious and learned choice of words. In this respect I entirely agree with those modern critics who assert that in order to move men to true sympathy we must use the familiar language of men."

KEATS

It is extraordinary how prominent a place in the history of our poetic style is taken by the work of Keats. The extent of his poetry is not large—there are only the three volumes published in his lifetime, and the posthumous pieces; yet to remove his name and his influence from our literature would be like removing one of the great Venetians from the galleries of European painting. He is the most opulent colourist in our literature. Picturesqueness has been a quality of our poetry since the time of Shakespeare, and in Keats it reaches its culmination. It is sometimes said that our poets are too much given to "verbal felicities," that they are too romantic. Yet without wealth of imagination, there is no value in clearness of design. And, on a broad view of Keats's work and character, it is evident that he was not content to luxuriate in the redundancy of his fancy. An excess of verbal elaboration certainly conflicts with the value of *Endymion* as a narrative, but the poem is frankly put forward as "a feverish attempt, rather than a deed accomplished" (Preface). To its countless poetic lines and expressions, we may surely apply the merciful comment of Dr. Johnson on another work: "Superfluities so beautiful, who would wish away?"

But of course, Keats is not simply a coiner of beautiful phrases.

[30]E.g., Keats, *Lamia*, 107.

Behind the lines of the poems, there is the character of the man. Keats's words are not only beautiful, they are intensely alive. He did not simply make phrases like "the far-foamed sands" or "cool-rooted flowers": he wrote the whole of the *Ode to a Nightingale*. Some of his finest passages are those in which the language is simplest, and he is as skilful in his use of the right word as of the rare word. He "looked on fine phrases like a lover," yet no one wished more ardently to wed poetry to life. His thought soon begins to reveal the outlines of a noble humanism. "Scenery is fine," he wrote, "but human nature is finer" (letter of March 13, 1818). It is the keenness and the depth of his poetic experience, and his awareness of the tensions within it, that give his work its lasting significance and his diction its vital power.

The verbal art of Keats changed and developed greatly during the three years or so of his poetic career, but two main phases may be distinguished. In the first, he is striving intensely after the pictorial phrase. In the words of his famous letter of May 3, 1818, he is still, for the most part, in "the Chamber of Maiden-Thought," and is "intoxicated with the light and the atmosphere." The volume of 1817 and most of *Endymion* (1818) belong to this earlier period. But already the Chamber is becoming "gradually darken'd," while he sees that "on all sides of it many doors are set open—but all dark—all leading to dark passages." At the same time there is a "sharpening" of his "vision into the heart and nature of Man"—convincing his "nerves that the world is full of Misery and Heartbreak, Pain, Sickness and Oppression." Hence, the faults of *Endymion* will not be repeated. Design will be preferred to tangled detail, and beauty, seen in its true relation to the rest of life and no longer as a tinted mist enveloping the whole, will grow at once simpler and more profound. It is in this later mood that the best of Keats's poems were written. The diction becomes more luminous, and at the same time, emotionally more real.

I

For Keats, as for many men of his generation, the golden age of English poetry was the Elizabethan. Unlike Coleridge and Shelley, he had no wide culture to temper his enthusiasm, and his study of Shakespearian English was as impassioned as Chatterton's self-immersion in the two preceding centuries. But Keats had none of Chatterton's antiquarian tastes. He was a modernist, and he loved the Elizabethans because they "taught him language." Except in a short passage of *The Eve of St. Mark*, he never used a style which was avowedly archaic. His early Spenserian stanzas are, like most imitations of the poet, more tense and compact than their fluid originals. In the art of grafting Elizabethan expressions upon a modern idiom, his chief teacher was Leigh Hunt, whose *Story of Rimini* was not a fortunate model. But Keats's lapses in taste were not so serious as Hunt's, and the critics had much less reason to include him in "the Cockney School." Of the few vulgarisms in Keats's diction, I shall say little, for they are not important. Nor shall I follow those scholars who have traced so many of his rare words to their sources in Spenser, Shakespeare, Drayton, Chapman, and other Elizabethans. For information of this kind, Dr. de Selincourt's edition of Keats and Sir Sidney Colvin's great biography are invaluable. My purpose is to begin with Keats's diction in his earliest poems and to trace the ripening of his art which proceeded in three years with such amazing rapidity. On this point several things remain to be added, even after the excellent remarks of Dr. H. W. Garrod, M. R. Ridley, D. W. Rannie, and many others.

From the first, it was Keats's instinct to embody new sensations in new words. Every poet, and almost every writer, has this ambition in some measure: but what is, at its lowest, no more than a technical problem was for him an impassioned struggle, with some likeness, towards the end, to a feverish race against time. His love of Nature was almost an intoxication. The discovery that this feeling held undetermined possibilities when made articulate in language was the beginning of his life as a poet.

> He ne'er is crown'd
> With immortality, who fears to follow
> Where airy voices lead.[31]

Keats's chief technical necessity, apart from ampler and less rigid forms of verse than those which still survived from the eighteenth century, was a reservoir of words to express new subtleties of sensation, new images. He discovered a resource in the liberties of Elizabethan grammar, which allowed the formation of new words, too fleeting or perhaps too strange for inclusion in the dictionary, but valuable for the more wayward purposes of the poet. In his earlier poems he took too many liberties with the language, producing at times effects of homely or childish simplicity. One fertile source of words was nouns formed from verbs, either by the addition of the termination *-ing*, or by the uninflected use of the stem. Thus, in *Sleep and Poetry* we notice—in addition to such accepted verbal nouns as *uplifting*—expressions like "aerial *limning*," "soft *floatings*," "the tender *greening* of April meadows."

---

[31]*Endymion*, II.211–13. Quotations are from *The Poetical Works of John Keats* (Oxford, 1920).

The practice continues in *Endymion*, with expressions like "a *yielding up*, a *cradling*"; a *conflicting*; "spicy *fannings*"; *lispings*; lute-*breathings; hoverings; shadowings; snortings; parchings; gulphing*; thunder-*gloomings; illuminings; pleasurings*. Uninflected verbal nouns are less numerous, but they are often made conspicuous by being coupled with an epithet. They occur in the later as well as the earlier poems, as in "with glad *exclaim*"; "with silent *creep*"; "honey-*feel* of bliss"; "silver *ramble*"; "the deadly *feel*"; "the *pierce* of woe"; "with fierce *convulse*"; "with cruel *pierce*." New or rare agent-nouns with the termination *-er* are very conspicuous, especially in the early poems, e.g. *spangler, mingler, hummer, budder, laughers, whisperer, lispers, hearkener*, "pale *unrelenter*"; and occasionally they appear in clusters of several together, as in *Sleep and Poetry* (11–16):

> [Sleep,] Soft closer of our eyes!
> Low murmurer of tender lullabies!
> Light hoverer around our happy pillows!
> Wreather of poppy buds, and weeping willows!
> Silent entangler of a beauty's tresses!
> Most happy listener!

He uses many new, or rare, adjectives formed from nouns by the termination *-y*, to produce picturesque phrases like "*lawny* fields," "*pebbly* water," "*liny* marble," "*nervy* knees," "*bowery* nest," "*spangly* light," "*sluicy* sands," and so on. He is also fond of adverbs from the participles of verbs which often fit into the fluid texture of his verse though they would have ill suited the style of the classical school, such as *blushingly, cherishingly, dyingly, drowningly, hoveringly, hurryingly, tremblingly*;

> Fearing to move or speak, she look'd so *dreamingly*.[32]

Other favourite types again are adjectives with the termination *-ful*, such as *spleenful, lifeful, freakful*; and with the termination *-ant*, such as *couchant, perceant, penetrant, discrepant*.

Keats's use of past participles provides several features of interest. First, he increases his vocabulary by the occasional nonce-use of intransitive verbs in a transitive sense. His purpose, again, is to produce a picturesque effect not to be gained by a commoner word. Thus,

> the whisp'ring roof
> Of leaves and *trembled* blossoms

of the *Ode to Psyche* is a phrase which would lose something by the

---

[32]*Eve of St. Agnes*, xxxiv. Such words are common in Shakespeare, e.g., *reportingly*; also in Browning.

substitution of "trembling." There is a similar advantage in "with horrid warning *gapèd* wide," compared with "gaping." There are many phrases, too, like "the *dinn'd* air," "the *rustled* air." Secondly, in forming quasi-participles from nouns, Keats prefers to give the termination -*ed* its syllabic value in the metre. Here he is following the Shakespearian precedent (*M.N.D.*, II.i.85) in a line like:

> Or in the beached margent of the sea.

Since the seventeenth century, this termination had been becoming mute except in poetic or archaic use. Hence, in nineteenth-century verse a phrase like "*globèd* peonies" certainly stimulates imagination more than "*glob'd* peonies." A glance at any of Keats's longer poems will show how numerous are his picturesque phrases of this type. In *Lamia*, for instance, one finds: "*hoofèd* Satyrs," "*wingèd* heels," "*chillèd* hand," "*slabbèd* steps," "*wide-archèd* grace," "*aislèd*[33] place." Such are the main features of the grammar of Keats's diction.

II

In the life of Keats there was, as I have said, a perpetual ripening of the poetic powers. The immature *Endymion*, so rich in promise, so imperfect in execution, was followed, almost at once, by some of his maturest work. *Endymion* is a mine of verbal wealth awaiting the hand of the refiner. Some passages are, of course, already perfect, and have no need of further polish. One is the first line, so happily altered in wording by an afterthought.[34] But most of the final touches were to be given in later poems. Keats simply remembered words and phrases of half-realized poetry in *Endymion* and recast them with slight changes in the work he was collecting for his volume of 1820. I will give a few instances. "*Wailful* gnat" is a sketch for the complete picture in *Autumn*: "Then in a *wailful* choir the small gnats mourn." "*Gordian'd*" used of braided hair recurs, with more force, in the description of the snake in *Lamia* (I.47): "She was a *gordian* shape of dazzling hue." "The *slabbèd* margin of a well" contains an epithet used more picturesquely in *Lamia* (I.380–2):

> a silver lamp, whose phosphor glow
> Reflected in the *slabbèd* steps below,
> Mild as a star in water.

---

[33]In text without accent.
[34]See Sidney Colvin, *John Keats*, p. 176 and note.

"*Wakeful* rest" reappears, more effectively, as "*wakeful* swoon," in *St. Agnes*. "Chill aguish gloom" contains the epithets but not the magic of the picture in *The Eve of St. Mark*:

> The *chilly* sunset faintly told
> Of unmatur'd green vallies cold,
> Of the green thorny bloomless hedge,
> Of rivers new with spring-tide sedge,
> Of primroses by shelter'd rills,
> And daisies on the *aguish* hills.

I have used the word "picturesque" of Keats's diction, but it is not an adequate expression. The visual element was predominant in his imagination, yet he never simplified poetry into word-painting. His descriptions, even in their sensuous aspect, appeal to more than the eye. His best passages, indeed, are not pictures but poems. He would make us *see* and *feel* the objects he describes: but still more, he would have us conceive them as living things. Many of his most vivid pictures hover on the brink of a myth, like that of the almost personified wave (*Endymion*, II.348–50):

> Old ocean rolls a lengthened wave to the shore,
> Down whose green back the short-liv'd foam, all hoar,
> Bursts gradual, *with a wayward indolence*.

It is the same in the lines on the sea in the sonnet "Bright star":

> The moving waters at their *priestlike task*
> Of pure ablution round earth's human shores.

Here the effect is of an entire image in which each word plays an integral part. On a lower plane of poetry are some of Keats's "lonely words," yet these too are often humanly suggestive as well as picturesque. Mr. D. W. Rannie, for instance, makes an excellent comment on the word *vineyarded* in the description (*Isabella*, xvii) of the two grasping brothers:

>   self-retired
> In hungry pride and gainful cowardice,
>   As two close Hebrews in that land inspired,
> Paled in and *vineyarded* from beggar-spies.

Here, he says, besides the pictorial image, there is the suggestion of the vineyard as the oriental symbol of riches: hence, the misers' wealth is a selfish barrier against the importunacy of their fellow-men.[35] Of Keats's compound words such as "*far-foamed* sands," "*sapphire-*

---

[35]*Essays and Studies by Members of the English Association*, III (1912), 98.

region'd star," "*moth-time,*" a good deal has been written elsewhere: they are, as Mr. Logan Pearsall Smith well says, "poems in miniature," and show an exquisite sense of language unsurpassed in its kind.

III

Hyperion, though it contains some of Keats's maturest poetry, did not satisfy him, and he left it a fragment. The reason most commonly repeated by critics is Keats's own admission, in his letter of September 21, 1819, to John Hamilton Reynolds, that "there were too many Miltonic inversions in it." This sentence has, I think, been given an undue prominence, while other self-criticisms of the poet in the same letter have been left unnoticed (not, of course, by writers so penetrating as J. Middleton Murry). The Miltonic inversions in *Hyperion* are not, in truth, very numerous. More important are the poet's other objections. The attempt to recapture Milton's style brought to light certain truths of which he was unaware when he began the poem. "Miltonic verse," he continues in the letter, "cannot be written but in an artful or rather artist's humour," and he proceeds to suggest that while some lines in the poem have "the true voice of feeling," others show only "the false beauty proceeding from art." Keats never had the power, and he now discovers that he has not the will to write an epic in a style which owes so much to literature as *Paradise Lost.* And he also feels, for the first time, that Milton's style is not a model of true English. He prefers Chatterton, "the purest writer in the English Language," adding a moment later that "English ought to be kept up." These, then, are the real reasons for the abandonment of *Hyperion*: the style is unequal; there is too much "art" in the poem; the language is not English of the purest kind.

The influence of Milton was an important episode in the development of Keats's art, but as Mr. Middleton Murry has shown, Keats was not fundamentally a poet of the Miltonic order. The true lodestar was Shakespeare. Milton's example, nevertheless, helped Keats to break free from many faults. It cured him of his Elizabethan redundancy and of his juvenile false taste. A comparison between *Endymion* and *Hyperion* shows that Keats thoroughly learned these negative lessons. In the second poem there are no homely expressions like "early budders" or "baaing vanities"; no vulgarities like "sea-flirt." But of Milton's positive merits, half at least were beyond him. His store of images was perhaps as great, but how could he rival Milton's knowledge of books and men? He could imagine scenes, he could compose half-lyrical passages in the highest order of solemn beauty. But the fighting speech of Enceladus is mere rant, and the "muster-rolls of names" are laboured. In fact, Keats is overstraining himself in about half the poem. And when he glanced back and found he had written phrases like "my lucent empire," "in opaque element," "his beard shook horrid," "tumults dire" he felt, no doubt, that he was succumbing to an alien spell. It was repugnant to him to use any phrase which did not answer vividly to his own experience or imagination.

IV

The Eve of St. Agnes is technically a more successful poem than *Hyperion,* and it is one of the masterpieces of poetic expression in the language. The poem might well serve as a starting-point for a treatise on the whole art of poetry. I wish, however, to emphasize only the stage it marks in the development of Keats's diction. In picturesqueness it equals any of his poems, earlier or later: but it also shows a quality which, though latent perhaps in all poetry, is present here in a conspicuous degree: the quality of symbolism. My attention to this aspect of the poem was first drawn by the frequent occurrence of the word *silver.* I then began to search for other key-words corresponding to the main currents of the poetic conception. The descriptions appear to be penetrated by the force of conflicting passions, and it is this that makes the language so effective and so harmonious.

The main theme of *St. Agnes* is a contrast between two opposites— a favourite conception in the poetry of Keats. There is a recurring conflict between the *warmth* of love and youth on the one hand, and the *cold* of chastity and age on the other. There is a slighter secondary theme of *silence* as symbolical of true bliss in contrast with the *noise* of revelry. These themes tend to influence the poet's choice of language; or, to regard the matter from another angle, they focus his mind on those aspects of the imaginary scene which are symbolic. We are, in fact, at a point where poetic invention and poetic expression are simply different aspects of the same thing. Let us see briefly how the two main themes are indicated by certain key-words: and how, conversely, these words are charged with a special power by their latent symbolism.

The note on which *St. Agnes* begins and ends is one of triumphant cold, a cold so intense that it subdues even well-feathered and warm-coated creatures—the owl, the hare, the sheep—and freezes the warm breath of man. The theme of coldness is continued to the fourth stanza, when it is momentarily interrupted by the secondary theme of intrusive music, played to welcome the noisy guests:

> The silver, *snarling* trumpets 'gan to chide.

To the absorbed Madeline ("St. Agnes' charmèd maid") the strains mean nothing at all:

> The music, yearning like a God in pain,
> She scarcely heard.

Next enters Porphyro "with heart on fire," who is taken by his good angel (Angela) to

> a little moonlight room,
> Pale, lattic'd, *chill*, and *silent* as a tomb.

Hearing of Madeline and the "enchantments *cold*," his passion breaks out with renewed ardour:

> Sudden a thought came like a full-blown rose,
> *Flushing* his brow, and in his pained heart
> Made purple riot.

He takes "covert" in the maiden's chamber, "silken, *hush'd*, and chaste," which Madeline shortly enters, having conducted the aged Angela to a place of quiet safety ("a safe, level *matting*") by the light of a silver taper. Now comes the pictorial climax of the poem in which the cold moonlight, shining through Madeline's window, produces a miracle of warmth and colour, a harmony of silver and rose:

> Full on this casement shone the *wintry* moon,
> And threw *warm gules* on Madeline's fair breast,
> As down she knelt for heaven's grace and boon;
> *Rose-bloom* fell on her hands, together prest,
> And on her *silver* cross soft amethyst.

Madeline, unrobing herself, unclasps "her *warmed* jewels," and then the thematic conflict is renewed:

> Soon, trembling in her soft and *chilly* nest,
> In sort of wakeful swoon, perplex'd she lay,
> Until the *poppied warmth* of sleep oppress'd
> Her soothed limbs, and soul fatigued away.

For a moment, the silence of the scene is broken by the counter-theme:

> The boisterous, midnight, festive clarion,
> The kettle-drum, and far-heard clarinet,
> Affray his ears, though but in dying tone:—
> The hall door shuts again, and all the noise is gone.

Meantime, Porphyro prepares a feast of delicacies in baskets "of wreathed silver,"

> Filling the *chilly* room with perfume light,

and seats himself passionately by the side of the chastely sleeping Madeline:

> Thus whispering, his *warm*, unnerved arm
> Sank in her pillow. Shaded was her dream
> By the dusk curtains:—'twas a midnight charm
> Impossible to melt as *iced* stream.

When Madeline awakes, and the lovers embrace, Porphyro is "flush'd, and like a throbbing star": she is his "silver shrine." Outside "the *iced* gusts still rave and beat," but the lovers escape to their home across the "*southern* moors," while the bedesman is left, forgotten, among his "ashes *cold*."

The first impression left by a study of the diction of *St. Agnes* is one of complicated harmony and symbolism. Naturally, the analysis might be pursued further than I have carried it here, but beyond a certain point it becomes too subtle to be handled profitably. The complete merging of poetic conception with poetic expression was the goal towards which Keats's instincts were always leading him—and this will become clearer in the remarks which I have to make about the Odes.

v

The Odes of Keats occupy a unique position in English poetry. An inner ring of three, though they may contain minute blemishes, are among the most intense expressions of beauty in the language. These are the *Nightingale,* the *Grecian Urn,* and *Autumn.* Two others, *Psyche* and *Melancholy,* contain passages of great beauty, but are clearly unequal. One or two odes stand on the border of the group: *Indolence,* which has some fine passages side by side with weak ones; "Bards of Passion," which is slight, and without the intensity of the typical odes; and *Maia,* which is only a fragment. A few inferior pieces called odes, may be omitted altogether. By the general term Odes, I mean the finest members of the group, together with those portions of the others which have the same significant quality.

The Odes are the maturest expression, in poetry, of Keats's spiritual experience: the whole of his poetic striving culminated in the substance and style of these poems. Other essential aspects of his thought are expressed in his letters and in *The Fall of Hyperion.* But the Odes express indirectly, and more profoundly, the same spiritual truths as are embodied in his best letters, the second *Hyperion,* and—let us add—in his life itself. For as Keats himself said (letter of Feb. 14, 1819), "a man's life of any worth is a continual allegory." Like all great poetry the Odes arise from a spiritual tension. As long as that tension continues the poet is dumb: with its relaxation, there is a release of words, and the words, like the source from which they flow, are intense. The classical but summary description of the process is Wordsworth's sentence: poetry takes its origin from emotion recollected in tranquillity.

The fundamental tension in Keats's mind at the time when he was writing the Odes arose from the conflict he felt between life and death. This universal experience was intensified in his own case by his poetic imagination on the one side and the facts of his life on the other. To enlarge his sense of life there were his consciousness of power, his ambition, and his "vast idea": to sharpen his sense of death there was his brother's sickness followed by his own, and of course the fearless and penetrative power of his imagination.[36] The other forms of tension are subsidiary to this, and are really only aspects of the same thing. The one uppermost in his mind was an agonizing insight into the nature of beauty—eternal in its essence, yet fleeting and frail in its forms. Beauty is Truth, yet there is a tragic truth at the heart of Beauty. The very passion for beauty compels the poet to probe it to its core. A similar tension is the awareness of Pleasure and Pain as subtly related to each other, and at times almost indistinguishable. Lamia in the poem (I. 191–2) was

> of sciential brain
> To unperplex bliss from its neighbour pain.

Dimly seen behind these perceptions was the great truth adumbrated in the last lines of *Hyperion*—that of death as the gate to life. Less poetically but more directly, this idea is expressed in the final couplet of the sonnet of March, 1819:

> Verse, Fame, and Beauty are intense indeed,
> But Death intenser—Death is Life's high meed.

We will consider first three pieces in which the absence of any spiritual tension or its slackness produces a total effect which falls short of the height attained in the finest odes. The *Fragment of an Ode to Maia* is in a style which Arnold would have called "akin to the antique." It is an early work (1818), and expresses a naturalistic or pagan attitude towards death: the style is correspondingly serene rather than intense. The poet aspires to the "vigour" of bards "who *died content* on pleasant sward, Leaving great verse unto a little clan," and his own song

> should die away
> Content as theirs,
> Rich in the simple worship of a day.

[36]See also his letter to Miss Brawne, July 25, 1819: "I have two luxuries to brood over in my walks, your Loveliness and the hour of my death."

The *Ode to Psyche*, also early, is lacking in complete harmony of style. The opening is in a picturesque narrative manner which, though exquisite of its kind, is not the most intimate poetry. Only at the fiftieth line do we hear the authentic note of Keats's great moments, and it is precisely then that the tension explicitly appears:

> Yes, I will be thy priest, and build a fane
>   In some untrodden region of my mind,
> Where branched thoughts, new grown with *pleasant pain,*
>   Instead of pines shall murmur in the wind.

There follow immediately two lines on pine-trees justly praised by Ruskin for their expressive conciseness, but at this point the tension is slackened and so remains till the end of the poem. The *Ode on Indolence* might seem, by its subject, to express a mood of relaxed tension:

> Pain had no sting, and pleasure's wreath no flower.

And this line does in fact express the true spirit of the ode except for a moment when the alien figures, Love, Ambition, and Poesy, break in upon the poet's indolence. *Indolence* is but a faint shadow of the greater odes: the three "phantoms" are bidden to depart, and the poem ends with an empty stanza—empty, for the poet has indolently renounced poetic effort and called his Muse a "demon."

The *Ode on Melancholy* is little inferior to the greatest of the group. The central conflicts of experience from which the poetry of Keats drew its power are brought together in four lines on Melancholy which are among the most penetrating the poet ever wrote:

> She dwells with Beauty—Beauty that must die;
>   And Joy, whose hand is ever at his lips
> Bidding adieu; and aching Pleasure nigh,
>   Turning to Poison while the bee-mouth sips.

The *Ode to a Nightingale* begins on a note of ecstasy which is also one of pain ("My heart aches") and its fiery progress ends as it must with "the journey homeward to habitual self" (*Endymion,* II.276). The words on the glory of spring are intensified into power by an agonized sense of man's mortal state:

> Where Beauty cannot keep her lustrous eyes,
> Or new Love pine at them beyond to-morrow.

From the idea of Beauty which is half Pain, it is a natural transition to that of Death in which neither Beauty nor Pain exists. But the revulsion from this thought to the strong affirmation in a major key:

> Thou wast not born for death, immortal Bird!

creates a tension out of which the simple words on Ruth in her loneliness come charged with the essence of poetry:

> Perhaps the self-same song that found a path
> Through the sad heart of Ruth, when, sick for home,
> She stood in tears amid the alien corn.

The intensity of the *Grecian Urn* is contemplative. In much of the ode the diction is of the utmost simplicity, and for five lines in the centre of the poem (stanza three), the poetry is sustained on little more than the epithet "happy," five times repeated. The word is poised on the tension between two ideas, the transience of earthly bliss and the imaginary passion of the eternal figures on the urn:

> For ever warm and still to be enjoyed.

But their love is *not* warm: their happiness is only a figment—indeed, the words in which it was asserted had an undertone of bitterness. As the contemplative trance dissolves, the daylight of truth enters in:

> Thou, silent form, dost tease us out of thought
> As doth eternity: Cold Pastoral!

And the "friendly" doctrine that Beauty and Truth are one is spoken from a serene height which mortal men cannot reach.

Only one of the greater odes conceals the spiritual struggle from which Keats drew the "thoughts that breathe, and words that burn": this is *Autumn*. But its serenity covers hidden fires: " 'Tis might half-slumb'ring on its own right arm." Written in a tranquil mood and in a tranquil season of the year, it is, in phrasing, the most perfect of all the Odes. Tension appears only in the contrast between Autumn as the season of fruitfulness (stanza 1), and Autumn as the prelude to winter (stanza 3). The style is not one of fire as in the *Nightingale*, but it is suffused with the golden glow of a September sun.

SCOTT, Byron, Campbell, and Crabbe were in one sense the true poets of the Napoleonic era. They were successful: they were popular in their own day. Their contemporaries, Wordsworth, Coleridge, Shelley, and Keats, did not write for immediate popularity, and their success lay chiefly in the future. Their very language was not of their time. Wordsworth's contests about "poetic diction" and Keats's passionate quest for fine phrases were aspects of a struggle to attain an utterance attuned to the ears of future generations. Many eminent men who lived far into the age of Queen Victoria felt much more at home with the Byronic than with the Wordsworthian group. The poets whom Macaulay genuinely admired were Scott and Byron: his praise of Wordsworth and Coleridge is little more than lip-service. Of all the poets of the age, the one most loved by Newman was Crabbe. The absolute superiority of one group cannot indeed be assumed as self-evident. Even in the matter of diction, it may be held that the merits are not all on one side, and that the fire of Scott and the careless strength of Byron produce results which we may sometimes miss in the philosophic simplicity of Wordsworth and the artistic perfection of Keats. Of course to say that Scott, Byron, or any of their group paid little attention to their diction would be misleading: yet, in comparison, it is perfectly true. Pope gave minute care to his words, so did Gray, so did Wordsworth, so also did Keats. They chose what seemed to them the *best* words; but for Byron and this group, the notion of the "best" barely existed. Byron, on his own confession, wrote to be *read*, and his criterion of the "best" was the taste of his readers. Much of his work, like that of Scott, is from the point of view of style no more than an index to what the public liked. But at his best, Byron did something more interesting than this. In his last phase, especially in *Don Juan*, he produced a style in verse which is outside the historic tradition of poetry altogether.

SCOTT

The position of Scott in the history of poetic style may be easily grasped if the essential qualities of his work are borne in mind. He was, first and foremost, a minstrel. That is to say, his spirit was martial, with a strong sense of the clan. It both stimulated and responded to the heroic temper of the age. In the great struggle against France, Scott was second only to Pitt in his power of kindling patriotic fervour. His love of the past had its practical and political side, for it helped to cement that rigid conservatism of the British people against which the force of revolutionary France broke in vain. At its best, his poetry burns like a steady, pure, transparent flame: as in the terse simplicity of the piece "Breathes there the man" and in the elegiac lines on Nelson, Pitt, and Fox. Here Scott is at his greatest, and at such moments he transcends his habitual style. But his ordinary style, in which he pours out his mind with a minstrel-like fluency, is of more interest to the historian. For the manner of Scott's lays was easily recognizable and often imitated, as it was widely popular. It has nothing of Virgilian beauty or refinement, and it was a mistake in Conington to adopt it for his translation of the *Æneid*. The manner of the lays is often hasty, unsifted, and diffuse, though redeemed by a general rapidity and vigour of rhythm. It is obviously incapable of expressing the finer side of the Romantic spirit, though its greater robustness is a compensation.

The most striking feature of Scott's diction is its use of historic colour. The ground-work in vocabulary is the modernized ballad-style. After a tentative use of frequent archaisms in the opening part of *The Lay of the Last Minstrel*, he settled into a plain virile diction, barely distinguished as poetic. But certain terms had long been associated with the "Harp of the North." Even the fastidious Collins had admitted words like *shiel* and *strath* into the classic lines of his *Ode on the Popular Superstitions of the Highlands of Scotland*. The impetuous current of Scott's verse could easily sweep along such words—and stranger ones—in its career. Accordingly, his diction is plentifully sprinkled with Scottish words, new or vaguely known, which do much to create the local colour dear to the taste of the time. Words indicative of regional customs and geography play a considerable part in his scheme. Examples, often recurrent, are: *slogan, foray, linn, pibroch*, which, with the rarer *correi, canna* (cotton grass), *chanter* (the pipe of the bagpipe), and others, combine with his skilful use of geographic names to produce a romantic northern atmosphere. Such words are as proper to the regional novel as to poetry; and it is a fact that most of the words, archaic or dialectal, to which Scott gave currency survive in the ordinary, not in the poetic, vocabulary: *raid, stalwart, smoulder, glamour*. After all, his genius was for broad general effects, and the finer forms of verbal artistry were outside his scope.

One is tempted to linger over various peculiarities of Scott's diction, such as his celebrated "ghost-word" *bartizan*; or the occasional distortion of Shakespeare, such as *vantage-coign* (both from *Marmion*, VI). But these are details. Of more general interest is his weakness for the "poetic" form of the adjective (or adjectival noun) with the super-fluous *-y*. In a single canto of *Marmion* (V) one notices "*steepy* limits," "*laky* flood," "*paly* gold," and "*reeky* fen." Most interesting of all his mannerisms is a type of phrase which stood for many years as the sign manual of the picturesque style until it degenerated into the stock-in-trade of the guide-book. An example meets the eye boldly at the begin-ning of *Marmion*: "Norham's castled steep." Familiarity begins to blunt the effect after we have had: "Whitby's cloister'd pile," "St. Andrew's cloister'd hall," "Roslin's castled rock," and "Barnard's banner'd walls."[1] It was a feature of Scott's style which was much reproduced by his imitators.

The *Last Minstrel* was presented to the world as an "artless Lay"; and Scott's whole style was basically that of a Border minstrel with added features from Percy's *Reliques*. All of this the poetry-reading public, led more by feminine taste than it had been in the age of John-son, both liked and expected. The poetic style of Scott is a lively version of the Romantic taste in language at the beginning of the nineteenth century. The popular appeal of Scott's style was due to words well out-side the limits of the Johnsonian vocabulary: words of the Scottish Border, words of medieval warfare and pageantry, appealing to a romantic sense of history rather than a purely poetic feeling. In style, as in the force of the romantic passion and the glamour of the romantic setting, Byron went one better than Scott. He takes it for granted that Scott was "beaten" by him, just as Scott did himself: "Sir Walter reign'd before me" (*Don Juan*, XI.57).

BYRON

The popularity of Byron was partly due to the great popularity of poetry itself just at the time when he arrived at an age to write. The cult of romanticism had been maturing steadily since the time of Horace Walpole's *Otranto* and Percy's *Reliques*. The whole national spirit be-came intensely romantic about the time of Trafalgar, and the Death of Nelson was the greatest romance of the age. The new spirit was at its height between Trafalgar and Waterloo: it survived a few years to fall into the mood of cynicism and disillusion which is expressed so forcibly in Byron's later bitterness and in Shelley's rebellious idealism. The new popular romanticism needed very different elements on which to feed from those which had supported it as a mere literary cult. It needed a

[1]*Marmion*, II; *Last Minstrel*, I, VI; *Rokeby*.

person who would be the living realization of its dreams. Byron became
that person. He embodied certain fashions which were as literary as they
were personal, and as personal as they were literary. Heroic poses,
rhetorical declamation, fine sentiments were as much in vogue as the
latest fashions in dress or slang. No author of the time in verse or prose
escapes the infection of the age. A writer so detached in spirit as Hazlitt
has many moments of romantic enthusiasm. The garrulous reminiscences of De Quincey alternate with passionate rhetoric. In the autobiography of B. R. Haydon we read of a life launched on a tide of
naïvely heroic emotions. Painter, poet, and actor alike knew that there
was always a ready market for "sublimity."

Byron's first serious appeal to the public was in a familiar manner,
with just enough seasoning of novelty to produce an exciting effect. In
substance, the first two cantos of *Childe Harold* are a poem of travel.
They belong to the Spenserian revival, begun long before by Thomson
and continued by Beattie. But Byron was a genuine traveller, and had
really been off the beaten track in Portugal, Spain, and the Balkans.
Life as well as literature inspired the work. The verse moves at a lei-
surely pace, scarcely faster than in *The Castle of Indolence*. Spenserian
archaisms from the eighteenth-century mint are frequent. We notice,
for instance, *withouten, ee* (eye), *hight, pleasaunce, eld, brast, whil-
ome, wight, ared* (from "areed"), *idlesse, yclad, ygazed*, and even the
Gothic *imbrown'd*, and *eremite's sad cell*. There is an open reminiscence from Collins in the line:

> Yes, Honour decks the turf that wraps their clay.[2]

Such diction was losing its spell in Byron's time, but it still served as
a foil to the newer and more daring romance which the poet brought
back as spoils from the East. Words like *caloyer, capote, santon, caïque*,
and *camese* were redolent of a life as mysterious as it was real, among
the mountains of Albania and the seas of Greece.

Byron soon learned that he had no need of the faded romance of
the Spenserian revival. There was romance enough in the real world—
provided one left the shores of England—and in his own passions. Nor
did Byron conceive poems in the form of a tension between two extremes
which it was the function of his art to transcend. It was the contest itself
that stirred his imagination. His poetic sympathies were kindled equally
by outlaws, renegades, pirates, mutineers, or any martyrs in the cause
of Liberty. He identified the spirit of rebellion with the spirit of man,
and if his heroes are always insurgents, they are also magnanimous.
Byron found much the same story in every age: in the life of Cain and of

[2]Quotations are from *The Poetical Works of Lord Byron* (Oxford, 1921).

the Corsair, in the fate of the Giaour and of the mutineers of the *Bounty*. He soon arrived, by a route of his own, at a position similar to that of Wordsworth when he declared that poetic diction was superfluous. Byron formulated no theory, but his practice speaks for itself. A story of strong suffering, like that of the Prisoner of Chillon, or a story of violent action, like that of Mazeppa, could dispense with the subtle interpretations of verbal art. The same diction served for every occasion, save only that a few rare words were added for local colour. It is a language elevated somewhat by the use of words long consecrated to metrical use, and by a few archaisms, biblical or quasi-biblical. Apart from that, it is the plain metrical English which varies little from one generation to another in the hands of any good writer who has escaped from the pressure of the age. But of his faults: Byron's diction is marred by not infrequent liberties with grammar and the true meaning of words; and in his more careless moods he admits phrases from the "poetic diction" of the eighteenth century which do not really harmonize with the Byronic temper.

A few illustrations of the main points will be sufficient. In *The Corsair*, the style is raised by such time-honoured poetic synonyms as *surge, deep, main*, and *strand* ("a safer *strand*," "the hated *strand*"). This is typical. Byron has an excellent sense of the value of such words, and there is no better illustration of the difference between *horse* and *steed* than in the quotation taken by A. C. Bradley from *Mazeppa*:

> Bring me a horse! the horse was brought,
> In truth he was a noble steed.

But if Byron was usually right on impulse, he was sometimes wrong through heedlessness. His style, which in its directness and vigour is nearly a model of its kind, is marred by carelessly admitted phrases like "the trembling fair" (*The Corsair*) and "the finny people" (*The Island*). He is also too fond of the merely verbal personifications which now had a very faded air. But probably the wide public for whom he wrote was uncritical of such niceties, and one may well wonder whether, in a poet of Byron's stamp, it is not a mistake to notice them. Words counted for little in the Byronic spell, and probably the only ones which added much to the zest of his readers were those of the kind already noticed in *Childe Harold's Pilgrimage*. Of such there is no want in any of the stories which are placed in distant and romantic settings. Thus, in *The Giaour*, we find *jereed, calpac, symar*; in *The Bride of Abydos*, *comboloio, gul, chibouque*; and even in *The Island*, where the scene is the South Pacific, Byron was at pains to collect Polynesian terms such as *gnatoo, tooa, cava*, and *tappa*. If the secret of Scott lay largely in his local colour, it is small wonder that Byron beat him. Byron was famous for his descriptions, but his method did not lie in the choice of apt single words. He preferred, like Scott, the use of accumulated details and broad effects. Only rarely do we find those single picturesque words so tellingly used by Keats, Tennyson, and Rossetti. A line from *The Island* contains one of those rare instances:

> The tropic bird wheel'd *rockward* to his nest.

Byron was most original when he broke entirely with the tradition of poetic language founded by Spenser. *Don Juan*, if not his most characteristic, is certainly his most interesting work. One is puzzled to say what he has done in this poem. Has he broken with the tradition of Spenser—his idealism and his pattern of a diction different from that of the age—or has he done more, renounced the very nature of poetry itself? There are signs that Byron realized the full extent of his literary revolution. His poem is not, in its earlier cantos, bare of romance; but when once the delightful episode of Juan and Haidee has been passed, the tone becomes more and more realistically cynical. In Canto IV, he clearly expresses the change which we are to expect in the remainder of the work (st. iii):

> And the sad truth which hovers o'er my desk
> Turns what was once romantic to burlesque.

And a little later there is a hint that he understood how far he was straying from the course which our poetry had followed since *The Faerie Queene*. The decline of chivalry as an institution had led, in Spain, to the creative prose fiction of Cervantes;[3] it had led, in Italy, to the mocking romance of Ariosto; but in England chivalry had been preserved under the guise of a new poetry, in which old words and the antique customs became the vehicles of "sage and serious" fictions. Spenser is not mentioned by Byron, but it is clear that Spenser, and what Spenser stood for, were in his mind when he alluded to Pulci. He is discussing the genre to which *Don Juan* belongs (IV.vi):

> To the kind reader of our sober clime
> This way of writing will appear exotic;
> Pulci was sire of the half serious rhyme,
> Who sang when chivalry was more Quixotic.

---

[3]It is perhaps true that *Don Quijote* is itself a romance: cf. Azorín (*Lecturas Españolas*): "D. Vicente Silvá, en su estudio sobre el *Quijote*, escribía las siguientes palabras: 'Su objeto no fué satirizar la esencia y fondo de los libros caballerescos, *puesto que aumentó su número*, sino purgarlos de los disparates e inverosimilitudes. . . .' Sí, esto es exacto!"

Since Spenser's time, until the dawn of the present, English poetry has been fundamentally romantic: that is to say, it has translated the memories of chivalry into terms of contemporary idealism. War was poetic when it was chivalrous war; love was poetic when it was chivalrous love; words were poetic when they were chivalrous words. Such was the lesson of *The Faerie Queene,* and such, in large measure, was the faith of the English people. Their affections long clung to the forms of chivalry; hence, English poetry remained romantic; and hence, a word or phrase skilfully chosen from the past often had power to evoke poetic suggestions. All this is implicit in Gray's admirable saying that "the language of poetry is never the language of the age." But the diction of *Don Juan* is the language of the age; or, to adapt Wordsworth's distinguishing phrase in his Preface of 1801, it is a "selection" from the language of the age. Once Byron has got his hero safely beyond the Isles of Greece his tone becomes partly lyrical, partly realistic and wholly modern. He discards the romance of war, the romance of love, the romance of Nature, and the romance of words. His poem becomes a novel in rhyme, far nearer in spirit to Thackeray's half-picaresque early stories than to *The Faerie Queene* or any of its many descendants. In VIII.lxxxvi, he explicitly takes his stand on the ground of realistic truth:

> But then the fact's a fact—and 'tis the part
>   Of a true poet to escape from fiction
> When'er he can; for there is little art
>   In leaving verse more free from the restriction
> Of truth than prose, unless to suit the mart
>   For what is sometimes call'd poetic diction.

But Byron has no intention of letting the mart for poetic diction interfere with the realistic spirit of his poem. The story must control the style, not the style the story. He breaks free from the traditional language of poetry. Even so unexceptionable a phrase as "driven snow" is dismissed with a sneer: "What bards call 'driven snow.'" He will force his verse to admit the most refractory words (VII.lxxviii):

> Bombs, drums, guns, bastions, batteries, bayonets, bullets;
> Hard words which stick in the soft Muses' gullets.

The presence of metre and rhyme are no more than a thin disguise to the true nature of the poem. Byron was so skilled a versifier that verse was to him less of a restraint than the discipline of prose, and if the reader is as practised in verse-reading as the author was in verse-writing, *Don Juan* may be read in precisely the same mood and spirit as a piece of prose fiction. In spite of the metre, no one need expect to be "disturbed with the joy of elevated thoughts." In a word, little distinctive of poetry has been allowed to remain.

Such being the general nature of *Don Juan*, its style does not call for any detailed examination. Two conspicuous features of the vocabulary are, however, of considerable interest in the history of literary style. One is the large number of French words and phrases which make *Don Juan* a true mirror of a Regency mode. Many are vogue-words, new or recent comers into the language. Some are actually introduced for the first time, and are printed in italics; and those which rhyme generally require the French pronunciation. The combined effect is to make the diction of the poem seem contemporary even to an exaggerated degree. Among the less anglicized French expressions are: *empressement, magnifique, gêne, agacerie,* and *espiègle.* In introducing *longueur,* he remarks: "We've not so good a word but have the thing"; and a foot-note to *mobility* makes the comment: "In French 'mobilité.' I am not sure that mobility is English. . . . It may be defined as an excessive sus-ceptibility of immediate impressions." The other outstanding feature of the style is the frequency of quotations from Shakespeare. The sig-nificance of this fact too is general rather than particular. Byron has no flair for Shakespearian phrases of unusual poetic beauty. He seems to remember at random. The great period of Shakespearian quotation was just beginning, and Byron, in practice, reminds us that Shakespeare enriched the literary language before his style became the common quarry of poetic phrases. The quotations in *Don Juan* are usually con-scious and deliberate: some are acknowledged in footnotes; some are accompanied by facetious remarks, such as "I like so much to quote." There are, on an average, perhaps, three or four Shakespearian quota-tions or reminiscences in each of the sixteen cantos; as specimens we may note, "Our hero quietly inurned" (I), "sweets to the sweet" (II), "cabin'd, cribb'd, confin'd" (IV), "spirits from the vasty deep" (VIII), " 'But heaven,' as Cassio says, 'is above all' " (IX), "Life's a poor player" (XI). Quotation from Shakespeare was, as Byron himself notes, in vogue, and neither these nor any other verbal reminiscences do anything to raise the style to a poetic level. Indeed, such a line as:

Juan slept like a top, or like the dead

is typical of the spirit of the whole, which consists in confounding dis-tinctions and reducing everything to burlesque. Side by side with echoes from *Hamlet* and *Macbeth* is a reference to the "incomparable oil" of Macassar.

Enough has been said to indicate the nature of Byron's biggest, and when all is said, most interesting experiment. *Don Juan* has brilliance, and it has power. It is non-Spenserian, non-romantic, and, according to one definition of the word, non-poetic. Byron, in his latest phase, is the opposite of Wordsworth. The one sought to raise common words to the sphere of poetry, and sometimes succeeded; the other sought to exorcize romance from all words, and seldom failed.

CAMPBELL

Thomas Campbell (1777–1844) was in every respect a popular Romantic poet of the Napoleonic era. In his diction, there is nothing which transcends the taste of his time; on the other hand, there is no writer who indicates so clearly what the public liked to read in didactic, narrative, and patriotic verse. It is as a patriotic poet that he survives best. The greatest of Wordsworth's sonnets on Natural Independence and Liberty rise to a height quite unattainable by Campbell; but as a stirring expression of the national war-spirit of the time there is nothing better than *Hohenlinden, The Battle of the Baltic,* and *Ye Mariners of England.* Campbell is the author of three quotations which are almost universally known:

> 'Tis distance lends enchantment to the view,
>
> Like angel-visits, few and far between,
>
> Coming events cast their shadows before.[4]

The lines are remembered still, but few have read the poems in which they occur: *Pleasures of Hope* and *Lochiel's Warning* now seem as hopelessly old-fashioned as they were once popular.

Campbell interests the historian rather than the pure critic. His *Pleasures of Hope,* as the title indicates, belongs to the long succession of didactic poems begun by Pope and continued by Johnson, Cowper, and Akenside; but in style, it forms a strong contrast to the icy hardness and exclusiveness of the Popian model at its best. The rigid didactic manner has been invaded by new tastes which are alien to it: sentimental Rousseauism, a sense of the warmth and colour in older poetic styles, and a certain rhetorical posturing which easily lapses into the absurd. These were all signs of decay: yet they aided rather than hindered the popularity of the didactic poem in its latest phase. Perhaps

[4]Quotations are from *The Poetical Works of Thomas Campbell* (London, 1846).

no epithet is so redolent of Rousseau as the much-used word *artless*: and Campbell has both "*artless* tear" and "*artless* savage." The taste for the sentimentally picturesque appears clearly in many expressions like "the hamlet's hawthorn-scented way," "the cot's romantic glade," and "broomwood-blossom'd vale." That Campbell had not inherited Pope's fine sense of the boundary between the right and wrong use of personification appears in the pompous apostrophe:

> Come, bright Improvement! on the car of Time,
> And rule the spacious world from clime to clime.

In these various features, added to the use of so trite an expression as "glittering tube" for "gun," we may see Campbell as a follower rather than a leader in literary taste.

Gertrude of Wyoming, his other long poem, was equally popular in its time and is equally old-fashioned today. It is a late work of the Spenserian revival, and is true to type in its blend of Spenserian phrases with local words drawn from a "romantic" region. The poets were now compelled to range further afield: Beattie's local colour was from Scotland; Byron's from the less known parts of Europe; Campbell's from North America. His romantic diction is not too outlandish, and it includes such words as *wampum, pirogues, sagamité, mocasins, condor* ("the condor of the rock"), and *cougar*, the last being explained as "the American tiger." *Gertrude of Wyoming*, as a story, remained popular into the Victorian age, but by 1860 at the latest the slender charm which its style may once have possessed must have nearly worn away.

CRABBE

To scrutinize the style of George Crabbe may almost appear an act of critical treachery. The task is one which obscures all the poet's merits and brings his failings into the light. Crabbe's sombre experience and narrow wisdom—often little more than prudence—disdain the higher forms of language. He was a poet almost in his own despite. His first group of poems appeared between 1781 and 1785. Then came a long gap, and he remained silent until 1807. Between 1810 and 1819 he published *The Borough, Tales*, and *Tales of the Hall* which contain together about four-fifths of his published verse. A poet who knew Burke and Johnson in the first part of his career, and in the second part, Wordsworth and Scott, whose work, too, was appreciated by all four is, apart from all else, a singular figure. Certain points in the language of Crabbe are of interest in the general history of our poetic style.

Crabbe was born in 1754, and his three early poems *The Library,*
The Village, and *The Newspaper* appeared respectively in 1781, 1783,
and 1785. Crabbe scarcely ever wrote except in couplets, and his diction varied little in his earliest and his latest work. In one point, he is
perfectly consistent: his dislike of sentiment and his dislike of ornament. In *The Library* there are some contemptuous lines on the imagery
and diction of the popular prose romances. In *The Village* the whole
plan is to give "the real picture of the poor." But while Crabbe is severe
on *The Deserted Village* and pastoral conventions, he accepts the current style of verse without sign of dissatisfaction. Like so many couplet-
writers in the 1780's, he is the pupil in diction of Pope and Gray, and he
repeats, without much discrimination, many of the favourite adjectives and
verbs which had become embedded in the couplet style. But amid much
convention, there are strong signs of the diction taught him by his own
observation, for instance in these couplets from Book I of *The Village*:[5]

> From thence a length of burning sand appears,
> Where the thin harvest waves its wither'd ears,

or

> Here joyless roam a wild amphibious race,
> With sullen woe display'd in every face.

Such poetry as Crabbe's style possesses arises from his pleasure in calling things by their right names. He is the poet of the uncheerful. Though
not without humour, he is chiefly amused by such things as the vanities
of a weak head (*The Learned Boy*) or the incongruity of an ill-matched
couple (*The Preceptor Husband*). The latter poem contains one of
Crabbe's most skilful passages in the sheer use of words—the description of a lesson in botany to an unwilling wife:

> Now o'er the grounds they rambled many a mile;
> He show'd the flowers, the stamina, the style,
> Calix and corol, pericarp and fruit,
> And all the plant produces, branch and root;
> Of these he treated, every varying shape,
> Till poor Augusta panted to escape:
> He show'd the various foliage plants produce,
> Lunate and lyrate, runcinate, retuse;
> Long were the learned words, and urged with force,
> Panduriform, pinnatafid, premorse,
> Latent and patent, papulous and plane,—
> "Oh!" said the pupil, "it will turn my brain."

Words which would be discordant in any other poetry, harmonize with

[5]Quotations are from *The Poetical Works of George Crabbe* (Oxford, 1908).

Crabbe's almost scientific temper. He takes a positive pleasure in words such as *mud*, to which he often adds the emphasis of rhyme. In what is perhaps the best-known passage in all his work—the lines on the solitary fishing of Peter Grimes—the adjective *dull* occurs no fewer than five times in fifty lines. By the lover of Crabbe, such words are forgiven, for there is more poetry in his "dullness" and "mud" than in his "nymphs" and "swains."

Crabbe's matter-of-fact temper nevertheless made him overlook many of the finer shades in the associations of words. He sometimes writes in a spirit of blunt accuracy, and pays the penalty in phrases of sheer bathos. There is nothing uncharacteristic of him in the flatness of these lines from *The Parting Hour*:

> Augmented pay procured him decent wealth,
> But years advancing undermined his health.

But he sometimes descends lower. There is a passage in *The Patron* in which a sensible father warns his son, who is about to visit a great house, to offer no opinion on food or wine. He continues:

> Thou know'st that all the science thou canst boast
> Is of thy father's simple boil'd and roast;
> Nor always these; he sometimes saved his cash,
> By interlinear days of frugal hash.

Crabbe was no pessimist, for he was a sincere Christian priest, but he believed that without Divine Grace human nature is corrupt, vicious, and weak. Possibly he was stiffened in this attitude by the growth of Rousseauism and its doctrine that man is fundamentally good. Mr. F. L. Lucas remarks that "his landscapes are, perhaps, the most permanent part of his work":[6] some of them, especially his riverside scenes, are as real as those of Dickens. Most of them are unrelieved by beauty: but they have a poetic sincerity and an almost religious conviction which make them like a defiant testimony to the fallen state of nature. Crabbe's epithets are sometimes inspired—not unhappily—by the spirit of contradiction, as, for instance, when he calls the cry of the fishing gull *tuneless*, pointedly reversing the stock epithet for the songs of birds, which was *tuneful*. But contradiction is only a minor motive of Crabbe's descriptive diction: its positive quality is the harsh tonic flavour of the earth with its tares, brambles, and scanty corn, and of the salt shore with its ooze and seaweed.

[6]*George Crabbe: An Anthology* (Cambridge, 1933), p. xxxi.

THOUGH Arnold was born thirteen years after Tennyson, and ten after Browning, all three poets belonged to the same generation and shared the same advantages or disadvantages which the age could bestow on its poets.[1] Keen dispute had been held about the diction of poetry by some of the writers of the previous generation, and the matter was still of vital interest to many of their successors. The position of the Victorian was not quite so enviable as that of the Elizabethan. In diction, the liberty of the Elizabethan poet was unlimited, for hardly any words were felt to be unpoetic. The liberty of the young Victorian poet was somewhat narrower, for Wordsworth's view that there is no essential difference between the language of prose and that of poetry had been generally rejected. On the other hand, the notion that a limited body of "poetic diction" had a special prestige had been completely exploded. All good poetry of the past was a quarry from which the modern poet might borrow the fitting word: Coleridge and Scott, Shelley and Keats had each discovered from his own reading new sources of verbal wealth. The generation to which Tennyson belonged had not the revolutionary ardour of its predecessor. Many of its members, like Tennyson himself, rated order as high as freedom, and had, like Tennyson, a taste for precision in poetry; there was less of that passionate originality so highly prized in the generation of Wordsworth. On the other hand, Tennyson had no intention of allowing any source of poetic enrichment to be closed to him. He read widely not only in English poetry but in Greek, Latin, and Italian. Like Milton he nourished his own diction from the best sources, native and foreign, thereby forming and strengthening the originality of his style.

TENNYSON

There were no profound changes in Tennyson's diction during the course of his long poetic career. It is true that in the *Poems* of 1830 the style is not mature, its elements being imperfectly blended, and it is

[1]This chapter is a reprint with a few alterations and additions of the author's S.P.E. Tract, no. LIII, *On the Diction of Tennyson, Browning and Arnold* (Clarendon Press, 1939).

also true that the poet adapted his style for particular purposes; there are, for instance, certain differences in the diction of the dramas as compared with that of the idylls. None the less, Tennyson attained a characteristic style early in his career and he never lost it; in language, at least, the child was father of the man. Naturally there was some change and development in the course of so long a life, but much less than in that of some other poets; no poems of Tennyson, for instance, differ in diction one quarter as much as *Michael* and *Laodamia*. One might illustrate the essentials of Tennyson's diction from the 1842 volume alone.

To judge from his practice, Tennyson would have agreed with Gray that "the language of poetry is never the language of the age." He would never have declared his diction to be founded on "the real language of men." It is palpably the product of art: this is a quality which is common to all his poems. There are of course varieties. There is far less visible artifice in the shorter lyrics than in the *Idylls of the King*; the diction of the impassioned parts of *Maud* is much simpler than that of *The Princess*. At rare moments, as in the lines "Break, break, break," Tennyson speaks to the reader's heart in words of perfect simplicity. But this is not his characteristic manner. His general attitude is not that of a man speaking to men, nor is he on quite easy terms with contemporary life. Some of his poems, like *The Lady of Shalott*, belong to the world of faery; some are on medieval themes; some are idylls of more or less artificial simplicity; some, like *In Memoriam*, are profoundly meditated and demand a vocabulary drawn from various sources.

To such a poet, the use of rare and archaic words was a necessity, and in many of his poems they play an important and calculated part. In his very early work he values them for their own sake. *Marish*, for instance, is an old word which has struck his fancy: he used it, together with *marish-flowers*, in *The Dying Swan*, and *marish-mosses* occurs in *Mariana*. *Lowlihead* (*Isabel*) and *eglatere* (*A Dirge*) are other examples of this kind of diction. As Tennyson's art matured, his taste for old and rare words grew more discriminating; in the *Poems* of 1842 and after, the flavour of antiquity, if introduced at all, is often varied to suit the occasion. In *St. Simeon Stylites*, for instance, the archaisms have an appropriate biblical cast, e.g., *the meed of saints, sawn in twain, spake, halt and maimed, smite . . . spare not.* The *Idylls of the King* are full of archaisms: *Morte d'Arthur*, for instance, naturally contains echoes of Malory, e.g., *lightly bring me word, lief and dear, slay thee with my hands.* In the later *Idylls* the archaism is less successful. Old and rare words are used which carry no distinct associations with them;

instead of adding colour to the style, they give it an air of spurious antiquity. Expressions like the following are frequent: "the *foughten* field," "*holp* me at my need," "Heaven *yield* her for it," "the little *fowl*" (birds), "*delivering doom*" (i.e., pronouncing judgment), "a *grimly* light," "many a costly *cate*," "this *frontless* kitchen-knave," "for *housel* or for shrift," "*approven* King," "*rathe* she rose," "sweetly could she *make* and sing," "there was *dole* in Astolat."[2] The effect of these phrases in their context may be fairly illustrated from the following passage (*Guinevere*), in which the diction, instead of being poetic, is no more than vaguely "old":

> and he,
> That did not shun to smite me in worse way,
> Had yet that grace of courtesy in him left
> He spared to lift his hand against the King
> Who made him knight: but many a knight was slain;
> And many more, and all his kith and kin
> Clave to him, and abode in his own land.

This tissue of archaic phrases illustrates in an extreme form the poet's avoidance of ordinary language. This is one of the least successful aspects of Tennyson's style, but I do not mean to disparage his occasional use of old or rare words, with more or less poetic associations, like *matin* for "morning," *sallow* for "willow," *herb* for "grass." In the greater part of his work, his use of these variants is eminently skilful.

II

We pass naturally from the consideration of Tennyson's old and rare words to a feature of his style which is more peculiar to himself. Many English poets use fanciful and witty expressions which offer a slight puzzle to the reader. Tennyson keeps his reader's mind active by the use of somewhat enigmatic words which not infrequently require explanation. Sometimes the poet solves the difficulty by a note of his own. He tells us, for instance, that the word *balm-cricket* (i.e., cicala), which occurs in his early poem *A Dirge*, is taken from a note on the word τέττιξ by Dalzel, an editor of Theocritus. He also explains that the *redcap* of *The Gardener's Daughter* is a "goldfinch." But he does not remove every difficulty, and he has left certain problems to the editors of the *Oxford Dictionary*. They explain the "budded *quicks*" of *In Memoriam* as "probably hawthorn," and comment on "her clear *germander* eye" (*Sea*

[2]The first two are from *The Coming of Arthur*, the next six from *Gareth and Lynette*, the next two from *Guinevere*, the last three from *Elaine*. References are to the Globe edition of Tennyson (Macmillan, 1950).

Dreams) as referring "to the beautiful colour of the flowers of *Veronica Chamædrys*." Some out-of-the-way words present no difficulty, and are simply a form of that graceful artifice of which Tennyson is a master. That most artificial of his poems, *The Princess*, abounds in far-fetched expressions: "*bosks* of wilderness," "a long low *sibilation*," "*linden* alley," "we . . . *perused the matting*," "not in this *frequence*," "free *adit*," and the like, and sometimes the artifice stands self-confessed, as when, describing the upbringing of two girl friends, the poet writes:

> They were still together, grew,
> (For so they said themselves) inosculated.

On occasion Tennyson somewhat clarified his phrasing in a later edition: the heroine of *The Brook*, on migrating to Australasia, was originally said to breathe "in converse seasons"; this afterwards became "breathes in April-autumns." No feature of Tennyson's language is easier to illustrate than this deliberate and often learned artifice of phrasing, but I will limit myself to a few further examples out of the scores which might be quoted: "cherish my *prone* year"; *glamour* for "magic"; *delivering* for "announcing"; "She lived a *moon* in that low lodge with him"; "I heard the watchman peal The *sliding season*"; *waning* for "fading"; "the fount of *fictive* tears"; "rust or *soilure*"; *sequel of guerdon*.[3] It would be a mistake to call these *recherché* expressions affected, for they are nearly always felicitous, and from Tennyson, whose mind was the reverse of simple, they come quite naturally. Moreover, he does not take himself so seriously as some of his critics imagine: a poem like *Amphion* shows with how slight a manipulation he could turn his usual style to a comic purpose.

A characteristic of Tennyson's style, somewhat akin to his use of the far-fetched word, is his use of periphrasis. Tennyson's periphrases are very various, some being pleasantly fanciful, some playful, a few rather commonplace or even ridiculous, and some exquisitely beautiful. Some of his phrases are merely allusive or slightly decorative, e.g., "him that died of hemlock" (*The Princess*), "the girls all kiss'd Beneath the sacred bush" (*The Epic*). The phrase "bristled grunters" in *The Princess* agrees with the mock-heroic tone of that poem, so does the playful description of a Chinese puzzle:

> Laborious orient ivory sphere in sphere.

[3]The first three examples are from *Gareth and Lynette*, the fourth from *The Last Tournament*; then follow two from *The Gardener's Daughter*; the last three are from *The Brook*, *Elaine*, and *Œnone*.

Some of the periphrases are, like much of Tennyson's language, over-elaborate; for instance, the lines in *In Memoriam*:

> Or where the kneeling hamlet drains
> The chalice of the grapes of God,[4]

may make the reader pause a moment before he recognizes the allusion to the Sacrament. But these lines are redeemed by that rightness of tone which Tennyson always commands when he touches a solemn subject; the effect recurs in the passage on Mary, the sister of Lazarus (xxxii):

> her ardent gaze
> Roves from the living brother's face,
> And rests upon the Life indeed;

and by the side of, or above, these examples, deserves to be set the exquisite periphrasis on the life of Jesus (lii):

> the sinless years
> That breathed beneath the Syrian blue.

Equally impressive is "the silent Opener of the Gate" of the late poem, *God and the Universe*. Tennyson often employs periphrasis for natural description: in *Morte d'Arthur*, icebergs are named "moving isles of winter," and the Aurora Borealis is "the northern morn." He calls the dandelion, in a delightful phrase (*Gareth and Lynette*),

> the flower,
> That blows a globe of after arrowlets,

and equally beautiful is his description of the kingfisher as "the sea-blue bird of March" (*I.M.*, xci). Some of Tennyson's periphrases, after the manner of the eighteenth-century poets, neatly fill a single line, e.g. (*The Princess*)

> A lidless watcher of the public weal

and sometimes, in the periphrastic manner imitated from Milton, an abstract is substituted for a concrete noun, e.g.

> Led on the gray-hair'd wisdom of the east;

> And all the pavement stream'd with massacre.[5]

Periphrasis may be a powerful weapon in satire, but the description of a preacher put into the mouth of the hero of *Maud*, "This broad-brimm'd hawker of holy things," does not strike very hard. Occasionally there is an elaboration of language which seems uncalled for, as when

[4]Section x.
[5]*The Holy Grail*; *The Last Tournament.*

a beard is called "the knightly growth that fringed his lips" (*Morte d'Arthur*). Some of Tennyson's periphrases seem to indicate a Victorian shyness to call things by their right names; the birth of children is a special occasion for this reticence. In *The Marriage of Geraint*, for instance, an anticipated baby is called

> another gift of the high God,
> Which, maybe, shall have learn'd to lisp you thanks,

and in *The Miller's Daughter* the birth and untimely death of a child are veiled in language of great mystery:

> The still affection of the heart
> Became an outward breathing type,
> That into stillness past again.

If Tennyson's periphrases sometimes resemble the manner of eighteenth-century verse, his occasional transference or adaptation of the parts of speech connects him with Keats and other writers who adopted that licence from Elizabethan English. Like Keats, Tennyson seldom or never uses the device for the evasion of difficulties, but to produce effects not otherwise attainable. His words in this class are mostly verbs, adapted for the occasion from adjectives or nouns. He is fond of the "verb" *gloom*:

> twilight *gloom'd*;
>
> The wan day
> Went *glooming* down;
>
> May her life . . . be never *gloom'd* by the curse.[6]

The transitive use of *tumble* enables him to form some expressive phrases, e.g. "*tumbled* fruit" (*The Princess*), "fragments *tumbled* from the glens" (*Œnone*), "Among the *tumbled* fragments of the hills" (*Elaine*). The verb "to orb" is something of a favourite. "Tennyson," says Mr. A. M. D. Hughes, "frequently uses the words to 'round' or to 'orb' of a star coming full face; as in 'orb into the perfect star' [*I.M.*, xxiv] . . ., 'all that orbs Between the Northern and the Southern morn' [*The Princess*, v]."[7] Other Tennysonian "verbs" are *voice* (*Lucretius*), *tongue* (*Tiresias*), *guerdon* (*The Princess*), *wann'd* (*Maud*).

The transference of the parts of speech is one of Tennyson's means of enriching his poetic vocabulary. Another device which he employs produces an effect like that of his *recherché* words—it widens the gulf

[6]*The Princess*; *The Last Tournament*; *The Wreck*.
[7]*Tennyson: Poems Published in 1842*, ed. A. M. D. Hughes (Clarendon Press, 1914), p. 327.

between verse and prose, and is sometimes an aid to euphony. This device is the use of rare forms or spellings of words, e.g. *thridding* for "threading," *knolling* for "knelling," *scymetar* for "scimitar" (see p. 161). His care for euphony appears in his preference for the form *Genovese* to "Genoese," but his use of *Ithacensian* for "Ithacan" is part of that display of rare language by which he enlivens the fantastic theme of *The Princess.* Tennyson makes full though not excessive use of those advantages which arise from a language not strictly standardized, and the use of verse in itself aids the relaxation of usage. Unlike Browning, he is seldom eccentric, never reckless, though in his early poem *The Merman* there is the form *almondine*, which is an error for "almandine." As a rule, his departures from custom either have good precedent, or are of so slight a nature as to be admissible. He uses, on occasion, *lissome* for "lissom," *landskip* for "landscape," *harken* for "hearken," *holly-hoaks* for "holly-hocks," *plowman* for "ploughman," *graff* for "graft," *turkis* (Milton's form) for "turquoise," and *hern* for "heron." He frequently uses the more phonetic *-t* instead of the *-ed* form of the preterite and participle, as in *dipt, dropt, past, slipt*.[8] Occasionally his accentuation of words is unusual or archaic, e.g. balúster, retínue,[9] chiválric.[10] The form *glode* as the preterite of "glide" in *The Battle of Brunanburh* is, in the phrase of the *O.E.D.*, "distinctly archaistic."

III

So far I have dealt with Tennyson's devices for giving his language the distinction which the use of metre demands. These devices do not, as in some poets, contrast strongly with the rest of his language, for Tennyson is far too skilful to be the dupe rather than the master of any device which he chooses to employ. He turns what might be and often has been a fettering convention into a means of displaying the resources of the English language and of his own art. It remains to consider those aspects of his diction in which he is writing more creatively; and naturally his language is most poetic when he is free to achieve effects of his own choice, and is not simply using an alternative expression in order to avoid a commonplace equivalent. But there is also an intermediate phase of his work which calls for notice, namely, his endeavour

[8]Tennyson's preferences in pronunciation, especially in vowel-quantity, were strongly marked. For instance, he insisted on "knōwledge" (*Tennyson and his Friends*, ed. Hallam, Lord Tennyson, p. 191). Further points of interest on this subject are mentioned in *Six Tennyson Essays*, by Sir Charles Tennyson (London, 1954), pp. 190–3.

[9]"The usual stressing in the 16th–18th centuries" (*O.E.D.*).

[10]"The pronunciation sanctioned by the poets" (*ibid.*).

to adapt the art of poetry to the needs of contemporary life and thought, a task involving the use of many expressions not previously associated with verse. Whatever our view of Tennyson as an original thinker, it is certain that he kept well abreast of the new movements in thought during his century, and he reflects the impact of those thoughts on the mind of his generation more clearly and completely than any other writer. During his life, the sciences gained much of that eminence in the intellectual world which they now possess, and Tennyson's position as Poet Laureate was a challenge to him to illustrate the truth of what Wordsworth had written in his Preface to the *Lyrical Ballads*: "If the labours of Men of science should ever create any material revolution, direct or indirect, in our condition, and in the impressions which we habitually receive, the Poet will sleep then no more than at present; he will be ready to follow the steps of the Man of science, not only in those general indirect effects, but he will be at his side, carrying sensation into the midst of the objects of the science itself."

That Tennyson met the situation with such success is a striking testimony to his mastery of language. In his more serious verse, he deals only with broad scientific conceptions, the names of which are mostly simple, and cause his verse little embarrassment. There is no incongruity in the use of such language in this stanza from *In Memoriam* (lv):

> Are God and Nature then at strife,
>   That Nature lends such evil dreams?
>   So careful of the *type* she seems,
> So careless of the single life,

or in *Lucretius*:

> Vanishing, *atom and void, atom and void*,
> Into the unseen for ever.

In his lighter moods, he delights in the technical problems presented him by uncouth names, and displays his skill in weaving them dexterously into the fabric of his verse. In *The Princess* is a well-known geological passage on the "stony names"

> Of shale and hornblende, rag and trap and tuff,
> Amygdaloid and trachyte,

also a mathematical line:

> Of sine and arc, spheroïd[11] and azimuth.

[11]The unusual form of this word (cf. French *sphéroïde*) no doubt represents a deliberate preference of Tennyson's.

Some of the new scientific words are rendered attractive to him by their sonorous syllables, like *mastodon*, or a botanical name will be interwoven into an alliterative line, "Sweeping the froth-fly from the fescue"; and though he poetizes an allusion to clockwork machinery as "every kiss of toothed wheels," he does not shun such terms of industrial progress as *trucks* and *trams*, or of finance as "dividend, consol, and share."[12] In one and the same poem (*Aylmer's Field*), he will use a plain colloquialism like "Call'd to the bar," and also summon up his powers of verbal elaboration to describe "the lawless science of our Law":

> That codeless myriad of precedent,
> That wilderness of single instances.

I doubt whether full justice has been done to the skill with which Tennyson reconciles the traditions of poetry with the new terms which were current in his lifetime among the Victorian clerisy.

IV

The Lancashire miner, Samuel Bamford, once wrote a letter to the poet which Lord Tennyson aptly reprints in the *Memoir* of his father. The letter ends with a few words of naïve but excellent criticism: "But your English! why it is almost unlimitedly expressive. This language of ours, what can it not be made to say? What height, what depth filled with all glorious hues, terrible glooms, and vivid flashes does it not combine and your poems exhibit all."[13] Tennyson is, indeed, wonderfully effective in his use of the fundamental words in our vocabulary; that is, words of Anglo-Saxon origin, old-established and fully naturalized words from Norse and French sources, and certain words of obscure or popular origin which are first recorded about 1200–1400 and are often peculiarly expressive. These groups of words form the foundation of our language, and Tennyson is the master of every device by which they can be made to strike home with special force. Sometimes the effect is produced by the apt placing of words in a particular context, as in the simple sentence, "The slow clock ticking," in *Mariana*. Sometimes it is done by metaphor, as in that phrase from *The Lady of Shalott* which was derisively italicized by the *Quarterly* reviewer:

> On either side the river lie
> Long fields of barley and of rye,
> That clothe the wold and *meet the sky*;

[12]*The Epic*; *Aylmer's Field*; *In Memoriam*, cxvii; *Maud*, X.i; *The Wreck*.
[13]*Tennyson: A Memoir*, by his Son (London, 1897), I, 286.

sometimes by metaphor aided by alliteration and metrical manipulation, as in the last line of a section of *In Memoriam* (vii):

> He is not here; but far away
>   The noise of life begins again,
>   And ghastly thro' the drizzling rain
> *On the bald street breaks the blank day.*

All readers who, in the excellent phrase of Walter Raleigh, admire Tennyson because they are fond of beautiful language, may probably find in these three quotations the types of many of their favourite passages. Occasionally it seems his deliberate purpose to illustrate the wealth of English in popular expressive verbs:

> The parrot scream'd, the peacock *squall'd* . . .
> The palace *bang'd* and *buzz'd* and *clackt*.[14]

With a fuller exercise of his skill he will so choose a particular verb that it gives life to a whole sentence, and in return receives life from it. Like other writers of the time, e.g. Ruskin, he is fond of producing this effect by verbs of motion, using them metaphorically in descriptions to suggest an imaginary or to emphasize an actual movement, as in:

> The narrow street that *clamber'd* toward the mill.
>
> The maiden splendours of the morning star
> *Shook* in the steadfast blue.
>
> The long light *shakes* across the lakes.
>
> The landscape *winking* through the heat.[15]

He produces many vivid effects from the metaphorical use of verbs associated with "burning," e.g.

> The helmet and the helmet-feather
> *Burn'd* like one *burning* flame together.
>
> Unloved, that beech will gather brown,
> This maple *burn* itself away.
>
> The light cloud *smoulders* on the summer crag
>
> The furzy prickle *fire* the dells
>
> Its stormy crests that *smoke* against the skies.[16]

And in many passages, which are surely the pride of every poet who can produce them, he makes us feel—by a delicate fitness of words to

[14]*The Day-Dream*: "The Revival."
[15]*Enoch Arden*; *Dream of Fair Women*; *The Princess*, iv; *In Memoriam*, lxxxix.
[16]*Lady of Shalott*; *In Memoriam*, ci; *Edward Morris*; *Two Voices*; *Lancelot and Elaine.*

a particular purpose—that familiar language is charged with a new potency of expression. This effect is produced, for instance, in:

> A still salt pool, lock'd in with bars of sand,
>   Left on the shore; that hears all night
> The *plunging seas* draw backward from the land
>   Their moon-led waters white.

> The chestnut *pattering* to the ground.

> The rooks are *blown about* the skies.[17]

But this quality cannot be fairly illustrated from a few quotations, for in varying degrees it pervades the whole of Tennyson's work.[18]

A close study of Tennyson's diction shows us that in him, as in most essentially poetic natures, language is inseparably blended with thought and sensation. It is often impossible to say whether the expression suggests the idea or the idea the expression, whether the sensation prompts the word, or the word stimulates the sensation. The interaction of feeling and language in Tennyson's mind may be illustrated by the following passage in *Lancelot and Elaine*:

> the blood-red light of dawn
> Flared in her face, she *shrilling*, 'Let me die!'

The reader may naturally consider that this unusual verb was chosen to suggest a particular cry, partly pathetic, partly hysterical; and this in a way is true. Yet it appears also that "shrill" was, for Tennyson, a useful but indeterminate verb capable of suggesting different sounds in different contexts. In *The Holy Grail* the verb "shrill" is used of the loud insistent cry of a man, in *Gareth and Lynette* of a woman's voice raised in petulance and contempt, in *The Last Tournament* of the excited voice of a Court Fool, and in *Merlin and Vivien* of a falcon's bells; and in each passage the verb seems peculiarly fitted to the occasion. The discovery and possession of words which will take on various shades of meaning is not only a powerful aid to a poet, it may be one of the impulses which prompt his invention. For Tennyson, a significant phrase was sometimes the nucleus of an entire poem. A sentence in *The Times*, "Some one had blundered,"[19] was the germ of his *Charge of the Light Brigade*; the words of a dying man, "God Almighty little knows what He's about taking me," were the occasion of *Northern Farmer, Old Style*; the phrase "too late" clearly suggested the maiden's song in *Guinevere*, and the words *Frater ave atque vale* are the motive of the poem so entitled. The lines *Far-far-away*, written in Tennyson's old age,

[17]*Palace of Art*; *In Memoriam*, xi, xv.
[18]Cf. Pope's verbs (p. 122).   [19]*Tennyson: A Memoir*, I, 381.

are built upon the title-phrase, words which, as the poet tells us, stirred in his boyhood what can only be called a "cosmic emotion":

> What vague world-whisper, mystic pain or joy,
> Thro' those three words would haunt him when a boy,
> Far-far-away?

Just as phrases are often the germ of poems, so words are often the germ of phrases, images, and poetic ideas. There is a wonderful continuity and connectedness of diction in Tennyson's work, and often the full poetic beauty of certain words is only apparent when they are illustrated by the same words in other passages. I do not undertake to supply a full list of Tennyson's favourite and characteristic words—the germ of much of his loveliest writing—but such a list would certainly include *glimmer, moan, verge, slope, gloom, windy, myriad, hollow, dip, flicker, crisp, droop, fret, level.* These are not all used very often, but they are many times the central words in passages of especial charm or beauty. To these must be added various verbs beginning with *sl-*, like the three which occur in one of the lyrics of *The Princess*:

> Now *sleeps* the crimson petal, now the white . . .
> Now *slides* the silent meteor on . . .
> Now folds the lily all her sweetness up,
> And *slips* into the bosom of the lake.

The favourites of this group are *slope* and *slant.* On the significance of many of these words, especially perhaps *slope* and *glimmer,* much might be written, but I will confine myself to the special interest attaching to the group *moan, boundless, deep.* Tennyson was a great sea-poet, and these three words seem to have dwelt in his mind in his broodings on the sea, slowly accumulating suggestiveness and meaning during the whole of his life. The culmination is reached in *Crossing the Bar.* In phrases from earlier poems one may watch the poet moving tentatively towards some unknown goal:

> The deep
> Moans round with many voices.

> And I from out the boundless outer deep . . .

> And the low moan of leaden-colour'd seas . . .

> But that one ripple on the boundless deep . . .[20]

Each of these passages is good in itself; yet all that is hidden in the three words is not fully revealed until that last sea-piece in which the poet prays that there may be "no moaning of the bar":

[20]*Ulysses; Sea Dreams; Enoch Arden; The Ancient Sage.*

When that which drew from out the boundless deep
Turns again home.

It was justly said by Tennyson's son, when he first read *Crossing the Bar*, "That is the crown of your life's work."

v

To the end of his days Tennyson was an active reader of the Greek and Roman classics, and he had in general no prejudice in favour of a non-literary or non-learned style. But he belonged to a generation which had been taught by Wordsworth to appreciate the beauty of simplicity. In some of his idylls he attempts a manner which is not natural to him, and Arnold rightly contrasts the "semblance of simplicity" of a poem like *Dora* with the "real simplicity" of a poem like *Michael*.[21] Tennyson's natural style is an eclectic one, a fabric woven of many colours. It is a blending of originality and conservatism, of invention and scholarship. He does not offer learning as a substitute for poetry. In *Ulysses* there are Homeric echoes—*barren crags* (κραναὴ Ἰθάκη), *windy Troy* (Ἴλιος ἠνεμόεσσα), *sitting well in order, smite The sounding furrows* (ἑξῆς δ᾽ ἑζόμενοι πολιὴν ἅλα τύπτον ἐρετμοῖς)—but the general tone is far from being coldly classical. Equally far is *Morte d'Arthur* from being narrowly medieval: the Virgilian line

This way and that dividing the swift mind

shows that the author's love of literary elaboration is not to be sacrificed to a pedantic doctrine of propriety. Nor are reminiscences of Greek poetry confined to poems on Greek subjects. The epithet *deep-meadow'd*, for instance, also in *Morte d'Arthur*, is from Pindar's βαθυλείμων. Latinisms in Tennyson's vocabulary are not infrequent, but they are scarcely common enough to constitute a marked feature of his style. He uses *eminent* in the sense of "projecting," *subjected* in the sense of "lying beneath," *fable* like the Latin "fabula," *frequence* for "crowd," *lucid* in the sense of "shining."[22] These are typical among Tennyson's Latinisms, and none are very striking or conspicuous words. Tennyson makes no effort to exclude the traces of classical reading from his ordinary style, but he does not rely on them for any important effect. In brief, the "classical" features of his diction show both his reading and his complete lack of pedantry.

On his use of compound words, especially of compound epithets,

[21]*On Translating Homer: Last Words.* See Macmillan ed. of the lectures *On Translating Homer* (New York, 1902), pp. 288–90.
[22]*Love and Death; Tiresias; The Gardener's Daughter; The Princess;* e.g. *The Lover's Tale.*

much of the poetic effect of Tennyson's style depends. He is not so prolific in his formations as Keats, nor does he pour such a wealth of imagination into them, but, with that single exception, no English poet is more felicitous in his compound words. I have enumerated elsewhere[23] the traditional types of the compound epithet in English poetry, and to one or other of these classes nearly all of Tennyson's formations belong; he is no lover of the "asyntactic" type, so much affected by G. M. Hopkins. His favourite kind is the parasynthetic compound, e.g. "*crimson-circled* star," "*million-myrtled* wilderness," "*deep-dimpled* current," "*horny-nibb'd* raven,"[24] and his most beautiful formations are those in which this type is combined with metaphor, e.g. "*dewy-tassell'd* wood," "*shadowy-pencill'd* valleys," "*ruby-budded* lime."[25] Another kind which he often uses I have called the bi-adjectival type, e.g. *human-amorous, wan-sallow, stately-gentle, silver-misty, divisible-indivisible* (world). His compound nouns are less frequent but, like the adjectives, they mostly have some verbal beauty, great or small, and scarcely one is an example of bare grammatical convenience or poetic licence. Specimen compound nouns are: *apple-arbiter, sea-cataracts, sea-voice, sea-lane, torrent-bow, foam-bow.* Some of Tennyson's compounds are in a lighter vein, e.g. "a *something-pottle-bodied* boy" (*Will Waterproof*), and a few seem rhetorical rather than poetic, like the phrase "*giant-factoried* city-gloom" (*Sea Dreams*), but as a rule Tennyson is true to his principle that the licences and conventions of verse must, whenever used, be justified by some touch of authentic poetry.

Like most of our chief poets since Spenser, Tennyson enriches his language with various words in which certain affixes have been used to form new compounds. It is sometimes difficult to determine whether the poet has himself formed such compounds, or has borrowed them from some little-known passage of an earlier date, but as a rule the distinction is without importance. Tennyson is too careful to overdo the use of any one affix, though like most writers he has his preferences. The prefix *dis-* is something of a favourite: he uses, for instance, the new or rare compounds *dislink, dishelm, discage, disprince, disedge, disroot.* He also makes some use of the prefixes *in-* and *en-*, as in *inswathe, immantle, encarnalize, empanoply, ensepulchre,* also of the suffix *-ful*, as in *mightful, prideful, gustful*; and like Carlyle he employs the suffix *-ism* for denunciatory or contemptuous formations such as *animalism, babyism, antibabylonianism*: *kitchendom* too is in Carlyle's manner.

---

[23]S.P.E. Tract no. XLIX, *The Formation and Use of Compound Epithets in English Poetry from 1579* (Clarendon Press, 1937).
[24]*In Memoriam*, lxxxix; *Lucretius*; *Gareth and Lynette*; *Battle of Brunanburh.*
[25]*In Memoriam*, lxxxvi; *The Daisy*; *Maud*, I.iv.1.

The somewhat rare prefix *counter-* appears as the first element in several compounds, e.g. *counterchange, countercharm, counterpressure,* and *counter motion* (printed as two words). Like many Victorian poets he has a taste for compound adverbs beginning with *a-*, e.g. *adown, anear, agrin, anight,* the first two of which were familiar in verse before Tennyson's time.

Some other features of Tennyson's diction remain to be mentioned, but as they do not raise points of much critical interest, they can be dealt with shortly. One is his use of onomatpoeia, whether in single words or in passages. Much has been written of Tennyson's direct verbal imitation of sounds in passages like that in *Morte d'Arthur*:

> Dry clashed his harness in the icy caves
> And barren chasms,

and it is true that such effects are fairly common. There is nothing very wonderful about them, and I agree with Mr. Geoffrey Tillotson, who in his excellent work *On the Poetry of Pope* remarks: "Onomatopoeia is a childish effect if it is carried to the extent to which, for instance, Tennyson carried it in the *Idylls.* In his tournaments Tennyson seems to be expecting to produce the actual sounds, rather than to suggest them." But scarcely anything Tennyson wrote is to be taken less seriously than these tournaments, which are perhaps too well known. Tennyson has suffered an injustice from the undue emphasis laid by critics, both friendly and hostile, on the onomatopoeic aspect of his style. How various is his command of poetic language I have in some measure already shown, and to speak of him as *par excellence* the poet of onomatpoeia would be as unjust as to quote Virgil's line

> Quadripedante putrem sonitu quatit ungula campum

as a representative specimen of the style of the *Æneid*. Tennyson has many lines of similar quality, such as this one from *Geraint and Enid,*

> The sound of many a heavily-galloping hoof,

and he is equally fond of onomatopoeia in short phrases and single words, but we need not pause long on this "childish" characteristic. I have already given instances of the vivid sound-effect which he elicits from familiar words: "The tempest crackles on the leads" (*Sir Galahad*) is an example which may be set beside "The chestnut pattering to the ground," and yet another is the reiteration of the name "Maud" (I.xii.1) to imitate the cawing of rooks: "Maud, Maud, Maud, Maud, They were crying and calling." Tennyson also makes frequent use of purely onomatopoeic single words, as in "*cheep* and twitter," "not a cricket *chirr'd*," and there is also an "echoic expressiveness" in

> the wood which *grides* and clangs
> Its leafless ribs and iron horns
> Together. . . .[26]

His well-known dislike of sibilants (except where a special sound-effect was required) and his taste for "hollow oes and aes, deep-chested music" naturally exerted some influence on his vocabulary. An illustration of his attention to detail is his change of *river's* to *river* in the line (*Lotus-Eaters*): "They saw the gleaming river's seaward flow." Like other masters of beautiful language, Tennyson had a sense of the music of proper names, but it is characteristic of his taste that he indulged this feeling very sparingly. In his earliest verse, names like Lilian, Madeline, and Oriana are prominent, sometimes excessively so; in his maturity, a line like (*The Princess*, ii)

> Clelia, Cornelia, with the Palmyrene

is a rarity. His manipulation of proper names in metre is always skilful. *The Daisy* contains examples which linger in the memory:

> But when we crost the Lombard plain
> Remember what a plague of rain;
> Of rain at Reggio, rain at Parma;
> At Lodi, rain, Piacenza, rain.

In *Boadicea* he shows with what dexterity he can handle unwieldy names like *Icenian, Catieuchlanian*, and *Prasutagus*.

It is a point of interest in Tennyson's general style that he finds use for several dialectal words in descriptive passages, e.g. "fast-falling *burns*," "sleeping *tarn*," "within the dark and dimpled *beck*," "down the shingly *scaur*," "the bushless *Pike*."[27] Tennyson's language is a very extensive subject; there are certain points which have not been touched upon, and many illustrations which might have been used have been omitted. But we must now turn to his contemporary who, though he shares the same Victorian background, is in many ways so strong a contrast.

BROWNING

It is now about seventy years since the death of Browning, and twenty-five more since the publication of *Dramatis Personae*, after which time

---

[26]*The Princess*, iv; *In Memoriam*, xcv, cvii.
[27]*Gareth and Lynette*; *Pelleas and Ettarre*; *The Miller's Daughter*; *Elaine*; *Ode to Memory*.

his style underwent a perceptible change. It is certain that much of Browning's poetry has kept its vitality, and it is unlikely that poetry written in the last century should be able to do this solely by its intellectual interest. There was a time when Browning's cleverest admirers thought principally of his meaning or "message," and it was interesting to point the contrast between Tennyson, the artist, and Browning, the philosopher. That view is no longer possible. In one respect at least Browning's technique needs no defence: Saintsbury's *History of English Prosody* establishes, once and for all, the high quality of his metrical art. The question of his language is more difficult. Its faults even in his best period are undeniable. Browning will never win admirers by the manifest attractions of his style. On the other hand, its merits are evident enough for those who choose to look, and one great merit, that of being "varied in discourse," was justly ascribed to Browning in the well-known lines of Landor. Browning's happy effects are not the result of mere luck, as has sometimes been suggested. An analysis of his dramatic monologues shows him to have possessed the poet's instinct of long self-preparation for new and original achievement, and many of the features of his style are, as we shall see, due to the exigencies of his favourite form. His early work may be regarded as a progress towards, and his later work as a decline from, the art of the dramatic monologue as he practises it in his best years—that is, during the period which begins about the time of his marriage and ends shortly after his wife's death.

Browning, of course, knew that his attitude towards poetry was unusual. In the last year of his life he wrote a letter to Professor Knight in which, as his biographer, Mrs. Sutherland Orr, remarks, "he states his view of the position and function of poetry, in one brief phrase, which might form the text to an exhaustive treatise": "It is certainly the right order of things: Philosophy first, and Poetry, which is its highest outcome, afterward—and much harm has been done by reversing the natural process."[28] This doctrine is in marked conflict with the theory that words and thought come simultaneously into the mind of the poet, that the poet knows what he wants to express by expressing it. Besides holding this theory of expression, Browning was a confirmed word-collector. As soon as he had chosen poetry as his vocation, he read through Johnson's *Dictionary*, and throughout his career he not only coined words, but adopted and adapted them freely from various languages. He had no fastidious shyness of influences: his inner life was

[28]Mrs. Sutherland Orr, *Life and Letters of Robert Browning* (London, 1891), p. 409. Quotations are taken from *The Poetical Works of Robert Browning* (London: Smith Elder & Co., 1910).

so robust that he delighted to rub shoulders with the outer world—the world of ideas and words, no less than the world of men and women. Hence his work reflects many aspects of the language of his time: it is a magazine of colloquial phrases, it is rich in learned and artistic terms, and it contains no less a wealth of words associated with poetry in general and Victorian poetry in particular. All these aspects of his diction will be noticed in turn; but I will first deal with his use of traditionally "poetic" words, as it is in this respect that his work offers the most striking and instructive contrast with that of Tennyson.

I

Although the language of Browning varies much in different poems, some use of "poetic" words is a fairly constant feature of his style. I imagine that most readers of Browning do not much notice these words: they are not so handled as to be conspicuous. In a few of his poems some traditional diction is almost inevitable. The theme of *Saul*, for instance, with its biblical atmosphere, impels the author to use various "poetic" words, and forms of words, in the familiar way: examples are *chaunt, 'gan, upsoareth, 'twixt, 'neath, inconscious, of yore, wot, ope, behest.* Such diction actually occurs in much of Browning's other work, but as often as not it is smothered and buried beneath a weight of alien associations. The following is a short list, which could be easily increased, of "poetic" words used in different parts of his work: *abysm, aëry, besprent, bosky, burthen, cinct, clomb, drear, dreriment, empery, hests, marge, marish, murk, pens* (feathers), *ope, steed, thrid, syllable* (verb). None of these words would cause the least surprise if met with in *Endymion* or *Hyperion*, and many of them are used by Tennyson. But in the effect which they produce the difference is great. Keats and Tennyson choose them for their atmosphere and associations, but to Browning they are more often than not the merest makeshifts. *Ope*, for example, occurs again and again; but it is simply a strange monosyllable in a context of ordinary English. When Tennyson writes:

> The circle widens till it lip the marge,

he gives an unhurried rhythm to the line which invites the reader to savour the words one by one, and the rare concluding word is in harmony with the rest; but when Browning uses the same word in *Instans Tyrannus*:

> Say rather, from marge to blue marge
> The whole sky grew his targe,

he seems to be clipping the final syllable partly in his haste, partly to fit the rhyme. So, too, in the line:

Twitch out five *pens* when plucking one would serve,

there is no apparent advantage in the poetic word for "feathers," except that as a monosyllable it suits the metre. These examples are typical. Browning rarely uses what the dictionary calls a "poetic" word to produce a poetic effect. He shows no more respect to one word than to another; he appears impatient of the finer tones of diction.

The variety of Browning's language is illustrated by his compound words, many of them new, formed by means of affixes. He has the Victorian taste for compound adverbs of which the first element is the prepositional prefix *a-*, as in *adrift*. Such words in the verse of the time usually have a romantic grace or charm. Some of Browning's also have this quality, but a great many are wholly different, being formed in a mood of jest or mockery. The following is a varied specimen list: *a-bloom, a-blush, a-bubble, a-chuckle, a-clatter, a-crackle, a-crumble, a-flare, a-flaunt, a-flicker, a-flutter, a-glimmer, a-grime, a-heap, a-seethe, a-simmer, a-smoke, a-spread, a-straddle, a-tangle, a-waft, a-whirl, a-wing.* A similarly mixed list might be compiled from the compounds formed with the prefix *be-*, though probably there would be a preponderance of jocular formations. Some affixes naturally lend themselves to a particular tone or style. For instance, Browning's compound verbs beginning with *en-* are mostly serious or romantic; even taken out of their context they suggest something of the pre-Raphaelite flavour, e.g., *enarm, enchase, encircle, enhaloed, enisled, enmesh, enwreathe.* His compounds ending with the suffix *-ry* are, as might be expected, of a very different quality: *archbishopry, cousinry, dupery, enginery, garnishry, gossipry, serpentry, stitchery, varletry*; perhaps the most serious formation in this group is *artistry*, of which Browning is perhaps the inventor. The use of adjectives ending with the suffix *-some* is characteristic of his style, e.g., *lightsome, toothsome, playsome, pranksome.* Such words agree with his prevailing colloquial tone; so do others of a similar type, e.g., *beseemingness(es), darlingness, uncomfortableness.* Many compounds he uses are rare or obsolescent, e.g., *lathen* (of lath), *griefful, blinkard, plenitudinous, morbify, immerd, dissheathe, celestiality.* These lists do something to suggest the vast range of the vocabulary which is needed when a mind so rapid, subtle, and original expresses itself in metrical form.

II

To do justice to Browning's style it is necessary to consider the special objects which he had in view. His most finished and elaborate works are the dramatic monologues of his middle period, and though it is of the essence of these poems that each is a highly individual work, yet they possess certain general qualities in common. For one thing, it is part of his plan to devise a situation in which the speaker should be able to unburden his mind with absolute freedom. Several of the speakers even pause to reflect on this frankness. For instance, Karshish in *An Epistle* (65-6) apologizes for troubling his correspondent with private matters:

> I half resolve to tell thee, yet I blush,
> What set me off a-writing first of all.

Bishop Blougram's visitor is one who imposes no restraint on the tongue of his host (929–32):

> Whereas I should not dare for both my ears
> Breathe one such syllable, smile one such smile,
> Before my chaplain who reflects myself—
> My shade's so much more potent than your flesh.

Caliban, at the end of his monologue (286–7), laments his indiscretion in talking so freely:

> There scuds His raven that has told Him all!
> It was fool's play, this prattling!

To suit the frankness of these self-revelations, Browning cultivates the utmost informality of style. His handling of colloquial idiom in little pieces like *The Lost Mistress* and *Confessions* is one of his finest achievements, and he shows the same skill on a larger scale in the best of the monologues. The excellence of the colloquial tone in poems like *Andrea del Sarto, An Epistle, Bishop Blougram's Apology*, and, one may add, *Cleon*—though there the manner is more stately—is evident, and equally evident are the subtle distinctions of style which mark off each poem from the others.

The mass of Browning's inferior work should not be allowed to obscure his masterpieces, but it must be admitted that few poets were so little formed by nature to woo perfection. Having mastered the colloquial style in verse, it was characteristic of him to go too far and become too colloquial. He had a bent towards the jocose, the disparaging, and the satirical, and in his later work he gave the impulse free play. This, of course, was partly due to his choice of imperfect and flawed characters as the main subjects of his poetry; but it was due as well to his own explosive vigour. His impatient energy impels him to give a ludicrous turn to the plainest statement. The line

> How both knelt down, prayed blessing on bent head

might have been written by Browning about the time of his *Pauline,* or
he might have composed it when in the rare mood of *The Guardian-
Angel,* but it is much more like him to write (as in fact he does in *The
Ring and the Book,* VI.378):

> How both *flopped* down, prayed blessing on bent *pate.*

Again, other men might have written the line:

> Pitted against a pair of juveniles,

but the version of Browning is, of course (*ibid.,* V.1356):

> Pitted against a *brace* of juveniles.

The mood of satire, whether gay or grave, is so common that it colours
Browning's whole style: in no other poet of the century is to be found
so large a store of contemptuous or disparaging words. Thus besides
pate for "head," he finds many occasions for *noddle;* for "speak" he
frequently uses *prate;* for "bow" he will substitute *lout;* for "child,"
bantling; for "move," *budge;* for "wrath," *bile;* for "bear" (verb),
spawn; for "go" or "march," *trundle.* "Daub his phyz" is quite Brown-
ingesque, so is "we drub Self-knowledge rather, into frowzy pate." He
searches out odd words of this abusive class, finding, for instance, *letch,
chouse, shag-rag,* and sometimes he enforces the effect by alliteration,
as in the line:

> And nuns a-maundering here and mumping there.

Many of these examples have been drawn from Browning's later work:
his style has less equilibrium after about 1864, the date of *Dramatis
Personæ;* but even in *Men and Women,* where his writing is most balanced, the note of exuberant mockery begins to be heard—for instance,
in *Holy-Cross Day.*

III

Verbal reminiscences from other poets are fairly common in Browning's work, and though they do not by themselves give a full idea of his
style, they suggest what its tendencies are. His early work shows some
traces of romantic diction, as in the line from *Sordello:* "That under-
current soft and *argentine,*" where the last word might have been borrowed from Keats; and there is a well-known echo of Keats's manner
in the song "Heap cassia" in *Paracelsus.* Reminiscences of the fine passages in other poets do not disappear from Browning's later writing,
but as the dramatic character of his work increases they come to be

chosen more and more for a dramatic purpose, like the quotations of Bishop Blougram in his reflections on Shakespeare (513–14, 517–19):

> He leaves his towers and gorgeous palaces
> To build the trimmest house in Stratford town; . . .
> Enjoys a show, respects the puppets, too,
> And none more, had he seen its entry once,
> Than 'Pandulph, of fair Milan Cardinal.'

Such references are characteristic of Blougram, but not of his creator. Browning's non-dramatic echoes of other men's words are of a more original type. The tendency towards abuse and disparagement which we noticed before is evident again here. Numberless English writers have shown their familiarity with Shakespeare's language, and Browning is among them, but it is not so much the highways of his poetry which he seems to know, as its bypaths and even its underworld. The phrases which he echoes from *Hamlet* are of this kind: "chop-fallen," "imposthume," "squeak and gibber."[29] From *Othello* he remembers "clink the cannikin" (Shak., "let me the canakin clink"), "prove a haggard": his phrase "nor cog nor cozen" is perhaps a variation of "cogging, cozening slave."[30] From *Macbeth* he remembers "lily-liv-ered."[31] "Mewls" is presumably from *As You Like It*, and "clapper-clawing" from *The Merry Wives of Windsor*.[32] "Just-lugged bear" sounds like a variant of "head-lugged bear" in *King Lear*, and "treads close on kibe" is Shakespearian, but not from any one passage.[33] From Milton, as might be imagined, he does not borrow much, but one word at least is a highly characteristic choice, viz. *scrannel*.[34] His borrowings from other writers are of a similar type: for instance, he uses Scott's *hellicat* (spelt "helicat") in *The Flight of the Duchess* (xiii). From Donne, with whom he has some affinity, he borrows the rare verb *out-streat* (*Ned Bratts*, 180). Of Bunyan, a spiritual fighter like himself, he was a close reader, and Bunyan provides him with several phrases. The allusion to Apollyon in *Childe Roland to the Dark Tower Came* (xxvii) is, of course, from *The Pilgrim's Progress*, and the description of Christian's fight with Apollyon who "stradled quite over the whole breadth of the way" leaves a trace in the phrase "a-straddle across its length" in *Ned Bratts* (222), which is a poem on two of Bunyan's converts. Browning also remembers the disdainful phrase bestowed on

[29]*Ring and the Book*, VI.134, VII.1145, XI.702–3.
[30]*Flight of the Duchess*, xvi; *Ring and the Book*, V.710; *Holy-Cross Day*.
[31]*Ned Bratts*, 86.
[32]*Aristophanes' Apology*; *Pietro of Albano*, 166.
[33]*Ned Bratts*, 201; *Ring and the Book*, X.1904.
[34]*Ring and the Book*, VI.1000.

Faithful in Vanity Fair: " 'a sorry scrub,' said Mr. High-Mind." The phrase is repeated in *Aristophanes' Apology*, and "a sorry little scrub" occurs in *Fra Lippo Lippi*. To illustrate Browning's verbal reminiscences I have drawn on only a few of his poems, but further examples would emphasize the same points.

IV

One element in the design of Browning's dramatic monologues is, as I have said, the unfettered freedom of the speaker's self-revelation. Another element, equally important, is the historical background which, to answer its purpose, must seem both real and accurate. Further, it is often a background of special significance. Browning loves to choose some moment of crisis, some period when great issues hang in the balance. In *An Epistle* and *Cleon*, the moment is one in which Christianity has just opened upon an unbelieving world; *A Death in the Desert* is dated a short time later. The Renaissance is one of his favourite periods: *The Bishop orders his Tomb at St. Praxed's, My Last Duchess, Andrea del Sarto* are all Renaissance poems, and *A Grammarian's Funeral* is headed "Shortly after the revival of learning in Europe." Even in *Bishop Blougram's Apology*, a more or less precise date is essential to the conception (414–18):

> Had I been born three hundred years ago
> They'd say, 'What's strange? Blougram of course
>   believes;'
> And, seventy years since, 'disbelieves of course.'
> But now, 'He may believe; and yet, and yet
> How can he?'

Sometimes, though not so often, Browning is equally explicit about place, heading the poems "Rome" or "Ferrara," or making it plain from the context that the scene is London, Florence, or elsewhere. But, binding himself in one way, he leaves himself free in another—the main character is either little known or wholly imaginary. Hence the detailed picture which he draws violates no familiar facts. On one occasion when he breaks this rule, namely in his portrait of Napoleon III, he secures some measure of freedom by calling the ex-Emperor "Prince Hohenstiel-Schwangau," but even this dialogue receives the precise and significant date, 1871.

In this scheme of producing the appearance of historical exactness, without sacrificing the poet's freedom of invention, diction plays an important part. Browning cares nothing for an atmosphere of vague romantic beauty, nothing for verbal melody or suggestion on their own account. He surveys remote lands and remote ages through a pellucid atmosphere: distance lends no enchantment to the view. The difference between him and his contemporaries is illustrated by his use of the word *argosy*. It is the historic element in this word that Browning brings out, not its vague romantic suggestiveness. The word occurs only in his play *The Return of the Druses*, where it is used four times, each time of *Venetian* ships. His scheme demands the accumulation of many small exact details of time, place, and circumstance. Hence the care bestowed on local colour, hence the frequent naturalization of foreign words, hence too the wealth of technical terms. His method is well displayed in his poem on the dying Bishop of St. Praxed's with his passion for architecture. The speaker's tastes are illustrated by the number and precision of his technical terms: *onion-stone* ("cipollino"), *antique-black* ("nero antico"), *lapis lazuli, gritstone, mortcloth, tabernacle, vizor, bas-relief, entablature, travertine*. The first seven words in this list are not used elsewhere by Browning—a proof of his careful differentiation of one poem from another. A similar effect is produced in *An Epistle* with its fitting display of medical terms: *snakestone, gum-tragacanth, sublimate* (noun), *tertian, viscid*: these words also are not used again in Browning's poetry. One wonders what other poet could have given such clear-cut reality to an imaginary letter from an Arab physician of the first century. It is more difficult to differentiate the language of a speaker who is not presented in his professional capacity or under any one aspect. Yet Browning succeeds here also. Bishop Blougram, for instance, is revealed less as a prelate than as a cultivated man of the world. Such a man, talking rapidly and intimately, will sometimes coin a word on the spur of the moment, sometimes use a rare word which he has perhaps never thought of before. It is thus that the Bishop does in fact speak: *decrassify* here makes its first appearance not only in Browning's work but apparently in the English language as well; *entourage, demirep, eventuality, experimentalise, excitation, fictile* occur in this dialogue and nowhere else in Browning. For the poet's peculiar method, great learning was necessary, and Browning's learning is generally to be trusted, though there are a few phantom allusions, such as that to the "Emperor Aldabrod" of *The Heretic's Tragedy*. It is true of Browning as of Milton that to appreciate him to the full is one of the rewards of consummated scholarship. His best work is strong enough to carry off some effect of strangeness in the language. Thus *loric* was not a word before Browning used it in his Roman poem *Protus*, but it suits the context and it dispels the intervening centuries better than "breast-plate." It is of course not the case in poetry that the end justifies the means.

The technical terms which Browning uses for a special dramatic purpose do not in his hands immediately turn into poetry, like the technical terms of Milton in the line:

> Cornice, or frieze with bossy sculptures graven.

Nor can the language of the arts have the same universal appeal as the common language of men. On that ground at least a cuckoo's cry is better described as a "twofold shout" than as a "minor third" (*Lovers' Quarrel*, 123). No poetry is safe in ignoring altogether the ideal of simplicity. It is characteristic of Browning that he so seldom approaches the plain dignity of biblical English. His diction is centrifugal: his restless activity impels him to avoid the norm; for him, as for Abt Vogler, the C Major of this life is a resting-place which invites sleep. Nor is he the man to use moderation. Some of his work, especially that of his later life, reads like a parody of his own method. The lines in *A Grammarian's Funeral*:

> He settled *Hoti's* business—let it be!—
> Properly based *Oun*—

produce a slight shock when first read, but, when familiar, they may give a kind of pleasure; so much can scarcely be said of lines in *The Ring and the Book* (VIII. 5, 6):

> *Amo -as -avi -atum -are -ans,*
> Up to *-aturus*, person, tense, and mood.

Nor is it clear why Count Guido Franceschini, who is not a physician, should call a pain in his shoulder-blade "an ailing in this omoplat" (V. 118). On the matter of technical terms in verse no two persons can possibly feel in the same way, a fact which in itself tells against them. For my own part, I can see why Browning in his character of dramatic realist should allude to the Pope's *cheirograph*[35] in *The Ring and the Book*, that being the correct term for "one of three forms in which the will of the Papal See is expressed in writing." I can also see some ground for the allusion to *tarocs* (i.e., playing-cards) in Caponsacchi's autobiographical sketch (VI. 349). But to form a nonce-word *baioc* (V. 542)[36] from "bajocco," the name of a small Italian coin, is simply unfair to the reader. Browning's declared principles in diction are cosmopolitan. He is naturally amused at "the sturdy Briton who, Ben Jonson informs us, wrote 'The Life of the Emperor Anthony Pie'—whom we now acquiesce

---

[35]Usually spelt "chirograph."

[36]Perhaps alliteration was the motive. The line is: "The broil o' the brazier, pays the due baioc"; see below, p. 240.

in as Antoninus Pius," but a little more insularity would have done nothing but good to Browning himself. Why, for instance, should he coin *ampollosity* from the Italian "ampolloso" rather than *ampullosity*, from the Latin "ampullosus"? The mere fact that he was writing a poem on Italian life is hardly reason enough. His refusal to latinize Greek names in the traditional manner, using instead such forms as *Olumpos, Phaidra, Phoibos, Sophokles, Klutaimnestra* is a small thing in itself, but it is significant of his attitude towards English usage. In his translation of the *Agamemnon* he aimed, as he tells us, at producing "the very turn of each phrase in as Greek a fashion as English will bear." He applies this principle to his diction in *Aristophanes' Apology*, giving us such expressions as: *dikast and heliast, kordax-step, peplosed and kothorned, choinix, barbiton, exomion* and *chaunoprokt.*

v

Some features of Browning's style are, as we have seen, the result of a particular end in view; they are necessary to his original handling of the dramatic monologue. But his language has other characteristics which must be considered in themselves, not in relation to any special purpose. Some of these points are of grammatical rather than of critical interest; some are blemishes which simply illustrate the weaker side of a powerful and brilliant writer; some suggest that in the obscurer parts of his nature this Victorian poet had affinities with the writers of an age very different and distant from his own.

A superficial but conspicuous feature of Browning's style is his use of the superlative termination *-est*, and less frequently the comparative termination *-er*, on occasions when it is more idiomatic to use "most" or "more" before the uninflected adjective or adverb. Other Victorian writers have this habit, Carlyle in particular, and less noticeably Ruskin and Arnold. Carlyle probably led the fashion. In Browning the practice begins early: *Sordello*, for instance, furnishes such examples as *distinctest, complexest, ficklest, notablest*; other poems contain *ineffablest, properest, directest, liberalest, dismalest, irreligiousest, sensitivest, heinousest, whimperingest, sagaciousest, benignantest, beauteousest*—a list which does not do much credit to Browning's ear. Examples of the rare comparatives are: *formidabler, truelier, clearlier, richlier, promptlier, safelier*. He freely uses or forms verbal compounds of the type in which the adverb comes first instead of second, as in normal prose usage. His favourite adverbial prefix is *out-*, as in *outbreak, outburst, outcourse, outflash, outpick, outpour*; another is *up-*, as in *upbear, upheave, uppatter*. He resembles Carlyle in his lavish use of the prefix *be-*, whether to form verbs like *becloud, bedaub, beflatter,* or to form participial adjectives in the manner of Carlyle's *bediademed, becoronetted, be-mitred.* In formations of the second type "the force of the be- is often merely rhetorical, expressing depreciation, ridicule, or raillery" (*O.E.D.*). In Browning are various examples, e.g.

> Lord So-and-So—his coat *bedropt* with wax.

> Its cobweb work, *betinseled* stitchery.

> Fop *be-flattered,* Hunks *be-friended,* Hag *be-lovered.*[37]

The eccentricity in the style of Carlyle and Browning is largely due to their ancestry and upbringing. Neither had any interest in that "Public School" and University English of which Thackeray and Arnold, each in his own way, are masters. Browning had a fine skill in the use of colloquial language, but the forms of it he knew best were those which are least cramped by insularity or class-consciousness. He brilliantly imitates the after-dinner conversation of a Roman Catholic bishop; with an Anglican he would not have succeeded so well. That he lived long out of touch with England is plain from his irregular or old-fashioned accentuation of certain words. I have noticed the following examples in *Aristophanes' Apology*: consúmmating, panégyric, demón-strated, cóntumély ("Whatever contumely fouls the mouth"). In *The Ring and the Book* are: súbjacent, promúlgate, revénue,[38] bastárd, marítal, and many more are certainly to be found.

VI

Though Browning could subdue his wayward impulses to the artistic end in view, his unruly passion for verbal eccentricity was always ready to burst out. Some of his subjects were of a nature to impose little re-straint upon him, and there were periods of his life when the passion for oddity was especially violent. The love of verbal freaks in a great master of English is a curious phenomenon, and its causes are complex. There was in Browning something of the antinomian, much of the humorist, much of the satirist, and scarcely anything of the scholar's conventional restraint. He had a close affinity with the spirit of the Re-naissance and sometimes reminds us of one of its cosmopolitan scholars, yet England inspires him with affection and pride, and there is no doubt of his patriotism. A more complex character does not exist among our greater writers. If to all this is added the recollection that he was an

[37]*Bishop Blougram's Apology; Red Cotton Night-Cap Country; Pietro of Albano,* 215.

[38]The usual accentuation in Shakespeare, and not uncommon in later verse.

impulsive writer who believed that the first fine careless rapture could never be recovered, and that revision is often an artistic crime, it will not be surprising if certain qualities of his style present the critic with a peculiarly difficult problem.

The purpose of Browning's rare words is often clear enough. Many in *Sordello*, for instance, have the same object as those in the best poems of *Men and Women*: they contribute to the local or historical colour. But one wonders why he so often chooses the unfamiliar form of a word which is itself sufficiently unfamiliar; for Browning is clearly not a Milton or a Tennyson to weigh the musical value of a single letter. Why, for instance, in *Sordello*, should he write *valvassor* for "vavasour," *truchman* for "dragoman," *plectre* for "plectrum," *trifoly* for "trefoil," *orpine* for "orpiment"? Possibly the pre-Raphaelites had an inkling of the answer, for some of these words have the medieval flavour which they liked, and Browning's early work helped to form their style. Throughout his career Browning had a taste for obscure and obsolete words and forms of words. For "frantic" he will write *frenetic*; for "restive," *restif*; for "swart," *swarth*; for "snigger," *snicker*; for "spit," *spawl*; for "canter" or "curvet," *tittup*. It is just like him to introduce the word *cue-owl*, a word used by himself and Mrs. Browning, but unknown, it seems, to the world at large. The strain which he puts on the use of rare words sometimes amounts to inaccuracy. In one of his poems, *catafalk*, which properly means "a stage or platform erected to receive a coffin," is used for "a kind of open hearse or funeral car"; in the same poem *encolure*, a French word for "the neck of an animal," is used to mean "the mane" (of a horse). Browning frequently forms or uses participles analogous to Milton's *increate* from "increatus," a practice common among writers of the sixteenth and early seventeenth centuries. Examples are: *exenterate, miscreate, saturate, contaminate, extravasate, unimplicate, undesecrate, consecrate, decollate, excommunicate, affiliate*, to which may be added *attent* from "attentus," and *porporate* from the Italian "porporato." Some of Browning's Latinisms seem to belong to the age of Burton or Browne rather than to the nineteenth century: for instance *benefic, crepitant, strepitant, mollitious*. The words in these last two lists, though queer and crabbed, at least bear the marks of scholarship, but occasionally Browning, like Spenser, incurs the reproach of "writing no language." There is, for example, his hybrid *ombrifuge* irregularly formed from ὄμβρος and -fuge, but this is not an extreme instance. Nor is his erroneous use of *lure* for "a trap or snare": here at least he is in company with others, including Disraeli. But in some of his verbal escapades he is apparently companionless. I do not suppose any other writer has adopted his *gadge*, which, the *Oxford Dictionary* informs us, is "used by Browning as the name of some instrument of torture"; nor has much further use been found either for *grudgment*, which is his rhyme for "judgment," or for *stomp*, which is "used by Browning (to obtain a rime) for *stump* or *stamp*."[39]

VII

Like most English poets, Browning frequently forms compound words, both nouns and adjectives. A number of his compounds are neat and beautiful in the manner of Tennyson; others show characteristic boldness or extravagance. He is fond of cumulative effects which are more energetic than euphonious: e.g., "That black-eyed brown-skinned country-flavoured wench"; "smooth-mannered soft-speeched sleek-cheeked visitor." Many of his compounds contain three or more elements: e.g., "bugle-bright-blackness," "middle-age-manners-adapter," "linden-flower-time," "hare-slice-and-peasoup-season," "bugaboo-and-baby-work," and—most extravagant of all—"monstr'-inform'-ingens-horrend-ous."[40] He is more effective when he shows more restraint, as in "the quiet-coloured end of evening," "an old pale-swathed majesty." As I have pointed out elsewhere,[41] his use of the asyntactic compound epithet, e.g. "*green-flesh* melons," anticipates some of the experiments of G. M. Hopkins.

Browning liked the vigorous effect of accumulated epithets; he also liked the emphasis of alliteration. In poems of his middle period, it is not uncommon to meet these two effects in combination: for instance in Fra Lippo Lippi's description of himself in his own painting,

> Mazed, motionless, and moon-struck,

and in the account which Karshish gives of his meeting with Lazarus:

> Out there came
> A moon made like a face with certain spots
> Multiform, manifold, and menacing.

Browning's taste for alliteration grew with years; and in some of his later work, when he gave free play to his satirical mood, an effect is pro-

---

[39]Browning's rhymes, as such, do not come within the scope of this study. His diction is, I think, bolder and more experimental in his blank verse than in his rhyming verse. But sometimes he certainly uses a word which he would not have thought of otherwise, for the sake of a rhyme, e.g. manage—*tannage* (*Flight of the Duchess*).

[40]*Æneid*, III.658: "monstrum horrendum, informe, ingens, cui lumen ademptum." Browning's compound occurs in *Waring*, iv.

[41]S.P.E. Tract, no. XLIX, *Compound Epithets*.

duced which is curious in itself and interesting to students of our early poetry. From the time of *The Ring and the Book* onwards, one meets with line after line, passage after passage, in which alliteration enforces the emphasis on certain key-words with remarkable vigour. I will quote a few examples from the large number which I have noticed:

> Proves a *p*lague-*p*rodigy to God and man.

> Look at my *l*awyers, *l*acked they grace of *l*aw,
> *L*atin or *l*ogic?

> Out with you! *Tr*undle, *l*og!
> If you cannot *tr*amp and *tr*udge like a man, *tr*y all-
> fours like a dog!

> *fl*at thus I lie nor *fl*inch!
> O God, the *f*eel of the *f*ang *f*urrowing my shoulder!—
> see!
> It *g*rinds—it *g*rates the bone.[42]

In these passages alliteration seems to be struggling to become the master-principle of the metre as it was in our ancient poetry, and when one meets a succession of lines like the following (*Ring and the Book*, XI. 1482–5), one feels that the spirit and manner of a long-forgotten past have mysteriously revived in this mid-Victorian writer:

> I tried chaff, *f*ound I *f*amished on such *f*are,
> So *m*ade this *m*ad rush at the *m*ill-house door,
> Buried my head up to the ears in dew,
> *B*rowsed on the *b*est: for which you *b*rain me, Sirs!

Alliteration has played a part in the verse of many English poets since the Elizabethan age, but for a parallel to this regular use of it upon three stressed words in the line we must go back to the alliterative poets before Wyatt and Surrey. In the tone of the passages which I have quoted, we hear something of the voice of Langland: he, like Browning, was a poet of headlong energy and unvarnished speech. But, for my own part, I am reminded even more clearly of the West Midland author of *Patience*, that poet of many moods, the tender, the humorous, the denunciatory. Surely there is something remarkably like certain phrases of Browning's style in the abuse which is showered on Jonah by the sailors in the ship bound for Tarshish (II. 196–200):

> What þe deuel hatȝ þou don, doted wrech!
> What seches þou on see, synful schrewe,
> With þy lastes so luþer to lose vus vchone?
> Hatȝ þou, gome, no gouernour ne god on to calle,
> þat þou þus slydes on slepe when þou slayn worþes?

[42]*Ring and the Book*, V.664, XI.1757–8; *Halbert and Hob*; *Ivàn Ivànovitch.*

This parallel is almost certainly due to the development of a natural tendency in Browning's style, and not to any study of early English verse. That a modern poet should revert, though but for a moment, to so remote an age, is surely a curious fact in the history of style.

VIII

I have dwelt freely on what I presume to call the "faults" of Browning's diction, yet it is clear that he was a great though irregular master of English. His influence on the language has been small in proportion to his powers. As we have seen, he is possibly the inventor of the word *artistry*, and a few of his phrases are current, e.g., "the first fine careless rapture," "the little more, and how much it is! And the little less, and what worlds away"; but his contribution to the language is much smaller than Tennyson's. In his lifetime, the influence of his style was not wide, but it was apparent in the work of two or three outstanding men. The pre-Raphaelites caught something of the spirit of his early style.[43] It is possible that D. G. Rossetti learned from Browning his idiom of the possessive noun + metaphor, e.g., "her neck's rose-misted marble" (Browning), "her eyes' o'erhanging heaven" (Rossetti). Certain features in the style of G. M. Hopkins are evidently borrowed from Browning, e.g., the accumulation of compound epithets, the asyntactic compound epithet (in which Hopkins is bolder than his master) and perhaps the use of emphatic monosyllables in a compact series. Browning's most profitable example to later poets lay in his use of colloquial English for the impassioned lyric. As G. K. Chesterton excellently puts it: "He substituted the street with the green blind for the faded garden of Watteau, and the 'blue spirit of a lighted match' for the monotony of the evening star."[44] In this respect Hardy is Browning's disciple, and from Hardy the example has spread far and wide into modern verse. That Browning's dramatic monologues have been little imitated is natural, for each piece has its distinct style, and to write a series of such poems would demand a combination of powers such as Browning alone possessed. Few writers have ever paid less regard to critics; he almost seems, like the fourteenth-century poets with whom I have compared him, to belong to a pre-critical age. "Tennyson," he noted, "reads the Quarterly and does as they bid him with the most solemn face in the world—out goes this, in goes that, all is changed and ranged. Oh me!" Browning could not have been what he was without his sturdy inde-

[43]In his early poems there are anticipations of the pre-Raphaelite manner in and repeated, for example, by Swinburne.
[44]*Victorian Age of Literature* (London, 1913), p. 176.

pendence; but it will surely act against his reputation in the future that
he implicitly denied one of the main disciplines which lead to literary
excellence: a consciousness that the rights of a reader make as just a
claim upon an author as his own instinct for self-expression.

ARNOLD

By his dates Arnold is a mid-Victorian poet. He has the amplitude
of mind and the seriousness of outlook which the best men of his generation possessed: it may be, indeed, that in these respects he surpassed
his contemporaries. He is untouched by the aestheticism of the later
Victorian age: poetry is to him a "criticism of life." Like Wordsworth
he strives to bring his poetic style as nearly as possible into line with
"the real language of men"; he dislikes any conscious attempt to widen
the gap between prose and poetry. His diction is more vital than Swinburne's, which is too literary, more real than Morris's, which is too
archaic. So much at least may be said in Arnold's favour; yet it must
be admitted that, in point of language, he is less interesting than either
Tennyson or Browning. The style of these two writers is, at all events,
strongly individual: Arnold's has much less character, it is individual
only in certain places. The very faults of Tennyson and Browning are
interesting, and bring us by a direct route to the most important problems of poetic expression. Arnold's faults are largely negative, and
therefore have less significance for the critic. It should be added, however, that Arnold's diction is not, like Tennyson's, his strong point;
further, that he wrote many poems and passages in a style beautiful
enough to satisfy the severest critic.

Though Arnold was in some senses an inheritor of the Romantic tradition, his relations with it were far less intimate than those of Tennyson
and Browning. He was, in fact, consciously on his guard against its
dangers. He underwent no youthful enthusiasm for its youthful poets.
He did not, like Tennyson, imbibe the spirit of Keats in his early man-
hood; he never had Browning's adolescent adoration of Shelley. The
poet of that generation whom he knew best and admired most was
Wordsworth, the master of the pure style; Byron he also admired, but
with a clear sense of his faults. The qualities which Arnold esteemed
in poetry were simplicity, restraint, austerity; how far this taste was
innate, how far acquired, it is impossible to say; but it is evident that
his mind was more closely moulded by formal education than the mind
of Tennyson or Browning. Some time for vagrant studies was probably
left by the classical curriculum in the Rugby of Arnold's day, but there

was certainly less freedom there for the "growth of a poet's mind" than at Hawkshead, or even at Louth or, Camberwell. In later life, Arnold acquired many new tastes of his own, but he remained faithful to the masters of whom his father most approved. Homer was to him always the infallible poet; of the Bible he remained an unwearied reader, nor did he ever fail in his admiration for Wordsworth. It was an invigorating education that Arnold received, but there was no escape from its influence, and it did much to determine the character of his poetry for good or ill.

I

A poet's choice of measures is always significant. The metres and rhyme-schemes of Arnold are mostly of the simple kind. He wrote a number of sonnets rhymed after the Petrarchan model, but his measures are usually much less exacting. His favourite forms are: blank verse (with far less artistry than Tennyson's), quatrains with alternate rhymes, six-lined stanzas of quatrain and couplet, and various forms of irregular verse, usually with easy rhyming-schemes, sometimes with no rhyme at all. Even in the stanza used in *The Scholar Gipsy* and *Thyrsis*, no end-word is rhymed more than once. As the measures are, so is the diction: it is sparingly adorned, and often austere. His early style is experimental, but there is a clear preference for simplicity. There is not much ornament in his prize poem, *Cromwell* (1843). His next volume, *The Strayed Reveller, and Other Poems* (1849) contains *Mycerinus*, a poem which Arnold often reprinted. Its style is modelled on that of Wordsworth's *Laodamia*, and though it falls far short of its original in concentrated strength, it has something of the same austerity, and something of the same Latinized diction. The reflective mood which is evident in the volume of 1849 becomes more pronounced in that of 1852, and to express it Arnold employs a style which he might have described in Dryden's lines on the heroic couplet:

> This unpolished, rugged verse I chose
> As fittest for discourse, and nearest prose.

Not only is Arnold's reflective verse often as near to prose as poetry can be, but there are passages in it which vividly recall the seventeenth-century manner. The following stanza (*A Farewell*, 73–6), for instance, is almost exactly in a style used by Dryden and Marvell:

> And we, whose ways were unlike here,
> May then more neighbouring courses ply;
> May to each other be brought near,
> And greet across infinity.

This note is rare in Arnold, but his reflective style shows a marked tendency to epigrammatic antithesis. He is fond of a sententious form of words like:

> Neither made man too much a God,
> Nor God too much a man.[45]

This kind of pointed expression is natural in the poetry which lies nearest to prose. There are poets with whom Arnold has a deeper affinity, but on the critical side of his nature he has much in common with Dryden. They have the same taste for simplicity, the same suspicion of false ornament.

Arnold said of Wordsworth "he has no style."[46] Something of the weakness which these words are meant to indicate is evident in Arnold's own work. His principle of composition seems to have been that of Horace:

> Cui lecta potenter erit res,
> Nec facundia deseret hunc, nec lucidus ordo.

There were a number of "res" which inspired Arnold with poetic eloquence; there were others which had not this power, and it is in writing of them that he betrays the lack of an habitual sustaining style. This point I will illustrate shortly: a minor but connected matter is his frequent disregard of verbal neatness. Arnold is not strong in the lesser virtues of style. Few good poets since the time of Pope have taken so little trouble to avoid the fault of hiatus. Phrases like "*the ills* we ought to bear," "the fight that crown'd *thy ills*," pardonable enough if exceptional, are in Arnold extremely common. Another characteristic, also tending to the slowness of his verse, is his practice of giving the value of two syllables to words like *spasm*,[47] *choir, fire, towards, flower, tired*. A more serious fault is his failure to produce "that subtle heightening and change" which are required for a "genuine poetic style."[48] It is not rare to meet in his poems passages which read like an excerpt from one of his essays cast loosely into the form of verse. In the following lines (*The Buried Life*, 55–69), for instance, though the value of the reflection is

---

[45]*Obermann*, 59, 60. Similar passages are: *ibid.*, 71–2, 95–6; *On the Rhine*, 19, 20; *Stanzas from the Grande Chartreuse*, 159, 160. Quotations are from *The Poems of Matthew Arnold* (Oxford, 1922).

[46]See p. 163.

[47]Contrast, for example, Milton, *P.L.*, XI.481: "All maladies Of ghastly spasm, or racking torture, qualms," etc.

[48]Preface to *Poems of Wordsworth*, chosen and edited by Matthew Arnold (1879); reprinted as "Wordsworth" in *Essays in Criticism*, Second Series.

undeniable, the effect of poetry is barely attained, and the last line is
completely prosaic:

> And many a man in his own breast then delves,
> But deep enough, alas, none ever mines:
> And we have been on many thousand lines,
> And we have shown on each talent and power,
> But hardly have we, for one little hour,
> Been on our own line, have we been ourselves.

Arnold's best work is free from such passages, but when his energy
flags he is apt to lapse into a bathos like that for which Wordsworth
has been so much blamed, the only difference being that Wordsworth's
bathos is one of platitude or rustic simplicity, while Arnold keeps his
literary manner. Lines like:

> By other rules than are in vogue to-day;

passages like:

> The other, maturer in fame,
> Earning, she too, her praise
> First in Fiction, had since
> Widen'd her sweep, and survey'd
> History, Politics, Mind,[49]

clearly belong to the prosaic rather than to the poetic criticism of life.

In his lectures *On Translating Homer*, Arnold has much to say on the
failure to render the grand simplicity of Homer's style. He condemns all
that is fanciful, eccentric, quaint, or rustic. Discussing a passage in Newman's version, he remarks that "as a matter of diction, the expressions
'O gentle friend,' 'eld,' 'in sooth,' 'liefly,' 'advance,' 'man-ennobling,'
'sith,' 'any-gait,' and 'sly of foot' are all bad," but he modifies the effect
of this by saying later: "Of the words which, placed where Mr. Newman
places them, I have called bad words, every one may be excellent in
some other place."[50] Arnold, for his own part, generally follows the
safe advice of Quintilian: "Consuetudo certissima linguae magistra,"
though one wonders, in passing, whether there is anything "quainter"
in Newman than the phrase "sustains the wise, the foolish *elf*" (*Empedocles on Etna*, I.ii.306), in which the last word is a synonym for
"man" chosen as a rhyme to "himself." Still, it is true that Arnold uses
comparatively few words or forms of words of the so-called "poetic" or
archaic kind. Among the examples which occur are *frith* (firth), *gulph,
sheen, marges, prore, wots, main* (sea), *steeds, eterne, drear, amain,
morns, eves, teen, wroth, frore*. I conjecture that several of these were

---

[49]*Empedocles on Etna*; *Haworth Churchyard*.
[50]*On Translating Homer* (New York, 1902), pp. 190, 248.

permitted as being nearer to their classical equivalents than the usual forms. Thus *prore* is nearer to "prora" than "prow"; *eterne* to "æternus" than "eternal." *Frith* is really a metathetic form of "firth," but it was commonly supposed to be allied to "fretum" in Arnold's time.

Verbal reminiscences from classical authors are common in Arnold's poetry, and have been the subject of various criticisms. One writer[51] points out some of the Homeric parallels: "the feeble shadowy tribes" (of Hell) and ἀμενηνὰ κάρηνα; "twittering ghosts" and τετριγυῖα ψυχὴ; "And is alone not dipt in Ocean's stream" and οἴη δ'ἄμμορός ἐστι λοετρῶν Ὠκεανοῖο; "long-necked cranes" and γεράνων . . . δουλιχοδείρων. Arnold has been blamed for treating the theme of *Sohrab and Rustum*, which is Persian, and that of *Balder Dead*, which is Norse, so much in the classical manner. Stopford Brooke, for instance, considers that "the Homeric tradition is out of place in *Sohrab and Rustum*" and calls *Balder Dead* "almost absurdly Homerized." I agree that in execution neither poem is wholly satisfactory, but these criticisms make the matter appear simpler than it really is. It cannot be maintained that Homeric echoes are only allowable in poems on a Greek theme: no one objects to the classicism in *Paradise Lost*. The point, rather, is that in *Sohrab and Rustum* and *Balder Dead* Arnold is not always in his natural element: parts are spontaneous, parts are laboured. In plain narrative Arnold is not like Homer; rather he is like Virgil, without Virgil's unfailing charm of style. What is lacking in a passage like the following (*S. & R.*, 197–9)—and it fairly represents the style in large portions of both poems—is the touch of verbal distinction which a Virgil or a Tennyson would have given it:

> The table stood beside him, charg'd with food;
> A side of roasted sheep, and cakes of bread,
> And dark green melons.

Here, as in many other places, there is none of "that subtle heightening and change" required for a "genuine poetic style." But when Arnold writes (*S. & R.*, 853–6),

> and from his limbs
> Unwillingly the spirit fled away,
> Regretting the warm mansion which it left,
> And youth and bloom, and this delightful world,

his feelings inspire a perfectly satisfying rhythm and diction. Arnold's good sense as a critic prevents him from spoiling the stories which he has to tell, but it is in the atmosphere, the background, the similes, and

---

[51] R. E. C. Houghton, *The Influence of the Classics on the Poetry of Matthew Arnold* (Oxford: Basil Blackwell, 1923).

above all in the reflective and elegiac passages that he proves himself a poet; in these he moves the reader because he is deeply moved himself. Had the author of *The Scholar Gipsy*, who voices so well "the sick fatigue, the languid doubt" of his own day, been able also to recapture some tones of the epic voice which he admired so much in Homer, he would have been the greatest poet of his generation. But this width of inspiration Arnold did not possess. Some half-dozen notes he can strike effectively; attempting more, he is evidently at a loss. He feels deeply as poet and scholar the beauty of classical myths and of the Oxford landscape; he is a stoic recommending moderate hopes, "close-lipp'd patience," and fidelity to the inward light; he knows the fickleness of joy and the rarity of peace, and clings all the more steadfastly to the things which endure, "what will be for ever; what was from of old." On these themes he always finds the right tone and the right words, and when he combines them in a single poem, he is one of the best of our elegiac poets.

II

A study of Arnold's characteristic words reveals both his strength as a poet and also his limitations. Inward austerity, as he tells us in the sonnet *Austerity of Poetry*, does not prevent the work of a poet from attaining outward radiance, and in Arnold's best poems, however severely planned, there is much beautiful diction. At the same time he appears, even in the comparatively small volume of his published verse, to be putting a strain upon his invention, for felicitous expressions in one piece are sometimes almost exactly repeated in another.

The repetition of words in poetry may be a sign of resource, or it may be a sign of limitation. I have shown elsewhere with what variety of effect Shakespeare uses the verb *gild*:[52] in some half-dozen contexts it produces the effect of as many different words. On the other hand, the repeated use of the adjective *dull* in some of Crabbe's verse is simply monotonous: the repetition is perhaps intentional, but the effect is like the continual striking of a single note. Arnold's work provides instances of both these kinds of repetition. One of his favourite epithets is *white*. This word he uses in various contexts, often with that touch of unexpectedness which is the life of poetic language: "*white* sleeping town," "*white* evening-star," "*whitening* hedges," "*white*-blossom'd trees." These phrases are vivid and fresh. But when we come to "*white* fog," "cold *white* mist," "*white* rolling vapours," "*white* peaks," "*white*

[52]"Some Kinds of Poetic Diction" (*Essays and Studies by Members of the English Association*, XV).

snows," the epithet begins to lose its force by familiarity. It was a happy thought to substitute *blanch'd* for *white*, and Arnold forms the beautiful compound epithet *moon-blanch'd*: but even this word is used twice, once with "green" and once with "street." In *Thyrsis*—a poem in which one is loath to find any fault—the epithet *pale* occurs three times in fifteen lines. Some of the repeated words do not lend themselves to differentiation. In the following phrases, for instance, "*high* unfrequented mountain spots," "*high* mountain pastures," "*high* the mountain-tops," "the *high* mountain platforms," "*high*-pasturing kine" the same note is struck each time, though it is a characteristic note which one enjoys and respects. Other words in Arnold are also characteristic, e.g., *austere* and the much-iterated *calm*. He is noticeably apt to repeat his felicities. For example, "blue *Midland waters*" in *The Scholar Gipsy* is an attractive phrase for the Mediterranean, but in *A Southern Night* we also come across "this *Midland* deep"; the pleasant simplicity of "the lights come out" in a description of the scattered farms near Oxford at evening (*Thyrsis*, 164) reappears verbatim in the lines on an autumn evening at Rugby (*Rugby Chapel*, 8).

A further examination of Arnold's diction, in its various phases, confirms these general impressions. Compound epithets are often characteristic of their author, and Arnold's follow this rule. In one group there are many traces of unconscious autobiography. The following list is very suggestive of their author's inner life: *heart-wearying, heart-wasting, care-fill'd, clearest-soul'd, high-soul'd, even-balanc'd* (soul); and the stoical self-discipline of Arnold's philosophy is indicated in the large number of formations in which *self-* is the first element: e.g., *self-sufficing, self-helping, self-ordain'd, self-govern'd, self-master'd*, and the group of four in the sonnet "Shakespeare": *self-school'd, self-scann'd, self-honour'd, self-secure*. Descriptive compound epithets are fairly numerous in Arnold's verse; they are one of the beauties of his two best poems, and no reader of *The Scholar Gipsy* and *Thyrsis* can have missed their effect in phrases like "*air-swept* lindens"; "warm *green-muffled* Cumner hills"; "*frail-leaf'd*, white anemone"; "dark *red-fruited* yew-tree's shade"; "*gold-dusted* snap-dragon." It is also in descriptive phrases that Arnold's somewhat rare use of metaphor appears most memorably: "white anemonies *Starr'd* the cool turf"; (some rich hyacinth) "a fragrant *tower* of purple bloom"; (of an eagle) "never more Shall the lake *glass* her, flying over it"; "where the nich'd snow-bed *sprays* down Its powdery fall"; "And from the boughs the snowloads *shuffle* down"; "Soon will the high Midsummer *pomps* come on"; "The *coronals* of that forgotten time."[53] Like Browning and other poets, Arnold shows a preference for particular affixes in forming compound verbs and participial adjectives: perhaps it is characteristic of him to prefer the negative ones, the prefixes *un-* (or *in-*), and the suffix *-less*. Some negative compounds, new or old, are used by him with remarkable energy. *The Scholar Gipsy* furnishes two examples in the vigorous lines:

> Still nursing the *unconquerable* hope,
> Still clutching the *inviolable* shade,

and *Thyrsis* supplies two more in the line:

> The *morningless* and *unawakening* sleep.

In descriptive use, negatives occur in "*unwrinkled* Rhine," "The *unplumb'd*, salt, estranging sea," "the west *unflushes*," and in the beautiful phrase "*uncrumpling* fern."[54] Arnold's sense of the impassivity of Nature is forcibly expressed in the negative epithets of the lines (*Empedocles on Etna*, II. 360–1):

> Over the *unallied unopening* earth,
> Over the *unrecognizing* sea.

Another prefix for which he shows a preference is *en-*, as in *enisled, enclasping, engarlanded, enkerchief'd*.

Of verbal reminiscences from other English poets there is comparatively little in Arnold's work. Critics have named Wordsworth as his principal English model, and Wordsworth is not a poet whose influence is traceable in the details of style. A close inspection of Arnold's language brings to light a few passages in which Wordsworth's phrasing has evidently been remembered. The style of *Mycerinus*, as I have already mentioned, shows a general resemblance to that of *Laodamia*. There is a description of pine-trees in the poem called *A Dream*:

> the morning sun,
> On the wet *umbrage* of their glossy tops,
> On the red *pinings* of their forest floor,
> Drew a warm scent abroad,

in which two words are obviously echoed from "the pining umbrage" of Wordsworth's *Yew-trees*. In a passage from *Sohrab and Rustum*:

> For he remember'd his own early youth,
> And all its bounding rapture,

[53]*Tristram and Iseult*, III.207–8; *Sohrab and Rustum*, 637, 570; *Parting*, 49–50; *Balder Dead*, III.319; *Thyrsis*, 62, 117.
[54]*On the Rhine*, 12; *To Marguerite* (1852), 24; *Thyrsis*, 163, 74.

the second line looks like a composite of "I bounded o'er the mountains" and "all its dizzy raptures" (ll. 68 and 85 of *Tintern Abbey*). Another possible reminiscence of the same poet is the opening sentence of *The River*, "Still glides the stream," which is identical with the first part of line 5 of the sonnet *After-Thought*. Here and there are echoes from other writers. For instance, "its *weary, unprofitable* length" (*Youth of Man*, 110) is obviously Shakespearian, and Arnold's use in description of *wailful, moss'd* (walnut-trees), and *summer eves*, all of which are characteristic of Keats and occur in his Odes, may be due to reminiscence of those poems. It is natural that so sedulous a reader of the Bible as Arnold was should show signs of its influence in his style, and it is not difficult to find examples: e.g., "seed-time and harvest," "We bear the burden and the heat Of the long day."[55]

Taken as a whole, Arnold's style is very unequal, and though he revised details of expression in successive editions of his poems, he was at heart much more concerned with the general plan of a work than with its execution. The mannerisms of his prose style have often been mentioned, and his poetic style has mannerisms which are not less conspicuous. Perhaps the most striking of these is the excessive use of lines consisting of three epithets or three nouns (e.g., Zealous, beneficent, firm; History, Politics, Mind). In *Rugby Chapel*, a poem of 208 lines, there are five examples of this type of line, viz. ll. 10, 43, 139, 158, 160. This mannerism occurs principally in the short-lined blank verse which is one of Arnold's favourite metres.

III

I have already alluded to the strong vein of reflective criticism which runs through Arnold's poetry. How successfully he wrote in this style is proved by the excellence of his quotable lines, for instance: "Who saw life steadily, and saw it whole"; "France, fam'd in all great arts, in none supreme"; "The pageant of his bleeding heart" (of Byron).[56] But the poetry of the Victorian age was the offspring of the Romantic movement, "a great movement of feeling," as Arnold calls it, not "a great movement of mind." He belonged to his age, and his deepest poetic impulse was an emotional one. Fundamentally he is an elegiac poet. The feeling from which nearly all his best work springs is summed up in the lines:

> Nature is fresh as of old,
> Is lovely: a mortal is dead.

[55]*Empedocles on Etna*, II.254; *Morality*, 9–10.
[56]*To a Friend; To a Republican Friend; Stanzas from the Grande Chartreuse.*

It is the symbolization of this contrast in alternate speeches in the second act of *Empedocles on Etna* that makes that part of the poem so immeasurably finer than the first act, with its monotonous exposition of an austere philosophy. Arnold needed a complex theme to unlock the full treasury of his language. That he had such a theme in *The Scholar Gipsy* and *Thyrsis* is the reason why those two works are his best poems. There he could express to the full the contrast between his love of the Oxford landscape and his delight in the poetry of the ancient world on the one hand, and his sense of the unrest and distraction of his own age on the other. Together, these themes drew forth the full passion and beauty of his poetic voice.

It is not my task to determine the full critical significance of the conclusions which have been reached in this chapter. It is clear, however, that any poetry which is widely read must leave some mark on the language in which it is written. Of the three poets who have been discussed, Tennyson's influence was far greater than that of his two contemporaries. Browning, it is true, anticipated some of the experiments of later verse, but no change in taste will ever make him popular in proportion to his intellectual vigour: the idiosyncrasies of his style will always form too great an obstacle. Apart from Tennyson's qualities as a poet, his influence is an historical fact of much significance. As Poet Laureate, he belonged to a succession of writers many of whom performed great services to their native tongue, and English is not less indebted to him than it is to Dryden, to Wordsworth, or to Bridges. Tennyson's faults, and in particular his over-attention to the minuter graces, fade into insignificance beside his command of a splendid vocabulary to which his many-sided talent continually gave new life. His example contributed in a hundred ways towards producing that high standard in the use of language shown by the later Victorians both in their verse and in their prose. By sympathy and interest he even had some contact with the contemporary advances in philology. He was a poet whose developing art was happily identified with the best interests of his native tongue. Without Shakespeare's sovereign mastery over words or Milton's power of impressing the stamp of his mind upon them, he rendered the language a high service by helping both to conserve and to refine it.

THE POSITION of D. G. Rossetti is one of crucial importance in the present survey. Any historian of English literature, from whatever angle he may be writing, will be drawn to choose one writer or group of writers as especially representative of the great changes in literature noticeable in the years round about 1870. The historian of prose style might choose Pater; the historian of the novel, Meredith or Hardy, or both; the historian of poetry, Swinburne, Rossetti, or Morris, according to his particular point of view. Swinburne's *Poems and Ballads* of 1866 probably appeared more revolutionary than anything else in the second half of the century, but the stir made by Robert Buchanan in his "Fleshly School of Poetry," in which Rossetti figured as the main culprit, was evidence of a conflict little less acute. In the limited field of the present study, Rossetti is certainly pre-eminent. In Swinburne's poems, diction is subordinate to a brilliant virtuosity in metre and rhyme, but for Rossetti's work, vocabulary was a paramount element. It is known that he ransacked old books in the British Museum for what he called "stunning" words. His influence on the next generation of poets was great: some adopted his idiosyncrasies; a few bettered his example. He helped to introduce a new school of poetry in which the diction diverged as far from the "real language of men" as in any part of the eighteenth century. The reaction in our own times against this movement has been as vigorous as that of Wordsworth was in 1801 against the "gaudiness" of false "poetic diction."

On the surface, there may not appear to be any profound difference between the diction of Rossetti and that of the slightly older poets. It has frequent echoes of Tennyson, and of Browning, as well as reminiscences of Keats. It is therefore not immediately apparent why it represented something new, almost revolutionary. The pre-Raphaelites, including Rossetti, had in general a high admiration for the early work of Tennyson—*The Lady of Shalott*, for instance, and the poems of 1842. But a small incident which occurred after the publication of Swinburne's *Atalanta in Calydon* illustrates the deep divergence of view between the older and the younger generations of poets. While expressing much admiration for the brilliant qualities of the new work,

Tennyson asked whether it was *"fair"* to use the language of the Bible in poems so antagonistic to the spirit of Christianity.[1] For Tennyson, it was a matter of poetic decorum and intellectual integrity to respect the historical associations of words and their religious implications. He disliked and denounced the attitude of the pure aesthete. Had he wished to express the sense of Swinburne's line in the *Hymn of Man*, "Glory to Man in the highest! for Man is the master of things," he would have found other words in which to do it. Rossetti had little of Swinburne's revolutionary violence, but on the aesthetic principle he clearly sided with him, rather than with Tennyson.

The view that different types of poetry demand a special diction of their own was commonly held in the age of Pope and Johnson, though the precise boundaries between the vocabulary of epic, drama, pastoral, and the other kinds were never laid down. The poets of Wordsworth's age still accepted this view, though the new ideas in poetry tended to throw it into the background. Further, as the personal element in poetry began to assume such large proportions, there was a latent inclination to assume that all poetic diction formed a single province, and that the only frontier was between poetry and prose. This opinion was never stated by Wordsworth, for Wordsworth did not hold, like some later critics, that the nature of poetry is essentially lyrical. It was a result rather than a cause of Romantic poetry, and probably it did not come to be widely expressed until after the time of Rossetti himself. Rossetti's aestheticism, however, is a large step in the same direction, though taken from a different starting-point. Tennyson, as we have seen, upheld a certain decorum or fitness in the choice of words against the practice of Swinburne. Rossetti, like Swinburne, acknowledged no consideration above the aesthetic. His diction, especially in the sonnets, which contain much of his richest verse, was largely formed on an appreciation of medieval art and love-poetry.[2] The sonnets and canzoni of Dante, which so deeply affected Rossetti's poetry, are sublimed by a spirit of religious adoration, for to Dante and his circle, earthly love is symbolic of heavenly. Deeply conversant with these poets, Rossetti transferred the style he had formed as their translator to his own love-poems, in which the heavenly element had no part whatever. The reader recognizes the language of religious mysticism, though the experiences are those of a purely earthly passion. Rossetti's admirers did not notice or

---

[1] "Is it *fair* for a Greek chorus to abuse the Deity something in the style of the Hebrew poets?" *Tennyson: A Memoir*, by his Son (London, 1897), I, 496.

[2] The list of Rossetti's favourite poets given by his brother W. M. Rossetti is illuminating. Special emphasis is laid on Dante, Keats, Poe, Blake, Tennyson, Browning, Chatterton, and Bailey (author of *Festus*).

did not resent this discrepancy. But the note of exaggeration and false emotional strain is now apparent, and Rossetti's sonnets, wonderful as they are in many ways, are written in a style which has been a good deal tarnished by time.

Before discussing the more general qualities of Rossetti's style, we must notice some of his technical experiments. As a translator of Italian verse, he naturally felt the comparative difficulty of finding rhymes in the English language. Especially was this so in the sonnet. This form, in English, has often been used with a certain laxity in the rhyme-scheme not consistent with its ideal symmetry. Rossetti felt this: and, as a remedy, endeavoured to increase the number of rhymes accepted as legitimate in English. Since the seventeenth century it has been the practice of English poets to admit certain approximate rhymes as conventionally correct. For instance, such pairs as *see–variety* or *tune–moon* have been admitted by the most scrupulous poets, and a certain limited number of "rhymes to the eye" such as *love–move* have been commonly allowed. Rossetti sought to increase the number of accepted rhymes. Probably few of his new rhymes are unprecedented, but they had not been used before as part of a system. One of his reforms, which gave him added flexibility of expression, was to adopt certain new approximate rhymes to the word "love." In his sonnets and elsewhere, *of* and *enough* are accepted as rhymes to *love*: thus we find the group *of–above–love* in one sonnet; *love–grove–thereof* in another; *love–of–enough* in a third. Rhymes on prepositions such as "for" are also frequent. Another device for obtaining new rhymes is to shift the accent from the beginning or middle, to the end of certain words, as in *playèr*, which thus provides an approximate rhyme to "here," "dear," etc.; or in *watèr*, which rhymes with "where" and "fair." Similarly, *visàge* rhymes with "foliage"; *complaisàunce* with "glance"; *lily* with "me." Accent-shifting is sometimes employed by Rossetti for its own sake, as a kind of archaic affectation, as in *Jùly* and *prelùde*, which occur in the middle of lines. The force of Rossetti's example in rhyming was limited; but in one region, that of the sonnet, ode, and elaborate lyric, it produced a very considerable effect.

A rich medieval colouring is a feature of many of Rossetti's poems. The youthful daring of Chatterton (a pre-Raphaelite favourite) was now replaced by calculation and scholarship. Rossetti's translations of early Italian poetry were executed with the aid of frequent Middle English and Middle French words, consecrated by their association with pre-Raphaelite art and poetry. He struck the key-note of his style in *The Blessèd Damozel* in which phrases like "citherns and citoles," as well as the title itself, are no small part of the poem: indeed, we are expressly told that the names Cecily, Gertrude, Magdalen, Margaret, and Rosalys "are five sweet symphonies." In the same poem we see how even a word like *herseemed* has a stylistic value; in others, *anhungered, alway, betwixen,* and the familiar *natheless* help to build up the archaic setting; and compounds like *circlewise, oftenwhiles, thiswise, therebeyond* contribute to the atmosphere of sacred remoteness. But the chief part is played by words which tend to group themselves into two opposing divisions of good and evil or, as Rossetti would have expressed it, of Love and Hell. We are reminded of his injunction on the art of sonnet-writing:

> Carve it in ivory or in ebony,
>   As Day or Night may rule.

The "evil" group is more comprehensive: it includes archaic words such as *ban, grame, dule, teen, shent, scathe, unweal, foredone, sufferance, malisons, disputeousness,* and phrases like "the nether clefts of Hell." In the "good" group are words like *guerdon*—a favourite with Rossetti—*pleasaunce, largesse,* and the much-used *aureole.* The last example is partly symbolic and pictorial, like *gonfalon* and others: and the symbolism of his colour words merits a study in itself. Archaisms which add little or nothing to the poetry, like *under,* an obsolete word for the middle of the morning, are sometimes admitted, but only rarely, for the artist in Rossetti usually predominates over the scholar.

His diction is marked by several other features which deserve to be characterized briefly, in view of his strong influence at the end of the century. First there are the various compound nouns recalling the prejudice in favour of "Anglo-Saxon" words then current. Examples are: *shadowkind, flood-brim* (i.e., horizon), *sundawn, song-craft, letter-lore* (i.e., learning).[3] As a stylistic contrast to this primitive note, Rossetti would often reserve a resonant word of Latin origin for a position of emphasis, especially in the last line of a sonnet. There is a certain mannerism in such conclusions as:

> The wind of Death's imperishable wing.
>
> The shame that loads the intolerable day.
>
> Sleepless with cold commemorative eyes.[4]

Another feature, too conspicuous to omit, is a semi-symbolical use of certain initial letters. Thus the title *Willowwood* given to a set of four sonnets is intended to suggest a mood of passionate melancholy which is sustained in the sonnets themselves by a repeated use of *w*-alliteration;

---

[3]*Sundawn* was used earlier by Browning in *Paracelsus* (I.404); *song-craft* appears in Longfellow's *Hiawatha,* Introd., 109.

[4]*House of Life,* iv, xcii, xcvii.

and a similar effect is produced in the conclusion of *The Stream's Secret*:

> Mine eyes that add to thy cold spring,
> Wan water, wandering water weltering,
> This hidden tide of tears.

One last feature of his diction is the choice of various words which, in an earlier period, would have been called "aureate." Besides exotic nouns such as those in the line "Hell-birth of *geomaunt*[5] and *teraphim*," one meets various rare Latinisms like *lustral* and *gracile*; and the "aureate" style is clearly marked in the precept which is given to sonnet-writers:

> And let Time see
> Its flowering crest *impearled and orient.*

Our final view of Rossetti's diction must, I think, be one of qualified admiration. Like his poetry as a whole, it is the result of "fundamental brain-work."[6] It is the diction of a poet learned in his art; a collection of choice words harmonized by a strong poetic personality into an instrument expressive of its own complex and passionate nature. It was adapted to lead a prevailing current in the literature of the time. In the mechanism of verse his influence was healthier than Swinburne's, for while Rossetti aimed at the flexible, Swinburne sought the fluent. But though the technical achievement of Rossetti is admirable, his poetry too often makes us uneasily aware of a discrepancy between the means employed and the results achieved. We feel ourselves to be in a room richly ornamented but confined and close, and with no view into the world without. For his language, with all its resonance, its imagery, its cross-currents of symbolism, is deficient in clear-cut expressive power. Here and there a picture stands out with fine distinctness, but too much is vague and veiled. The diction is overloaded with literary reminiscence. We are evidently entering an age of literary sophistication in which poetry is too much seduced by the splendour of its resources, and too conscious of its own medium to assert the liberty and energy which are the parents of great works.

WILLIAM MORRIS

William Morris, after some years of close fellowship with Rossetti, parted company with him and pursued a path of his own. Between the two poets we find, as might be expected, certain points of resemblance

[5]I.e., "geomancer." Apparently from Ital. *geomante* (*O.E.D.*).
[6]Rossetti's phrase in a letter to Sir Hall Caine; see O. Doughty, *A Victorian Romantic* (London, 1949), p. 614.

as well as many points of contrast. Both drew much inspiration from medieval poetry and art; but Rossetti's Italian models made little appeal to Morris, whose chief delight was in French and English works, and later, in Icelandic. What Dante was to Rossetti, Chaucer was to Morris. But apart from their favourite fields of reading and study, there was a deeper diversity of spirit and aim. In spite of its medieval trappings, Rossetti's work was fundamentally an expression of the modern spirit; while Morris, notwithstanding his strenuous exertions to influence the life of his time, lived far more in the past—an idealized past, it is true. Nothing he wrote reveals the natural bent of his imagination more than the two lines (*Earthly Paradise: An Apology*):

> Dreamer of dreams, born out of my due time,
> Why should I strive to set the crooked straight?

The difference between the two writers is vividly brought out if two of their early poems—each among the best of its author's work—are set side by side. *The Haystack in the Floods*, one of the most intense and dramatic of Morris's pieces, is like a flash of lightning illuminating a moment of history. Rossetti's *Jenny*, notwithstanding archaic touches in the style, is as much a study of contemporary life as his celebrated pre-Raphaelite painting on a similar subject, entitled *Found*.

Besides this difference of temperament there is a radical divergence of type in the work of the two poets. Rossetti, introspective and brooding, excelled in lyrical and meditative poetry; Morris, an outward-looking man, intensely interested in the crafts and pageantry of bygone ages, excelled in narrative. These differences are clearly reflected in their style. Of the two, Rossetti's exercised a deeper influence, for it was adapted to the emotional life of the time. The discrepancy between means and result, previously noted, was itself a modern feature, for the age (especially the seventies and eighties) was torn by violent emotional, intellectual, and religious conflicts. The style of Morris has none of the inward tension of the time. The words which he uses are of a piece: their associations are harmonious. But they are also less effective than Rossetti's, as their task of interpretation is much simpler. The toils and strife of Argonaut and Viking can hardly affect us deeply unless fused with the modern spirit by some prodigious effort of style. Morris simply seeks to kindle our interest in the tragic and picturesque elements surviving in these wonderful legends. An admirable attempt: but not one to call forth a major exertion of poetic power.

Archaism, a return to simpler methods, is therefore an integral part of Morris's plan. No doubt his style varies in the stages of his evolution as represented by *The Defence of Guenevere, The Life and Death of Jason, The Earthly Paradise*, and *Sigurd the Volsung*. Still, in some respects his work possesses the same character throughout. A pre-Raphaelite in art, he was a pre-Spenserian in poetry. He had no rigid program, it is true, and he took no pains to exclude every post-Spenserian touch from his vocabulary. Some compound epithets and other marks of the long tradition of poetic diction since Elizabethan times linger in his verse. But in general he eschewed nearly the whole complex art of poetic expression, in metre as in diction, which had been built up by the followers of Spenser. His favourite measures (apart from the long line of *Sigurd*) are octosyllabics, the Chaucerian decasyllabic couplet, and the stanza of *Troilus and Criseyde*. It was clearly impracticable to apply the vocabulary of Chaucer to a nineteenth-century poem. Morris (except in *Sigurd*) seldom uses a word not easily intelligible to an educated reader of the time; and on the other hand, he admits many words from various sources, learned and popular, which were unknown in the century of Chaucer. His aim, however, is poetic, not philological; and by his great reduction and simplification of vocabulary he largely banishes the memory of Shakespearian drama, of Miltonic epic, and of most Romantic nature-poetry, and creates the atmosphere he desires—one fit for

> sweet stories by the poets sung
> From ancient days.

To the nineteenth-century reader, there was something very novel in the type of poetry offered by Morris. Not the intensity of great moments in succession, but the diffused interest of an ever-moving action—this is what Morris gives in his great narrative poems, *Jason* and *The Earthly Paradise*.

The difference between Morris and most poets of the century appears significantly in his descriptive adjectives. The poets in the Romantic tradition were ever in search of the unusual epithet. Morris preferred the true epithet, whether rare or not. The point must not be laboured. At times, he will use a phrase like "the spray-arched cave" in the typical manner of the time. But this is not his characteristic style, which consists in a naïve reliance—or what seems such—on the plain truth to produce its proper effect. If Nature repeats her colours, what can the painter-poet do but repeat their names? Thus, in *Jason* we hear of *red* roses, *red* rubies, *red* wine, *red* lips, *red* blood, *red* flame; of the *green* grape, the *green* sea, *green* trees, *green* grass, the *green* earth, *green* waves, *green* billows. The mere names of the primary colours are a

major element in Morris's style and his descriptions are never better
than when two appear in conjunction, as in the lines:

> until the broad sun, growing low
> Reddened the green sea;

or,

> And while their oars were whitening the green sea;

or,

> And all unheeded did the mackerel shoal
> Make green the blue waves.

In these descriptions the combined colours produce the "rare" effect—
the slight shock of surprise—which the use of metre leads us to expect.
But the constant repetition of the single names makes us sometimes
wonder whether the painter or dyer in Morris has not obtained the
upper hand over the poet.

How far Morris's style was really affected by his practice as painter
and craftsman, how far it was a matter of pure literary choice is too
specialized a subject to be discussed here. The points, so far as they
concern general criticism, are so admirably put by Dr. Alfred Noyes
in his book *William Morris* that I cannot do better than quote his remarks in full:

It is . . . probable that Morris—who stoutly denied that "inspiration" had
anything to do with artistic craft—was in some ways hampered by the wealth
of ornament that lay ready to his hand, in books, in pictures, in tapestries,
and in stained windows. Out of all these things, too often perhaps disre-
garding the fount within himself from which he might have drawn directly,
he made a kind of poetic dictionary that at first sight would seem to have
very little bearing upon the realities of life, and in one sense seriously limited
his great poetic energies. His work, in a word, was as highly conventionalised
as that of Pope, though the conventions were new, the product of a romantic
period, and for the most part brought together by his own hand. These conventions he used as a kind of literary shorthand, and he limited himself to
them in a very extraordinary way. There is only a certain and narrow range
of natural objects which he will allow himself to mention—whether they be
of the earth or the sea, flower or fish, or bird or beast. He will speak of roses,
for instance, of lilies, of sunflowers, of violets, and of daisies. But "Ragged
Robin" or "Old Man's Beard" or "Shepherd's Purse" would be as impossible
to him as it would be possible to Shakespeare or to Tennyson. The lark and
nightingale and a few other birds he will allow; but the bullfinch and the
yellow-hammer, the white-throat and the herring-gull are all, we may say
beforehand, avoided by him as if they were turkeys. There are many more
which might or might not appear in almost any other English poet from
Shakespeare to Tennyson, but would at once be dismissed by a practised reader
as impossible to Morris, who in nine cases out of ten would be content with
some such phrase as "the brown bird's tune." It is the same with his sea-

scapes. In place of the marvellous succession of exquisitely true and beautiful pictures of the sea which glimmer and recede and foam and roar through the poems of Tennyson, from that marvellous description of a North Sea wave in the *Idylls of the King* to that

> scream of a madden'd beach dragg'd down by the wave

in *Maud*,—in place of these we have in Morris a series of conventional drawings of a singularly limited range. For the most part his waves are "green," a little less frequently they are "blue"; and beyond that he has—in energetic moments—"white" and "tumbling" and perhaps two or three words more, all of which he uses over and over again. In less energetic moods he is usually content with the quaint inversion "the water wan," which occurs some hundreds of times in the course of his works, and certainly scores of times in *Jason* alone.[7]

In the poems of his best years the simplification of which Alfred Noyes speaks is the outstanding feature of Morris's diction. But in his later works the language loses something of its poetic originality: it becomes "more strange and less new." Like many writers of the time he seems to have felt that Teutonic archaisms were a legitimate ornament of poetry and prose. The historian Freeman did much to foster the tendency to idealize all things Old English which was very common at this time: philologists and grammarians joined in by asserting the superiority of the "Saxon" element in English. In *Jason*, Morris uses archaisms like *folk* for "nation," *spill* for "destroy," *acre* for "field," and *bane* for "slayer." We also find *likely-head, hardihead, goodlihead, dreary-head* as well as *agone* for "ago" and the participle *bursten* for "burst." After his studies in Anglo-Saxon and Icelandic his tendency to Teutonize became much more pronounced. He acted as co-translator of *Beowulf* and of several sagas, and he saturated himself in the spirit of the Icelandic epic cycles. The finest fruit of these studies is *Sigurd the Volsung* (1876). While admiring Morris's splendid re-telling of this great story, the critic can hardly doubt that he has injured his work by using a diction which gets awkwardly between the reader and the poem. Not that Morris makes any real display of philological learning, though it is clear that he has read his sources in the original. The truth rather is that *Sigurd* is a kind of clearing-house for all the "Saxonism" of the century, true and false. It is interesting to sort out the various kinds of "Old English" which figure in the poem. First, we may note examples of pseudo-antique grammar or spelling, such as *torch-litten*[8] for "torch-lit," *wotted* for "wist" or "knew," *whileome* for

---

[7]Alfred Noyes, *William Morris*, "English Men of Letters Series" (London: Macmillan, 1908), pp. 45–6.
[8]Cf. "Dim with the dew of *moon-litten* hours" (Bulwer Lytton).

"whilom." Next, there is the use of the superfluous suffix -*ward*, as in *to usward*, "a cry from *withoutward*."⁹ Thirdly, we notice the use of obsolete words which are ambiguous in modern use through being identical in form with other words of different meaning, as in phrases like: "in the *tide* when my father fell" (for "time"); "clouds beneath the *lift*" (for "sky"); "men drink the *bridal* of Sigurd" (for "bride-ale"); and the word *waxen* meaning "grown." Again, there are the biblical phrases, chosen, one feels, in deference to the prevailing view that the Bible was a store-house of "noble Saxon English," not because such expressions had a natural fitness on the lips of Sigurd or Brynhild. Many quotations like the following could be made:

> He laughs to scorn the treasure where thieves break through and steal,
> And the moth and the rust are corrupting. . . .

Finally, we are sometimes reminded of the ill-advised attempt to replace certain well-established words from a foreign source by artificial equivalents of native origin: as in the well-known suggestion of *folk-wain* in place of "omnibus." *Yea-saying* is not a happy substitute for "assent"; still less is *Welsh-wrought war-gear* a good way to convey the sense of "foreign-made weapons." Morris's Teutonic diction wears a still odder look in his translation of the *Odyssey*. In such a work, the reader is probably accustomed to a certain set of words, and it is startling to find a phrase like νεφεληγερέτα Ζεύς rendered, not by the time-honoured *cloud-compelling*, but by the strange expression "the god that driveth the lift." In leaving this subject, however, it is only fair to remark that *Sigurd* is not one of the poems in which the diction plays a primary role. An enthusiastic critic like Alfred Noyes naturally writes little about the language and much about the metre, which is, as he says "managed with marvellous skill"; and one may entirely agree when, in his praise of the battle-scene in which Brynhild stabs herself, he maintains that the "heroic triumph" "is perhaps conveyed to us more by the music and cadence and general spirit of the poem—as in some great symphony of Beethoven, rather than by any 'array of terms.' "¹⁰

SWINBURNE

The space given to Swinburne in this study might appear to be less than that which is due to a poet of such marvellous technical accomplishment. But Swinburne, who drew so deeply upon the vital powers

⁹This was also a mannerism in Carlyle's prose.
¹⁰Noyes, *William Morris*, p. 121.

of the English language, added to it little of his own vitality in return. Several critics have agreed in holding that he rather closes than opens a great poetic era. With this view I am in full agreement, and it is a conviction which the study of Swinburne's diction has done much to produce. I have, throughout this book, endeavoured to emphasize those aspects of a poet's diction which are creative within the Spenserian tradition: and while few poets stand more securely within that tradition than Swinburne, few have done less, in proportion to their powers, to renew its vitality by the creative qualities of their own style. It is, of course, impossible not to be impressed by the garnered wealth of Swinburne's poetic vocabulary. He was a man of immense reading, of what Sir Edmund Gosse well calls "assimilative genius." The same critic quotes an amusing admission by Lord Lytton who, in reading *Poems and Ballads*, had been so carried away by the virtuosity of the new poet that he had failed to notice anything else. "The beauty of diction and mastership of craft in melodies," he wrote, "really so dazzled me that I did not see the naughtiness till pointed out."[11] The critic who observes style only cannot be a true critic of style. Yet the mistake of Lord Lytton was perfectly natural. It is true that Swinburne's poetry is largely made up of rhythm and diction, and in reading it one is reminded of the remark by a late Greek critic that an over-rhythmical style gives a feeling of the rhythm only, not of the sense.

Johnson's complaint against *Paradise Lost*, "the want of human interest is always felt," is much more applicable to the poetry of Swinburne. The emotional note heard in his poem *The Triumph of Time* is not often repeated. His great passion was for literature, and his real heroes were Landor, Victor Hugo, and Baudelaire. It was natural that he should have expressed himself so fully in verse and prose criticism, and that some of his most vital work should have been his brilliant literary parodies. Observers agree in noting the impression he gave of being not quite human, and for a poet he was strangely aloof from the human affections. Even the interest which he latterly showed in little children was not unconnected, it seems, with Hugo's *L'Art d'être grand-père*.[12] Apart from literature, his deepest passion was for the sea, and it is in the splendid sea-descriptions of *Tristram of Lyonesse* that his style becomes most vividly alive and his diction charged with its maximum of expressive power.

The diction of Swinburne is extremely "poetic" in the literary sense

[11]Edmund Gosse, C.B., *The Life of Algernon Charles Swinburne* (New York: Macmillan, 1917), p. 153.
[12]See *ibid.*, p. 304.

of the term: it is poles asunder from the vocabulary of analytic, scientific, or realistic prose. Poetry for Swinburne, as for Rossetti, is a self-contained province, and his diction is of the most exclusive kind. It rejects most words not sanctioned by literary association, or without the power of contributing to melody of verse or to wealth of rhyme. As Tennyson said, not meaning to be severe, "He is a reed through which all things blow into music." Swinburne's diction is not archaic in the manner of Spenser's, but it is no less remote from common life. No English poetry is more biblical in phraseology, and no English poetry is more pagan in sentiment. When, in *Tristram of Lyonesse* (VI), Ganhardine asks of Tristram on behalf of his sister:

> what evil hath she done, to be
> Mocked with mouth-marriage, and despised of thee,
> Shamed, set at nought, rejected?

it is, one sees well, for their literary glamour alone that Swinburne prizes the biblical phrases. It has been noted that his "ornate melody" does not exclude such "unpoetic" monosyllables as *bloat, pinch, rind, fang, wince.* But even such words are not so alien to literature as they may seem: Shakespeare himself might have used them in much the same way.[13] It is indeed the bookish origin that strikes one as the distinctive feature of Swinburne's diction, next to its marvellous union with his metrical skill. For one rare or striking word which he has stamped with his own individuality, there must be a score which he has simply remembered and repeated. To give a few examples: "Foam" being one of Swinburne's favourite words, one might well suppose that *afoam* (*Atalanta in Calydon*) is of his own making: but it had, in fact, already existed for some years, having been used by Charlotte Brontë of whom Swinburne was a great admirer. *Frondage* and *flowerage* are just such ornate words as he might have been supposed to coin himself: yet the first had already been used by Aubrey de Vere and the second by Tennyson. In affecting such verbal forms as *paven* for "paved," *shapen* for "shaped," and *unslaken* for "unslaked" Swinburne is simply following a fashion of the time. He uses many of the "revived" words of nineteenth-century poetry such as *burgeon, benison, guerdon.* He borrows the epithet of a typical phrase coined by William Morris, "the *sundering* sea," and applies it to "death." *Westering* as a word associated with the sunset begins its career in *Lycidas*, and it was "in very common use c. 1840" (*O.E.D.*); it was this word of general literary currency that Swinburne repeats in his phrase "the westering sun"

[13]*Bloat* and *pinch* do in fact occur together in *Hamlet*, III.iv.182–3.

(*Tristram*, VIII). Much of his diction is of course drawn from remoter sources, and though it is more Victorian than is at first apparent, its chief origins are Elizabethan, Jacobean, and Caroline. Thus, in "The very dawn was . . . *freaked* with fire" (*Studies in Song*, 15), "freaked" is no doubt a direct reminiscence from *Lycidas*. Rare words of Shakespearian (or Elizabethan) origin such as *pleached* and *incarnadined*, contribute in like measure to the impression of glamorous sophistication given so consistently by Swinburne's poetry. Conciseness and simplicity are the last qualities to be looked for in Swinburne: rather one may expect a liquid fluency and swiftness, purchased at times by a heedless redundancy of words. The sonorous polysyllabic participles used so effectively by Rossetti often serve the more doubtful purpose in Swinburne of enriching the music of a line or phrase with only the slightest advantage to the sense. The word "regenerate" may not be wholly superfluous in the phrase "requickened to *regenerate resurrection*" (*Death on Easter Day*), but it is hard to attach any but the most tenuous sense to "reverberate" in the line (*Tristram*, ix),

> Inseparable as *reverberate* day from night.

Every reader of Swinburne must have observed the diluting effect which the use of such words produces both in his poetry and in his prose.

Swinburne's diction, as we have said, is most creative in his descriptions of the sea. He also shared with contemporary poets an impulse to add to the vocabulary new words or compounds expressive of a fanciful or lingering observation of times and seasons, and the processes of Nature. Thus, *day-dawn* may, in one sense, be a superfluous word: used, perhaps invented by Coleridge (in *Remorse*), it had become a poet's word, and is repeated by both Morris and Swinburne. So, too, *sun-dawn*, appearing in Browning's *Paracelsus*, is one of Swinburne's words: he may himself have invented *moon-dawn* and *star-dawn*.[14] Like many other poets he uses the ancient poetic word *sun-bright* and he repeats the newer *snow-bright*, which had appeared in Shelley's *Revolt of Islam* (xii, xli). *Sea-line*, an alternative for "horizon," which enjoyed a vogue in the poetry of the eighties, finds its way into Swinburne's verse and is one of the numerous compounds of which "sea" is the first element. A fertile and constant feature of Swinburne's imagination is an impulse to conceive land and sea as the counterparts of each other: and this conception leaves many traces in his language.

---

[14]*Sun-dawn* appears in *Marino Faliero*, Ded., vii. The *O.E.D.* example of *moon-dawn* is dated 1895, but it occurs in *Tristram of Lyonesse*, ii (1882). For *star-dawn* see *After Sunset*.

"The great sea" is to him "faultless as a flower" (*Félise*), and in his figurative descriptions there is a marked mutual attraction between the words "flower" and "foam." Expressions like *"flowers of foam," "foam-flowers,"* and *"foam-flowered* sea"[15] are scattered over his work. So too, there are *sea-bloom, sea-flower, sea-fruit, sea-blossom,*[16] and similar words spring up everywhere. It is characteristic that the rare word *seashine* should have been used by him in the description of a *land*-scene (*Studies in Song,* 179):

> Streak on streak of glimmering seashine crosses
> All the land.

Swinburne's love of the sea as a source of energy to his entire style is, I think, the most interesting feature of his diction, in its creative aspect.[17]

[15]*Love at Sea; A Leave-Taking; Erechtheus.*
[16]*Rondel:* "Kissing her hair"; *Ave atque vale; Triumph of Time; Chastelard.*
[17]Very few of Swinburne's word-formations have been repeated, but one possible example (so it appears from the *O.E.D.*) is *slumberland.* Some readers may think this characteristic.

THOMPSON AND BRIDGES

AN ALLUSION was made by the late Sir Edmund Gosse in a public lecture given shortly before 1914 to the problem facing the poets of the time who had to work with the "worn-out counters" of literary currency. In our survey of the diction of poetry from Spenser onwards we have reached a time when the problem mentioned by Gosse was felt by an increasing number of poets. The traditional attitude to language and metre which had survived many shocks and had served the needs of the most diverse poets was at last beginning to prove no longer tenable. Whether it would have to be totally abandoned or would adapt itself to the needs of a distant future was a question which did not yet arise. Nor was every poet and critic aware of the crisis. Even after Swinburne many poets were to produce work of finished beauty within the time-honoured traditions. Yet the changes in the whole climate of civilized life were making it more certain every year that those who clung tenaciously to the past would pay the penalty in the narrowness or unreality of their work.

Tennyson was the last great poet who could work, without sense of restriction, within the poetic order established by Spenser and Milton. His aim was to produce a body of poetry beautiful in all its details— an object which accorded with the spirit of his age. In Browning, as we have seen, a new impulse was astir. He was the precursor of many other poets who sought some alternative to the Tennysonian blend of high expressiveness with finished beauty. The example of William Morris in his modified revival of pre-Spenserian diction also had its results. It was followed, for instance, by Charles Doughty in *The Dawn in Britain*. New ambitions in the life of the nation called for new modes of expression. For the imperialistic spirit which became vocal in the latter part of the nineteenth century the older traditions were too urbane and too moderate. The diction of Kipling, the poet of imperialism, is a blend of the ultra-modern and the primitive: its outstanding elements being the slang of the army and echoes from the Old Testament. Of a far higher order is the vital and concentrated style of Hopkins whose creative handling of syntax held much significance for the future. His diction, as Mr. Charles Williams well says, is the outcome of "a passionate emotion which seems to try and utter all its words in one."[1] But it was long before the work of Hopkins was to have its full impact in the field of letters.[2] Another poet of the age, Thomas Hardy, must on the whole be ranked with the innovators. He was, it is true, a tireless reader of the great poets of the past—his quotations show it—but his special affinity was with Browning, of whom he is the greatest successor. There are, of course, many phases in Hardy's diction, but its original features are most fully developed in *The Dynasts*, his inclusive and culminating poem. Mr. Edmund Blunden, in his book on Hardy, convincingly relates the nature of the great drama to the peculiar qualities of its diction. He notes that the words especially needed by Hardy are of the following kinds: "the local, graphic, primitive, hard, and the psychological, subtle, abstract."[3] All these innovating poets were abandoning the fashions of diction which had been consecrated to poetry for three centuries, and they therefore lie outside the scope of our survey.

The subject-matter of our last chapter has been drawn from the poetry of Francis Thompson and the earlier poetry of Robert Bridges. In the poetic order to which these writers belong, they are late, but they are not decadent. As a *fin de siècle* figure, A. E. Housman might have been chosen in preference to Bridges. But the astonishing power of Bridges in developing new modes of expression in his last years places him as a link between the Spenserian past and the unknown future. His latest work is not discussed in this book, but it gives him an added title to close the series of poets here dealt with, as it reminds us of the deeper continuity of our poetry.

THOMPSON

The links with the past were still strong in the last decades of the century, and it had been shown by Rossetti and Fitzgerald what power was still latent in the cult of "beautiful" language. Critics like Pater and Gosse were wholly on the side of continuous tradition, and the motives which underlay the style of the "innovators" and "eccentrics" were little understood. Francis Thompson (1859–1907) was not the man either by condition or by temperament to challenge the standards of his time. The Catholic poets with whom he was associated, Coventry Patmore and Mrs. Meynell, were content with the traditional diction and metres,

[1]Introduction to *Poems of Gerard Manly Hopkins* (Oxford, 1933), p. xv.

[2]The present writer has discussed one aspect of Hopkins's diction in *The Formation and Use of Compound Epithets in English Poetry from 1579*, S.P.E. Tract, no. XLIX (Clarendon Press, 1937).

[3]Edmund Blunden, *Thomas Hardy* (Macmillan's Pocket Library, 1951), p. 236.

though they differed from Thompson—Mrs. Meynell in particular—in cultivating a style of far more restraint and economy. Thompson's taste for verbal opulence has more than a hint of the baroque manner of seventeenth-century Catholic art, but it is equally due to his own temperament and the intellectual atmosphere of his age. After some miserable years in London, in which he resorted to opium, he was taken into the house of the Meynells to whom he owed his survival as a poet. The inspiration of his poems lay in two or three profound experiences: that of the pursuit of his soul by its Divine Lover (*The Hound of Heaven*); that of overwhelming gratitude to his benefactress (*Love in Dian's Lap*); and a troubled, baffled struggle towards a higher and clearer spiritual life (*Sight and Insight*). Inspiration so narrow, inward, and intense was bound to reflect itself in a certain exaggeration of style, and this appears in the radiant but often tortured imagery of Thompson's verse, as well as in a lavish display of the "beauties" of diction, in which his work recalls the "aureate" style of earlier times.

The same features of style are apparent in nearly all the poems that Thompson wrote, though there is a special simplicity in some of his shorter lyrics such as the *Poems on Children* and a special restraint in others, such as *The Kingdom of God*. For description of his general style one need go no further than his own poetry: he speaks (in *Retrospect*) of his "heaven-sweetened tongue" and the "skiey-gendered rain" of his music; and elsewhere (*Sister Songs*, II) of

> this treasure-galleon of my verse,
> Fraught with its golden passion, oared with cadent rhyme,
> Set with a towering press of fantasies.

It is difficult to conceive of Thompson as writing in any language but that of poetry: yet, though his diction is laden with reminiscences, it is also stamped with his own personality. Sometimes we hear a word from Shakespeare or Keats; more often from Shelley or Rossetti: but he can absorb suggestions from the most diverse sources. Within the compass of his small output there is an echo from nearly every one of our greater poets, and his style might be described as the quintessence of "poetic diction." It is impossible that what he did should ever be done again. He lived at a time when it was natural for a sensitive man of letters to cultivate a refined receptiveness towards the best work of the past, and he excelled his contemporaries because he was, among the poets of the time, the most naïve and the most exuberant. In Thompson's work, we are clearly watching the last phase of a long tradition.

The dominant influences on Thompson's diction are the poets already mentioned: Shakespeare, Shelley, Keats, and Rossetti. That poets so contrasted in type as Shelley and Keats—the inspired and the artistic— should have an equal share in Thompson's diction is itself a proof of his wide receptiveness. He repeatedly uses words, when they suit him, from the discarded diction of the eighteenth century. He also echoes the manner, if not the words, of the "metaphysical" poets, especially Donne and Crashaw. In common with Gosse and other critics of the time, he admired the work of Sir Thomas Browne, and that great master of rhetorical prose must be reckoned among the formers of his style. Finally, he uses many words and forms of words which are marked "poetic" in dictionaries, though to the critic they appear to belong to the diction of verse rather than of poetry. A new "verse-diction" had grown up in the nineteenth century, and Thompson admits it freely into his vocabulary.

To begin with the Shakespearian words. Some of them are the long-established ones like *o'ercanopies*; but the novelty in Thompson is his preference for Shakespeare's rarer word-coinages. There is a lavish use of new "verbs" formed from other parts of speech, and the direct borrowings are equally numerous. We find, for instance, four distinct echoes from *Antony and Cleopatra*: *lethed*, *terrene*, *lackying*, and *dumbed*.[4] Words like *antre* and *rondure*—both Shakespearian—are also of the more *recherché* variety, and the "verb" *sultry* is in the late Shakespearian manner.[5] Thompson did not inherit the disgust felt by the early Romantic poets for the trite diction of the eighteenth century, and he freely admits words like *fulgence*, *beamy*, *vernal*, *gelid*, and *conscious*[6] ("the conscious gates of morn"), which had been out of fashion for nearly a century. "Storied urn,"[7] which comes direct from Gray's *Elegy*, may be added to the list. It is likely that Thompson's admiration for Browne prompted some of his rare Latinisms: the fact that the title of a poem *From the Night of Forebeing* is a quotation from Browne lends support to the conjecture. In any case, many of the participial adjectives might have come direct from *Urn Burial*: e.g., "*constellate* dreams," "others, not yet *extricate*," "the *purpurate* shine," "*immitigate* fangs," "*discinct*,"[8] and the same might be said of words like

[4]The first three are from *Sister Songs*, "The Proem," I, II; the fourth is from *The Way of a Maid*.

[5]The first two are from *Sister Songs*, I, II; *sultry* is used in *Ode to the Setting Sun*.

[6]*Fulgence* and *beamy* appear in *Sister Songs*, I; *vernal* in *Sister Songs*, II; *gelid* and *conscious* in "*Manus animam pinxit*" and *Orient Ode*, respectively.

[7]*Sister Songs*, II.

[8]*Constellate* (also in Bailey, and in Browning) and *extricate* are found in *Sister Songs*, I; *purpurate* is from *The Poppy*; *immitigate*, from *Sister Songs*, II; *discinct* from *The Night of Forebeing*.

praevenient, vidual, coerule.[9] Echoes from Shelley are somewhat rare in later poets, and the indubitable examples in Thompson are therefore the more conspicuous. "Destroyer and preserver," "earthquake and eclipse," and "revolving year" are obvious quotations: "aërial hyaline" is an imitation of Shelley's manner.[10] The blending of the two strains, the Latinized and the Shelleyan, is sometimes a little odd:

> Some, with languors of waved arms,
> Fluctuous oared their flexile way;
> Some were borne half resupine
> On the aërial hyaline.

Shelley's style is an influence diffused over the whole of Thompson's poetry: Keats's style appears in vivid flashes of verbal reminiscence. In the following lines, for instance (*Sister Songs*, I),

> If Even burst yon globèd yellow grape
> (Which is the sun to mortals' sealèd sight)
> Against her stainèd mouth,

the imagery is a composite recollection from the *Ode on Melancholy* ("globèd peonies," "burst Joy's grape against his palate fine") and the *Ode to a Nightingale* ("purple-stainèd mouth"). Also in the manner of Keats are various epithets, rare or newly formed, on the pattern of *rumorous*, such as *arborous, flavorous, tremorous*.[11] Among many signs of Rossetti's influence are the epithet *gracile*[12]; the "medieval" imagery of *gonfalon* and *aureole*[13]; and rhymes (rare or strained) such as *drouth-mouth; love-thereof*. The "floating" diction of Victorian verse in represented by the smooth-sounding "weak" participles *bereaven, over-shaden, folden* and by the typical formations *a-dream, a-flaunt*, and *a-lurk*.[14]

This record of Thompson's indebtedness to previous poetry is, of course, far from complete, and it certainly conveys something less than the truth as to his saturation in the language of his favourite authors. The analysis has not been made with the object of minimizing his

[9]All three words are from *The Night of Forebeing*; *coerule* is in Spenser (*Virgil's Gnat*).

[10]*Orient Ode* (and *Ode to the West Wind*); *To Monica, Thought Dying* (and *Revolt of Islam*); *The Night of Forebeing* (and *Adonais*); *Sister Songs*, I.

[11]*Sister Songs*, II; *The Night of Forebeing*; *To a Poet breaking Silence*; *Orient Ode*.

[12]*Sister Songs*, I (also Rossetti's *Love's Nocturn*).

[13]*The After Woman*; *Any Saint*.

[14]The history of the prefix has been studied in J. H. Neumann's "A Nineteenth-Century 'Poetic' Prefix" (*Modern Language Notes*, April, 1943); Mr. Neumann's statistics "show that 110 of the 270 words with *a*-plus substantive or verbal forms occur first in the 19th century"—see *Year's Work in English Studies*, 1943.

originality. His poetry, even at its weakest, is much more than a laborious in-gathering of fine phrases. At its best—but not always—it adds new lustre to what it borrows. A manner of his own, innate and inalienable, is clearly audible in a passage like this, from *Sister Songs*, I:

> I had endured through watches of the dark
> The abashless inquisition of each star,

and indeed throughout the whole of his stronger poems, especially *The Hound of Heaven*. The point to be made is that Thompson, like many of his contemporaries, but in a greater degree than they, is embarrassed, almost overwhelmed by the wealth of his poetic inheritance. He is betrayed into a fluency of splendid phrases under which his meaning is in danger of being buried, and the simpler style in which his poems sometimes conclude scarcely makes amends for the previous complexity. His admission, "I who can scarcely speak my fellows' speech" (*Sister Songs*, II), indicates his own feeling of disability. After the lapse of nearly a century, a situation like that which Wordsworth describes in his Preface of 1801 had arisen once again, but this time it was not merely the neo-classicism of two generations, but the great tradition of beautiful language begun by Spenser that had grown decrepit. The question for poetry was: Must the tradition be discarded altogether, or could it be reformed by the self-denial and austerity of poets, and by reinvigoration from neglected sources?

ROBERT BRIDGES

No one made so impressive an effort to recover the freshness of the past as Robert Bridges, in whose work phrase and rhythm are selected with unhurried and scrupulous care. Unlike Tennyson he had no temptation to write for popularity; his poetry—especially that which precedes *The Testament of Beauty* (1929)—suffers from a certain aloofness, and he was too remote from the minor pains of life to interpret the harsher side of the modern world. This detachment lessens the human appeal of his poetry, but it was the condition of his almost unrivalled craftsmanship. A. E. Housman, a fastidious judge, called the *Shorter Poems* of Bridges "the most perfect book of verse ever written."[15]

Like many other English poets Bridges excelled in the descriptive lyric, and his finest work is in his collections of pieces such as *Shorter Poems* (1890), *New Verse* (1925), and certain sonnets; and, in addi-

[15]Edward Thompson, *Robert Bridges, 1844–1930* (Oxford University Press, 1944), p. 11.

tion, in detached passages from his poetic dramas and *The Testament of Beauty*. In his narrative poem *Eros and Psyche* (1885) the lyrical element is absent, but nowhere are his descriptions fuller of light, colour, and beauty. The great gifts of Bridges were an inventive mastery over the music of metres and syllables and an unfailing response to the beauty of Nature as he knew it in the spacious, varied, and friendly landscape of southern England. In addition, he had an intimate interest in words themselves, and in his later years was a friend of the philologist Henry Bradley. He had begun life as assistant physician to a hospital, and he always kept something of his scientific attitude: he certainly never forgot that an element of science has entered into the composition of some of the best poetry, and one of the qualities which made Milton his principal model among English poets was the rational art underlying the most magnificent and complex of his verbal harmonies.

All true poets seek to use "the best words," in Coleridge's phrase; but the phrase is susceptible of various meanings. For Keats and Tennyson the best words were those most charged with expressive power: hence, epithets were key-words. Many readers of poetry in the nineteenth century held this opinion—"l'épithète rare, voilà la marque du poète." Mr. Edward Thompson tells us that "when he [Bridges] was appointed Poet Laureate in 1913, an influential journalist disgustedly accumulated a selection of Bridges's adjectives, to show how dull and undistinguished they were, and complained that his grass was always green, instead of emerald or flashing, his skies blue and not turquoise or azure or sapphire."[16] The truth is that Bridges refused to take part in the race for rare epithets, knowing that such a contest could only lead to sophistication in poetry, and the exhaustion of the language itself. Nor had he the other ambition of his age, to cultivate a style of strongly marked individuality. Arthur Symons remarked truly that some of his finest lyrics "might have found their place . . . in an Elizabethan song-book. . . . They are very personal, but personal in a way so abstract, so little dependent on the accident of what we call personality, that it seems the most natural thing in the world for him to turn to a style which comes to him with a great anonymous tradition."[17]

The art of Bridges passed through several phases, and it might appear dangerous to speak in general terms of the style of a writer whose first volume was published in 1873, and who in 1929 produced a poem of an entirely new and original type. Yet through all the work of Bridges

[16]*Ibid.*, p. 21.
[17]*Studies in Prose and Verse* (1904), pp. 210–11; quoted by Edward Thompson, *Robert Bridges*, p. 12.

there does run a certain consistency of style. It is true that if we look
at his more conventional work—the weaker sonnets, for example—we
may find nothing but a kind of negative perfection. But in the whole
body of his vital poetry we are aware of an unsleeping metrical sense
which, in his middle and later work, becomes a conscious aim to harmonize the accepted rhythms of verse with the cadences of living speech.
This was something new in its day and at first was not appreciated. But,
to quote Mr. Thompson again, "You had merely to read the verse as
if it were ordinary prose, and fresh subtleties came crowding in, so
that the rhythm imaged forth perfectly the picture which imagination
imposed on the words and lines. The best-known example of this is of
course *London Snow* . . . the words seeming to follow the movement
of the flakes—pausing whenever they pause, drifting aside when they
drift aside—finding their way down unhurriedly and casually and yet
certainly."[18] The final stage of Bridges's metrical experiments came in
the "loose alexandrines" of *The Testament of Beauty*, but there the
balance is upset: the speech-rhythms have overcome the counter-move-
ment of metrical regularity, and the verse loses that recurrent pattern
which keeps poetry distinct from rhythmical prose.

The work of Bridges, then, has a certain analogy with Wordsworth's
in that he revived the traditional metres by infusing them with "a selection of the *rhythms* really used by men."[19] His conscious artistry was
bestowed first and foremost on the music of verse, but his diction,
chosen with infinite care, is a true embodiment of his poetic character.
In his use of words Bridges was no radical reformer—his temper was
opposed to extremes. By accepting Milton as his model, he ranged himself with the Spenserians, and he made no effort to discard a moderate
use of verse-diction. The poets whom he studied most naturally left
their traces on his style, and he uses plenty of Miltonic expressions,
such as *frore, dewy eves, freak'd* (with blue), *wide-water'd*. From
Keats, of whose odes he made a minutely detailed study, he once incorporated the entire phrase "summer hath o'erbrim'ed their clammy
cells" (*Testament of Beauty*, II.355) and the epithet *wailful* may be
presumed to come from the same poem. Now and then there are touches
of Shakespeare as in "winter's icy fang" (*Growth of Love*, 10), and
certain rare words such as *unhouseld* (*Low Barometer*). These are no
more than random examples, but if the full account were made up it
would not be a large one. Bridges was a very self-critical and indepen-

---

[18]*Robert Bridges*, p. 17.
[19]Cf. "a selection of the real language of men in a state of vivid sensation";
Wordsworth's Preface.

dent writer: if he needed an expression from the work of an author whom he respected, he borrowed it frankly, but no one could have more consistently avoided the repetition of those second-hand "poetic" expressions which slip so stealthily into verse. Among the few words which got past his critical scrutiny is a handful of adverbs like *aquiver, arow, ascare, aslant,* which are among the most "dating" features of nineteenth-century literary style, but even these he used in moderation.

The critic who complained that in Bridges the grass was always green and the sky was always blue certainly missed the delicate unobtrusive beauty of his style. He was wrong in more than one way. His chief mistake lay in concentrating on the epithets and ignoring the verbs. Mr. Thompson justly remarks that "felicity is present as a constant effect," and he quotes two lines (*Shorter Poems,* IV.15)—

> The pinks along my garden walks
> Have all shot forth their summer stalks

commenting on "the almost colloquial vigour of the verb" which indicates "the seeming suddenness with which the spring flowers arrive in their places."[20] It was partly by putting more force into his verbs and relying less on rare epithets that Bridges attained his freshness of style. In such a line as "The lazy cows wrench many a scented flower" (*Shorter Poems,* II.5) the fitness of the verb is typical.

There is a short poem of Bridges's (*Shorter Poems,* IV.6) which has been quoted in full in two fine critical studies and it may fitly be repeated here, for it illustrates the constant qualities of his best work: the absence of the self from the theme he has chosen, with a corresponding confidence that beauty will emerge out of faithful observation and record; and secondly, the exquisite handling of metre, rhyme, and rhythm which "superadd" charm and freshness to the accuracy of the words:

April, 1885
> Wanton with long delay the gay spring leaping cometh;
> The blackthorn starreth now his bough on the eve of May:
> All day in the sweet box-tree the bee for pleasure hummeth:
> The cuckoo sends afloat his note on the air all day.
>
> Now dewy nights again and rain in gentle shower
> At root of tree and flower have quenched the winter's drouth:
> On high the hot sun smiles, and banks of cloud uptower
> In bulging heads that crowd for miles the dazzling south.

In this poem there are slight signs of verse-diction in *drouth, afloat,*

[20] *Robert Bridges,* p. 22.

uptower, but the delightful impression it leaves is due in the main to homely words sweetened by their delicate rhythmical setting. This is the constant quality of Bridges's good work, and now and then a line of extra felicity, such as "With sudden flap of pigeon wings in the sky" (*Shorter Poems*, V.4, *The Garden in September*), will give that pleasant "shock of mild surprise" without which the use of metre is unjustified.

It should be remarked that Bridges had a talent for warmth of colour in style as well as for the silvery chastity which is habitual with him. In *Eros and Psyche* there is an almost lavish display of beauty in image and phrase; and there are stanzas, like those on the names of Aphrodite's attendant Nereids, which recall the "prodigality" if not the "pomp" of Milton's proper names. Bridges was so genuine a lover of landscape and language that he was bound to write passages in the Virgilian manner of Tennyson, such as that (*New Poems*, no. 14, *November*) on the old-fashioned ploughing which he loved:

> The teams following and crossing far and near,
> As hour by hour *they broaden the brown bands*
> *Of the striped fields*,

or the line on the sea-shore (*New Poems*, II.7, *The Downs*):

> Of waves on rocks dashing and *searching* the sands.

So too, his delight in the beauty of flowers will sometimes fashion a line worthy of Keats, as in the lovely phrase (*The Garden in September*):

> The nectaries of deepest-throated blooms.

His love of beauty in language was wide enough to embrace the aesthetics of spelling. In this he had precedents enough among English poets, though he went further than they in his use of forms like *coud, ifso, spredd, desolat, pictur* and others, which suggest the systematic reformer rather than the pure artist in words.

It is partly in virtue of his deliberate labour for the preservation of the English language as an instrument of beauty and precision that the name of Bridges seems especially worthy to close the present study. The Spenserian tradition has not yet ended; Bridges reset it more firmly in its rightful course and infused it with a new spirit for its future career. His work has some analogy with that of the National Trust for the preservation of scenes of natural beauty and with that of the "Friends" of various cathedrals: to ignore this side of it is to minimize his contribution to English letters. He was aided in his twofold task by the very limitation of his poetic powers, as well as by his uniquely fortunate circumstances. The truest admirers of Bridges have admitted that the note of passion is almost totally absent from his work, and the result is that his love of beauty never has the full significance which it possesses in the greatest poetry. In fact, with all his refinement, Bridges lacks power. The note of suffering is not present in sufficient force to give his verse the deeper harmonies: there is little of that tension between the sense of beauty and its transience to which the sonnets of Shakespeare owe their piercing sweetness, nor had he that feeling of the issue between pleasure and pain, beauty and death, that gives the Odes of Keats their penetrating power. Bridges was grateful for the rare happiness of his life:

> For a happier lot
> Than God giveth me
> It never hath been,
> Nor ever shall be,[21]

but there is something in his poetry, something in the painless perfection of his rhythms, which suggests that this happiness is partly one of circumstance as well as of the spirit. Yet no poet was a better craftsman, and his influence which increased so much in his later years, came at a most timely moment. Beyond all other writers of the age, he had a poet's insight into the past, present, and future of the language.

[21]*Fortunatus Nimium.*

INDEX

•